Against Facts

Against Facts

Arianna Betti

The MIT Press
Cambridge, Massachusetts
London, England

MIT Press books may be purchased at special quantity discounts for business or sales promotional use. For information, please email special_sales@mitpress.mit.edu.

This book was set in Stone Sans and Stone Serif by Toppan Best-set Premedia Limited. Printed and bound in the United States of America.

Library of Congress Cataloging-in-Publication Data

Betti, Arianna, 1970–
Against facts / Arianna Betti.
    pages cm
Includes bibliographical references and index.
ISBN 978-0-262-02921-6 (hardcover : alk. paper)
1. Facts (Philosophy). I. Title.
B105.F3B48 2015
111–dc23
2014048123

10 9 8 7 6 5 4 3 2 1

Ai miei genitori, Tina e Roberto

Contents

Preface

This book has taken more than ten years to complete. My original motivation to write it was my own need for a book like this while writing my PhD thesis on the metaphysics of truth and time from Bolzano to the Lvov-Warsaw school. I wanted to know when facts emerged in the history of thought, and why. More fundamentally, I wondered: what are facts? I was unable to find literature that explained in a clear and articulate way exactly what facts are, how many kinds of facts there are, what problems facts are supposed to solve, and how facts differ from propositions, relations, circumstances, situations, states of affairs, substances, thick particulars, events, and mereological complexes. The relation between facts and complexes especially puzzled me, although it was crucial to my work. No single book or article could tell me just how things stood in this regard, even though talk of facts was all-pervasive in nearly every field of research both inside and outside philosophy. While investigating the history of facts, I kept stumbling upon systematic questions and was led to try to solve these as well, by that time having become convinced that we do not need facts at all. So, after my PhD I set out to write a book that would both explain in detail what facts are and how they relate to cognate notions, and also show why, ultimately, there is no need for facts. I hope that *Against Facts* will be especially helpful to every young researcher who, like me back then, is struggling with these questions.

Originally, *Against Facts* included a long historical chapter on the history of facts from Aristotle to David Armstrong, which is now scheduled to appear as a separate book. While I find this separation of historical and systematic material somewhat unfortunate, I also feel that this shorter, fully systematic version of *Against Facts* might do a better service to its readers. Still, to me, philosophy and its history are inextricably related. A philosopher had better have an excellent grasp of the history of the notions she investigates, and vice versa—a historian of philosophy had better have an excellent systematic grasp of the notions she investigates.

Chapter 2 contains excerpts from a paper published in 2008 in *Dialectica* and coauthored with Jan Willem Wieland. My thanks to Dialectica for allowing me to lift material from that paper without having to obtain formal permission to do so.

Against Facts was made possible mainly by funding for fundamental research from the European Research Council (TRANH No. 203194). I am particularly grateful to them for enabling me to set up my own research group, and to devote myself fully to research for five years. An ERC grant is truly the most fantastic grant scheme a young researcher can hope for. Life has never been the same after that. I am sure that any other ERC grantee feels the same way.

The ideas contained in this book were presented in talks all over the world. This involved many institutions and many people. The three main institutions that have supported work on *Against Facts* are the VU University Amsterdam, the University of Amsterdam, and the University of Gothenburg, where this book was completed while I was visiting as Marks Professor Nr. 2. The image of (what I take to be) Hargle the hedgehog on pp. vi, xxvii, 2, 38, 83, 106, 121, 157, 194, 224, 231 appears courtesy of TattooTribes.com.

It is practically impossible on this occasion to mention all those colleagues and students who in these years have been so kind to interact with me on the topics of this book. I won't do this here, for I would surely unwittingly leave someone out. I have endeavored to mention in footnotes everybody to whom I owe substantial discussion on specific points. I do want to mention six colleagues here, who have been crucially supportive at difficult moments of the publishing history of this book. Wolfgang Künne, Anders Lundberg, Anna-Sofia Maurin, Kevin Mulligan, Jeroen Smid, and Jan Willem Wieland: you have been wonderful, and you know why. Many thanks to all of you.

Gothenburg, June 25, 2014

Introduction

Argle Bargle! Look what I found!
Bargle A hedgehog! Cute! Does it have spines?
Argle Of course. All hedgehogs have spines.
Bargle Right.
Argle So it's a fact that all hedgehogs have spines?
Bargle Yes.
Argle And this fact is what I talk about when I say "The fact that hedgehogs have spines is well documented"?
Bargle Well …
Argle And so this fact is in the world, with all its constituents—hedgehogs, spines, and maybe also the relation of having?
Bargle What? Wait, that can't be right … (*takes out a smartphone and looks up "fact" on Wikipedia*)

This is a book against facts. It argues that we have no good reason to accept facts in our catalog of the world, on the major metaphysical theories of facts known to us. It holds that neither of two major such theories are tenable: neither the theory according to which facts are special structured building blocks of reality, nor the theory according to which facts are whatever is named by certain expressions of the form 'the fact that such and such'. There is reality, to be sure, and there are entities in reality that we are able to name, but among these entities there are no facts.

These conclusions will chiefly interest metaphysicians and philosophers of language, but the book is also written with other readers in mind. Anyone working with an applied notion of fact—philosophers of science, linguists, legal theorists, and also sociologists—should all find something of their interest here.

The structure of the book is simple. There are two parts, each devoted to one conception of facts argued for on the basis of one central argument, and each of which is criticized in three chapters focusing on crucial premises of that central argument. The first part ("Compositional Facts") is about present-day mainstream metaphysics and compositional facts—facts as special structured building blocks of reality. The second part ("Propositional Facts") is about topics in the philosophy of language and linguistics, and propositional facts—roughly, whatever is (allegedly) named by certain expressions of the form 'the fact that such and such'. The central argument of the first part is Armstrong's *truthmaker argument*; that of the second part is (what I call) the *argument from nominal reference*, an argument inspired by— but merely inspired by—Quine's criterion of ontological commitment.

In the three chapters of part 1, I criticize compositional facts and Armstrong's truthmaker argument. Chapter 1 ("Compositional Facts") offers an immediate, intuitive grasp of the notion of fact, and, as a successive step, a rough idea of the discussion in philosophy and the key technical concepts involved. Here I introduce the truthmaker argument and develop some conceptual tools to help set out the important distinctions between facts and several other related entities that are important to the chapters that follow. Chapter 2 ("The Unity Problem") discusses the most pressing problem for compositional facts, the unity problem, and offers a criticism of Armstrong's position. Chapter 3 ("Solving the Unity Problem") offers a dissolution of the problem. Mereological (i.e., part/whole) considerations and the difference between nonmereological facts and mereological complexes play a crucial role here. This part of the book draws mainly on research in present-day metaphysics.

In the three chapters of the second part, I criticize propositional facts and the argument from nominal reference. The strategy I adopt in chapters 4 ("Reductio") through 6 ("A Fallback Position" (1) and (2)) is that of a reductio. For the sake of argument, I assume the methodology of language-based or *descriptive* metaphysics, as well as claims about facts often made by philosophers of this conviction. I show that the claim, common to such philosophers, that there are facts because there is reference to them in natural language is untenable, even by their own standards. Chapter 4 introduces the argument from nominal reference and offers a criticism of its central assumption. Chapters 5 and 6 offer a fallback position and show that this fallback position is untenable as well. I round off the discussion by offering some critical remarks on the methodology of language-based arguments in analytic metaphysics, within which I bring together the critical conclusions of both parts of the book on compositional and propositional facts. I conclude that it can't be shown convincingly that there are facts.

You may wonder why one would spend nearly 300 pages only to say that facts are not there. One reason is that talk of facts is all-pervasive in nearly every field of research, both inside and outside philosophy, though it is quite unclear what this talk really is about. This might strike one as odd, since facts are much debated in analytic philosophy. This debate is often confined, however, to a very specialized area of investigation and framed by strong tacit assumptions. Frequently the debate proves unclear in one or more of these four areas: which notions of fact are at issue; how they relate to cognate notions (circumstances, situations, states of affairs, Fregean propositions, Russellian propositions, substances, thick particulars, tropes, events, relations, mereological complexes, etc.); why we need facts (if at all); and, from a more general methodological point of view, what sorts of arguments there are for acknowledging facts, especially those based on the workings of natural language, and on what grounds any such argument may be considered effective. These are four broad and basic questions about facts. The pages that follow address them in detail. One thing this book clarifies, for example, is that there are two kinds of facts, compositional and propositional, which are argued for in philosophy in completely different ways. The facts allegedly named by certain that-clauses, or by nominals of the form 'the fact that p', can't be compositional facts; they can only be propositional facts. Therefore, contrary to what one might think at first, the arguments based on that-clauses that are advanced in favor of propositional facts do not carry over to compositional facts. The two theories of facts, compositional and propositional, originated from one single conception, but they have developed in recent history into quite different construals of what facts are. The first kind of theory is more popular now, whereas the second was more popular in the 1960s and '70s, but it is still around: you find it in Peter Strawson's work and, in a hybrid version, in some theories working with possible worlds, such as Alvin Plantinga's. So, what *Against Facts* tells you, first of all, is what philosophers talk about when they talk about facts, and to a certain extent how this relates to talk about facts outside philosophy.

It should be made clear that the book's systematic message, namely that compositional and propositional facts, as we find in chapters 2–3 and 5–6, should be rejected, is merely negative. No effort is made to propose or defend any metaphysical theory in particular. I do highlight the merits of new variants of existing theories that I find interesting (such as the mereological complexes of either tropes or universals, in chap. 3), but this is an outcome rather than a starting point. I'd say that the most important message of *Against Facts* is metaphilosophical—at least its approach is a strongly metaphilosophical one. In assessing facts critically, I am especially interested in the way this can best be done; in the methods, that is, used to argue for and against them. I argue that the introduction of compositional facts is an indefensible ad hoc move, and chapter 2 contains an extensive critical analysis of that move. I argue that propositional facts have arisen as a result of a methodology in philosophy that can rightly be criticized, and chapters 4–6 explain why. Metaphysicians should stop worrying about facts, and philosophers in general should stop arguing for or against entities on the basis of how we use language. Philosophers seem to be stuck with facts, among other reasons, because they still believe theories about language that no other qualified scientist seems now to believe. This is a bad reason to hang on to facts. Or so I argue.

What's in the book exactly? In the "Synopsis" below, I give a quick and, as such, quite dense overview of the argumentative structure of the book. As this may make for a tough read, you may consider skipping it and starting on chapter 1. Before I pass to the overview, I want to stress one point. Although they appear rather different, the two parts of the book and the main argumentative strategies they employ against facts are unified by a single core assumption (although, as said, the way I proceed in the two parts is quite different, owing to the specifics of the arguments involved and the circumstance that my second argumentative strategy is a reductio). The core assumption is this: we can't assess claims concerning the existence of metaphysical items such as facts unless we have explicit and shared criteria to do so, and the latter should tell us which arguments to use in favor of facts or against them. The arguments in question are arguments to the best explanation: the shared criterion I follow is based on the degree of explanatory power of a theory accepting facts with respect to a certain problem vis-à-vis other theories that do not accept them. In the first part of the book, I show that the most celebrated argument for *compositional* facts to the best explanation, the truthmaker argument, fails. In the second part, I show that a Quine-like argument based on the ontological commitment of language to *propositional facts* also fails. Although the latter is not in itself an argument to the best explanation, I submit in my conclusion that even if this Quine-like argument succeeded (and it does not), it would not show that propositional facts exist, because such facts are unable to play any sensible explanatory role.

Note that the above seems to commit me to the following: claiming (i) that facts do not exist is to claim (ii) that we should not accept (the existence of) facts because theories accepting (the existence of) facts do not explain some important metaphysical phenomenon or solve a certain metaphysical problem better than any other theory. One might hold that this commitment is unacceptable, because showing (ii) does not allow me to conclude (i). Whoever holds this holds a legitimate view and, according to this view, this book does not show that facts do not exist; it shows only something weaker, namely that facts are unmotivated. To someone holding this view, I can only say that we legitimately disagree on some deep convictions about truth and existence in metaphysics. These are convictions on which there is no consensus. For whether claims about the existence of metaphysical items are different from claims about such items being motivated depends on our take on introductory arguments in metaphysics. If we agree that introductory arguments in metaphysics are all arguments to the best explanation, then the claim that *those* arguments fail for facts and the claim that facts do not exist turn out to be identical for all intents and purposes. (If, instead, we agree that the only introductory arguments in metaphysics are Quine-like arguments regarding the ontological commitment of language, then the claim that *those* arguments fail for facts and the claim that facts do not exist turn out to be identical.) But if we instead disagree on this point, then you'll take my conclusion in this book to be just that all major arguments in favor of (the existence of) facts fail. That's fine. I won't argue further for my preferred position here (namely that facts don't exist) and the book can be read as staying neutral on this principal issue. This might make some readers feel as if I shift constantly between facts being unmotivated and facts not existing. But one should rather keep in mind that it is matter of debate whether claiming the former is the same as claiming the latter.

In addition to stressing the core assumption outlined above as to explicit criteria to reply to the question *Do xs* (i.e., facts) *exist?*, I also want to stress a second, similar assumption I make at two crucial argumentative junctures about explicit criteria to reply to another question, namely *Are xs ys?* (e.g., is 'the fact that *p*' a singular term?). Questions of the latter kind are raised when we want to classify a certain item under a certain label. For this, we normally rely on a shared definition or characterization of some sort. If a definition is not available, then we reason by analogy (Are *xs* like *ys* in all relevant aspects that make them *a*s? Then *ys* are *a*, too). If analogy fails, however, then we are entitled to say that the label is inappropriate for the item in question (or for the concept of that item). Saying that it is appropriate is unmotivated or ad hoc. The first juncture at which I use this move explicitly is my argument against the nonmereological composition of Armstrongian facts in the first part, to the effect that facts are ad hoc because their nonmereological composition is sui generis even in a framework in which we allow for *some* notion of nonmereological composition; the second juncture is my argument to the effect that 'the fact that *p*' is not a singular term. Since we don't have a definition of singular term, we reason by analogy; but there is no salient analogy between 'the fact that p' and (expressions considered to be) singular terms. Therefore, 'the fact that p' is not a singular term. As things stand, it is unmotivated or ad hoc to say that it is.

Again, one might want to hold that saying that it is unmotivated or ad hoc to say (in a so-called essential predication), that xs are ys (for example, that the expression 'the fact that p' is a singular term), does not allow me to conclude that xs are not ys, or to conclude that it is *false* that xs are ys.

Again, to whomever holds this view, I can only say that we legitimately disagree on the role that analogy and classification criteria or *definitional arguments*, as this kind of reasoning may be called, should play in methodology—and not only within philosophy, but also outside it.

Let's now see in compressed form what this book has to say.

Synopsis

The book has two parts: part 1, against compositional facts, and part 2, against propositional facts. A conclusion brings the two parts together.

Part 1: Compositional Facts. The argument against compositional facts in the first part goes as follows.

In chapter 1, I discuss *what* compositional facts are and what they are *for* in connection with Armstrong's truthmaker argument, of which I offer a reconstruction. To this end I distinguish five roles that various entities can play in the theoretical space at the intersection of language and world (sec. 1.1.1, "Semantic Roles"), and characterize compositional facts as entities able to play two semantic roles: the role of what linguistic statements in our language are about (*sentence-object*), and the role of what makes our sentences or judgments true (*truthmaker*).[1] Consider the true sentence 'Hargle is on Argle's lap'. According to Armstrong, the truth of a sentence such as this must have an ontological ground, that is, something in the world in virtue of which the sentence is true: a *truthmaker*. This truthmaker is a fact: the fact that Hargle—Argle's pet hedgehog—is on Argle's lap, or *Hargle's being on Argle's lap*. Armstrong's main point is that compositional facts are the only (or the best) candidates for the truthmaker role. This is, according to Armstrong, a crucial reason why we should accept them (sec. 1.2, "Compositional Facts: Why").

In Armstrong's view and that of many others, compositional facts are the most desirable truthmakers because they possess certain peculiar ontological characteristics. I individuate seven ontological characteristics that facts are taken to possess and which together form the seven conditions of the (working) definition of the notion of fact I propose in this book: a compositional fact is a complex entity with a fixed number of constituents (minimally two) that is part of the furniture of the world, and whose composition is formal, nonmereological, and heterogeneous both from the ontological point of view and from the point of view of the categories involved (sec. 1.3, "The Nature of Compositional Facts"). Together with the semantic roles, these seven ontological conditions are useful to fix not only what facts are, but also what they are not; that is, they serve to clarify other notions discussed in the book: along with the notions of *Fregean propositions*, *Aristotelian propositions*, *states of affairs*, and hybrids of propositions and states of affairs such as *Meinongian Objektive* and *Russellian propositions* (sec. 1.4, "Facts versus Propositions, Facts versus States of Affairs"), these ontological conditions help fix the notion of *trope* and *event*, and, to some extent, the notions of *integral whole* and *complex*, which are important to my argument in chapters 2 and 3. The most salient difference between (compositional) facts and complexes is that compositional facts, but not complexes, have a nonmereological composition.

This difference occupies center stage in chapters 2 and 3. Armstrong's truthmaker argument presupposes that facts serve to provide unity and structure to the world: facts, therefore, play both this unifying role (premises 5 and 6 of the argument) and that of truthmaker (premises 4 and 7 of the argument), and can play the latter *only on the assumption that they play the former*. The compositional fact *Hargle's being on Argle's lap*, it is argued, is an object with a special, nonmereological composition: it is not a mere collection of Hargle, the relation of *being on*, and Argle's lap, but something more, a fourth thing over and above these three constituents. The reason that fourth thing is needed, according to Armstrong and others, is the following. The existence of Hargle, the relation of *being on*, and Argle's lap does not yet bring about the existence of the fact in question. Suppose that Hargle is running happily across a meadow in Keuru, Finland, and Argle is munching on a Gruyère sandwich on the grass of Museumplein in Amsterdam, and there is something on Argle's lap, say, a colander. Then Hargle, Argle's lap, and *being on* all exist, but *separately*: that is, Hargle is not resting on Argle's lap. In other words, Hargle, Argle's lap, and the relation of *being on* must be *brought together*, arranged in some way. In short, facts—entities *over and above* their constituents—are needed because their constituents alone cannot get us a world where relations (*being on*) relate their relata (Hargle, Argle's lap). In Armstrong's "primitivist" view, facts simply *are* constituents brought together. This position is the best available on the view of compositional facts as unifiers of the world, since it qualifies as a solution to the problem without igniting Bradley's relation regress as other solutions do (sec. 2.1, "Compositional Facts and the Unity Problem"). Yet, I argue, this primitivist solution is not a good one, because it is ad hoc, and, in the presence of better alternatives, should be dismissed as implausible. In figure S.1, I present the

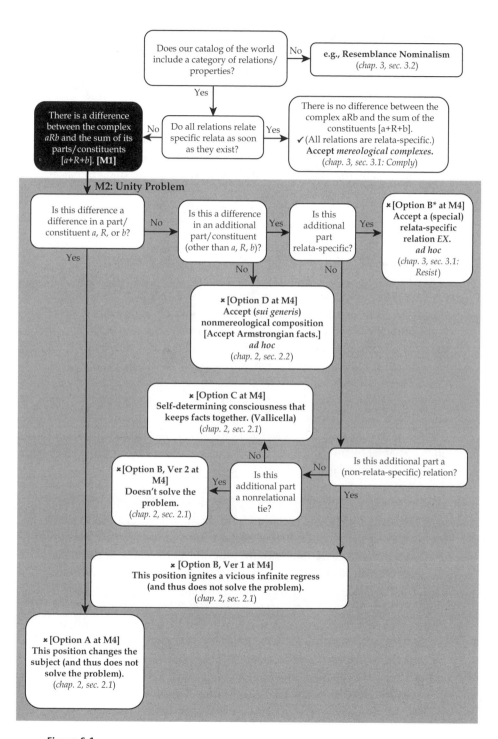

Figure S.1
The arguments against facts in chapters 2–3.

argumentative strategy I follow in the second and third chapter in a flow chart. Note, however, that the order in which the steps are presented below does not match the order I follow in those chapters. The reason for this is didactic. In chapter 2, I start from the problem of unity first in order to make it understandable; then I guide the reader to the available solutions. I refrain from immediately introducing a number of distinctions needed to present my preferred solution, as they might be confusing when offered all at once and make the chapter less readable. The flow chart presented here reconstructs matters by way of choice points in a more systematic and less narrative way.

The central move in the argument outlined in the flow chart against Armstrongian facts (see the cross at Option D at M4) goes further than simply rejecting facts as magical (as David Lewis does) or incoherent (as William F. Vallicella does), and involves an extensive discussion in two steps preceded by a methodological account of the use of ad hoc criteria in theory choice in metaphysics. The first step is to show that facts are ad hoc. It consists in showing that there are no direct or indirect arguments in favor of the nonmereological composition characteristics of facts independent of the need to solve the unity problem. My reasoning at this step draws from the debate on material constitution, and focuses on the claim, central to this debate, that there is a difference between *real unities* and *mere aggregates*. I apply elements of this debate in an effort to seek arguments in support of facts as nonmereologically composed entities. I conclude that this effort is ineffective (sec. 2.2, "Step One: Facts Are Ad Hoc Entities"). I round off this chapter by showing that theories that accept (obtaining and nonobtaining) states of affairs are, a fortiori, worse off than facts (sec. 2.3, "The Unity Problem in an Ontology of States of Affairs"). The second step, which I take in chapter 3, consists in showing that superior alternatives are available. If a certain common assumption on the nature of relations is abandoned, namely the assumption that relations are *relata unspecific* (where the relata-specificity of a relation is not the same as its externality or particularity), and it is instead assumed that relations are relata specific, then mereological complexes of relations and their relata alone will suffice to provide unity in the world (sec. 3.1 1, "Step Two: A Fact-Free Dissolution of the Unity Problem"). The solution I advance should be preferred because it is not ad hoc, or, in any case (if we'd rather not rely on ad hoc avoidance), it presents the fewest costs and most benefits (sec. 3.2, "What Problem? Relational Unity, the Unity Problem, and Truthmaking"). I point out that mereological complexes can take up the role of truthmaker—a role that, according to some philosophers, is nonnegotiable—instead of facts. This is possible because mereological complexes involving relata-specific relations share with facts certain modal characteristics that enable truthmaking as necessitation. However, that truthmaking as necessitation can be obtained only by assuming entities with certain modal characteristics shows that Armstrong's truthmaker argument is not sound: it is at most an elucidation of a scenario in which we make explicit on the one hand what constraints we want to put on truth (namely truthmaking) and on the other what metaphysical constraints should be accepted once these constraints on truth are in place (namely, we have to accept entities with certain suitable modal properties). Note that, as stated, my aim is not to defend any specific metaphysics in this book, so I am not making the strong claim that an ontology of mereological complexes including relata-specific relations (on which I say deliberately little) is the one most likely to be our ontology— our world. I am making the weaker claim that *if* we want an ontology including relata-specific relations, then we should favor a world of mereological complexes where all relations are relata specific rather than a world of (Armstrongian) facts.

Part 2: Propositional Facts. At this point I wonder whether there are not, after all, other arguments in favor of facts, such as arguments from language use. In part 2, I first show that these arguments cannot support acceptance of facts of the compositional kind, but at most support only facts of the propositional kind; then, second, I show that these arguments are also unable to support propositional facts.

In the part's introduction, I propose the *argument from nominal reference for facts*. This argument, inspired by Quine's criterion of ontological commitment, is a reconstruction of the way in which philosophers who rely on the working of natural language tend to argue for or against entities. It is built around three conditions for ontological commitment that facts allegedly fulfill. The first condition regards singular reference in natural language to propositional facts by means of that-clauses, a condition I show to be unfulfilled in chapter 4 by arguing that there is no reference to facts. The second (successful) condition regards identity conditions for facts. I argue in chapters 5–6 that, under the assumption that there is, per absurdum, reference to facts, we have no acceptable identity conditions for propositional facts, or at least the identity conditions given for propositional facts by their proponents collapse them into true propositions. The third and final condition regards the ineliminability of quantification over facts in natural language, a condition I show to depend on the first condition, and therefore consider rejected when this first condition is not met. A detailed overview of chapters 4–6 is best given by displaying the argument from nominal reference itself and how its steps get rejected. This is the argument in the most analytic version I consider (see also the conclusion of chap. 4):

✓   (*Quine-Like*) Facts exist if and only if statements of natural language are true that are ontologically committed to facts.

A statement *s* of natural language is true that is ontologically committed to facts if and only if

✓   (*First Conjunct*) *s* implies a true first-order statement of the form $\exists x Fx$ (indefinite reference) where 'F' is 'is a fact'.

✓   (*SuffFirstConjunct*) A sufficient condition for *First Conjunct* is that *s* contains singular terms for facts in natural language (definite reference).

✗   Sufficient conditions for *SuffFirstConjunct* are

✗   (*SuffSuffFirstConjunct 1*) Some (kinds of) that-clauses are singular terms referring to facts. (chap. 4, sec. 4.1)

✗   (*SuffSuffFirstConjunct 2*) 'The fact that *p*' is a singular term referring to the fact that *p*. (chap. 4, sec. 4.2)

✗   Necessary condition for *SuffSuffFirstConjunct 1* and *SuffSuffFirstConjunct 2* is

                    (*NecSuffSuffFirstConjunct 1 and 2 = Singular Terms*) That-clauses are singular terms

                    where

✗   necessary conditions for an expression *x* to be a singular term (that is, an expression purporting to pick out exactly one object) are

✗   (*NecSingularTerms 1*) *x* is substitutable by a coreferential singular term salva veritate and congruitate;

✗   (*NecSingularTerms 2*) *x* is able to replace an individual variable in an open sentence in a first-order logical theory (i.e., a variable that can be bound by a nominal quantifier);

✗   (*NecSingularTerms 3*) *x* is substitutable by a kind-restricted natural language particular quantifier;

✗   (*NecSingularTerms 4*) *x* is able to function as structural subject of natural language sentences (NP in Spec, IP).

✗   (*NecFirstConjunct*) A necessary condition for *FirstConjunct* is that 'is a fact' functions genuinely as a predicate in predications of the form 'x is a fact'. (chap. 4, sec. 4.3)

✗   (*Second Conjunct*) We have identity criteria for facts. (chaps. 5 and 6)

✗   (*Third Conjunct*) The quantification over facts in natural language is ineliminable. (chap. 4, sec. 4.3)

Claim *Quine-Like* is a (definitional) statement fundamental to the argument above, and I assume it for the sake of the argument throughout chapters 4 through 6. I criticize *SuffFirstConjunct* in the first two sections of chapter 4. Section 4.1 ("Against *SuffSuffFirstConjunct 1*: That-Clauses Are Not Singular Terms") is directed against *SuffSuffFirstConjunct 1*; section 4.2 (Against *SuffSuffFirstConjunct 2*: 'The Fact That p' Is Not a Singular Term, in Particular Neither a Definite Nor an Appositive Description") criticizes *SuffSuffFirst-Conjunct 2*: 'the fact that *p*' is not a singular term—a conclusion for which I rely in part on the finding that 'that *p*' is not a singular term either. Section 4.3 ("Against *NecFirstConjunct*: 'Is a Fact' Is Not a Predicate") is directed against condition *NecFirstConjunct*. *NecFirstConjunct* is a necessary condition for *First Conjunct*, which is crucial to *Quine-Like* and therefore crucial to the claim that facts exist. Notice, however, that although the claim that that-clauses are singular terms for facts is only a *sufficient* condition to derive $\exists xFx$, this claim is a *necessary* condition for *NecFirstConjunct*, which in turn is necessary to *First Conjunct*: for the expression 'is a fact' to function as a predicate in 'that *p* is a fact', 'that p' must be a singular term. Therefore, by rejecting that that-clauses are singular terms we do something more than merely reject a sufficient condition to get to $\exists xFx$ in natural language. By rejecting the first sufficient condition, we also reject the necessary condition for deriving $\exists xFx$. By this reasoning, anyone sharing the methodology set out in the argument has to conclude that facts do not exist. For this conclusion is warranted by the shared criterion that is part and parcel of the argument from nominal reference, namely an argument fixing when we are entitled to say that something exists (under the assumption, mentioned above, that assessing such arguments is all we can do to decide on questions of existence; as noted, one might disagree, see pp. xvi–xviii above). There is no genuine quantification over facts in natural language, and it is illusory to think that there is.

   In chapters 5–6 I review a fallback position, by supposing per absurdum that the thesis that some that-clauses refer to facts (which is rejected in chapter 4) still stands, and showing that it is still problematic. Even if we could account for all counterexamples to this thesis, it would still be self-defeating since it would entail the collapse of (true) propositions into facts. Put in other words, in chapters 5–6 I show that even if the first and third conjunct held, the second conjunct would not: we do not have satisfactory identity criteria for propositional facts as distinct from true propositions. I proceed as follows. In section 5.1 ("Fact Reference Refined and Strengthened: Fact Reference*_{Power!}*"), I introduce and discuss the thesis that *factive* that-clauses refer to facts while *nonfactive* that-clauses refer to propositions.

In sections 5.2 ("Propositional Facts") and 5.3 ("Fact Reference$_{Power!}$ Commits Us to Propositional Facts") I show that the only kind of facts that factive clauses could refer to are so-called *propositional facts*. In section 5.4 ("The Collapse of Propositional Facts into True Propositions") I argue that propositional facts are identical to true propositions, and reject five attempts to block this identification. In section 6.1 ("Sixth and Final Attempt: Linguistic Evidence Cannot Motivate the Acceptance of Propositional Facts Alongside True Propositions"), I investigate whether linguistic evidence can be used to reject the identification of propositional facts and true propositions and support an acknowledgment of propositional facts as distinct entities. I conclude the evidence in question cannot be used to make a case for propositional facts, and thus that this sixth and final attempt to make that case is a failure: language alone cannot establish a difference between facts and true propositions. Therefore, since it is false that some (kinds of) that-clauses refer to propositional facts while other (kinds of) that-clauses refer to true propositions, *even if* that-clauses were singular terms, it would still not be the case that there are two kinds of that-clauses, one referring to facts and another referring to propositions. The only defensible position, should that-clauses turn out to be singular terms, is one that takes them to refer to propositions and *only* to propositions, to the effect that factive that-clauses refer to *true* propositions (sec. 6.2, "No Reference to Propositional Facts as Distinct from True Propositions"). There is thus no category of facts alongside true propositions to which that-clauses refer. Section 6.3 ("Exit Fact Reference$_{Power!}$, Together with Singular Terms") makes sure that the argument against Singular Terms I offer in chapter 4 is also effective against the somewhat different kind of literature—literature from linguistics—I use in chapters 5–6.

As noted, the discussion in chapters 4 through 6, which is based on a methodological attitude known as *descriptive metaphysics*, is a reductio. I myself prefer an attitude called *revisionary metaphysics*. I make this clear in the conclusion, where I round off the book by arguing that the only sensible position on reference to facts is one according to which facts are taken to be the semantic value of certain expressions *by stipulation* ("Conclusion"). This, however, requires that we can show with arguments other than purely linguistic ones that we must assume facts. These arguments must be arguments to the best explanation: they need to show that nothing in our ontology is better able than facts to play certain roles, on which philosophers have to agree widely in every case that they must be played. However, as I argue, it can't be maintained that roles such as truthmaker and object of a sentence—as well as, one can maintain, unifier of reality and referent of (certain) that-clauses—*must* be played come what may; on the contrary, I suggest that among the five roles I have introduced in chapter 1, the only roles that we might sensibly insist be played by entities are that of truthbearer and that of sentence-subject. Even if it can be maintained, I argue, that the roles of truthmaker and sentence-object must be played, they aren't best played by facts. Facts, according to the major theories known to us—whether compositional or propositional—are either metaphysically unacceptable as items at the level of reference or, in any case, they aren't preferable as players of such roles in terms of costs and benefits to, for example, complexes of relata-specific relations plus their relata (or bearer-specific properties plus their bearers) or propositions. Therefore, facts must be abandoned.

1 Compositional Facts

You are reading this book. "A fact!" many would say. A robust piece of reality involving you, reading, and a book. What could be more evident? You most certainly exist, this book most certainly exists, and the relation of reading that relates you and this book most certainly exists.

The reading by you of this book: what could be more obvious than that reality in this moment contains such a unified structure? Oh, plenty, I say. It isn't evident at all, nor is it plausible that there are such things in reality.

That sounds dramatic, doesn't it? But I am not saying that these three things do not exist: you, this book, and the relation of reading. What I am saying is that at most there are *just* these three things. There is no *fourth* thing—you reading the book—which is a special 'being together' of these three things *over and above* them. Philosophers call these special 'being together' entities *compositional facts*. This is what the first part of this book is about.

My treatment of compositional facts will span three chapters. I will first say what compositional facts are. Then I will discuss why philosophers think we need them, highlighting the place of facts in the systematic debate in metaphysics. The most famous argument in favor of facts, Armstrong's truthmaker argument, will function as a thread running throughout part 1.

In chapter 1, I aim to offer an immediate, intuitive grasp of the notion of fact, and, as a successive step, a rough idea of the discussion in philosophy and the key technical concepts involved. In this chapter I develop some conceptual tools to help set out the important distinctions between facts and several other related entities that are important to the chapters that follow. In chapters 2–3, I discuss the most pressing problem for compositional facts: the unity problem. This part of the book draws mainly on research in present-day metaphysics, with a marked attention to mereological themes.

My conclusion is that we don't need compositional facts.

1 Compositional Facts

Russell writes:

The first truism to which I wish to draw your attention ... is that the world contains facts, which are what they are whatever we may choose to think about them, and that there are also beliefs, which have reference to facts, and by reference to facts are either true or false. ... If I say 'It is raining', what I say is true in a certain condition of weather and is false in other conditions. The condition of weather that makes my statement true (or false as the case may be), is what I should call a 'fact'. (Russell 1918–1919: 500)

Is it, as Russell says, a truism that the world contains facts? No, it is not. In what follows, I argue that it is implausible that the world contains facts.

This passage, like so many of Russell's, is marvelously deceitful. Russell uses everyday terms and makes appeal to seemingly intuitive notions: truth, facts, statements like 'it is raining', those statements' being true or false, the opposition between beliefs and facts, weather conditions, and so on. But the content of the passage, behind its plain surface, is highly technical. It is almost pure jargon—however paradoxical this might sound. It contains at least seven technical terms: *fact, belief, reference, true or false, statement*, perhaps *the world*, and surely *making true*. Even, as we shall see in chapter 4, the phrase *that the world contains facts* is technical. Far from expounding a truism, Russell is appealing to controversial views of the world, of language, and of the way in which world and language are related. It is with these controversial—albeit widespread—views that I will take issue in this book.

My main critical focus in the three chapters that follow will be the technical notion of *fact* that Russell assumes here. Facts have become part and parcel of the toolbox of analytic philosophy today. Russell worked with a notion of fact known as *compositional*. For him, facts are not *simple* entities; they are composed of other entities. 'A condition of weather' is to be interpreted here in a rather specific way: as a term referring to a complex object in the world involving the weather (conceived as an *object*) and a certain condition (conceived as a *property*).[1]

In these first three chapters I will also pay some attention to Russell's coining of the phrase *making true*, since, thanks to the work of David Armstrong and others, truthmaking and facts have come to be regarded as strictly connected. I will not offer a criticism of the notion of truthmaking, for my aim is rather to offer a comprehensive criticism of the notion of fact. Besides, as I will show, facts are able to play the role of truthmakers only insofar as they are able to play the role of unifiers of the world. I will discuss this point in detail in chapter 2.

In the following sections I introduce compositional facts. Section 1.1 introduces five semantic roles that facts and related notions are or are not fit to play,[2] and seven ontological conditions that serve jointly as a working definition of fact. I then use (dis)similarity with respect to semantic roles and ontological conditions in sections 1.2 through 1.4 to distinguish the notion of fact from other notions in its metaphysical surroundings (*events, tropes, integral wholes*, and *complexes* in sec. 6.3, and two theories of *propositions* and *states of affairs* in sec. 6.4). I connect this analysis to the fundamental ideas behind the most well-known argument for compositional facts: Armstrong's truthmaker argument.

1.1 Compositional Facts: What

What is a fact? The state of the art answers:

Facts, philosophers like to say, are opposed to theories and to values [A], they are the objects of certain mental states and acts, they make truthbearers true and correspond to truths [B], they are part of the furniture of the world [C]. (Mulligan & Correia, 2008)

This characterization echoes that which Russell offers in "The Philosophy of Logical Atomism," quoted above: facts "are what they are whatever we may choose to think about them." Both characterizations suggest that facts are in some sense *raw* items—that they are independent of how they are thought about by us, (social) individuals who interpret and evaluate them (A).

According to the theories of facts described in the passage, our judgments and beliefs, on the other hand, are said to be correct, and our claims true, depending on whether and in the extent to which they correspond to facts (B). Finally, facts are in the world, in the sense that they are *constitutive* of it (C). The last point is important, for facts may be raw, uninterpreted items functioning as epistemic and semantic constraints (that is, they are taken to be literally what we can *know* and *talk about* truly in language), but they aren't taken to be raw *data* or *information units*: they are part of the world, they enter its catalog, the catalog of what there is, like children's comic books—and friendships, milk, hedgehogs, colanders, and shopping receipts, and our own limbic states and those of others. Note that I am not saying that facts *must* be included in the catalog of the world, that they *exist*: my view is just the opposite. What I am saying is: *according to what certain philosophers like to say*, facts are such-and-such items. We need this characterization first to get clear on what facts are according to these views, so that, when I speak of facts, it is plain that I speak of facts in that sense. Then we can ask: is it plausible that facts in this sense exist? And to this I shall answer: no, it is not plausible that facts as fixed by that characterization exist.[3]

In this chapter, I shall concentrate on two aspects of Mulligan and Correia's characterization: the ontology of facts (C) and the theoretical roles that facts are supposed to fulfill (B). I do not take issue with the so-called *fact/value dichotomy* involved in (A),[4] nor with the relation between beliefs and facts—not, that is, with the relations generally between mind and world—but instead concentrate on the relation between language and world.

Mulligan and Correia's characterization might appear, in one sense, aptly broad. Although it does not capture all the various theories of facts that philosophers have put forward, it seems at first sight to capture the main two theories that I will discuss in this book. One is the *compositional view* of facts already mentioned. This view, which I discuss in this chapter and the next two, is associated mainly with David Armstrong. The other is a noncompositional view known as the *propositional view*, associated with

John Searle and others, which I discuss in the second part (chaps. 4–6). I have said that Mulligan and Correia's characterization *seems* to fit both of these views because, as we shall see in chapter 4, however eagerly defenders of propositional facts like Searle might want their facts to fit that characterization, on a serious analysis propositional facts actually don't fit it at all, or do so only poorly. The main difference between compositional and propositional facts is that the latter aren't parts of the world (C) that are able to *make truths true* (B)—and, as I show in chapter 5, cannot plausibly be such.

Mulligan and Correia's characterization is not a definition, nor is it a description uniquely characterizing compositional facts. The reason is that it is too broad: it also captures other items that we might take (and which sometimes philosophers do take) to play the roles that facts play, such as *events, tropes, integral wholes* (or substances), and *complexes*. Thus, before I discuss arguments against facts in chapter 2, I devote section 1.2 below to the elaboration of a somewhat more precise characterization of the nature of facts and discuss in section 1.3 the ways in which facts differ from events, integral wholes, and tropes. The difference between complexes and facts— given its importance for what I say in this book—will receive an extended treatment in chapter 2. The reason I want to be clear on this philosopher's toolbox, so to speak, is that I want to be critical of facts only, and of whatever can be rightly thus considered a fact, not of events, tropes, substances, or what have you. For the same reason I distinguish facts from propositions and from states of affairs in section 1.4. The notion of proposition, that of state of affairs, and that of fact are three related but different notions. Those should be distinguished regardless of whether or not one embraces in her theory propositions, states of affairs, or facts. Again, if we want to reject something, we had better know what we're rejecting.

As noted, the theories of facts I shall consider in the three chapters of this part of the book are exclusively compositional ones. No matter their variety, compositional theories show fair agreement on this much: that (in the simplest case) facts are complex objects (i.e., not simple); that they have a fixed number of *constituents* arranged in a special way; that of these constituents, at least one is an individual concrete object; and that facts belong to metaphysics, not semantics—that is, facts are *in the world*, and do not transcend themselves to reach out to the world as do meanings or referring entities such as linguistic expressions.

What does this mean exactly? And can we be more precise? This means, first, that facts occupy a specific place in, say, the "theoretical space" at the intersection of language and world; and second, that they have a specific nature. The first point is semantic and relates to B in Mulligan and Correia's characterization, and the second point is ontological and relates to C.

As to B, facts relate to semantic notions such as truth, meaning, and reference in a distinctive way. The way in which they relate to those semantic notions determines the details of the theories of facts that are accepted. In the following I propose to characterize compositional facts as entities capable of playing two roles in the theoretical space of language and world (the *semantic space*): the role of what linguistic statements in our language are about (in a sense yet to be defined: i.e., *sentence-objects*) and the role of what makes our sentences or judgments true (*truthmakers*).[5] As we shall see, two roles in the semantic space—these two, as I say, semantic roles—enable us easily to distinguish facts from *propositions*. The two semantic roles together also capture part B of the characterization we saw above:

Facts ... make truthbearers true [*truthmakers*] and correspond to truths [*sentence-objects*] [B]. (Mulligan & Correia, 2008)

In the next section, I shall introduce the two semantic roles that specify B as two out of five semantic roles that can be played by entities in general.

As to C, the specific nature of facts, I have said that a fact is a complex object in the world with a fixed number of *constituents* arranged in a special way (including at least one individual concrete object). Is there more to say about this? Yes: we can spell out C by saying that a fact (in the simplest case) satisfies seven conditions:

Condition 1: A fact is a *complex* object with a *fixed* number of constituents (in the simplest case minimally two and maximally three) which it comprehends in its *reticulation*.
Condition 2: A fact is *categorically heterogeneous*.
Condition 3: A fact is *in the world*.
Condition 4: A fact is *semantically idle*.
Condition 5: A fact is *ontologically heterogeneous*.
Condition 6: A fact is *structured in a formal way*.
Condition 7: A fact has a *nonmereological composition*.

These seven conditions aim to be both necessary and sufficient—the full articulation of C:

Facts ... are part of the furniture of the world [*fulfilling 1–7*, C]. (Mulligan & Correia, 2008)

In saying that conditions 1–7 are the "full articulation" of C, I mean not that facts must obey 1–7 to be part of the furniture of the world, but that 1–7 give the full specification of the *way* in which facts are supposed to be part of the furniture of the world. The list above is a checklist of symptoms of (compositional) *factness*, together constituting a criterion: check whether an entity has all of them; if it does, you can call it a fact. The list is supposed to capture no more and no fewer kinds of entities than compositional facts.[6] It also fixes by way of definition my use of 'compositional fact' throughout the book.

Let's first have a closer look at the semantic roles related to B, and then at the seven ontological conditions related to C. The introduction of roles and conditions in this chapter sets the stage for the critical arguments in chapter 2, and indeed in the rest of the book, as well as assembling a philosophical toolbox by clarifying the notions and the terminology I use. In chapter 2, I will focus critically on the ontological nature of facts and show how the seven ontological conditions taken together are implausible.

1.1.1 Semantic Roles

I shall consider five semantic roles in total, namely:

Role 1: Sentence-subject
Role 2: Sentence-sense
Role 3: Sentence-object
Role 4: Truthbearer
Role 5: Truthmaker[7]

What exactly does playing these roles consist in?

Alyosha, Dmitri, and Ivan are three cosmonauts. To comfort his days in outer space, Dmitri brings, together with his cat, a bottle of vodka carefully wrapped in thin paper. One day the vodka is gone, and Alyosha looks bad. While glancing at Alyosha, Dmitri says to Ivan:

(0)   Alyosha stole the vodka.

What are the *subject* and the *sense* of this sentence?

Role 1: Sentence-Subject The subject of a sentence is what a sentence is about, in one sense of 'about'. According to this sense of 'about', (0) is about Alyosha the man, and (possibly) the vodka, depending on what theory one accepts.[8] If we take a sentence to have as many sentence-subjects as there are *referential terms* occurring in it, the number of sentence-subjects will depend on how many of those terms (i.e., syntactic-semantic units) our preferred analysis of sentences yields.[9] We could end up with just one term, that is, only Alyosha, and therefore with only one subject. This was a popular view until the end of the nineteenth century. But we could end up with both Alyosha and the vodka and thus two sentence-subjects; we could end up with three, since the relation (or relational property) of stealing could also qualify as a referential term and thus as subject. Be that as it may, Alyosha will definitely be a sentence-subject, on all theories.

Role 2: Sentence-Sense   Of course, 'Alyosha stole the vodka' is not precisely what Dmitri says. While glancing at Alyosha, Dmitri in fact says to Ivan:

(1)   он украл водочку.[10]

This sentence—the words actually pronounced by Dmitri—*says that* Alyosha stole the vodka. This is its *sense*: what that sentence says. But the sense of a sentence is not the same as its *conventional linguistic meaning*, which is translation invariant, and which, in this case, would be preserved in English by translating (1) as

(2)   He stole the vodka.

Both (1) and (2) have the same linguistic meaning, while 'Alyosha stole the vodka' does not, although all three sentences have the same sense. If Dmitri had said to Ivan

(3)   он украл водочку

while glancing at his cat, (3) and (1) would have had the same linguistic meaning, but not the same sense: the sense of (3) but not of (1) would be the same as the sense of 'The cat stole the vodka'.

In the following, the difference between linguistic meaning and the sense of a (declarative) sentence will not play a role. I will speak about the sense of a sentence as what a linguistic sentence *says* or *states* (or *claims* or *asserts*), with all circumstances of utterance taken into account—that is, the particular language in which the sentence is formulated, time, location, and any other frame of reference. Some philosophers would deem it appropriate to say that what I just said means that I am considering sentence *tokens* rather than sentence *types*. The distinction between type and token is simple. In the previous sentence three letter *s*'s occur: these are three tokens of just one letter *s* type.

Some philosophers—by no means all—conceive of the role of sentence-sense in a quite substantial way as a role that must be played by some *entity*, in fact quite a special one. So, alongside the *words* of which sentences are composed, and the *objects* those words are about (like cats and cosmonauts, their material parts, and their actions, thoughts, and feelings), such philosophers introduce a third, special kind of entity that plays the role of sentence-sense. This entity is called, in technical prose, a *proposition*.[11] In this section, I shall say little on what propositions are: I shall discuss theories of propositions and their difference with facts in section 3 below. Propositions will also feature extensively in part 2 (chaps. 4–6).

Role 3: Sentence-Object   The notion of the object of a sentence is complicated and, in fact, a very recent addition to the philosopher's toolbox. The object of a sentence is what a sentence is about, but in a different sense of 'about' than that of sentence-subject (and of judgment-subject). Take the sentence

(4)   Alyosha looks bad.

According to this different sense of 'about', (4) is not about Alyosha and, perhaps, the property of looking bad, but about something else. A common choice in present-day metaphysics is that this something else is a *fact*. This sense of 'about' is indeed the one closest to the idea of *correspondence* in part B of Mulligan and Correia's characterization:

Facts ... are the objects of certain mental states and acts, they make truthbearers true and *correspond to truths* [B] (Mulligan & Correia, 2008; my emphasis)

In the sense of 'about' linked to sentence-object, sentences *as a whole* correspond to something. In this sense, (4) is about *the fact that Alyosha looks bad*—with the proviso that one accepts facts. We can also say, expressing ourselves with a gerundive nominal instead of a that-clause, that (4) is about *Alyosha's looking bad*, or about *the having by Alyosha of (an instance of) the property of looking bad*. What does it mean that truths correspond to facts? 'Correspondence' is an ambiguous notion. I take any view of truth to be a correspondence theory that is

explicitly embracing the idea that truth consists in a relation to reality, i.e., that truth is a relational property involving a characteristic relation (to be specified) to some portion of reality (to be specified). (David, 2009)

This characterization is quite minimal. There are stronger variants of it. Indeed, the role of sentence-object in the sense we are considering points to one of these stronger variants, which was crucial to the introduction of *states of affairs* (which in sec. 1.4.2 I will distinguish from facts).

Sentence-objects are the ontological counterparts of *entire* sentences. They are those cuts of the world that sentences considered as unities *project onto*, as I shall say. This idea finds considerable agreement among philosophers today, although they might disagree on what exactly the cuts of the world at issue might look like and whether *all* sentences, and not only true (and simple) ones, yield such worldly cuts. The general idea is that a sentence *as a whole* has a unique, minimal, or privileged counterpart in the world, and that there is a two-place relation between a sentence as a whole and a special piece of the furniture of the world, a relation that, following the literature, I shall call *projection* (see, e.g., Smith, 1999, 2002; Gregory, 2001; Schnieder, 2006a). Note that acknowledging projection is not the same as acknowledging that sentences are *names* of facts (or of whatever their sentence-object is) as some have done. I shall come back to this point in chapter 4, section 4.1.

In keeping with the above, irrespective of the *kind* of object we choose as the object of (4) as a whole, in the sense of 'about' we saw in the case of the role of sentence-object, the following sentence

(5)   Alyosha kisses Ivan

is not about Alyosha and, eventually, Ivan and kissing (as it was in the sentence-subject case), but about something else. It is about, for example, *Alyosha's kissing Ivan.*

The object of a sentence is not necessarily a fact, however. Other options are possible. According to a recent idea, what (4) is about is its "total projection" (see Smith, 1999, 279). This is a rather complicated complex object, but in any case it includes as a part a *particular, specific* property of looking bad that is exclusively Alyosha's, called a *trope.* I'll say more on tropes in section 1.2 under condition 2.

That special piece of the furniture of the world, the semantic cut, counterpart, or projection of a sentence is, in some (but by no means all) important theories, what determines, in part or wholly, the *truth* of the sentence (see below, "Role 5: Truthmaker").[12]

Role 4: Truthbearer A truthbearer (or truth-value-bearer) is whatever object may aptly be called *true* (or false—or frue, or talse, or whatever truth-values you wish to have—although here I consider only the two conventional truth-values). If we take (having) truth-values as properties (as I shall do throughout this book), that which can have such properties is called a *truthbearer.* Like Mulligan and Correia do in B, sometimes I shall speak of *truths* and *falsehoods* instead of truth-value-bearers that are true and truth-value-bearers that are false. The *role* of truthbearer itself is a fairly innocent one, for truthbearers are needed whenever the notion of truth is at issue; no philosophical disaster lurks behind the label 'truthbearer'. The choice of *candidates* for the role, however, is usually not a neutral and independent matter with respect to other aspects of one's metaphysics and theory of truth and meaning.

Candidates that have been proposed for the truthbearer role include propositions, statements, assertions, (type or token) sentences, and (type or token) judgments.[13] Judgments were considered the primary truthbearers until the beginning of the twentieth century. In the tradition before this time, sentences depended on judgments as to their semantic behavior, and often sentences were not taken to stand in for judgments in all the roles I am considering. For the purposes of this book, we don't need to distinguish sentences from judgments as truthbearers. Yet note that taking one or the other as the primary actor in semantics has far-reaching consequences for the arguments that might plausibly be advanced for questions such as whether we should accept a complex object of judgment and how exactly this should be conceived.[14]

Role 5: Truthmaker Unlike that of truthbearer, the role of truthmaker is theory laden. Truthmaker theories are a strong, popular, and peculiar present-day version of correspondence theories of truth. Like some other notions featured in this book, 'truthmaker' is a twentieth-century addition to the philosophical vocabulary, and it is by no means unproblematic. A proper criticism of truthmaking would go beyond the aims of this book, and since this book is directed against facts, in the following I shall sometimes talk of truthmakers without much ado (although I do not find truthmaking an attractive version of correspondentism; see also the end of chap. 3).

A truthmaker is, intuitively put, that *in virtue of which* truths are true. Truthmaker theories do not necessarily include entities in virtue of which *falsehoods* are false, but they might (such 'falsity-makers' are sometimes called 'truthmakers' as well; see sec. 1.3 below). A truthmaker for a certain truth is not, as a rule, another truth (although Bolzano, e.g., thought it was), but something suitable for being a sentence-object—and usually it *is* indeed the sentence-object for that very truth. For instance, the fact *Alyosha's hugging Ivan* as the sentence-object of 'Alyosha hugs Ivan' would be considered a suitable truthmaker for that sentence. Consider again:

Facts ... are the objects of certain mental states and acts, they *make* truthbearers *true* and correspond to truths [B] (Mulligan & Correia, 2008; emphasis added)

We saw above that what a sentence *projects onto* is a sentence-object in the sense of role 3. We can also indicate truthmaking as the *converse of projection* (though note that this can be said only for theories in which both relations are explicitly thus acknowledged). Truthmaking is a relation *from world*, that is, sentence-object, *to language*, that is, to truthbearer, while projection is a relation *from language*, that is, truthbearer, *to world*, that is, sentence-object. That both projection and truthmaking are acknowledged is by no means a matter of course. Although in theories that do acknowledge both relations the roles of sentence-object and truthmaker are often played by exactly the same entity, the roles as such must be kept separate. One reason is that a philosopher may accept that the sentence-object role must be played and yet might reject truthmaking, that is, might deny that the truthmaker role should be played, or simply not acknowledge the notion of truthmaking at all.

A second reason to keep the roles distinct, related to the first, is that truthmaking in present-day theories is conceived either as *necessitation*, that is, it is held that truthmakers *necessitate* the truth of (certain) assertions, or as *explanation*, that is, it is held that truthmakers *explain* the truth of (certain) assertions. Neither aspect is given once projection *alone* is given. Such characteristics of truthmaking need to be separately theorized and are by no means guaranteed by the mere introduction of a relation of projection from a sentence (or in general from a truthbearer) to the world.

A third reason to keep the roles of sentence-object and truthmaker distinct is that one might also just have truthmaking, and no projection. It seems that it is rather this scenario that best represents the position adopted by the Russell of "The Philosophy of Logical Atomism" (1918–1919). This historical circumstance might explain why the scenario in which there is truthmaking without projection is the one that was adopted in the early age of modern truthmaking.[15]

A fourth reason to keep the roles of truthmaker and sentence-object distinct is that fairly recently there have been attempts to give a somewhat more precise account of truthmaking (and thus solve some problems posed by characterizations of truthmaking as necessitation) by relying on the following scenario. Truthmaking has two aspects: necessitation and projection. What a sentence projects onto is not necessarily identical with its (minimal) truthmaker (Smith, 1999). This requires that the roles of truthmaker and sentence-object be kept distinct.

Now we have seen all the semantic roles one needs to consider to understand facts, and to achieve some clarity concerning just what exactly propositions and facts are. I am not saying that merely distinguishing facts and propositions with the aid of the roles they are or are not able to play shows that facts and propositions exist; I hold exactly the opposite, namely that keeping these notions apart does not show anything as to whether these entities should be acknowledged (on this, see chaps. 5–6). I am also not claiming that all five of these roles should be played by entities: in fact, I will maintain at the end of the book that there seems enough good reason only to accept two such roles: the role of truthbearer and that of sentence-subject.

In the following section I shall apply our analysis of the five semantic roles to introduce the role played by facts in the most influential argument in favor of facts, David Armstrong's *truthmaker argument*. As we shall see, the circumstance that facts are the only candidates or even the best candidates for the truthmaker role is, according to Armstrong, a crucial reason why we should accept them. In chapter 2 I shall criticize Armstrong's claim and argue that the truthmaker argument is unsound. To understand the objection I will be making in chapter 2 in full, we will need to have a firm grasp on the seven ontological conditions that facts fulfill, which I shall introduce in section 1.3 below. As will become apparent in chapter 2, Armstrong's position is the best position one can take on facts. This is also why Armstrong figures so prominently in this book in general, and in these first three chapters in particular.

1.2   Compositional Facts: Why

In *A World of States of Affairs*, Armstrong says that the most fundamental argument for facts is what he calls *the truthmaker argument* (Armstrong, 1997, 115). In this section, I will briefly introduce that argument and the conceptual distinctions involved in it. I shall discuss the core of the argument in chapter 2. The truthmaker argument is the following:

Why do we need to recognize states of affairs? ... If *a* is *F*, then it is entailed that *a* exists and that the universal *F* exists. However, *a* could exist, and *F* could exist, and yet it fail to be the case that *a* is *F* (*F* is instantiated, but instantiated elsewhere only). *a*'s being *F* involves something more than *a* and *F*. It is no good simply adding the fundamental tie or nexus of instantiation to the sum of *a* and *F*. The existence of *a*, of instantiation, and of *F* does not amount to *a*'s being *F*. The something more must be *a*'s being *F*—and this is a state of affairs. (Armstrong, 1989, 88)

What does this mean exactly? This passage adds another handful of technical terms to our list: *states of affairs, universals, instantiation, tie or nexus of instantiation,* and *sum*. The first is easily placed: Armstrong uses *states of affairs* for what we have spoken of as a *fact*. I shall come to this and the other four terms below (for states of affairs, see sec. 1.3; for ties, sec. 1.2, condition 1; for universals and instantiation, sec. 1.2, condition 2; for sum, sec. 1.2, condition 7). For now, here's an easier and more analytic reconstruction of the argument sketched in the passage above. The line numbers below indicated within parentheses on the right of each line of the argument do not signal a formal connection, but a far loser one— something like '(partially) on the basis of' or '(partially) because', and by this I do not mean that each step is motivated *only* by the previous; for instance, 3 is itself an assumption, though one that is also motivated by 1 and 2. I come back to each of these steps below.

(1)   Empirical truths concern real objects in the world.
(2)   There are empirical truths, for instance:
      (*)   A hedgehog is lying on Argle's lap,
which concerns a particular hedgehog, Argle's lap, and *lying on*.
(3)   A particular hedgehog, Argle's lap, and *lying on* play a role in the truth of (*) (1, 2).
(4)   For (*) to be true, (i) we need a (real) truthmaker, where (ii) a truth-maker is something in the world in virtue of which (*) is true.
(5)   Disconnected from each other, a particular hedgehog, Argle's lap, and *lying on* are no truthmaker for (*): their connection is a truthmaker for it.
(6)   The fact *a (particular) hedgehog's lying on Argle's lap* is the connection of a particular hedgehog, Argle's lap, and *lying on*.
(7)   This fact is the truthmaker of (*) (3, 4 ii, 5, 6).
(8)   We need facts (4, i, 7).

Note that, actually, the argument so far only shows that we need at least *one* fact as truthmaker, that is, a (particular) hedgehog's (Hargle's) lying on Argle's lap. (Note also that the hedgehog on Argle's lap is Argle's pet Hargle, who is sick.) However, the argument can easily be made more general to match Armstrong's original formulation (see also Armstrong, 1997, 115).

Thus reconstructed, Armstrong's argument nicely makes clear what place facts occupy in the theoretical space between language and world and why we might feel the need to acknowledge them. The role of *truthbearer* (role 4) in the argument is taken up by (meaningful) sentences (Armstrong, 1997, 131, 8.53), that is, sentences equipped with a sense or meaning, and no special object is assumed to play the role of sentence-sense (role 2).[16] Note that for our purposes, the truthbearer (*) 'a hedgehog is lying on Argle's lap' is just a linguistic variant of 'Hargle is lying on Argle's lap'. In other words, we can here disregard problems related to the reference of general names plus indefinite article ('a hedgehog') as different from that of a singular name ('Hargle'). I will address questions related to specific functions of parts of speech in chapter 4.

According to this reconstruction, what our truthbearer (*) is *about* (role 1, sentence-subject) is three separate things: Hargle, Argle's lap, and *lying on*. These objects all play a role in the truth of (*), but they are not its truthmaker, even taken together. The truthmaker (role 5) of this truth, here identified with the object (role 3) of this truth, is the fact that Hargle is lying on Argle's lap—*Hargle's lying on Argle's lap*. The difference between these three separate things and the unified object that Armstrong chooses to play truthmaker—a fact—shall occupy us throughout the whole of chapter 2 and 3 below.

From Armstrong's truthmaker argument we see that a fact is well cast as a sentence-object (role 3) and as a truthmaker (role 5). It is not well cast as a sentence-sense (role 2) or as truthbearer (role 4). This is a paradigmatic situation in present-day analytic metaphysics.[17] In fact, one might also not agree with Armstrong that *facts* can play (well or at all) the truthmaker role, but in general whoever agrees that *something* has to play that role will accept a very similar argument.

Importantly, in some special cases, facts can also be sentence-subjects (role 1), but these are quite specific cases in which the nominalization of a fact figures as a term in (true) sentences (second-order cases). Suppose Argle and Bargle watch *All about Eve*. Argle says to Bargle:

(M)   Margo's looking at Eve while smoking was enthralling.

Margo's looking at Eve while smoking is a fact, here in the role of sentence-subject. The object of (M) is also played by a fact, but by a *different* one: *Margo's looking at Eve while smoking's being enthralling*.

Let's now have a closer look at the argument. (1) is a kind of definition. Then the following assumptions are made. (2) is an existential and semantic assumption; (3) is a semantic assumption linked to (1), and is stronger than (2) insofar as it supposes that objects in the world have a role in determining the truth of sentences; (4) and (7) are very strong assumptions introducing the conceptual apparatus of realistic truthmaking theories. The truthmaking apparatus requires argumentative support, but as stated I will not challenge this assumption here (I will be somewhat more critical of it at the end of chap. 3). The two assumptions that I shall discuss in much detail in this chapter and in the following two are (5) and (6).

Let's look at (5) first. If at one and the same time Hargle is running happily across a meadow in Keuru, Finland, and Argle is munching on a Gruyère sandwich on the grass of Museumplein in Amsterdam, and there is something lying on Argle's lap, say, a colander, then Hargle, Argle's lap, and *lying on* all exist for sure, but *separately*: that is, Hargle is not resting on

Argle's lap. In other words, Hargle, Argle's lap, and the relation of *lying on* must be *brought together*, arranged in some way. (6), which says that facts *are* things brought together, is the fundamental ontological assumption for friends of facts. As we shall see below, it can take several different forms. And as we shall see in the next chapter, they are all problematic.

At this point one might wonder whether facts are truthmaker-candidates only for *relational* predications such as 'Harle is on Argle's lap'. The answer is no: changing the example in (*) into 'Hargle is sick' would make no difference to the argument; facts provide truthmakers also for nonrelational predications such as those. In other words, the need for facts as truthmakers as advanced by Armstrong does not depend on the example being a *two*-place or relational predication of the form *Rab*: the same argument would hold also for *one*-place predications of the form *Fa*—and indeed Armstrong's passage above was concerned with the latter. To see this, consider the following.

(1′) Empirical truths concern real objects in the world.

(2′) There are empirical truths, for instance:

  (**) 'Hargle is sick',

which concerns Hargle and *being sick*.

(3′) Hargle and being-sick play a role in the truth of (**) (1′, 2′).

(4′) For (**) to be true we need a (real) truthmaker: something in the world in virtue of which (**) is true.

(5′) Disconnected from each other, Hargle and being-sick are no truthmaker for (**): their connection is a truthmaker for it.

(6′) The fact *Hargle's being sick* is the connection of Hargle and sickness.

(7′) This fact is the truthmaker of (**) (3′, 4′, 5′, 6′).

(8′) We need facts (4′, 7′).

Again, the end-of-line numbers do not indicate a logical relation of *following from*. Notice the parallel between (5) and (5′) and (6) and (6′): the point concerns the need for some object that accounts as a *unified* entity for the truth of 'Hargle is on Argle's lap' and 'Hargle is sick' and does not depend on whether the two or three separate entities involved in the truth of those sentences are relations.[18] What is important is the difference between individuals (Hargle, Argle's lap), properties (being sick), and relations (lying on) *taken separately* (5, 5′) on the one hand, and their actual—well, *factual*—connection (6, 6′–8, 8′) on the other, which is, according to the argument, the only thing that in this case can function as truthmaker.[19]

To see what is involved in (5) and (6), we have to understand the nature of facts, and to see this, we need to look more closely at the seven ontological conditions that facts fulfill. As noted, we are setting the stage for objections to come in chapter 2. The most important thing to stress is that (5) and (6) show that if facts aren't real unities—if they can't play the role of unifiers of the world—then they can't be truthmakers. Here again are our seven ontological conditions:

Condition 1: A fact is a *complex* object with a *fixed* number of constituents (in the simplest case minimally two and maximally three), which it comprehends in its *reticulation*.
Condition 2: A fact is *categorically heterogeneous*.
Condition 3: A fact is *in the world*.
Condition 4: A fact is *semantically idle*.
Condition 5: A fact is *ontologically heterogeneous*.
Condition 6: A fact is *structured in a formal way*.
Condition 7: A fact has a *nonmereological composition*.

Let's now look more closely at them one by one.

1.3   The Nature of Compositional Facts

The first of the seven ontological conditions that facts fulfill is the following:

Condition 1: A Fact Is a Complex Object with a Fixed Number of Constituents (Minimally Two and Maximally Three in the Simplest Case), Which It Comprehends in Its Reticulation   What does this condition exactly prescribe? Let us consider again premises (5) and (6) of the truthmaker argument:

(5)   Disconnected from each other, a particular hedgehog, Argle's lap, and *lying on* are no truthmaker for (*) 'A hedgehog is lying on Argle's lap': their connection is a truthmaker for it.
(6)   The fact *a (particular) hedgehog's lying on Argle's lap* is the connection of a particular hedgehog, Argle's lap, and *lying on*.

(5′)   Disconnected from each other, Hargle and being sick are no truthmaker for (**) 'Hargle's sick': their connection is a truthmaker for it.
(6′)   The fact *Hargle's being sick* is the connection of Hargle and sickness.

If a fact is the connection of other objects as (6) says, then a fact is a complex item, which is just to say that it is *not simple*. Of what is a fact composed? How many constituents does a fact in the simplest case have, involve, or, as I will say, *reticulate*? Let us assume that the truthmakers of (*)

and (**) are instances of simplest cases.[20] In the first examples we have Argle's lap, Hargle, and *lying on*, and in the second example we have Hargle and sickness. Argle's lap and Hargle are particular individuals, also called *concrete particulars*, sickness is a property, and *lying on* is a relation. So, in the simplest case, a fact has minimally two constituents, a concrete particular and a property, or else three, two concrete particulars and a relation.

In light of the above, we should consider then at least *two* basic forms of facts: relational and nonrelational. Whereas nonrelational facts reticulate an individual and a property, facts of relational form reticulate two (or more) individuals and some relation R.[21] Could we have just one basic form, and treat relations just as we treat properties? In principle we can, but some metaphysicians assign great significance to the distinction between properties and relations.[22] Besides, special problems arise with relational facts, as we shall see in chapter 2, which make it important to observe the difference. But this said, most of what I say against facts applies already to the simplest case of atomic, nonrelational states of affairs and a fortiori to relational ones. When the relational versus the nonrelational status of facts is irrelevant I will freely use examples of either kind.[23]

Some say, however, that two constituents (in the nonrelational case) or three (in the relational case) are not enough for a fact. The reason is that, as (5) in the truthmaker argument points out, some connection or *unifying glue* is needed between the particular and the property or the two particulars and the relation, something that accounts for the reticulation. One way to interpret this connection is to take it to be an additional special constituent. So, some claim, facts should have minimally three constituents: a particular, a property, and a *tie* (or four: two particulars, relation, and a *tie*). We get:

(I)   two-kinds-of-constituent theories (with two basic forms of facts, relational: *a-R-b* and nonrelational: *a-F*);

(II)   three-kinds-of-constituent theories (with two basic forms of facts, relational: *a*-tie-*R*-tie-*b*, *a*-tie-*R*-tie-*c*-*R*-tie-*b*, etc., and nonrelational: *a*-tie-*F*).

Note that ties and relations are different entities: special, nonrelational ties are usually accepted alongside relations.[24] The relation R that relates a and b may be a different (kind of) relation: a and b may be in a relation of being friends, of being more boring than, of hugging, of exchanging drafts of unilateral global disarmament, and so on.[25] By contrast, the tie will be always the *same* (species of) tie, whatever its nature. One could object that I have not rendered the case involving ties accurately enough in (I) and (II), for it suggests that there are only two-place ties, whereas there might be many different ties with different adicities. But, to anticipate one point I will discuss in the next chapter, it seems difficult to say more than what I have. It seems difficult in particular to specify exactly what a tie, or at least *this* particular tie typical of facts, is: often the only explanation you get, if you insist, is "you know, the thing that holds facts together."[26] I will discuss ties in chapter 2, section 2.1, option B.

Condition 2: A Fact Is Categorically Heterogeneous   According to (5) and (6) in Armstrong's truthmaker argument, facts are complex entities composed of other entities, and these other entities are individuals, properties, relations, and perhaps nonrelational ties. This quickly reveals that facts involve first of all a "categorial heterogeneity" of constituents (Smith, 1989, 422). In the examples I took to illustrate Armstrong's truthmaker argument, Argle and Hargle are *concrete* objects and belong to different *categories* than sickness and *lying on*, which are *abstract* objects.

What are abstract objects? Abstract objects are often taken to be *ideal* objects, objects having an intrinsically timeless status like square roots, hexagons, conic sections, and virtuous ideals. This way of construing 'abstract' is not the one I will adopt in this book, for it would not serve us very well. What I mean here by 'abstract' is 'qualitative' (Maurin, 2002, 23). We can put the distinction in this way: those objects are called abstract that can be *had* by other objects, not in the sense in which Hargle has spines, but in the sense in which Hargle has courage (Bolzano, 1837, §80, I, 379). Some would prefer to say, in more technical jargon, that abstract objects are those that are *exemplified by* or *instantiated in* other objects: Hargle exemplifies courage, or courage is instantiated in her. Objects that are not qualitative and cannot thus be had (exemplified, instantiated) in the way a quality is had are concrete. Facts themselves are concrete objects (at least in Armstrong's version).

The two ways in which abstract objects can be said to be related to concrete objects, *exemplification* and *having*, match two different theories of properties. On both views, properties are abstract entities (as we saw, this means *qualitative*), but on the first view properties are *universal*, and on the second they are *particular*:

(*Universal properties*)   A property is universal if and only if exactly similar properties are numerically identical with it.

(*Particular properties*)   A property is particular if and only if exactly similar properties are numerically different from it.

Something similar holds of relations:

Universal relations   A relation is universal if and only if exactly similar relations are numerically identical with it.

Particular relations   A relation is particular if and only if exactly similar relations are numerically different from it.

What does this mean? How can properties and relations be *exactly similar*? What is meant here by 'exact similarity' is the sense in which Bolzano speaks in the following passage of 'two reds':

Bolzano's Zwei Röthen   This red (numero idem) can be found in [*an*] no other rose. The red found in any other rose can, if you wish, be *similar, very similar* to it, but it cannot be the *same*, just because it is not the same rose; for *two* roses *two* reds [*Röthen*] are needed (Bolzano, 1833/1935, 32–33).

Importantly, the properties and the relations that a fact reticulates can be universal or particular. Suppose that Hargle is sad and Bargle is also sad. If we take sadness as a universal property ('Sadness', to give it distinction), and we follow Armstrong, there is a fact that has as constituents Hargle and Sadness, that very same Sadness, the only Sadness there is, that is also a constituent of the fact that has Bargle as a constituent. Similarly, when Argle is sad, there is another fact that has as constituents Argle, a particular, and Sadness, that very same Sadness, the only Sadness there is, that is a constituent of the fact that has Bargle as a constituent, and also of the fact that has Hargle as a constituent. And so on. If we take sadness as a particular property or as a *trope*, as it is usually called, then if Argle, Bargle, and Hargle are sad, a different and distinct trope of sadness is reticulated in each of the three different and distinct facts reticulating Argle, Bargle, and Hargle, respectively.

Something similar holds for relations. If *a* and *b* are in the relation of standing two feet away from each other, and *c* and *b* also are in such a relation, are we then dealing with one relation or two? If the relation of standing two feet away from each other between *a* and *b* is *numerically different* from the relation of standing two feet away from each other between *c* and *b*, then those properties are particulars, or in other words, *tropes*; if those relations are, in fact, numerically one and the same, then they are *universals*. The universal/particular distinction is then a matter of number.[27]

What are tropes, then, exactly? Tropes are *abstract simple particulars*. Sometimes they are called 'particular(ized) properties', and up until the nineteenth century they were sometimes called 'metaphysical parts' to distinguish them from the physical parts, that is, the *pieces* of an object.[28] Meet Donald, busy taking apart lollipops:

Since we cannot find more parts of the usual gross sort, like the stick, to be wholly similar from lollipop to lollipop, let us discriminate subtler and thinner or more diffuse parts till we find some of these which are wholly similar. ... Just as we can distinguish in the lollipops ... the gross parts called "sticks," ... so we can distinguish in each lollipop a finer part which we are used to call its "color" and another called its "shape"—not its kind of color or shape, mind you, but these particular cases, this reddening, this occurrence or occasion of roundness, each as uniquely itself as a man, an earthquake, or a yell. (Williams, 1953, 4–5)

These "subtler and thinner or more diffuse parts" are tropes.[29]

Armstrong's facts are composed of concrete particulars and universals. Note that nothing rules out that facts reticulate concrete particulars and tropes.

Condition 3: A Fact Is in the World   So far, we have seen that according to Armstrong's truthmaker argument, facts are categorically heterogeneous, complex, concrete objects composed of other concrete and abstract objects. The argument also assumes that facts are in the world. When one says that facts are in the world it may be hard to understand immediately what 'the world' refers to, and in what sense facts are 'in the world'. Sometimes this phrase is taken to be unproblematic, and to refer simply to all there is in a rather plain sense, the one that includes animals, cities, cells, jars of sambal badjak as well as their lids and their owners and producers—that is, *things*. But we might also want to include in the world barkings, smiles on a face, the warmth of the sun's rays on Lake Baikal, the size and mass of cells, and so on. These are not things, but rather *events* involving things, and *states* of things, their *qualities* and *modifications*. So we would put in the world both abstract and concrete objects (both objects that *have* and objects that *are had*, as we put it under condition 2). We might also welcome other interesting kinds of entities: holes inside empty sambal badjak jars, their edges and borders, and the waves on the surface of the Lake Baikal. Maybe the last group of entities I mentioned is more controversial (why say that *holes* are things? Why not say instead that some things are perforated?). Perhaps; but what is important to us is that no matter how strange, so far we have put in the world only time-bound entities, entities existing through time and in time as causes or effects in a causal chain. These entities I will call *real*. Among real entities we also find tropes. Our catalog of the world might include even more, however. It might include (kinds of) entities existing at all times or at no times, that is, existing outside time, and not entering the causal chain. For instance, we might want to include (on some particular view of mathematics) the number seven among all other numbers, continuous functions, conic sections, power sets, and so on. These time-unbound entities I shall call *ideal*. Among ideal entities we also find universals.[30]

Now, as long as we have *ideal* entities like concentric spheres in the same bag with *real* stuff such as animals and cities and all their qualities and lacks and borders, and we call it 'the world', then we might think that what we are talking about is clear: entities that are *there* in an interesting sense, (a collection of) spatiotemporal perceptible entities (including their limits), plus imperceptible, non-spatiotemporal ones. But it still won't be clear enough what 'the world' means, for we can go on adding even more abstruse kinds of objects to the bag we call 'the world', and still not have what other people talk about when they talk about 'the world'.

One way to get clearer on what 'the world' means is to speak in terms of the distinction between *sense* and *reference*, a distinction by now part of philosophical lore (it comes from Gottlob Frege, but it is also present in a psychological variant in Twardowski, like Husserl a pupil of Brentano, and in Bolzano). Consider the two phrases '4' and '2+2'. They have the same reference but not the same sense: they speak of the same referent in different ways. The world as I have meant to introduce it here when I say that compositional facts are in the world is at the level of *reference*, not of *sense*. The world is not at the same level as (the collection of the) *ways* we talk about things: it is at the same level as the things themselves.[31] Compositional facts are in the world just as things are in the world. Some other philosophers put the world at the level of sense, and call 'the world' the (successful) ways in which we speak about things (see chap. 5, n. 8).

Saying this allows us, as we shall see below, to distinguish several positions in order to analyze them. First, we have the position in which a fact like *Hargle's being sad* is a real object and part of the world at the level of reference exactly as concrete particulars like animals are. This is the case in Armstrong's theory. Second, we have the position in which a fact is an *ideal object* like conic sections, and is in the world at the level of reference like the reference of '4' and '2+2'. We might also consider a third position that accepts that facts are both at the level of sense and of reference (or at neither level), because that distinction is simply not made. However, as we shall see, the objects we are dealing with in that case aren't actually facts: I shall call them (*Russellian*) *hybrids*, blurs or propfacts, as I need to distinguish them from other entities. On this, see the end of the last subsection in section 1.4. We could also distinguish a fourth position according to which by 'facts' we mean objects that are ideal and at the level of sense, *not* in the world and at the level of reference. Again, these objects are not facts, but rather, as we shall see, true (*Fregean*) *propositions*. I come back to this position in chapters 4 through 6 when I will introduce *propositional facts*—facts that are noncompositional objects at the level of reference and thus distinct from the compositional facts I discuss in this and the following two chapters.

Here we establish that compositional facts—the facts featuring in the truthmaker argument—are in the world at the level of reference (in the construal outlined above), regardless of whether they are real or ideal.

Condition 4: A Fact Is Semantically Idle   A point related to the above discussion is this: we assume that language has the capacity to transcend itself and reach out to things by devices of reference and expression. Facts do not work like that. Facts have no capacity to transcend themselves in this sense. It is nonsense to ask: what is the reference of *Hargle's being sad*? Facts are at the level of reference, and that's all.[32] Here is one way to make the point:

It is nonsensical ... to speak of a state of affairs as being "about" the entities which it involves. The state of affairs of *a* being green is not *about a* being green, for example, since it simply *consists in a* being green. (Aquila, 1977, 58–59; on state of affairs versus facts, see sec. 1.4.2)

In connection with the point just discussed as to facts being in the world: we can say that whereas facts are entities in the world which are semantically idle, linguistic expressions (and, if they are accepted, senses) are entities in the world which are *not* semantically idle.

1.3.1   Toolbox: Facts versus Events
That's the way the needle pricks
That's the way the glue sticks
—William Burroughs and Tom Waits, "That's the Way," from *The Black Rider*, 1993

At this point, before moving on to the remaining three conditions, I shall introduce the first set of conceptual tools in our toolbox, tools to distinguish facts from other entities with which facts might be confused: *events*, *integral wholes*, *propositions*, *states of affairs*, and *complexes*.

So far we have seen four characteristics of facts. Are facts the *only* things that are (taken to be) (1) complex objects with a fixed number of constituents (two/three or three/four in the minimal case), (2) categorically heterogeneous, (3) part of the world, and (4) semantically idle? Doesn't this description fit *events* as well, for example? That depends on what we mean by 'event'.

We might divide events into *activities, accomplishments, achievements,* and *states* (Vendler, 1967, 106–107). Intuitively, we say that events are things that happen in the world, and, however creative we might be in understanding 'happen', events—as things that happen—will be *real.* They will be, that is, part of the world at the level of reference, and they will be semantically idle.[33] Since facts are entities of this kind, the question thus arises: can events satisfy (1) and (2), that is, be structured entities with a fixed number of categorically heterogeneous constituents? Why do we say that *Hargle's being sad* and *the stomach's rumbling* are facts if we could say that they are a kind of event, namely a *state*?

In some views of events, such as Kim's and Goldman's (Goldman, 1976; Kim, 1973, 1980), events are indeed seen as a thing's exemplifying a property, and thus as structured entities matching all the characteristics we have ascribed to facts so far. This amounts to *identifying* events with facts. We can describe these theories of events as, indeed, theories of facts, or as theories exploiting the notion of fact to explain what an event is. A similar position can be ascribed to Armstrong (1997, 37, 95). But if we don't want that, then how do we distinguish facts from events?

Let us first ask this: why is it so important to keep events and facts distinct? The main reason is the following. Suppose you need events for some reason in your ontology. If your theory merges facts with events, and I manage to convince you that you do not live in a world of facts, some objections of this book will seem to apply to events as well, and, if these objections convince you, may make it seem as though you should also abandon events. This is, possibly, quite bad for your ontology. So, we should not mix the two.[34]

A philosopher taking facts as *ideal* entities could base the opposition between facts and events fully on the idea that facts have no spatiotemporal boundaries and cannot be perceived, whereas events have spatiotemporal boundaries and (often) can be perceived.[35]

An alternative view of events takes them to be real but unstructured entities. On such a view, events are *tropes*.[36] The same reasoning that we saw in the case of universals versus particular properties applies also to events: exactly similar explosions can be counted as one or many. On the view in which an event, say, Caesar's death, is a trope, that event is not a structured object reticulating Caesar and the property of being dead or of dying (and possibly some kind of gluing tie). It is a *particular* happening at a particular time located at a particular place. The death of Caesar is Caesar's and no one else's. This does not mean that Caesar is a constituent of the thing named by 'Caesar's death' (nor that the time and place of its occurrence are). It is rather the other way around: we are speaking of a 'diffuse part', something said to be *in* Caesar, in some sense of *being in*. And on the view that events are tropes, only *that* 'diffuse part' is what we call, metaphysically, an event.

So: unlike (compositional) facts, events are not categorically heterogeneous complex objects with a fixed number of constituents, although they are part of the world and semantically idle like facts.[37]

1.3.2 Toolbox: Facts versus Integral wholes

Let us now introduce our second set of tools. As we have seen, a fact is a complex object, but not all complex objects are facts. There are, actually, three kinds of complex objects relevant to our discussion: *facts*, *integral wholes* (sometimes also called *substances*), and *complexes*. I shall briefly introduce complexes under condition 7 below. I will return to the difference between facts and complexes, and between complexes and integral wholes, in the next two chapters. For now I discuss only integral wholes.

Integral wholes are concrete structured objects, but unlike facts they do not have a *fixed* number of constituents in the minimal case. No matter how many constituents a fact has (two or three in the minimal case, with no specific maximum bound), the identity conditions for a fact are given by the number of its constituents and the arrangement in which they stand, including identity through time.[38] There is a fair agreement among philosophers that this is not how integral wholes like grasshoppers are individuated, since integral wholes may lose or acquire parts and undergo change of properties: (1) a grasshopper might lose a feeler and still be the very same grasshopper (the denial of this being *mereological essentialism*—i.e., the view that all parts of an object are essential to it—see Chisholm, 1973, 1976); (2) a grasshopper may survive the hungry beak of a bird and become a poor, shocked, sad grasshopper, and still be the very same grasshopper. None of the kind applies to facts.

This is important because although philosophers usually do not identify integral wholes with facts, some do take integral wholes to be facts. Again, as in the case of events, a theory of facts such as Armstrong's exploits the notion of fact to account for integral wholes. If integral wholes are facts (either big complex facts or agglomerates of facts), rejecting facts would mean rejecting integral wholes. We may not care much for events, but most philosophers are content with integral wholes and would be unhappy to see them depart from the ontological inventory together with facts. So, what can integral wholes be other than facts? There are several options, one being that integral wholes are agglomerates of tropes (either just tropes, as in trope bundle theories, or tropes plus a bare particular, as in trope substratum theories; see Loux, 2002, 85–92). This is by no means the only option, but it is not important which one we choose here: it is enough that we are not forced to take integral wholes to be facts. The difference between integral wholes and facts will play a crucial role in chapter 2.

Condition 5: A Fact Is Ontologically Heterogeneous   We saw that, in contrast with facts, events are simple, and integral wholes do not have a fixed number of parts or constituents (for the difference between parts and constituents, see condition 7). Let us now return to our seven ontological conditions. By 'ontological heterogeneity' I mean either of the following:

(i)   that facts have at least one constituent whose *ontological status* is different from the ontological status of the other constituents;
(ii)   that all the constituents of a fact have the same ontological status, but the ontological status of the fact itself *as a whole* is different from that of its constituents.

By 'ontological status' I mean the way of being of an object—yet this still explains little. Recall our distinction between *real* or time-bound and *ideal* or time-unbound entities from condition 3. Onto this distinction I shall now map another distinction between *existence* and *subsistence* as two different modes of being: sometimes I shall say that spatiotemporal objects such as lakes and hedgehogs *exist* (but not that they subsist), and that timeless, spaceless objects such as the number four and a recursive function *subsist* (but not that they exist).

The ideal/subsisting versus real/existing terminology just introduced is a little cumbersome, and neither necessarily nor always useful or clarifying.[39] One might prefer to say that real objects *exist by being in time*, while ideal objects *exist by being outside time*. But sticking to the subsistence/existence distinction allows us to take into account a spectrum of philosophical positions that would be difficult to capture without it. Actually, sometimes I'll be forced to go beyond even that. (I am speaking of the notion of *obtaining*. I will return to this when discussing states of affairs in sec. 1.4.2 below, and in chap. 4.)

According to condition 2 above, all facts are *categorically* heterogeneous in the same way: they all reticulate concrete and abstract objects although they themselves are concrete (they are not *had* by anything). Condition 6 now says that all facts are also *ontologically* heterogeneous, but they can be so in different ways, namely the following three. According to some theories of facts, facts have both ideal and real constituents, while the facts themselves are ideal. (This is Russell's position, both with regard to his early 'propositions' and his later facts. The same holds for Russell-inspired positions, on which see, e.g., Fitch, 1994). According to some other theories, facts have both ideal and real constituents, while the facts themselves are real (this is Armstrong's position).[40] According to still other theories, no matter whether facts have all real or all ideal constituents, they are themselves ideal (early phenomenologists like Meinong, Husserl, and Twardowski hold this view; see chap. 4, sec. 4.2). It is very difficult to understand what exactly grounds these choices from an intrinsic point of view. We are given not arguments, but slogans, such as "This is the victory of particularity" (Armstrong, 1997, 126), or its defeat (Russell, 1918–1919). But never mind this. For us, the interesting thing is how these three options fare vis-à-vis the problems they face. We will consider the most pressing of these problems in chapter 2.

Condition 6: A Fact Is Structured in a Formal Way   Let's take stock: compositional facts—the facts that are established by the truthmaker argument—are complex objects reticulating a fixed number of constituents (two to three or three to four), categorically and ontologically heterogeneous, part of the furniture of the world, and semantically idle.

Admittedly, 'reticulate' is a weird term even for a philosopher. But it has an advantage: it signals that facts indeed have a special relational nature, that is, a special articulation or arrangement.[41] Because of this relational(-like) nature, a fact is different from a property. But it is also different from a relation, because a fact *comprehends* the constituents that it relates in its relational articulation. I know of no metaphysical theory of relations in which relations *include* the relata.[42] This is particularly clear in the case in which relations are taken to be tropes, for these are, as we've seen, simple, that is, *unstructured*, entities.

For many a philosopher, the relational articulation that glues together the constituents of a fact is a *logical* articulation.[43] Only linguistic entities, or entities coming sufficiently close to linguistic entities, can strictly speaking have syntax. Facts are neither linguistic nor languagelike, because they are that of which the world is made, and the world is not made of linguistic or languagelike entities *at the lowest level of reference*. Thus, the articulation of a fact cannot be logical in the sense of being syntactical. It is a categorical mismatch to say that there is a *syntactical* articulation between a lizard and light green or an alto sax and its price. We thus say that facts have a *formal* articulation, meaning by this that no matter what the constituents are (no matter their subject matter), they are always arranged in the same way. For Russell, facts have a formal articulation by having a certain *form*, a notion he introduces in the following way:

Two facts are said to have the same "form" when they differ only as regards their constituents. In this case, we may suppose the one to result from the other by *substitution* of different constituents. For example, "Napoleon hates Wellington" results from "Socrates loves Plato" by substituting Napoleon for Socrates, Wellington for Plato, and *hates* for *loves*. (Russell, 1919, 278)[44]

There are a number of possible variations on the details of how we should conceive of the 'formal reticulation' of a fact, and on whether there are one or more ways in which facts are seen as formally structured; but at bottom the idea is that the constituents of all facts are all arranged in a certain way. Philosophers keep these ways (or 'forms') at an extremely low number. Ideally, there is one single way to arrange (or form) a fact in this sense. Armstrongian facts are no exception to this.

Condition 7: A Fact Has a Nonmereological Composition   We've seen so far that compositional facts are complex objects with a fixed number of constituents in a formal reticulation, and that they are categorically and ontologically heterogeneous, part of the world, and semantically idle. Now we shall examine condition 7, which is really crucial. Consider again the following:

(5)   Disconnected from each other, a particular hedgehog, Argle's lap, and *lying on* are , no truthmaker for (*) 'A hedgehog is lying on Argle's lap': their connection is a truthmaker for it.
(6)   The fact *a (particular) hedgehog's lying on Argle's lap* is the connection of a particular hedgehog, Argle's lap, and *lying on*.
(5′)   Disconnected from each other, Hargle and *being-sick* are no truthmaker for (**) 'Hargle's sick': their connection is a truthmaker for it.
(6′)   The fact *Hargle's being sick* is the connection of Hargle and sickness.

The objects reticulated by facts in their structure are almost never called 'parts', but rather 'constituents' (see, e.g., Russell, 1919, 278). Why is that? Because, it is argued, facts have a nonmereological composition, and this explains why philosophers tend to avoid using 'parts' for the objects reticulated in a fact: 'parts' here would be misleading (if not plainly wrong). We shall see this point more clearly in chapter 2, section 2.2. In chapter 2 we shall also see better in what sense the nonmereological composition of facts is responsible for the difference between facts and *mereological sums* (of which some are *complexes*)—and for endless difficulties. Often a fact is said to be something more than the *mere* (as many like to say) mereological sum of the objects of which it is composed. In theories conceiving of facts as special articulations of concrete particulars and universal properties (or relations), for instance, the mereological sum of the constituents of the fact *Hargle's being sad*, that is, of Hargle on the one hand and of property of sadness on the other, exists in the universe once Hargle and sadness exist in the universe, irrespective of whether *Hargle's being sad* exists in the universe. Differently put: 'Hargle is sad' is true if and only if the fact *Hargle's being sad* exists, while it is not the case that 'Hargle is sad' is true if and only if the mereological sum Hargle plus sadness exists in the universe. The reason why this is so will be dealt with at length in chapter 2, but the crucial point is this: philosophers who do accept facts say that when Hargle is sad, alongside these *two* things (Hargle and sadness) there is also a *third* thing in the world: a special 'being together' of these two things in a real unity *over and above* the two things—a *compositional fact*. Philosophers who don't accept facts say that at most there are *just* these two things: Hargle and sadness.[45] Now, this might sound confusing, because I mentioned above something called 'the mereological sum Hargle + sadness', which seems itself to be one *single* object, not two. But the problem, as we shall see, is that mereological sums are still taken to be mere collections, as a flock of sheep is a collection of animals or a puzzle a collection of pieces. Aggregates of this kind could be considered as one thing, but such things do not have what is normally called *a real unity*. By contrast, a fact, it is said, *really is* one unified thing.[46]

The upshot of the above is that, in short, a compositional fact is a complex entity with minimally two constituents that is part of the furniture of the world, and whose composition is formal, nonmereological, and heterogeneous both from the ontological point of view and the point of view of the categories involved. If we examine a theory in which some complex entities in the world appear with a minimal number of two or three constituents that are unmereologically and formally structured, and categorically and ontologically heterogeneous, then they are facts.

Now we ask: what makes compositional facts different from propositions and states of affairs?

1.4 Facts versus Propositions, Facts versus States of Affairs

Let us return to semantic roles to help us understand the difference between compositional facts, propositions, and states of affairs. Doing so, we can add two new sets of tools to our toolbox. This analysis will come in handy in chapter 2 (states of affairs) and chapters 4 through 6 (propositions).

'Proposition' is an ambiguous label. There are several competing notions of proposition in philosophy. Given this variety, some of my terminological choices in the following might sound odd.[47] This situation is unavoidable, however, if one aims, as I do in this book, to offer conceptual analyses of notions such as fact, state of affairs, and proposition that are as general as possible. The criterion I follow is this: I am interested in keeping the notions of proposition and fact separate, so I am especially interested in discussing notions of propositions that come close to that of fact but cannot be identified with it. The purpose of doing this, again, is to make explicit the characteristics of the entities involved, so that we can get a clear grasp on the extent to which the arguments against facts I formulate in this book do or do not apply to (different notions of) propositions.

1.4.1   Toolbox: Fact versus Propositions

Propositions, like facts, are complex entities with a formal composition of minimally two or three parts,[48] but unlike facts, propositions are *not semantically idle*, are *not in the world* at the level of reference (though they might be at the level of sense), are *categorically* and *ontologically homogeneous* entities, and have a *mereological* composition. To say that the composition of propositions is mereological is certainly controversial, but we'll let it pass for the moment. In chapter 2 I return to it briefly.

Let us first look at two theories of propositions that can be considered variants of the notion of proposition just introduced. Call the first the *Fregean theory*:

(i)   Propositions are nonlinguistic objects; they are (or function as) the meaning or content of linguistic expressions (sentences).

(ii)   The parts of a proposition have the same ontological nature as the whole, and have, like the whole, a semantic function.

(iii)   Propositions so conceived are what is primarily true or false (the primary truthbearers); the sentences expressing them are only derivatively true or false.

(iv)   Propositions are *independent* of being expressed in language, and they subsist outside of time and space.

Both Bolzano and Frege are representatives of this view.[49]

According to the second theory of propositions, call it the *Aristotelian Theory*:

(i′)   Propositions are syntactico-semantic meaningful unities: inscriptions engraved or series of sounds pronounced by someone equipped with meaning or sense (which is not a separate entity).

(ii′) The parts of a proposition have the same ontological nature as the whole, and, like the whole, have a semantic function.

(iii′) Propositions so conceived are what is primarily true or false.

(iv′) Propositions are *dependent* on being expressed in language (or in thought). Meaning cannot exist without being expressed in words (or thought).

We have seen that Armstrong can be seen as an advocate of this view, which was standard in the Middle Ages and was held earlier by Aristotle.

The two notions of propositions just elucidated correspond to Alonzo Church's 'proposition in the abstract sense' (our Fregean view) and 'proposition in the traditional sense' (our Aristotelian view; see Church, 1956, 3). An Aristotelian proposition is a *real* object: a declarative sentence in use taken together with its (dependent) sense or meaning, which we can't take to be an entity (even less an ideal one). A Fregean proposition is an independent, *ideal* object.[50]

As we saw in the previous section, facts are categorically heterogeneous entities because they reticulate concrete and abstract constituents (individuals and properties/relations), though they are themselves concrete (i.e., qualitative). Further, they do not themselves have the same ontological status as their constituents (which can instead have the same ontological status with respect to each other). But propositions, no matter whether Aristotelian or Fregean, are wholes composed of categorically homogeneous parts, and these wholes have the same ontological status as the parts. Take the example of an entity obeying our description of a Fregean proposition, a Bolzanian *proposition-in-itself*. It is composed of exactly three parts: *ideas-in-themselves*, and these have the same ontological status as the proposition; both wholes and parts are ideal. Mutatis mutandis, the same holds for Aristotelian propositions. This makes both views *compositional views of propositions*.[51]

It might be argued that a proposition is categorically heterogeneous, though heterogeneous only in a sense quite different from the heterogeneity of the constituents of a fact. The heterogeneity we have in the case of propositions amounts to the fact that propositions have, on the one hand, parts that have been variously called *copulas*, functionlike *unsaturated entities*, and *syncategorematic terms* ('is sad'), and on the other hand, namelike parts that have been variously called *saturated entities* and *categorematic terms* ('Hargle'). Or, at least, this is how things work in some idealized or regimented language (which might look quite different from how natural language is actually spoken). But all these subpropositional parts of propositions (parts of propositions that are not themselves propositions) are not at all a mix of concrete and abstract entities in the sense in which I use these terms here. This is so even though some kind of subpropositional parts might be able to *express*, *denote*, or *refer to* concrete entities, and other kinds of subpropositional parts might be able to do so for abstract, that is, qualitative entities. Therefore, at most, it can be said that propositions are *linguistically*, syntactically (or semilinguistically, semisyntactically) heterogenenous. For the parts of propositions are all *concrete* entities, because they are not themselves qualitative and are not *had* by other parts of propositions, such as being sick is had by Hargle; rather, they are had by such parts as a spine is had by Hargle.

We can set apart facts and propositions by appealing to roles 1–5 in the following way.[52] Fregean propositions are suitable for playing the role of sentence-sense (role 2), yet they cannot be sentence-objects (role 3, barring second-order cases) or truthmakers (role 5).[53]

What about Aristotelian propositions? Like Fregean propositions, they fulfill the role of truthbearer (role 4) but do not fulfill that of sentence-object (role 3) or truthmaker (role 5) (in first-order cases). There is no difference on these points between the two theories of propositions. The point on which they do differ is the way in which each takes the roles of sentence-sense to be fulfilled by propositions. In this sense, Aristotelian theories are a mixed bag. But generally an Aristotelian proposition will not, strictly speaking, itself *be* either a sentence-sense; a declarative sentence will rather *have* a sense or meaning.

You might be an Aristotelian or a Fregean propositionalist; either way, the fundamental distinction between propositions and (compositional) facts in terms of semantic roles still stands: facts cannot be truthbearers, nor have any semantic properties or representational aspects of any kind. This aspect is closed under parthood: decomposing propositions, no matter what kind, will always give you meaningful parts or meaning-parts, never the objects that these parts are *about*. By contrast, decomposing facts will give you instead the *objects* that parts of propositions are about—those objects are not themselves "about" anything. The exception here are facts reticulating constituents that have semantic capacities like *The word 'ice-cream''s being a compound*; however, even these facts are, as a whole, semantically idle: they do not *mean* anything, they do not *refer* to anything, they are not *about* anything (in either sense of 'about').[54]

Moreover, propositions divide into (at least) true and false. This is fundamental to their role as truthbearers, so much so that it's quite implausible for a philosopher to acknowledge just true propositions without also acknowledging false ones. One can have more truth-values than just true and false, but no fewer. Nothing of the kind holds for facts.

Let's now fix things as follows: what the above means is that *if* in some theory the semantic roles I mentioned *are played at all*, then they are played by facts and propositions in the way indicated. Of course, for a role to be played, you need an actor: that is, you must make it plausible that facts and propositions belong to the catalog of the world (if for no other reason than that they are needed to play those roles, with the proviso that no other object can do a better job). But, as said, here I am just *describing* possible roles and actors: I am claiming neither that all these roles should be played nor that they should be played by facts and propositions. Alongside the arguments against facts that I give throughout the book, in chapter 4 I will offer an argument against Fregean propositions (which are among the actors I am considering in this section) based on the function of that-clauses.

1.4.2 Toolbox: Facts versus States of Affairs

Suppose your Dutch boyfriend tells you

(1)   Jan Peter Balkenende keeps a herring as a pet

and you believe him. However, you are mistaken in believing him. What exactly does your mistake consist in? According to Arthur Prior,

surely error consists in some sort of misapprehension of fact, not in the quite successful apprehension of something quite different.[55]

This passage is about *error*—about what it means to hold as true something which is not. One way to extract the gist of Prior's point here is that a proposition such as (1)—or if you prefer, the proposition, or judgment, expressed by (1)—is false because it does not do its job properly: it does not pick out *a fact*. It is not the case that (1) is false because it does pick out a funny object like *Jan Peter Balkenende's keeping a herring as a pet*. Jan Peter Balkenende does not keep a herring as a pet. There is no Jan Peter Balkenende's keeping a herring as a pet among the pieces of the furniture of the world. And this means, for some, that Jan Peter Balkenende's keeping a herring as a pet is not even an object.

For others, however, this means that Jan Peter Balkenende's keeping a herring as a pet is a genuine object, but it's just *not there*: it is a *nonobtaining state of affairs*. Some philosophers thus accept both nonobtaining states of affairs, such as Jan Peter Balkenende's keeping a herring as a pet, and obtaining ones, such as Berlusconi's owning a secret antinuclear bunker in an ecologically protected area in Sardinia. In these theories, facts are *obtaining states of affairs*.[56] Berlusconi's owning a secret antinuclear bunker in an ecologically protected area in Sardinia is a fact (i.e., an obtaining state of affairs). Propositions can be true or false, states of affairs can obtain or not, but nothing of the kind can be said about facts. Facts are just there: 'obtaining fact' is redundant, and 'nonobtaining fact' is contradictory (see Russell 1918–1919, 504). If it does not sound too repulsive, you can also think of states of affairs as *possible facts*.[57] For one thing, this makes clear that states of affairs and facts would form but one category.

Recall the distinction I made between 'existing' and 'subsisting' (sec. 1.3, condition 5). Does 'obtaining' mean the same as 'subsisting'? No. 'Obtaining' is supposed to mean something like *being there*, present in the catalog of the world, often in some unspecified sense. For some reason, philosophers who acknowledge states of affairs do not seem to want or to be able to say exactly what 'obtaining' means.[58] They must feel it is inappropriate to use either 'existing' or 'subsisting'. *Obtaining* seems to stand for some shadowy neighbor of *validity*, or *truth*, or even *being the case*. This is very confusing.

But perhaps we can make things clearer at least for our purposes by setting up a classification in which we merge the terminology introduced so far with ideas on modes of being borrowed from Meinong and Twardowski. According to table 1.1, nonobtaining states of affairs are objects that don't have any mode of being (so they neither exist nor subsist) but are still objects in their own right—that is, they are part of the catalog of the world all the same. This helps in one sense to distinguish propositions from states of affairs. We saw that there are true and false propositions. This distinction is not an ontological one, that is, a distinction concerning modes of being: the mode of being of a true proposition is not different from the mode of

Table 1.1

Objects				
Obtaining				
Real or Existing (*Dasein, Existieren*)		Ideal or Subsisting (*Bestehen*)		Nonobtaining
Concrete (Hargle)	*Abstract* (Hargle's sadness)	*Concrete* (The concept of sadness)	*Abstract* (the property of Sadness)	Nonobtaining states of affairs (*Balkenende's keeping a herring as a pet*)

being of a false one. The difference between a true and a false proposition is more like a qualitative one, such as the difference between being black and being white: the difference between obtaining and nonobtaining states of affairs is more like the difference between reality and fiction. The classification of states of affairs into obtaining and nonobtaining states of affairs *is* ontological.[59]

Now, facts and states of affairs, as we saw, are entities in the same category. Whereas philosophers who accept compositional facts tend to take them to be real, philosophers who accept states of affairs, and identify facts with obtaining states of affairs, tend to take them to be ideal. As mentioned in a similar connection above under condition 5, there seems to be no metaphysical criterion for either choice. In chapter 2, section 2.3, we will see that ideal facts pose problems of their own: the unity problem gets particularly sticky for ideal facts, and the question of how we should conceive of the reticulation of concrete particulars in an ideal fact remains a mystery.

One view of states of affairs is quite peculiar. On this view, Fregean propositions and facts are merged and put at the level of reference (not of sense). There might be four main reasons why the distinction between Fregean propositions and states of affairs gets blurred in this way in such theories. The first, second, and third are that states of affairs and propositions are both ideal, have a similar structure, and are taken to be spoken about by means of that-clauses. When the formal reticulation of a fact is not kept distinct from a *propositional* or *syntactical* arrangement, it becomes tempting to identify facts with (true) propositions and conflate them with states of affairs.[60] The temptation is all the stronger since, as I said above, propositions, like facts, are often designated by nominalizations of declarative sentences that are syntactically articulated, typically by means of that-clauses: the proposition *that Hargle is sad*, the fact *that Hargle is sad*. This use is ambiguous. I shall say more about it in chapters 4 through 6. Here I will just say that throughout this book I will consistently employ an alternative nominalization for facts—*A's being b (Hargle's being sad)*—to prevent confusion.

The fourth and perhaps most important reason for this is that theories that merge propositions and states of affairs are very popular in some quarters. Theories of this kind are defended by Chisholm and the direct reference theorists ("Russellians" or "Millians").[61] Direct reference theory, which holds that there is no level of sense that functions as a go-between between a sentence and a Russellian proposition, is the mainstream present-day semantic paradigm in the philosophy of language. Some go so far as to declare the tenets of direct reference theory "immovable" (Bach, 1997,

217). The common terminology in these discussions is 'Russellian propositions', as opposed to 'Fregean propositions'. I shall speak of Russellian propositions sometimes as 'blurs' or 'hybrids' or as 'propfacts'.

The merge results in an entity that satisfies all conditions for facts but
plays essentially two semantic roles—that of truthbearer and that of truthmaker—to the effect that these entities are said to be true if and only if they
exist (or 'obtain'). This is the most problematic entity that we shall see in
this book.

In the following I shall speak of facts, states of affairs, and hybrid entities
like Russellian propositions as 'factlike' entities, that is, entities that satisfy
all seven ontological conditions for facts. I will not use the term 'factlike
entities' for propositions.

1.5 Conclusion

In this chapter we have seen, in all generality, *what* facts are and what they
are *for*. That is, we have seen the nature of facts, and why philosophers
think they need to acknowledge facts in their account of the universe or
"catalog of the world," as I have called it, which is linked to the semantic
roles facts are taken to play—roles in the theoretical space in the intersection of language and world.

We have seen five semantic roles that entities can play; we have seen a
working definition of facts with seven conditions; and we have seen the
most celebrated argument in favor of facts, Armstrong's truthmaker argument. Compositional facts are entities that satisfy all seven of the ontological conditions I have introduced: they are complex entities with minimally
two constituents, whose composition is formal, unmereological, and heterogeneous both from the ontological point of view and the point of view
of the categories involved; furthermore, both their constituents and the
facts themselves are part of the furniture of the world, and they have no
semantic capacities. Facts are apt to play two semantic roles in the intersection of language and world (sentence-object and truthmaker). Also, I have
introduced a large number of technical terms and three sets of conceptual
tools: the notions of *event, integral whole* as a kind of *complex, proposition*,
and *state of affairs*, which I set apart from the notion of fact on the basis of
the ontological conditions and semantic roles. We have seen several kinds
of facts, actually, among which the paradigmatic example is the kind of fact
that features in Armstrong's truthmaker argument.

In the next two chapters we shall discuss the most serious problem for
facts: the unity problem. It will turn out that Armstrong's *primitivist* theory

of facts is the most plausible theory of facts in circulation, that is, the least problematic. However, we shall see that even the most plausible theory of facts provides only an ad hoc solution to the unity problem. It can be shown that the latter claim applies to all entities—no matter what they are called—that obey the seven ontological conditions I ascribe to facts. As we shall see, one of these ontological conditions in particular is tricky: that according to which facts have a nonmereological composition. It is essentially because of their nonmereological composition that facts are taken to be able to play a certain *ontological* role we have yet to see: the role of unifier of the world. The question is whether to play this role we need facts as unifying entities that are in addition to what is to be unified, that is, their constituents. I argue that we don't. We shall see in what sense this makes the truthmaker argument unsound.

2 The Unity Problem

Stat rosa[1] pristina nomine, nomina nuda tenemus.
—Bernard of Cluny, *De contemptu mundi* (1125)

Facts are stupid things.
—Quote from Ronald Reagan's address to the 1988 Republican convention, sprayed on Frank Zappa's office wall

In Russell's *Theory of Knowledge* we find a cryptic passage:

An entity which can occur in a complex as "precedes" occurs in "A precedes B" will be called a *relation*. When it does occur in this way in a given complex, it will be called a *"relating relation."* (Russell, 1913/1984, 80, my emphasis)

What is Russell talking about? He seems to point to a difference between a relation and a *relating* relation. What is this difference exactly, and how is it relevant? As we shall see in this chapter and the next, this is the question raised by the difference between things taken separately, on the one hand, and facts as the unity of these things, on the other. We have seen this at play already in Armstrong's truthmaker argument in the previous chapter: it's the difference between, on the one hand, Hargle, *lying on*, and Argle's lap taken separately, and their unity, that is, the fact *Hargle's lying on Argle's lap*, on the other. Here we shall examine this issue in detail, and from the very beginning.

It seems odd at first to speak of 'relating relations' as Russell does above. It sounds like 'completing completion' or 'gluing glue'. But frankly, is it not the business of a completion to complete and the business of glue to glue? Is it not the business of a *relation* to *relate*? Indeed: the business of a relation, so goes the slogan, is to relate (Blanshard, 1984, 215). So what is going on here? Does Russell mean, perhaps, that there are good relations and bad ones—just as there is good glue and bad glue—and that a relating relation, like gluing glue, is just the good kind that gets the job done?

Yes and no. What Russell means is that relations might well be the *sort* of things that relate relata, like glue is the sort of thing that glues together the pieces of a broken plate, but for a *relating* relation something more is needed. The analogy with gluing has its limits, as we shall see, but it serves well enough for a start. For we get an actual relating only when relations *actually* apply to relata, just as we get actual gluing only when glue is actually applied to the pieces of a broken plate. A relation, by itself, does not necessarily relate; if it does, it is a 'relating relation'. This is the difference at issue, and it is this difference that lies at the core of the problem that will occupy us in this chapter and the next: the unity problem. What is the unity problem exactly? The passage from Russell we started with draws attention to the difference between relations and relating relations, but does not tell us what exactly *explains* or *grounds* this difference. What is it that makes relations do actual relating? In virtue of what do relations relate? This is, in a nutshell, the unity problem. Let's look at it more closely.

Relations, says Russell, *can* occur in a *complex*. The relation *precedes*, for instance, does so. By 'complex' Russell means here a unity of a relation with certain relata (in due course I shall distinguish between *complexes* and *facts*, but for the time being I won't).[2]

Suppose you're playing chess. There are all sorts of relations that *can* occur between chess pieces, in particular between pawns. Suppose now that at move 12, white pawn 1 precedes white pawn 2. Suppose that by move 27 it's the other way around: white pawn 2 precedes white pawn 1. So *precede* is a relation and it is the sort of thing that can occur between pawns—and, as a matter of fact, at move 12 that relation *does* actually occur between white pawn 1 and white pawn 2, and at move 27 *does* actually occur between pawn 2 and pawn 1. But it could have been otherwise: for instance, there could have been no preceding whatsoever between pawn 1 and pawn 2; or there might have been neither *that* preceding nor any other preceding between pawn 2 and pawn 1. Russell's point in the passage as applied to our example is this. At move 12 there is a complex, *white pawn 1's preceding white pawn 2*, then at move 27 there is another complex, *white pawn 2's preceding white pawn 1*. So, the relation *precedes* is, in these complexes, a *relating* relation: not only *can* it relate pawns generally, it actually *does* relate specific pawns in these specific cases.

One important thing to notice here is the modal language I used in the last paragraph: 'can' versus 'does'. In the former case we have a possible situation, in the latter an actual one. The fundamental aspect of the difference between relations and relating relations is the modal difference between what *could* be related in the world and what *does* actually get related in the world in specific cases. As we shall see in detail below, no difference other than the modal one between being possibly related on the one hand and actually so on the other seems to be involved here—for instance, there is no difference in parts that the objects involved acquire or lose.

Another important thing to notice is that the modal difference at issue does not depend on *precede* being an asymmetric relation, that is, a relation where the *order* of the relata matters. The same point holds for symmetric relations, such as *being two squares away*. Suppose, for instance, that at move 15 white pawn 1 is two squares away from white pawn 2. *Being two squares away* is a relation, the sort of thing that *can* occur between pawns, and at move 15 it actually *does* occur between pawns 1 and 2. Thus the same difference between a relation and a relating relation can be detected in this case.

That there is a difference between relations and relating relations is a fundamental metaphysical assumption in Russell's framework (Russell, 1903, 99; 1910, 374). I shall call it *Russell's claim*.

Russell's claim There is a difference between relations and relating relations.

The problem we have is this:

Unity problem What grounds this difference? What makes relations into relating relations?

As I am going to show in this chapter and the next, Russell's claim is based on two deeper and mutually related metaphysical assumptions: one about the nature of relations and a second assumption I shall call "the unity versus aggregates assumption." These assumptions are at the core of the unity problem.

Discussion of the first assumption, the one that regards the nature of relations, will be postponed until chapter 3. We will wait a while, then, before coming to what I consider a fundamental way to solve—or better, *dissolve*—the unity problem; we begin, instead, with an analysis of what goes wrong with attempts at a solution when this assumption is in place. Note that the problem of relational unity carries over immediately to properties. Consider Russell again:

> Wholes occur, which contain ... what may be called *predicates*, not occurring simply as terms in a collection, but as ... *qualifying*. (Russell, 1903, 136; emphasis added)

If for 'wholes' we read 'complexes' and for 'predicates' we read 'properties'—unimportant differences here—we can formulate the problem for both relations and properties as a question: what makes something a *unity* of a relation and its relata, or of a property and its bearer, instead of a heap of these things? In other words, both the problem of the difference between relations and relating relations on the one hand, and the problem of the difference between properties and qualifying properties (i.e., properties that are, say, *really being had* by their bearer) on the other, are basically just the problem of finding out what unifies categorically heterogeneous constituents into complexes (which is also, if you will, the problem of what unifies relations and properties into concrete particulars, at least if we take complexes to be such 'really unified' structures). This is the unity problem from another point of view. The problem of relating relations, then, is a special case of a more general unity problem regarding the unity of properties with their bearers as well, and, if we conceive of properties as monadic relations (as I said I would do, following Russell), then it is immediately clear that the problem is one and the same: how to account for the unity of relations with their relata and for the unity of properties with their bearers (I shall henceforth take for granted that properties are monadic relations). This brings us to the second assumption on which Russell's claim is based.

This second assumption regards the idea that there is an important difference between composite objects that are mere collections, heaps, or *aggregates* of things, and composite objects that are real *unities*, such as for instance integral wholes that are concrete particulars. This assumption is intuitively very appealing. It also seems to be firmly nested in commonsense reasoning: a prickle of hedgehogs does not have the same kind of unity as a hedgehog like Argle's pet Hargle, and having all pieces of an IKEA kitchen is not the same as having the kitchen mounted with all the pieces in the right place (one would say). Note, however, that no matter how intuitive we find this reasoning, there are basically two ways to do justice to the idea of the difference between unities and 'mere' aggregates: at level of sense, taking the difference between collections and integral wholes to be a *conceptual* difference, and at the level of reference, taking the difference to be an *ontological* one. Consider a small house made of Tinkertoys. Clearly, a bunch of Tinkertoy pieces is not the house. You could make a tractor out of the wood, instead of a house, for one thing. And if you make a tractor, then the wood is still there, but the house is not. Now, if we take the difference between the wood and the house to be at the level of sense, then what we are saying is that there is *one* thing in the world, which we talk about in two ways, that is, *as* 'the wood' and *as* 'the house'. If instead we take the difference to be at the level of reference, then what we are saying is that there are *two* things in the world: the wood and the house. The house is an object *over and above* the wood, something more than just the wood. It is something extra—and therefore different. Many philosophers, Russell included, place the difference at the level of reference and turn it into a genuine ontological datum: there are objects in the catalog of the world that *really are* unities of constituents, and objects that are not such, because they are *just* the stuff or the aggregate of constituents of which unities are composed.[3] Let us fix this as follows:

The unity versus aggregate assumption   There is an ontological difference between real *unities* and mere *aggregates* (Russell, 1903, 136).

If you accept this assumption, there is a difference in number between unities and aggregates of objects. You have to count unities alongside their constituents or constituting stuff: there is the house *and* there is the wood of which it is composed. If you do not accept this assumption, then there is no difference in number between these things. You do not have to count unities alongside aggregates: there is just the house; or there is just the wood—but not *both*.

The difference made in this assumption between unities—entities that are *really* unified—and mere collections or aggregates, and the difference between relations and relating relations in Russell's claim, connect in a fundamental way: in a framework such as Russell's, the latter difference is taken to be a special case of the former. The unity versus aggregate assumption is a rock-bottom assumption for defenders of facts (or states of affairs), although it is often not made explicit—as frequently happens with the vital assumptions of a well-entrenched perspective. In the rest of this chapter and the next I will not dispute the unity versus aggregate assumption, though I will dispute Russell's claim (i.e., that there is a difference between relations and relating relations), as an instance of the assumption.

It is important to realize that the unity problem—the problem of how to account for the difference between relations and relating relations (and properties and qualifying properties)—does not simply concern the difference between what we *count* as many and what we count as one, but rather the difference between what *is* really one—a genuinely unified entity—and what is not. I say this because one might think that the unity problem can be solved by accepting the *principle of unrestricted mereological composition* (or *unrestricted mereological sum* or *unrestricted mereological fusion*), a principle of mereology thanks to which for any plurality in the universe, say, four particular nuts, there is their mereological sum, say, the mereological sum of those four nuts.

Principle of unrestricted mereological composition   For any number of distinct objects $x_1 \ldots x_n$ in the universe, there is an aggregate $x_1 + \ldots + x_n$ in the universe that consists of all and only those objects.[4]

This principle is 'unrestricted' because it says that *any* given objects in the universe yield a sum. Also, arbitrary mereological sums of scattered and gerrymandered objects, like the object composed of the Concertgebouw and a particular farmer in Virginia named Bill, are sums in their own right: this sum is a whole with two scattered parts, the Concertgebouw and Bill, and it is as individual as its parts (so it is not an ideal object like a set; notice also that there are no empty sums, i.e., there are no sums with no parts). The principle of unrestricted mereological composition is a strong one. Many philosophers, independently of the discussion of the unity problem, find the principle suspect and reject it. I do not find it suspect, but this is not relevant, for accepting it or not has no bearing on the unity problem. Consider again line (5) of Armstrong's argument:

(5)   Disconnected from each other, a particular hedgehog, Argle's lap, and *lying on* are no truthmaker for [the truth "A hedgehog is lying on Argle's lap"]: their connection is a truthmaker for it.

The problem occurs whenever we have several disconnected things that need to be connected. (Forget for a moment the truthmaker talk here: as we shall see, in Armstrong's particular case, solving this problem of unity is key to solving another, namely the problem of finding truthmakers, which are objects with the role of necessitating truths; I return to this double problem shortly.) Now, *even* accepting the 'grossly overstrong' (Thomson, 1983, 203) principle of unrestricted mereological composition does not solve the unity problem. To see why, let's return to our example: if you accept that mereological composition is unrestricted, then there will be in the universe, among all sorts of other sums, a mereological sum of Hargle, Argle's lap, and *lying on*, but, as I explain more fully below, there will *still* be a difference between this sum and the fact *Hargle's lying on Argle's lap*. Why? Because a sum is not necessarily a unity.[5] In other words, the principle of unrestricted mereological composition does not give you unities, or unities by default. It only gives you a way to *count* objects as one instead of counting them as many. Some of the sums yielded by the principle will also be unities, but by no means all. For what kind of unity do the Concertgebouw and Bill have? Let's put it like this: if we knew when we have a sum that is also a unity, if we knew how to supplement the principle of unrestricted mereological composition in such a way that it enables the selection of those sums that are unities (for instance, by assuming some adjunctive principle), we would have solved the unity problem, because we would know when something is a genuine unity and not a heap of things. In the terms just presented, the problem seems merely epistemological, but it's not—it's metaphysical. At issue is the question: What is the metaphysical difference between sums that are unities and sums that are not? Is it, for example, something added to the sum? If not, what else could it be? This is the question we seek an answer to. This means that accepting the principle of unrestricted mereological composition does not grant the connection of the parts we need to have unified in a complex or fact. The parts of a sum can be separate and have no interaction whatsoever, and still form a sum: Hargle running happily on a meadow in Keuru, Finland, Argle munching on a Gruyère sandwich on the grass of Museumplein in Amsterdam, a colander lying on Argle's lap—Hargle, Argle's lap, and *lying on* all exist for sure, and so does their sum, but these entities are still separate, also in the sum, even though the sum is one and not many. The problem is that since there is a difference between the collection of Hargle, Argle, and *lying on* and their *actual reticulation*, something must be the ground of the actual reticulation of those objects together: something *in virtue of which* such constituents form a unity. What is it? That's the unity problem.[6]

There is an immediate link between these three—the unity problem, Russell's claim, and the unity versus aggregate assumption—and facts as I introduced them in the previous chapter. In the previous chapter we saw that a (compositional) fact is a composite entity with minimally two constituents the composition of which is formal, which is (typically) ontologically and categorically heterogeneous and, most importantly, *unmereological*. By contrast with a heap of objects, a fact is a really unified object—so goes the theory—and in this it also differs from the collection of its constituents taken separately. Collections are best conceived as *mereological sums*, that is, composite objects governed by principles of (extensional) mereology, whereas facts, like any real unity, do not obey those principles: their composition is *unmereological* (or so goes the theory).[7] We saw this in connection with two assumptions of Armstrong's truthmaker argument. Let's consider that argument again:

(1)   Empirical truths concern real objects in the world.
(2)   There are empirical truths, for instance
        (*)   'A hedgehog is lying on Argle's lap',
which concerns a particular hedgehog, Argle's lap, and *lying on*.
(3)   A particular hedgehog, Argle's lap, and *lying on* play a role in the truth of (*). (1, 2)
(4)   For (*) to be true we need a (real) truthmaker (i): something in the world in virtue of which (*) is true (ii).
(5)   Disconnected from each other, a particular hedgehog, Argle's lap, and *lying on* are no truthmaker for (*): their connection is a truthmaker for it.
(6)   The fact of a (particular) hedgehog's lying on Argle's lap is the connection of a particular hedgehog, Argle's lap, and *lying on*.
(7)   This fact is the truthmaker of (*). (3, 4 ii, 5, 6)
(8)   We need facts. (4 i, 7)

In the argument, (5) and (6) are immediately related to the unity problem. In fact, it is clear from these premises that Armstrong considers facts to be themselves a solution to the unity problem because he conceives of facts as entities that are the 'being together' of a relation with its relata. When is a relation actually relating? Answer: When it is involved in a fact. If a relation forms a fact with its relata, then it is a relating relation, because facts are unities of relations with their relata.[8]

   In light of this, we now can see an aspect of the truthmaker argument that we did not see before. The argument highlights two different roles for facts: the *semantic* role of truthmaker as we have seen in chapter 1, and the *ontological* role of unifier, that is, that which secures unity and structure in the world. The role of unifier is related to one of our seven specific ontological conditions of facts, namely to their unmereological composition, which is in turn connected to the unity problem.

It is important to stress that whereas facts as a solution to the unity problem concern the ontological structure of the *world*, facts as truthmakers have to do with truth in *language*: assumptions (5) and (6) in the truthmaker argument are related to the first issue, assumptions (4) and (7) are related to the second. It is important to note that these issues are not the same: the unity problem, on the one hand, and the problem of providing truthmakers for empirical truths, on the other, are not the same problem. This is the case even though for Armstrong facts provide a solution to both problems at once, for they do so by playing what are actually two different roles.[9] Still, facts can play the truthmaker role insofar as they can play the role of unifiers of the world. In other words, the unity problem is a more basic problem than truthmaking. *Given a certain framework* (on which more in chap. 3, sec. 3.2), it is simply not possible to run a truthmaker argument without presupposing some solution to the unity problem. The unity problem is a truly basic problem to solve for any metaphysics involving a certain kind of properties and relations, and so a fortiori for any metaphysics coupled with a truthmaker theory of truth. This consideration will prove important in the next chapter.

In the first two sections of this chapter and the first section of chapter 3, I deal only with the role of facts as unifiers and with the unity problem. I argue for two claims: first, that we have no good reasons to assume that facts play the role of the unifiers of the world; and second, that the role of unifier of reality need not be played by any special entity, such as a fact, additional to the constituents involved. In section 2.1, I deal with the unity problem by means of a master argument. After considering the solutions on offer, I argue that the best theories of facts to meet the unity problem are those that accept (Armstrongian) facts. But in section 2.2, I claim that Armstrongian facts can't be considered a good solution to the unity problem, because that solution is (maximally) ad hoc. My argument will go roughly like this. Armstrong solves the unity problem by assuming facts as special objects that just *are* the unity of their constituents. The solution is a primitivist one: facts are taken to be *primitive nonmereological* unities of their constituents. But we can find no independent argument in favor of the existence of this specific nonmereological composition of facts, except that it is needed to solve the unity problem. Therefore, facts are ad hoc entities. In contrast to other existing lines of argument, I do not say that facts are contradictory objects, nor do I reject nonmereological composition altogether. I merely argue, after providing an attempt to show the contrary, that the specific nonmereological composition ascribed to facts by their defenders is left unsupported by arguments. Now, as I make clear, that a theory assumes ad hoc entities to solve a problem is not enough, by itself, to reject that theory. But if we have better alternatives, or if the problem does not actually need to be solved, than yes, the theory should be rejected. In chapter 3, I discuss two alternative theories to facts, both based on mereological complexes, that fare better in this respect. In one of these theories—the one I will focus on as the best solution—the problem simply does not arise: I maintain that this first fact-free theory should be favored over the second fact-free theory, at least if we want to keep relations (and properties) in our ontology. I also argue that, no matter the weight we put on the theory-choice criteria of ad hoc avoidance, both of the alternatives I will discuss fare better than any theory of facts can do in terms of criteria such as economy, generality, and simplicity. I conclude that the problem of unity at issue here is created by assuming that there must be a difference between relations and relating relations (Russell's claim), and that, on the best position on offer, the problem is dissolved once this assumption is rejected. In chapter 3, section 3.1, I show how we can plausibly abandon Russell's claim, yet still get a world where relations relate their relata. To show this more clearly, in chapter 3, section 3.2, I push the analysis a bit further and reexamine my metametaphysical strategies.[10] My conclusion, as we shall see in section 3.5, has immediate bearing on the truthmaker argument, which as a result appears unsound.

In short, the scenario I will discuss can be put like this:

Argument for facts
Facts—entities *over and above* their constituents—are needed because their constituents alone cannot get us a world where relations relate their relata.[11]

Rejoinder against facts
If it can be shown that constituents *alone* can get us a world where relations relate their relata, then facts—entities *over and above* their constituents—are not needed.

Recall that philosophers who do accept facts say that when Hargle is sad, alongside these *two* things, Hargle and sadness, there is also a *third* thing in the world: a special, 'being together' of these two things in a real unity *over and above* the two things, a *compositional fact*. Philosophers who don't accept facts say that at most there are *just* these two things, Hargle and sadness. Whether the second position can be held depends on whether we can show that Hargle and sadness alone suffice for a world where relations relate relata (in this monadic case: where properties are had by their bearers). In chapter 3, section 3.1, I show that constituents alone can get us a world where relations relata their relata, and that therefore we do not need facts. My critical focus in arguing for this position will be the unmereological composition of facts: I contend that the mereological composition of constituents (i.e., mereologically composed complexes that are not entities over and above their constituents) suffices. Once the rebuttal of facts in this sense is complete, I will round off this chapter by discussing in what way and to what extent my criticism of facts carries over to theories that accept (obtaining and nonobtaining) states of affairs.

In chapter 3, section 3.2, I discuss to what extent mereological complexes can serve as adequate truthmakers (for empirical truths), and also why it is important to keep apart the ontological role of unifier and the semantic role of truthmaker. For although according to Armstrong and others, both roles—unifier of reality and truthmaker—need to be played, they are two different roles, and having them played by one entity, or having both roles played at all, are just possible options. Valuable alternatives surface when the roles are considered separately.

To my mind, *neither* role—neither truthmaking nor unifier—should be played. But arguing that the unifier role should not be played involves considerations of quite a different kind from arguing that the truthmaker role should not be played, as will become clearer in the following. The need for a truthmaker depends essentially on the theory of truth that we defend, whereas the need to account for unity in the world in order to solve the unity problem depends on other issues, such as how we conceive of worldly structures. If we think that such structures require a difference between relations and relating relation as an instance of the difference between aggregates and unities, and that this difference must be accounted for ontologically, then we might find it reasonable to assume facts to play that role, as Russell did. The early Russell is an interesting case for us, because he did assign facts (a.k.a. Russellian propositions) the unifier role, but he did not assign them the truthmaker role, because, from a systematic point of view, given his theory of truth, the truthmaker role did not need to be played (and, from a historical point of view, truthmaking did not yet even exist).[12] This confirms that the unity problem is a more basic problem than truthmaking, and needs to be solved first so long as our theory of truth requires truthmakers.

For the case I want to make in this book, I need only show that we do not need facts, not that we do not need truthmakers. To be sure, once facts are rejected *as unifiers of the world* (because we have better alternatives) Armstrong's truthmaker argument will also be rejected as an argument in favor of facts *as truthmakers*, for the latter role depends on the former. But this

does not mean that my arguments dismiss the need for truthmakers altogether. I am only arguing against the effort to make facts play that role.
Other entities can play the role of truthmaker (*if* we think that role must be
played).

In the following I accept the principle of unrestricted mereological
composition—as many do in this discussion—for two reasons. First, as indicated above, discussing the unity problem in a framework that accepts the
principle of unrestricted mereological composition makes clear that we
might be very liberal about composition (we have *always* a sum of whatever
objects), yet still not solve the unity problem.[13] The arguments I survey go
through even without accepting this principle, but putting the point as I
shall in terms of 'mere' sums versus facts (or aggregates versus unities)
makes the argumentation easier and more perspicuous. Second, the principle plays no role in my criticism—that is, the parties involved on both sides
of the debate accept it.[14]

2.1   Compositional Facts and the Unity Problem

If the unity problem concerns the difference between relations and relating
relations, won't simply acknowledging this difference be enough to solve
it? Does the problem not disappear exactly by assuming that there are *two*
kinds of relations? No: the relation and the relating relation cannot be two
kinds of relations. Far from that, they have to be *identical*. It is exactly the
same object that in a collection is an *inert* building block, a brick in the
structure, and that in a complex or fact is a unifying element, the cement
(Russell, 1912, 74; note the anaphoric reference of 'it' in the opening passage). And this is the problematic bit: how can something be (numerically)
the same *and yet be different*? Finding answers to questions such as these
may not seem like a genuine metaphysical task, and indeed, as shall become
clear in the following, I think such questions don't need to be raised. But by
this I do not mean that they are *nonsense*: I mean, rather, that they are generated by the metaphysical framework we accept, and that once we step
outside that framework such questions simply do not arise. But I shall discuss this option only after having dismissed several alternative answers—
those that need to address that question, including facts. But let's start from
the beginning.

In virtue of what do relations relate? Several solutions to the unity problem for relations have been proposed in recent decades (see the excellent
discussions in Vallicella, 2000, 2002, 2004). A widely shared assumption in
this debate is that we need *something* that accounts for the difference,

something that makes relations apply to relata and get an actual relating, like glue needs someone to apply it to the pieces of the broken plate. For, it is argued, relations cannot do their relating work alone. It is not really like fixing a broken plate—the analogy is too crude—but still something is needed to *make* the relation relate its relata. The solutions come in four kinds. Here I will dismiss them one by one.

I present the point in the form of a master argument.[15] Suppose a relation R holds between a and b. Then:

(M1: Russell's claim)   There is a difference between the complex aRb and the sum of constituents $a + R + b$.

(M2: Unity problem)   Something—an ontological ground—must account for this difference. What is it?

(M3)   The ground can only lie in (A) the constituents a, b, or R; (B) one or more additional constituents of the complex; (C) something outside the complex; (D) the complex itself.

(M4)   A, B, C, and D are implausible.[16]

(M5)   Hence, there is no plausible ground for the difference between complexes and sums.

(M6)   Hence, there is no plausible difference between the complex aRb and the sum of constituents $a + R + b$ (vs. M1). (M2, M3, M4)

Again, as was the case in the truthmaker argument in chapter 1, the steps here are not supposed to follow in a strictly logical way. Note also that in the master argument Russell's claim and the unity problem are worded slightly differently than I worded them in the introduction to this chapter; however, this is harmless. I shall reconsider the formulation of the unity problem in the next chapter, where I present its dissolution and evaluate it. We come to the last step in this way: since the only options A, B, C, and D are implausible (M4), there is no plausible way to account for the ground for the difference at M1 (M5); but if nothing can explain it—and no difference is without plausible explanation, or ontological ground (M2)—then we should conclude that there is no plausible difference between aRb and $a + R + b$ (vs. M1). The question is how we can show plausibly that there is no difference between sums and complexes, that is, that the unity problem at M2 does not arise, but still get a world in which relations relate their relata.

In the following I will spell out these steps one by one. I shall continue throughout this section to speak of a *complex* as a unity of a relation with certain relata (which I mark aRb), and of a *sum* as the mereological collection or aggregate of a relation and relata (which I mark $a + R + b$). I use '+' for mereological composition. In certain cases (e.g., option D) it would be more appropriate to speak of facts right away instead of 'complexes', since the complexes involved in the master argument are actually facts. However, I will start out with a terminology that will enable me to speak generally of complexes and, until a certain point at least, to keep the matter open. This procedure has the advantage of showing that facts are meant to be a solution to a certain problem and are by no means a category of objects corresponding to an absolute metaphysical given. For the same reason, I will make no difference between *parts* and *constituents* until later in the text.

My conclusion will be that there is no need for a ground for the difference between the complex *aRb* and the sum of constituents $a + R + b$, because we don't need to assume a difference between the two. I arrive at this conclusion after discussing M1–M4 and assumptions regarding the nature of relations. The latter are hardly ever made explicit in the literature, but are crucial to the solution—or actually the *dis*solution of the unity problem—that I consider in the next chapter. So, let's start by examining the unity versus aggregate assumption, M1.

M1 (Russell's claim)   There is a difference between the complex *aRb* and the sum of constituents $a + R + b$.

We saw that the difference between the complex *aRb* and the sum of its constituents $a + R + b$ assumed in M1 is that the relation R in the complex *actually relates* the relata a and b, whereas R in the sum fails in this. We are dealing with a unity problem (Vallicella, 2000, 241; 2002, 13; 2004, 163): the complex *aRb* is a unity of R, a, and b, whereas the sum $a + R + b$ is *just* a collection of three items for which the unity is by no means guaranteed. This is easier to see, perhaps, if we look at the conditions under which the complex and the sum in question exist: the mereological sum $a + R + b$ exists once a, b and R exist, independently of any connection between them, whereas for the complex *aRb* this is not the case. The complex *aRb* exists only in the case in which a, b, and R form a unity.

Let us suppose that Argle and Bargle stand two feet away from each other. In this case, we have a complex formed by Argle (*a*), Bargle (*b*), and the symmetric relation of standing two feet away (*R*). Suppose now, as a second case, that Argle and Bargle stand three feet away from each other and that they also both stand two feet away from a plate of crackers (*c*). In this case, we do not have a complex formed by Argle, Bargle, and the relation of standing two feet away, although we have, still, the mereological sum Argle + standing two feet away + Bargle. (We do have, of course, the complex *aRc* formed by Argle, the plate of crackers, and the relation of standing two feet away, and the complex *bRc* formed by Bargle, the plate of crackers, and the relation of standing two feet away.)

It is important to note that this reasoning depends on a cluster of additional assumptions that one may very well find controversial. One of these assumptions is fundamental and regards, as I mentioned in the previous section, the nature of relations. I shall come back to this in the next chapter. Another assumption, which I have also mentioned in the previous section, is the principle that the mereological sum $a + R + b$ exists once a, b, and R exist (*principle of unrestricted mereological composition*). This assumption is not fundamental. The reasoning can be easily reformulated so that it does not depend on this principle—we can just talk of *three* objects being there in the one case—a multiplicity without a unity being formed—and, in the other case, of a unity. I will keep working with the principle of unrestricted mereological composition in what follows because it makes exposition easier, and I shall explain more of its consequences below. One word of clarification about the principle of unrestricted mereological composition that will come in handy later: my examples so far might suggest that the world contains mereological sums of objects only when, in some sense, appropriate objects exist, such that it might seem as though restrictions on sums are in place in the reasoning I am considering. For instance, I took as examples sums of *two* objects and *dyadic* relations that *fit* them such as Argle, Bargle, and standing two feet away from. These restrictions do not follow from the principle of unrestricted mereological composition, however. The reason I considered exactly these sums is that I want to stress the difference between sums and complexes in the master argument. But this is a selection I myself make among all the sums that the principle yields unrestrictedly. To better grasp this, consider the following example. The world contains herrings, the relation of *keeping as a pet*, and Dutch politicians: the mereological sum of a herring named Reddy (a), *keeping as a pet* (R) and Dutch ex–prime minister Jan-Peter Balkenende (b) is *also* contained in the world with no additional conditions than the existence of the objects involved. However, the world as it stands does not contain a unified complex formed by J-P Balkenende, Reddy, and *keeping as a pet*—whatever the order of ownership might be. So far, this is an example similar in every respect to the others I gave. Now, the point is that Reddy + J-P Balkenende + keeping as a pet is a sum of *fitting* objects: it might be funny or implausible or whatever, but the relation of *keeping as a pet* is a dyadic one, and it is the kind of relation that obtains between two objects, a non-human animal and a human one, and indeed, the objects involved were exactly such (Reddy and J-P Balkenende). Now: it is not the case that *only* mereological sums of, say, fitting objects exist. The principle of unrestricted mereological composition allows for mereological sums of *any kind* in the world with no restrictions on the kind and numbers of the parts involved and the resulting wholes. So, consider all the objects in the world as if they were points on a circle: any selection of those points, however distant or unfitting, gives you a mereological sum. If you also accept abstract objects in your world, such as numbers or Fregean propositions and their parts, those will also be among the points, and enter sums. So, if you accept the principle, there are no good or bad sums: all sums are on a par, also scattered and gerrymandered ones. The combination of all the objects there are—considered as proper parts of those wholes we call sums—is totally free. So the sum of a Dutch herring like Reddy, the feet of an armadillo, two of Hargle's spines, the times I have been late, and the 27th president of Australia, Julia Gillard, will be in the world—once the world contains all such things.[17] However, the one I just indicated is an uninteresting sum in daily life: we tend to consider sums that are interesting for some purpose, and for these we usually have (proper) names. David Lewis's famous example is the sum of the head of a trout and the body of a turkey (Lewis, 1991, 79–81). This is a much-quoted example to show how weird this principle is, but we can also say that fundamentally this sum is just uninteresting and useless.[18]

The sums that interest us most, and those that happen to be most relevant for my argument here, are instead sums that are in all respects similar to unified complexes—namely those that have exactly the same parts as the unified complexes we are interested in—and that *could possibly be* complexes except they are not. And so we ask: what grounds this difference?

(M2: Unity problem)   Something—an ontological ground—must account for the difference between aRb and $a + R + b$.

The quest for the ontological ground for the difference between aRb and $a + R + b$ comes down to this: in virtue of what does R do its relating work in the complex, but not in the sum? Simply stated, the problem is that a, R, and b might be constituents of all sorts of complexes: R might relate other relata (to come back to our simple example, the very same relation of standing two feet away relates in our first case Argle and Bargle, and in the second case Argle and the plate of crackers, as well as Bargle and the plate of crackers), and a and b might be related by another relation (Argle and Bargle are related by the relation of standing two feet away in the first case and by the relation of standing three feet away in the second), such that the existence of the mere mereological sum $a + R + b$ is not enough to yield aRb.

The question in these terms runs: in virtue of what do a, R, and b come together as aRb? What makes them form a complex rather than a mere sum?

This question is not about the *empirical cause* of aRb: the answer is not something along the lines of 'Argle's moving toward Bargle until the distance between them is two feet'. We are searching instead for an ontological ground of the difference between aRb and $a + R + b$ (Vallicella, 2002, 26–27). To see this clearly, let us put the problem in somewhat different terms. When Argle and Bargle stand two feet away from each other, we have not only the sum Argle + standing two feet away + Bargle, but *also* the complex in which Argle and Bargle are unified by the relation of standing two feet away. In other words, we have *two* distinct and coincident objects. Note that, to my knowledge, nobody puts things this way, and no one seems to address the question of coincidence explicitly in debates of the unity problem, but to hold that if you have a complex aRb you thus automatically have the sum $a + R + b$ (e.g., Vallicella, 2002, 12), and to hold that complex and sum are numerically different, is to accept that there are two different objects exactly at the same place and at the same time. This coincidence issue will play an important role in my discussion of option D in section 2.2. For now, let's ask the following: granting that there is an ontological difference between complex and sum—that the complex is more, as it were, than the mere sum of constituents—what is responsible for the difference? What grounds this *more*?

Without such a ground, one seems to face the inadmissible inconsistency that a complex is the same as and yet at once more than the sum of its constituents. On the one hand, the complex is composed of the three items $a + R + b$, and is therefore identical to this sum. On the other hand, the complex is not identical to but is more than the mere sum, because only in the complex does R relate its relata. If complexes involve an inconsistency, we cannot admit them in the catalog of the world. But if relations are to relate, and if they do so only in complexes, it cannot be allowed that there are no complexes. So an ontological ground for the difference between aRb and $a + R + b$ is required. But what is it?

(M3)   The ground of the difference between aRb and $a + R + b$ can only lie in (A) the constituents a, b, or R; (B) one or more additional constituents of the complex; (C) something outside the complex; or (D) the complex itself.

Let us look at options A through D one by one. D deserves a section of its own. Going through A, B, and C will make clear both why D is the best option, but also, as we shall see, why it is still implausible.

Against (A): The Ground Cannot Lie in the Constituents

The ground of the difference between aRb and $a + R + b$ cannot be a difference in the constituents a, b, or R, because the underlying assumption (M1) is that the constituents are the same. One might deny this assumption by holding that there is a difference between R in the sum and R in the complex. However, this does not solve anything, for the question would then become: why does R in the sum differ from R in the complex? This is merely a restatement of M1's problem, not a solution to it. So R must be exactly the same object both in the complex and in the sum. Furthermore, saying that the ground of the difference is not a difference in R but a difference in the relata of R would just mean changing the subject: our problem is finding a ground for the difference between aRb and $a + R + b$, not between something else, say, $a'Rb$ (where a' is a different constituent) and $a + R + b$.

Against (B): Additional Constituents Ignite Bradley's Relation Regress or Do Not Solve the Problem

No one puts flowers
On a flower's grave

—Tom Waits, "Flower's Grave" (2002)

If seeing the ground in the constituents of the complex is not an option, we might say that what holds the constituents together, the glue so to speak, is an additional constituent present in every complex. It soon becomes clear, however, that the ground of the difference between aRb and $a + R + b$ *cannot* lie in additional constituents of the complex. Let's see why not.

There are two variants of option (B), depending on the nature of the additional constituent. The first is the addition of a binding or exemplifying *relation* to the sum, call it *EX*. This variant involves Bradley's relation regress (Bradley, 1893, 27–28). The second is the addition of a *nonrelational tie*, call it *NEX*. This does not ignite the relation regress, but it is no help in solving the unity problem.

Let us first have a closer look at Bradley's relation regress. Here's a scheme of it:

(T)   R relates in aRb, but not in $a + R + b$.
(S1)   In virtue of what does R relate the relata a and b? In virtue of relation *EX*, which unifies R with a and b.
(S2)   In virtue of what does relation *EX* relate the relata a, R, and b? In virtue of relation *EX**, which unifies *EX* with a, R, and b.

(S3) In virtue of what does relation EX^* relate the relata a, R, EX, and b? In virtue of relation EX^{**}, which unifies EX^* with a, R, EX, and b.

(S4) And so on, ad infinitum.[19]

Now the problem in this infinite regress is that the additional constituent postulated, EX, is itself a *relation*. The thought that any theory igniting an infinite regress should be rejected belongs to standard lore. But, as Anna-Sofia Maurin puts it, infinite regresses by themselves neither prove nor disprove anything (Maurin, 2007, 1–2). One has first to determine whether or not the regress at issue is vicious. Could Bradley's relation regress be harmless after all? Maurin argues that there is but one adequate criterion to separate vicious from harmless regresses, namely, the direction of dependence of its steps. In general, a regress is vicious if and only if the answer to its first question in S1 depends on the answers to all the other questions in S2–SN; if this is not the case, and each question can be tackled independently of the questions and answers in subsequent steps, then the regress is just a strange side effect of its underlying theory. Is Bradley's relation regress vicious according to this criterion? Does the answer in S1 depend on the answers in S2–SN? Yes. The unity problem is not solved in the first step. If the complex aRb forms a unity in virtue of the relation EX, then we can ask in virtue of what the larger complex $aEXRb$ forms a unity that makes it different from $a + EX + R + b$, and if the complex $aEXRb$ forms a unity in virtue of the relation EX^*, then we can ask in virtue of what the larger complex aEX^*EXRb forms a unity that makes it different from $a + EX^* + EX + R + b$, and so on. The unity of aRb depends on the unity of $aEXRb$, which depends in turn on the unity of aEX^*EXRb, and so on. Hence, EX indeed ignites a vicious infinite regress.[20]

But what if we postulate a nonrelational tie, NEX, as some have suggested? Indeed, one way out of Bradley's regress could be to say: but *of course* it's not a relation, this glue that holds together complexes. It is a (nonrelational) *tie*. So, in a complex reticulating an n-adic relation and n relata or an individual and a property, the tie is the glue. Note that in a complex reticulating two individuals—say, the hedgehog Hargle and Argle's lap in *Hargle's being on Argle's lap*—the relation R itself (here, *being on*) will not be the glue; the glue will still be the tie NEX connecting R to the two individuals (as in the case of the relation regress, where the new relation EX served as the glue, not R itself).

Because NEX is not a relation, it does not generate the relation regress. The tie, however, is no solution to Bradley's regress, for two reasons.

First, one cannot simply *state* that a tie is different from a relation without providing any analysis of what a tie is in the first place, as regularly happens in the literature. Taking the tie as primitive would thus not solve the problem, unless we construe being primitive as immunity from any philosophical doubt whatsoever, or being made self-evident by a philosopher's act of will or by the wonderful powers of italicization:

> But [a 'fundamental tie'] is *very* different from anything that is ordinarily spoken of as a *relation*. (Armstrong, 1997, 118)

There is no performative act that creates ties the way mayors institute marriages and popes once made emperors. If the difference between a tie and a relation is itself in need of a ground, then it's clear that this move comes down to just restating the problem, for the problem is exactly finding a difference between a relation and a relating relation. If you just *rename* 'relating relation' as 'relation-*cum*-nonrelational-tie', you have indeed merely renamed the problem, not solved it. We shall see more on brute solutions of this kind in the last, 'primitivist' option, D.

The second and more important reason why the tie is no option is that *NEX* solves nothing. Since *NEX* is an additional constituent, we can now consider *aNEXRb*: what is the ground of the unity of *aNEXRb*? In what way would *aNEXRb* be different from a + R + NEX + b? The problem presents itself again, only in a fashion involving more constituents. *NEX* might tie *R* to *anything*, so why is it tying *R* to *a* and *b*?

Even if *NEX* was, by analogy to a Fregean function, an unsaturated entity, _NEX_ in need of completion, and reticulated in both the sum and the complex, the sum a + NEX + R + b would still be different from the complex *aRb*. Why? Because *NEX* might be saturated by any particular object of the right kind, so why by these specific a and b (Vallicella, 2000, 241–243)? Something similar holds for taking _R_ itself to be such an unsaturated entity. Actually, one wonders why we would take *NEX* to be an unsaturated entity in need of saturation if R itself can be taken to be such. The problem that is important to note here is that the idea of unsaturatedness does not work at the level of *specific* individuals: unsaturatedness is a form of *generic* dependence. The relation of being two squares away can, for instance, be saturated by chess pieces, but why is it saturated by those specific, particular pawns as in the first example above? In fact, Russell's claim can be reformulated easily in terms of unsaturatedness and actual saturation: there is a difference between unsaturated entities that can be saturated by objects and unsaturated entities that are actually saturated by objects. Note that this observation is important to our understanding of where the problem really lies, and what a solution could be. I shall come to that in the next chapter. At this point, the ontological ground we seek is still to be found.

Against C: The External Operator Is Unbelievable

We might say that the ground lies outside the complex. This position is taken up by Vallicella (2000), who proposes an external operator U to unify R with a and b. The idea is that there would be numerically one and the same operator for all complexes, and further that the unifying operations of U are grounded neither in a, R, and b, nor in the nature of U itself. But if the unifying operations of U are accidental, wouldn't we need another operator to ground these operations? If so, we find ourselves stuck in an infinite regress of ever more operators, and nothing is solved. If not, U must have the special capacity of grounding its own accidental operations, something that R is not able to do. This means that there is an ontologically grounded difference between on the one hand the complex U<a, R, b>, where U contingently self-determines the actual relating, and on the other the mereological sum $U + <a, R, b>$, where U does not do that (Vallicella, 2000, sec. 5; 2002, 28–31; henceforth I will sometimes write '<aRb>' to delimit complexes). The U-operator is an entity that unifies all relations with their relata, and which at the same time grounds its own accidental unifying operations.

This option has no intuitive support. Imagine Bargle accidentally breaking the plate with the crackers in two pieces and then holding the pieces together so that Argle will not notice that the plate is broken. What this position holds is that the difference between the complex Bargle<piece 1, piece 2> and the sum Bargle + <piece 1, piece 2> is Bargle's contingent self-determination of keeping the two pieces together: the moment he stops doing that, the sum of constituents Bargle + <piece 1, piece 2>, but not the complex Bargle<piece 1, piece 2>, would continue to exist. U is, by analogy, an All-Purpose Big Bargle. But just what kind of metaphysical fiction is U? Metaphysics often posits entities that strain credulity, such as binding relations like EX and nonrelational ties like NEX, but this seems to go a step too far.[21] Can we do better? Let us see.

Against D: The Brute Fact Theory or Primitivism

According to our last option, D, the ground of the difference between aRb and $a + R + b$ lies in the complex *itself*. Theories of this kind are not threatened by Bradley's regress and do not postulate a nonrelational tie. They come down to a *primitivist* solution to the problem.[22] Defenders of this position seem at first to detect a brute difference between sums and complexes, something in the fashion of a foot-stamping "Sums differ from complexes because sums differ from complexes." Unified complexes in these theories are just accepted as a (hypothetical) datum—as the building-block of reality that is simply *there*. According to Vallicella (2002, 18–19), this amounts to claiming that the difference has no ontological ground and therefore amounts to a rejection of M2, the premise that an ontological ground must account for the difference between relations and relating relations. Now, there is a sense in which Vallicella is right, and, as we shall see, whoever endorses option D does actually endorse the foot-stamping claim that complexes differ from sums because complexes differ from sums. But this means that we lack independent arguments except the need to solve the problem, and thus we can't plausibly maintain that there is a difference between complexes and sums. This conclusion needs to be supported by more theoretical work, however, than what's on offer at the moment. For one thing, it remains for the moment dubitable that option D amounts to denying M2, since defenders of option D do argue for the difference between complexes and sums and therefore do maintain M2 (or at least their position can be presented in these terms). The point is, rather, that these defenders can't come up with any convincing arguments to back up M2. Or so I shall argue.

We can start by observing that we can take primitivism, that is, option D, as maintaining M2 and claiming that the ontological ground for the difference lies in the *unmereological composition of the complex*: sums and complexes are both composed entities, but the composition of the first kind of entities is mereological whereas the second is not. This position requires attention, for in all generality unmereological composition has its followers. Armstrong is famous for acknowledging unmereological composition, and many others are happy to share this view.[23] Option D says thus that the complex aRb results from the same constituents as the sum $a + R + b$ but that the difference lies in the complex itself, insofar as aRb is unmereologically composed whereas $a + R + b$ is mereologically composed (see Armstrong, 1989, 88–93; 2004, 141–142).

A first problem with option D is the following. The unmereologically composed complex aRb turns out to be *identical with* and yet something *other than* the sum of its constituents (or, as often maintained, something *more* than the sum). Option D seems thus to embrace an inconsistency. As Bradley puts it, D runs into a "flat contradiction" (Bradley 1910, 179), and thus it cannot be adopted. This conclusion is followed by Lewis (1992, 200) and Vallicella (2000, 247).

The defender of option D can reply that the objection misses the point: unmereologically composed objects are precisely *not* the mereologically composed sum of their constituents. So, says the defender of D, there is not *one* thing that both is and is not the sum of its constituents. There are *two* things: one is a mereological sum of parts, the other is a *fact*, which is the unmereological unity of those parts, called the 'constituents' of the fact.

In turn, we can observe that this (namely the claim that the complex *aRb* is a nonmereological fact) seems to be no more than a verbal trick. We can restate the problem immediately: What grounds the difference between mereological and nonmereological composition? What is this nonmereological composition? If these nonmereological complexes, these 'facts', are more than mereological sums, what accounts for the difference between them? The claim is merely that complexes are *more* than mereological sums, but in what this *more* lies is never made clear.[24] As we shall see in the following, this is the difficulty the defender of option D cannot finally overcome. But let's proceed in order.

The defender of D could object as follows to the objection just described: We can't ask each time for a different ground, can we? We must stop somewhere, mustn't we? There must be *something* that we have to take as ontologically primitive: something such as, in Armstrong's view, a primitive difference between mereological and unmereological composition.

The problem with this reply, however, is that we can't appeal to primitivity simply to avoid further questions. That is, what we take as primitive can't be exactly the controversial notion we are unable to explain.[25] What we take as primitive must be plausible, and this plausibility must, in addition, ideally enjoy a consensus that is as large as possible. But what exactly can ensure plausibility in metaphysics? This is a controversial question. At the very least, we can say the following. Whatever we think of unmereological composition, a satisfying theory of unmereological composition that served the purpose cannot be ad hoc. That is, the unmereological composition of facts cannot be assumed for the *sole aim* of grounding the difference between facts and sums. In particular, even though, as mentioned, nonmereological composition has its followers, an appeal to general acceptance of nonmereological composition is not enough to support the kind of primitivism defended in option D. Why is this? Because of the following. Suppose we grant that *a certain kind* of nonmereological composition, call it *Comp+*, is plausible. Then we have two options: either (I) we show that the nonmereological composition of the complexes at issue, namely, facts, is exactly the same kind of nonmereological composition as *Comp+*, or a special case of it (*indirect arguments*); or (II) if the nonmereological composition of facts is *not* exactly the same kind of nonmereological composition as *Comp+*, we give good reasons to accept the particular non-mereological composition of facts, reasons independent of the need to solve the Unity Problem (*direct arguments*). Both options would give us convincing reasons to accept facts alongside mereological sums. If no such reasons can be given, however, then facts will result to be *ad hoc*, entities assumed for the sole purpose of solving a problem. In the following section I investigate whether convincing reasons to accept facts can be given. I conclude that they cannot, and that, ultimately, Option D, like Options A, B and C as discussed above, is implausible. It is important to note that if Armstrongian facts (or similar primitivist solutions) are rejected, the last possible way to account for the difference between sums and complexes *ad* M1 will also be rejected. At least, this holds under a certain assumption about the nature of relations which underlies the master argument as outlined above, and which I discuss in greater detail in the next chapter. In the next chapter, I will show that when the assumption about the nature of relations just mentioned is rejected, interesting alternative solutions emerge. In the Conclusion, a flowchart sums up all the steps I highlight in this connection.

Since, as I argue, Option D relies on an ad hoc ontology, its dismissal as implausible will take more theoretical work than merely the dismissal of options A, B and C.[26] Ad hoc ontologies can't be dismissed just because of their ad hocness. An ontology is ad hoc always with respect to a certain problem. Because of this, ruling out ad hoc ontologies can be done in two ways: (1) if the problem in question is genuine, i.e., if its solution is non-negotiable, we show that other theories are available that do the job without assuming special entities, i.e., that these theories are not ad hoc or, at least in some sense, less so; (2) if the problem is not genuine, then it does not need to be solved; and so, a fortiori, not solved in an ad hoc way. I will come back to ad hoc reasoning in chapter 3, section 3.2.

In more detail, and described within a somewhat more general framework, the situation is this. Good reasons must be given to add any new category of objects to our catalog of the world. These reasons can't be based on what we can call *purely definitional arguments*. We have a purely definitional argument whenever certain differences between kinds of objects simply follow from defining those very objects as having certain characteristics. Arguments of this kind are popular in metaphysics and, in fact, are important and needed, because by means of them we specify exactly which objects we are introducing (we could also call such arguments *ontologically introductory definitional arguments*). However, these arguments *alone* are not convincing: they must be accompanied by adjunctive constraints, for obviously, virtually any entities can be introduced in one's ontology on their basis. One such adjunctive constraint is that the entities we introduce must have a metaphysical function, that is, they must play some metaphysical role, must solve a genuine metaphysical problem X (Check 1).[27] Another constraint is that the entities we introduce should not be introduced for the purpose of solving problem X *only*, that is, they should not be ad hoc (Check 2). In the case at issue, we introduce facts to play a metaphysical role, that is, to play the role of unifiers of the world and thus solve the unity problem. (Note that exactly this is the function of line (6) in Armstrong's truthmaker argument: introducing facts as unifiers of the world.) This is the point where I differ from the diagnosis of others: I do accept that facts pass Check 1, and thus are a solution to the unity problem. But to conclude that facts should be acknowledged it is not enough simply to define them as different from sums *because* the latter are mereologically composed while the former are unmereologically composed. We need more, that is, we need *independent reasons* to introduce facts as we define them; reasons to accept nonmereological composition that are independent of the need to solve the unity problem. If we don't have such reasons, we are merely engaging in an ad hoc definitional exercise. As in the case of ties or of Vallicella's U-operator, we *say* we are solving a problem by simply defining a new class of objects with certain characteristics, but so long as we can't give good reasons to assume such objects we can't say that our problem has been solved. For in this case we are not *really* solving the problem, we are just restating it in other words: we don't pass Check 2. Now, one could say that an unsatisfactory solution of this kind is still a solution, though perhaps not very convincing. That is correct: ad hocness is an alarm, but not the last word. We need a *Check 3*. So we ask: is problem X genuine? If so, we look for alternatives that are not ad hoc, or at least that are less so, with respect to assuming new (categories of) entities, that is, that solve the problem with entities already available in our ontology. If instead the problem is not genuine, then we look for alternatives in which the problem does not even arise. Finding alternatives of the latter kind is the most attractive option.

In the light of the above, under the assumption that facts do solve the unity problem (pass Check 1), the dismissal of option D will thus require two steps: first, we must show that the nonmereological composition of facts is ad hoc (step 1: alarm, don't pass Check 2); second, we must show that there are better alternatives (step 2: defeat, don't pass Check 3). The issue at step 1 is whether option D can ground acceptance of the particular nonmereological composition of the complexes it acknowledges, namely facts. If this cannot be done (and it can't), we may conclude that facts are ad hoc entities. Note that taking step 1 will require two substeps: showing both (i) that there are no direct arguments in favor of the unmereological composition of facts; and (ii) that also it is not possible to construct an indirect argument by analogy drawing on the plausibility of the unmereological composition that philosophers most commonly accept, that is, the unmereological composition of integral wholes (which, to my knowledge, is the only good example of what I somewhat fictitiously called *Comp+* above). Actually, the only difference we will be able to find between unmereological facts and mereological sums *ad* option D is the very one that defines the problem we are trying to solve: namely the modal difference between a possible (sums) and an actual (facts) unity of constituents. That is, as one could say, facts are maximally ad hoc. This is a problem for line (6) in the truthmaker argument, and thus for the argument as a whole.

Step 1 will be accomplished in the next section: facts are ad hoc entities. Step 2 is accomplished in the next chapter. There I present alternatives to facts, one of which shows that the unity problem is not a genuine one: according to this alternative, there is no difference between relations and relating relations, ergo no need of an ontological ground for it, a fortiori no need for facts. The unity problem vanishes.

Let's proceed with step 1. Are there good reasons to believe that there are indeed two kinds of composition at issue here: unmereological (complexes) and mereological (sums)? I say there are no such reasons.

2.2   Step 1: Facts Are Ad Hoc Entities

2.2.1   Step 1, I: Direct Arguments Fail
Let's reconsider option D. It says that the difference between the complex *aRb* and the sum *a + R + b* is that the complex is a nonmereologically composed fact and the sum (just) a mereologically composed sum of the very same constituents. What arguments could be given in favor of this? In chapter 1, we saw Armstrong's truthmaker argument, which Armstrong himself and many others with him consider the strongest argument in favor of facts at option D. However, as mentioned earlier in this chapter, the truthmaker argument is not an argument establishing an ontological thesis like the one we are seeking to establish, for it is not an argument in favor of the nonmereological composition of facts and their ontological role as unifiers of the world. The truthmaker argument is an argument in favor of facts as truthmakers, *given a world of facts as unifiers of the world*. The argument is itself based on the assumption that certain objects—facts—are given, and

that these objects have certain ontological characteristics thanks to which they can play the role of unifiers of the world. And *because of this*, the objects in question, facts, are able to serve in the semantic role of truthmakers, that is, as that which makes truths true in the sense in which this expression is used in certain correspondence theories of truth.[28] But why should we accept that there are such nonmereological objects in the first place? What is the argument for *this* claim? In other words, the truthmaker argument is not an argument for that claim, for in the argument nonmereologically composed facts are simply assumed.[29]

Are there prima facie reasons to accept the nonmereological composition of facts? One such reason, one might think, is the following. Take *a*, *R*, and *b*, where *R* is not symmetric: *two* different facts can be composed from the same constituents, namely *aRb* and *bRa* (Russell, 1904/1994, 98; Armstrong, 1989, 90), but those constituents form only *one* sum, namely *a* + *R* + *b*. The general point here is that mereological composition would be such that the arrangement or *mode of combination* of the constituents plays no role, and unmereological composition would instead be such that the combination of constituents is most important. For instance, who's keeping whom as a pet seems to be important.

There are at least three problems with this reasoning.

First, it does not explain how the nonmereological composition of facts is possible, but simply takes it for granted: *given that there are* nonmereologically composed facts, which are such that the mode of combination is important, then, this reasoning presumes, in appropriate cases we have two facts *aRb* and *bRa* but only one sum *a* + R + *b*. But since we are looking for good reasons to accept the nonmereological composition of facts in the first place, taking it for granted obviously does not do.[30]

Second, we also need to explain the nonmereological complexity of relational symmetric and nonrelational facts (*Fa*): even if the observation just made about order were to convince us to accept facts reticulating relations other than symmetric ones, it would not be convincing as an argument for facts reticulating symmetric relations, nor as an argument for nonrelational facts. In other words, the difference between facts and sums with respect to order will simply, by definition, just stem from assuming that there are nonmereological facts alongside mereological sums. Once we take for granted that there are *two* things, a sum and a fact, then a number of claims about their difference will follow, one of which is that the order is important in the fact but not in the sum. Now, this very assumption—that there are facts alongside sums—cannot, obviously, be employed in turn to argue that there are facts alongside sums. And as noted, it would not give us reason to think that there are facts other than the relational ones for which order matters.

Third, modes-of-combination talk is problematic.[31] Once we ask how we can account for such 'modes of combination', it becomes clear that the Russell–Armstrong suggestion either (i) is nonexplanatory or (ii) fails to show that the composition of facts is unmereological.

Regarding (i): If we say that aRb consists of the three items a, R, b combined in a certain manner, and that aRb *is* the mode of combination of the sum $a + R + b$, then one option is to say that we are stating something like $aRb = aRb<a + R + b>$. The main problem with this proposal is that the phrase 'aRb' reappears on the right-hand side of the identity statement (see Vallicella, 2002, 31). We are identifying the complex as whole with something (possibly, a proper part) *in* or *at* it as an internal or external addition, and that cannot be the case. Perhaps this problem can be dealt with. But the point is that we would not progress much anyway, because the complex mentioned on both sides of the identity is composed of the three items a, b, and R, and consequently the very same problem returns of its mode of combination. This is nonexplanatory, because nothing seems to have been gained by recurring to unmereological modes of combination in our explanation. So, generally, a complex cannot be wholly identical to the mode of combination of its constituents in the sense indicated. The same reasoning—to the same effect—can be applied to the complex bRa.

Regarding (ii): If we now say that aRb consists of $a + R + b$ *plus* the mode of combination of these constituents, and that this mode of combination is different from both $a + R + b$ and aRb, such that $aRb = a + R + b + $ mode of combination$_1$ (as also $bRa = a + R + b + $ mode of combination$_2$), the question arises whether the items we are talking about are not *mereological* instead of unmereological complexes. If complexes are sums of constituents plus modes of combination, we find ourselves actually at option B (the additional constituents option), not D (the 'brute facts' or primitivist option).[32] Indeed, modes of combination are very much like EXs: they are binding relations with extra combinatorial or ordering roles: as such, they involve Bradley's relation regress.

Let's dwell for a moment on this third problem, and consider the general strategy of reasoning against nonmereological complexes according to (i) and (ii). Are these objections really effective against option D? As to the first objection, (i), it seems that no one of the Armstrongian mold is saying that a fact is identical with something like a part of the sum of its constituents;

so (i) seems like a straw man move. Moreover, both objections (i) and (ii) seem to have a question-begging flavor. Why is that? Because of the use of '+' and *only* '+', that is, of mereological composition, in the reasoning. Detractors of unmereological composition appealing to (i) and (ii) seem, thus, just flatly unwilling to accept any composition other than a mereological one. Defenders of D such as Armstrong do *not* think that the difference is in a *part*, a constituent, or any entity whatsoever that can be added or subtracted by mereological composition. Therefore, it cannot be a good strategy to argue against D by asking: so, what's the part that makes the difference? Defenders of D are not giving an answer to that question, and we cannot blame them for this, since from their position the question does not arise. In general, we can't raise effective objections against D that simply assume that there are only mereologically composed objects. An effective objection would instead have to be one that does not presuppose this. Insofar as we are told that facts are not mereological complexes with parts but special unmereological entities with *constituents*, we cannot reject facts by holding that they are and yet are not identical with the sum of their *parts*, for this begs the question against Armstrong and other defenders of D. For them, we have two things: the fact and the sum.[33] This said, we do need an account of the alleged nonmereological composition of facts, and the burden of the proof remains with the defenders of D, because it is they who insist that we must accept additional, special nonmereologically composed facts *alongside* mereologically composed sums. The mereological composition of sums is not in question; the unmereological composition of facts is. If no arguments can be found, then nonmereological facts will turn out to be ad hoc entities introduced alongside mereological sums for the sole purpose of solving the unity problem. That would be a serious blow to their credibility, although, as I stressed, not a final verdict. We need an argument that justifies the assumption of nonmereologically composed facts in the first place. What could this argument be?

Before we answer this, and in order to see what exactly is at stake, let's call to mind again the difference between facts and sums. The salient difference between the mereological composition of sums and the unmereological composition of facts as defended by option D is this: that mereological sums obey the extensionality of parthood (EP), a principle of extensional mereology, while facts do not.

Extensionality of parthood   If x and y are composite objects with the same proper parts, then $x = y$.[34]

This principle embodies clearly from the mereological point of view the nominalistic idea behind the motto "No difference without a difference maker," that is, that objects with the same proper parts are identical (Varzi, 2008). An important observation in this context is the following. It is seemingly in keeping with the circumstance that facts violate EP that Armstrong, who is the most representative defender of option D, claims that facts have *constituents*, not *parts*, and that the same constituents can compose different facts:

Armstrong 1   "The complete constituents of a state of affairs are capable of being, and may actually even be, the complete constituents of a different state of affairs. Hence *constituents do not stand to states of affairs as parts to whole*" (Armstrong, 1989, 92, emphasis added)

Armstrong 2   "*a*'s loving *b* and *b*'s loving *a* might both be states of affairs, and states of affairs quite independent of each other. This is to be contrasted with mereology. ... If parts are summed mereologically to make a whole, *then there can be no more than one whole that they make*" (Armstrong, 1997, 118, emphasis added)

So *Armstrong 1* and *2* take the circumstance that the same constituents give rise to different facts to mean that facts have a fundamental and peculiar nonmereological form of composition; *Armstrong 2* seems to suggest that this applies to facts reticulating symmetrical relations, that is, to facts in which order matters. But—and this is connected to the first and second problems mentioned above—isn't it the case that *all* facts are supposed to be nonmereological complexes with constituents, not only those facts in which order matters? Yes. And this means that, contrary to what *Armstrong 2* might suggest, in any option D world *any* fact must fall outside the scope of the extensionality of parthood. The problem of order must be an adjunctive one. And, indeed, it is. We might think that only certain specific types of facts reticulating relations other than symmetric ones (such as *Argle's preceding Bargle*) fall outside the scope of the extensionality of parthood. But, actually, this is the case for any most basic fact, that is, any atomic, nonrelational fact such as *Bargle's being hungry* or *This thing's being a hydrogen atom* falls outside the scope of EP. Why is that? Because one who defends D, like Armstrong, is committed to the colocation of nonidenticals. This calls for explanation.

Consider the case in which the world is such that at time *t* it contains *Bargle's preceding Argle*. In that case the world does *not* contain *Argle's preceding Bargle* at that very time *t*, although it *does* contain at that very same time (and place) the mereological sum Bargle + Argle + *preceding*. Similarly, a world containing *Bargle's being hungry* will also contain, at the same time and place, the mereological sum Bargle + *being hungry*. And this will be the case with all facts. In general, in a D scenario, whenever we have a fact we have two coincident entities with the same parts/constituents: both the fact and the mereological sum of its constituents *at the same time and place*. This has nothing to do with order, and I say that *this* is the most fundamental reason why facts fall outside the scope of the extensionality of parthood. It is also their most fundamental characteristic insofar as it best captures their nonmereological composition. Take the following examples of facts: one involving an object and a property, one involving two objects and a nonsymmetric relation, and one involving two objects and a symmetric relation:

At *t*	Same proper parts	Two different coincident objects
Case 1: Fa ('Bargle is hungry')	Bargle, being hungry	(1) Bargle + being hungry, (2) *Bargle's being hungry*
Case 2: aRb ('Argle is smaller than Bargle') (*R* nonsymmetric)	Argle, Bargle, being smaller than	(1) Argle + Bargle + being smaller than (2) *Argle's being smaller than Bargle*
Case3: aRb (*R* symmetric)	Argle, Bargle, standing three feet away from	(1) Argle + Bargle + standing three feet away from (2) *Argle and Bargle's standing three feet away from*

In other words:

(*Armstrongian or D-coincidence*)   For every fact *Fa* with constituents *F*, *a*, there exists a sum *a* + *F* with parts *a*, *F*, coincident with the fact.

This idea is part and parcel of what we can call 'dualism about composition' in option D, which amounts to saying that objects can be combined in two ways: mereologically and nonmereologically.[35] Armstrong's world is a particularly clear example of such a dualist universe. By mereological composition, objects give rise to mereological sums *with parts*; by nonmereological composition, the very same objects (may) give rise to nonmereological facts *with constituents*. The parts entering the mereological sums can be said to obey EP and other principles of extensional mereology, while the constituents entering facts cannot be said to obey principles such as EP—these latter principles simply do not apply.

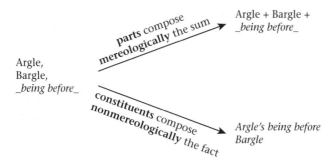

Figure 2.1

(*Armstrongian or D-dualism*)   For every object $x_1 \ldots x_n$ (of suitable category and adicity) $x_1 \ldots x_n$ can form facts $y_1 \ldots y_n$. coincident with sums $x_1 + \ldots + x_n$ according to unmereological principles and $x_1 \ldots x_n$ *do* compose sums $x_1 + \ldots + x_n$ according to principles of (extensional) mereological composition.[36]

The crucial question, thus, is this: can any defender of Armstrongian facts offer acceptable reasons for being a dualist about composition in this sense, that is, for assuming that the world is one of coincident unmereological facts and mereological sums?

As noted above, here the defender of option D has two strategies at her disposal: (1) she gives *directly* good reasons to accept (the unmereological composition of) facts and thus also the dualist world just sketched, reasons independent of the need to solve the unity problem; or (2) she identifies some kind of nonmereological composition that we are prepared to accept for other reasons, and shows that the nonmereological composition of facts is either exactly the same kind or a special case of it.

We've seen no direct arguments for facts, and to my knowledge none are on offer. On this basis we have to conclude that strategy (1) is unviable, and so we may conclude the first substep of step 1. But strategy (2) is still open. For there is a certain kind of non-mereological composition, that of integral wholes, which enjoys a rather large consensus, is defended in debates unrelated to the unity problem, and is often framed in scenarios that resemble the dualist D scenario sketched above. This seems promising: we can thus check whether arguments given in those debates to assume complex non-mereological entities alongside the mereological sums of their constituents can also be applied in our case. If so, then we could have an argument in favor of facts. Let's see whether we can take this route. I will argue that we can't.

2.2.2   Step 1, II: Indirect Arguments Fail

Stephanie   Dammit! Look at whatcha did!
Number Five   Error! Grasshopper disassembled! Reassemble!
Stephanie   Huh?
Number Five   Reassemble!
Stephanie   I can't reassemble him. You squashed him. He's dead.
Number Five   Dead?
Stephanie   Right. Dead, dead as a doornail.
Number Five   Reassemble, Stephanie, reassemble!
Stephanie (*sweetly*)   I know you don't understand, but when you're dead, you're
dead. That's just the way it is. Dead is forever.
Number Five   Squashed. Dead. Disassembled. Dead. Disassembled! Dead! (*runs away*
in panic)
—*Short Circuit* (dir. John Badham, 1986)

In this section, I explore an indirect argument for the nonmereological
composition of facts on behalf of defenders of option D. It works by analogy and involves the rich and lively debate on material constitution and
identity, composition, and principles such as the extensionality of parthood, along with the evidence generally offered in support of unmereological composition. As we shall see, my attempt fails in such a way as to reveal
a rather deep problem with assuming Armstrong-like facts to solve the
unity problem. It shows that facts provide an unsatisfactory solution to the
problem insofar as they provide a (maximally) ad hoc solution to it. This
means that if alternatives are available that are not ad hoc (or less so, or
even equally ad hoc but which present other significant advantages over
option D), then facts should be abandoned. This will conclude step 1 in the
dismissal of facts. In the following chapter I examine alternatives that will
give us the final step in the dismissal of facts (step 2). This will enable us to
argue in the second section of that chapter that the truthmaker argument
is unsound.

The debate on material constitution and identity seems at first to have
nothing to do with the problem we are considering, but this isn't so, as we
shall see shortly. This debate centers on one issue: the intuitive distinction
between the conditions of identity of *integral wholes*, and those of 'mere'
mereological sums, in particular the nonidentity of colocated individuals
such as a statue and the clay out of which it is made.

When you squash a grasshopper, as Number Five does in John Badham's
Short Circuit (1986), you cannot merely reassemble its parts to bring it back
to life. If we assume that no part of the poor grasshopper got lost in the

squash, then the dead grasshopper is the same sum of parts as before, but is no longer an integral whole (and cannot be "reassembled"). Or consider the statue made yesterday by Argle and broken today by Bargle into twenty-three pieces: when Argle gets back twenty-three pieces of clay, he is not getting back the statue, right? Examples of this kind are often cited in support of the view that there is a difference between on the one hand mereological sums of parts or pieces of organisms or artifacts, which, it is argued, are 'mere' aggregates, and on the other the organisms and the artifacts themselves, which, it is argued, are unities. There is, therefore, an important similarity between this debate and the fundamental issue of this and the next chapter. Recall:

The unities versus aggregates assumption   There is an ontological difference between real *unities* and mere *aggregates*.

This very same general assumption, acknowledged implicitly by defenders of facts such as Russell and Armstrong when they argue that there is a difference between relating relations and relations and between complexes and sums, is also acknowledged explicitly by defenders of the idea that there is a difference between, say, the statue and the clay of which it is composed. Statues, as it is argued by one side of this debate on material identity, are not identical to the material of which they are composed: in particular, statues (in contrast to the sum of the parts of which they are composed) do not obey principles of extensional mereology.

There is, however, also a dissimilarity between the debate on material composition and the debate on facts that is crucial for us to keep in mind. The real unities involved in this debate are (to my knowledge) integral wholes, *never* facts. The integral wholes involved in this debate are ordinary objects, that is, particulars such as tables, chairs, grasshoppers, wooden houses made of Tinkertoy pieces, kids, plants of Tuscan kale, Michelangelo's *David*, buildings like the church of St. Maria del Carmine in Florence and Mont Blanc with all its *neiges* ('middle-size dry goods'). The mereological sums that we should or should not consider as being different and distinct from these daily entities are the mereological sums of the parts of these objects (or the stuff of which they are composed): for example, the mereological sum of all the single cells constituting a grasshopper, or the mereological sum of its small body plus its feelers versus the grasshopper as a whole.[37]

The circumstance that the question of the unity of facts never plays a role in this debate is to the advantage of my position rather than to its disadvantage. I draw upon the debate on material constitution and identity in the present context because this debate seems to be the only one in which the unity versus aggregate assumption is defended *with arguments*. So, as I said, a good way to proceed seems to be to look into whether such arguments can't conveniently be borrowed to support the defenders of option D, namely those assuming facts: if we can, then this position would be provided with grounds for accepting the unmereological composition of facts; if we can't, then the conclusion stands that facts are ad hoc entities. This enables us to secure step 1 and go further than both Lewis, who just rejects unmereological composition (calling it 'magic'), and Vallicella, who states that the position in question is inconsistent.

So the crucial point for us is, first, understanding on what grounds we should acknowledge a difference between sums and integral wholes, and then asking whether the answer to this question provides support for the position that says that we should accept facts as unities alongside mereological sums as aggregates. The answer, as we shall see, is no. There are no reasons for this that are independent of the need to solve the unity problem, or so I shall argue. The grounds on which we acknowledge a difference between sums and integral wholes do not provide support for a difference between sums and facts. To show this, it will be important to note once again the modal talk used in the formulation of Armstrongian dualism. Let me point out that I am *not* arguing against the unity versus aggregates assumption in general: I am arguing just for the weaker claim that the difference between *facts and sums* is not an instance of it.

Let us start by considering a typical discussion about material identity involving a wooden house made of Tinkertoys and the wood of which it is made. Let us denote by 'α' the house that is now on the shelf and by 'β' the wood that is now located where α is located (see Varzi, 2008). The question routinely posed in the debate on material composition is: is α identical to β? Typically, it is argued (i) that α, but not β, would survive the annihilation of a single Tinkertoy piece, or (ii) that α is in the Victorian style whereas β isn't, or again (iii) that taking the Tinkertoy pieces apart would destroy α but not β, that is, that α is necessarily house-shaped whereas β isn't. On the basis of these considerations, it is concluded (by one side of the debate) that α ≠ β: there is a difference between the wooden house and the Tinkertoy pieces of which it is composed. And, from this, it is further concluded that we need to acknowledge that there are two (coincident) objects, not just one: we have a nonmereological integral whole (the wooden house α) alongside a mereological sum (the collection of Tinkertoy pieces β). More schematically, the reasoning goes like this:

T1   In virtue of what does α differ from β?

T2 α differs from β in virtue of one or more of the following properties:

    (i) α is in Victorian style, whereas β isn't;

    (ii) α, but not β, would survive the annihilation of a single Tinkertoy piece;

    (iii)   taking the Tinkertoy pieces apart would destroy α but not β, that is, α is necessarily house-shaped, whereas β isn't.[38]

T3 α and β behave as T2 says.

T4   Therefore, $\alpha \neq \beta$.

Let's now apply this reasoning to the difference between facts and the mereological sums of their constituents. Recall that we're trying to see whether grounds for reliance upon the unmereological composition of facts can be given by reliance upon the unmereological composition of integral wholes, since no direct arguments are available in favor of the former. As I mentioned, the debate on material constitution, composition, and identity seems to be the only one in which unmereological composition is discussed on the basis of arguments (rather than going on foot-stamping that there *is* unmereological composition).

Let us denote by 'γ' the fact *Bargle's being hungry* and let us denote by 'δ' the mereological sum Bargle + *being hungry*. Notice that γ and δ are, like the house and the Tinkertoy pieces, coincident: at the same place at the same time (see the previous section for this claim). I will additionally make the assumption that Bargle and *being hungry* are both atoms, that is, that we are dealing with the simplest (for ease of presentation, nonrelational) kind of facts, atomic ones, having two simple constituents. This means that the coincident sum Bargle + *being hungry* will also have atoms as parts (recall that we are working under the assumption that the sum and the fact do not differ in any part or constituent). This assumption is unproblematic and easily justified. We are interested in understanding how the nonmereological complexity of facts is at all possible alongside the mereological complexity of sums. If we granted that there is *already* nonmereological complexity in any constituent of the fact, we won't be able to make any headway in our discussion. So we need to assume that the constituents/parts involved are atoms.[39]

Let us now ask: can we also say in this case $\gamma \neq \delta$ (T1)? That depends on whether γ and δ behave as T2 says (T3). Let's have a look at T2, and ask on what grounds we can say that $\gamma \neq \delta$. It will result that, in contrast to the case of the wooden house above, all parts/constituents involved here are necessary *and* sufficient *both* to the fact and to the mereological sum, except in one respect, namely, the modal difference I mentioned at the beginning of this chapter.

As to the *annihilation/survival* at (i): The way integral wholes are dependent on their parts is different from the way in which *both* facts *and* mereological sums are dependent on their constituents/parts. It can be shown that a version of essentialism holds for both facts and sums: all their parts (constituents) are essential to the whole (sum or fact). Mereological essentialism—the position according to which all parts of a whole are essential to it—is considered controversial, for a grasshopper with only one feeler, it can be argued, is still a grasshopper. But the controversy regards only integral wholes, not facts or sums: the latter are clearly such that all constituents/parts are essential to them. And whatever one thinks of mereological essentialism, it seems impossible to deny a version of it for facts, that is, to argue that the constituents of a fact are *not* all essential to it. All constituents of a fact are essential to it. Therefore, neither γ nor δ would survive the annihilation of any of their parts or constituents, that is, Bargle and *being hungry*. So (i) does not hold for either facts or sums. There is no difference between sums and facts in this respect.

As to (ii), it is rather difficult to talk sensibly about aesthetic properties in the case of nonmaterial objects. One could thus say that properties of this kind simply can't apply to the case we are considering. Alternatively, one can, with some imagination, perhaps speak of a kind of 'shape' that objects of the kind involved can have, however metaphorically (maybe as if we were to picture these objects graphically). In this case, say, both α and β are *Bargle's being hungry*-'shaped', that is, they are actually unified or brought together in the way they are. (Recall that here I am talking of the mereological sum coincident in time and space with the fact.) So, (ii) holds for neither facts nor sums; there is no difference between sums and facts in this respect. Note that the point at issue in (ii) is not that the sum is *necessarily Bargle's being hungry*-'shaped', because that's false: the point is that the sum happens to be *actually* such. The point about possibly versus necessarily being *Bargle's being hungry*-'shaped' is (iii).

As to (iii), taking parts/constituents apart would destroy γ but not δ: γ is *necessarily Bargle's being hungry*-'shaped', whereas γ isn't. So, (iii) *does* hold for facts and sums. There is a difference between sums and facts in this respect.

Let's take stock. The only ground that we were able to find for the difference between facts and mereological sums is the difference given in (iii). But if this is so, then the only difference between sums and facts is the modal one that the fact is necessarily a unity of its constituents, whereas the sum is not. But, and this is now the crucial datum, *if* the modal difference at (iii) is—by contrast with the differences between sums and integral wholes—the *only* difference that we can indicate between mereological sums and facts (being the only similarity between integral wholes and facts), then the facts defended for option D are (maximally) ad hoc entities, for the very point of the difference between a relation and a relating relation (as between a property and a qualifying property, as we've seen) is that very modal difference. It could have been different, the defenders of the difference in question maintain; *happiness* could have been instantiated in Argle instead of being instantiated in Hargle, which comes down to this: the world could have contained the fact *Argle's being happy* instead of *Bargle's being happy*, or *happiness* could have qualified a totally different bearer.

This means that we have shown that, in order to justify the difference between the nonmereological composition of facts and the mereological composition of the coincident sums of their constituents, we can't reason by analogy with the difference between the nonmereological composition of integral wholes and the mereological composition of the coincident sums of their constituents: the former difference is neither the same as nor an instance of the latter. What is more, the latter difference proves to be exactly identical to the difference we are trying to account for. If this finding is correct, we are left with no argument in support of the nonmereological composition of facts, for we have reached the point at which it is clear that option D amounts to a foot-stamping assertion that sums differ (modally) from complexes because sums differ (modally) from complexes. But without any argument in favor of the nonmereological composition of facts (excepting the need to solve the unity problem), there is little plausibility for the claim that we have found the ontological ground for the difference between sums and facts in the fact itself, that is, in the nonmereological composition of facts.

We cannot, then, plausibly maintain that there is an ontological ground for the difference in question, though we have agreed from the very beginning that we need it—that we need it *if*, at least, *we are to maintain a difference between relations and relating relations*. If we have to maintain that difference, then we have to accept a merely ad hoc solution. If we are instead prepared to drop the request for a difference between relations and relating relations, then other scenarios open up.

Before we examine these other scenarios in the next chapter (see the flowchart in the conclusion of that chapter for a full overview), note that two considerations seem to be in place. First, one might think that the conclusion I draw from considering the properties distinguishing facts and sums at T1–T4 is too strong. Isn't it possible that other differences in properties (e.g., a δ to be added to α, β, γ) can be found between facts and sums, such that the difference in modal status is not the only one we can find? Perhaps. However, that would not disprove my point and would not make facts any less of an ad hoc solution—it would just make them, say, less ad hoc than maximally ad hoc. For note that when advancing a proposal for the difference-making properties (α, β, γ) at issue here, two things should be kept in mind.

First, the argument I offered above works by analogy: first, we accept as a datum that the nonmereological composition of *integral wholes* is plausible and that there is a difference between integral wholes and mereological sums. Then we check whether properties normally invoked to ground this difference can also ground the difference between nonmereological *facts* and mereological sums (and we have found only the modal property indicated above). So, any additional properties one might want to propose as relevant here, that is, as able genuinely to ground a difference between facts and sums, will fit the bill if and only if the properties in question are properties that (1) (can be plausibly invoked to) ground the difference between *integral wholes* and sums, and that (2) can *also* be used to ground the difference between *facts* and sums. If this is not the case, and the properties we have in mind can be invoked only to ground the difference between facts and sums, then such properties won't do, because our move would be non-explanatory. In other words, we have, once again, to avoid reasoning as follows: there is a difference between nonmereologically composed facts and mereologically composed sums *because by definition* there is a difference between nonmereologically composed facts and mereologically composed sums.

Second, we must be able to show that the relevant difference-making properties are fully independent of the modal property that we have indicated as the only difference between facts and sums, that is, we have to take care that those properties are not simply entailed by that very modal property.

It seems quite difficult to come up with any property that could fit the bill, and I doubt that such properties can be found, though I would not want to say it is impossible. Again, and importantly, even if such properties could be found, that alone would not make option D any more plausible. To see this, suppose, as a fallback position, that we find a property that does fit the bill. Then the following consideration suggests itself.

As we saw, there is no full overlap between properties distinguishing integral wholes and sums on the one hand and properties distinguishing facts and sums on the other: in the property in (i), all parts/constituents of both fact and sum are essential to both. This means that the kind of non-mereological composition typical of integral wholes is a *different sort* of nonmereological composition from the nonmereological composition that the defenders of D acknowledge as typical of facts. This means that the defender of option D is assuming a sui generis kind of nonmereological composition, one that is nothing like the kind of nonmereological composition most commonly accepted by philosophers (namely that of integral wholes) on the basis of arguments independent of the unity problem. This does not make things any easier for Armstrongian facts, because the objection will still stand that facts under option D are entities assumed for the sole purpose of solving the unity problem: they are ad hoc entities.

Note that the arguments given in favor of the existence of colocated integral wholes alongside the sums of their constituents or stuff are not merely definitional. They seem to be well anchored in our daily practice and to depend on intuitive empirical observations. For instance, our daily practice tells us that not all grasshopper's parts are essential to it. No such thing can be said of the difference between facts and sums. I say this because one might say that nonmereological composition of integral wholes does not rest on any better arguments than definitional ones. One might be dissatisfied with arguments from daily practice or intuitions supporting integral wholes, but the only thing relevant here is that no such argument is available for facts, which are theoretical constructs about which we can hardly say that we have direct experience (at least not in the same sense as we have experience of integral wholes). It is of course possible to argue that the nonmereological composition of integral wholes is also implausible. But that would make things even worse, for in this case we won't have any reason whatsoever left to believe in any kind of nonmereological composition, including a fortiori that of facts.

2.3 The Unity Problem in an Ontology of States of Affairs

At this point, one may wonder to what extent the unity problem is a problem for other entities in the neighborhood of facts, such as propositions and states of affairs. I will not examine this question in detail; it suffices to say the following. We know what the unity problem is and how it arises. States of affairs and propositions will face this problem too, depending on whether or not they require a nonmereological composition that makes them fall prey to the unity problem, for which no solution that is not ad hoc will be available.

It follows immediately from the considerations I put forward in the previous sections that states of affairs not only fall prey to the unity problem, but they have an adjunctive problem as well—they have, so to speak, a double dose of the unity problem. To see this, recall that states of affairs come in two kinds: obtaining and nonobtaining. This double nature is their sole difference from facts, for *both* these obtaining and nonobtaining states of affairs match all seven ontological characteristics of facts; for example, they are both entities reticulating an object and a property (in the minimal, nonrelational case). But because of their double nature, the defender of states of affairs will have to assume *two kinds of nonmereological composition* or reticulation: one that gives us a difference between the mereological sum of the constituents of an *obtaining* state of affairs and the state of affairs itself, and another that gives us a difference between the mereological sum of the constituents of a *nonobtaining* state of affairs and the state of affairs itself. One kind of states of affairs obtains, and the other does not obtain—but what grounds this difference? Some would call it a difference in ontological status. But how do we explain that? Take the nonobtaining state of affairs *Jan Peter Balkendende's keeping a herring as a pet*. In what respect is this object different from the obtaining state of affairs *Argle's keeping Hargle as a pet*? We cannot say that the difference is that in the case of Jan Peter Balkendende's keeping Reddy the herring as a pet there is in fact no such thing *because* there are only these three separate objects, Jan Peter Balkendende, *keeping as a pet*, and Reddy the herring (or the sum of them), and no unity of them. This can't be the reason, for if those three objects (or the sum of them), which most certainly are 'obtaining', were unified, that state of affairs would obtain: it would be a fact. But it is not: so what is the ontological difference between a state of affairs that does *not* obtain and one that does? In the case of *Jan Peter Balkendende's keeping a herring as a pet* we are talking of a complex of three things that are not the quite the three things in a unity making up a fact. To account for this, we have to suppose that there are two kinds of reticulation: something like a 'loose' (nonmereological) reticulation, which is typical of all states of affairs, and a 'tight' (nonmereological) reticulation, which is typical only of obtaining states of affairs. But how can we account for *two* kinds of unmereological reticulation when we are unable even to account for one?

The very same reasoning applies to Russellian propositions. Russellian propositions are, as we have seen, hybrids of propositions and facts. Since there is a difference between the mereological sums of their constituents and Russellian propositions, the latter pose exactly the same problems as do states of affairs. So, one should reject Russellian propositions as well.

As to propositions, if propositions (in whatever version, Fregean or Aristotelian) obey mereological extensional principles, as I boldly stated without argument in chapter 1, then they have nothing to fear. But if propositions do *not* obey such principles, then the same reasoning we have in the case of states of affairs applies to them, and they are doomed, exactly as states of affairs are doomed. This conclusion has bearing on what I will say about propositions in chapter 5. However, I am optimistic that propositions—at least Aristotelian propositions—can be kept safe from the perils of the unity problem.

2.4 Conclusion

In this chapter, I have discussed a number of options that have been advanced to solve the unity problem. The unity problem is the problem of accounting for the difference between, on the one hand, facts as 'really unified' complexes of relations and their relata (the *constituents* of the fact), and, on the other hand, the 'mere' mereological sums of those very same objects, that is, relations and their relata (the *parts* of the mereological sum). We have seen that the problem starts with accepting the following claim:

Russell's claim   There is a difference between relations and relating relations.

We set up a master argument in which this claim figures, in a somewhat derived form, as the starting assumption:

M1 (*Russell's claim*)   There is a difference between the complex aRb and the sum of constituents $a + R + b$.

This assumption prompts the unity problem. We then asked:

M2 (*Unity problem*)   Something—an ontological ground—must account for this difference. What is it?

We then worked our way through four attempts at a solution. The four options we considered are represented in the provisory flowchart in figure 2.2.

In this flowchart, the options we saw are ranked from top to bottom according to whether they solve the problem, and if so, how (note, however, that it might be disputed whether version 2 of option B is indeed better than version 1, but I will leave the issue open here). The first option holds that the difference between a fact and the mereological sum of its

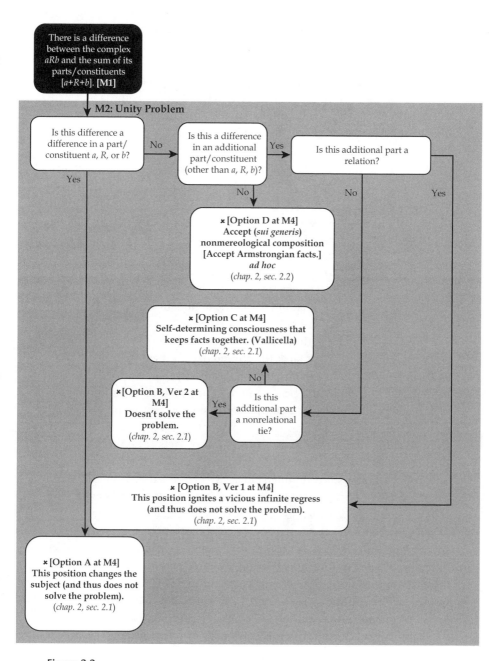

Figure 2.2

constituents lies in the constituents of the fact themselves. We rejected this option (*Against A*) because it changes the subject, and therefore does not solve the problem. The second option consists in adding a constituent to the fact, and either ignites a vicious regress when the additional constituent is itself a relation, and thus does not solve the problem (version 1) or, when the constituent is a so-called nonrelational tie, renames the unity problem instead of solving it (version 2) (*Against B*). Option C, according to which there is a Big Unifier keeping all facts together in acts of self-determination, seemed to be too far-fetched, costly, or in any case of limited acceptability (*Against C*). Option D appeared to be the best option available; however, as I showed, under this option facts turn out to be (maximally) *ad hoc* entities (*Against D*), that is, entities assumed exclusively for the purpose of solving the unity problem. The argument against facts as ad hoc entities was two-fold (sec. 2.2): first I showed that there are no direct arguments in favor of the nonmereological composition of facts (sec. 2.2); subsequently, I showed that there are no indirect arguments in favor of the nonmereological composition of facts, either (section 2.2.1). The argument I used to show that indirect arguments fail was built in this way: we first accept, in contrast with other critics of facts, that facts are not contradictory or magic entities, and that M2 is satisfied insofar as the ground of the difference between facts and sums is that facts are nonmereologically composed while sums are mereologically composed. Then we find an acceptable sort of nonmereo-logical composition, one that enjoys strong support among philosophers, namely the nonmereological composition of integral wholes. We then show that the nonmereological composition of facts is neither the same (sort of) composition nor an instance of the nonmereological composition of integral wholes, since nonmereologically composed facts are different from mereologically composed sums exclusively in this modal respect: that facts are necessary reticulations of their constituents whereas sums aren't. This means that, since the nonmereological composition of facts is of a very special kind, in fact coming down to representing exactly the ontological difference needed to solve the problem, no more and no less—it is ad hoc, assumed for the sole purpose of solving the unity problem. I concluded that facts are ad hoc entities. In section 2.3 I then showed that the unity prob-lem is even more serious for states of affairs, as I introduced in section 1.4.2 of chapter 1, and that all the criticisms I have directed against facts hold a fortiori for states of affairs.

At this point, however, option D—assuming facts as primitive entities—has not yet been dismissed, even if facts are ad hoc entities. As we saw, dis-missing ad hoc solutions takes two steps: (1) showing that a certain option is ad hoc, that is, that the option in question is strictly speaking a solution to the problem, though ad hoc, and thus suspicious (step 1, *Alarm*), and (2) finding a better alternative (step 2, *Defeat*). As we saw, and as we shall see more clearly in section 3.3 of the next chapter, ad hoc solutions cannot be dismissed at step 1, that is, just because they are ad hoc: we might be in a situation in which a solution to the problem at issue is nonnegotiable and there is no better alternative to the ad hoc solution. Therefore, if we want to dismiss an ad hoc solution, a second step is needed: we need to show that there are better alternatives. If we manage to do that, these alternatives will be more attractive than the ad hoc solution, especially if they imply that the problem for which we are seeking a solution does not need a solution. This allows us to dismiss the ad hoc solution as less desirable.

In the following chapter I will show that there are alternatives to assuming facts in order to solve the unity problem, and according to one of these solutions, which I deem to be the most desirable, that problem does not need to be solved because it does not even arise. I'll distinguish between the unity problem, stated in terms of relations and relating relations, and a general problem of relational unity, the solution of which does not require that distinction.

The conclusion we have arrived at raises other two issues. First, my general use of ad hoc avoidance might be questioned. I discuss this point in section 3.2 of the next chapter. Second, from my analyses in the last section, we can see that by assuming facts we are just assuming what we want to ground, namely, the modal difference in Russell's claim (that there is a difference between relations and relating relations). But if this is so, then a problem arises for the truthmaker argument: that argument will now be unsound, because one of the premises presumes that facts are a satisfactory solution to the unity problem under Russell's claim (in fact, it supposes they are the best solution). As pointed out above, the truthmaker argument does not establish the need for facts: it just fixes that facts, which are taken for granted as unifiers in the argument, can be used as truthmakers. I shall come back to the repercussions of the findings of this section for the truthmaker argument in section 3.2 of the next chapter.[40] First, let's see the alternatives to facts.

3 Solving the Unity Problem

In the previous chapter we've seen four options for solving the unity problem (A, B, C, and D). All of these options have been shown to be problematic. Option D turned out to be the best option. As we have seen, however, that option is ad hoc. By showing that Option D is ad hoc, we have taken the first step toward dismissing it as a good solution. Our task in this chapter is to see whether we can take the next step: can we find any better alternatives to option D and dismiss D entirely? Yes, we can.

I proceed as follows. Let us assume that option D definitely fails alongside A, B, and C. If so, then the master argument stands.

(M1: *Russell's claim*)   There is a difference between the complex aRb and the sum of constituents $a + R + b$.

(M2: *Unity problem*)   Something—an ontological ground—must account for this difference. What is it?

(M3)   The ground can only lie in (A) the constituents a, b, or R (a, or F); (B) one or more additional constituents of the complex; (C) something outside the complex; or (D) the complex itself.

(M4)   A, B, C, and D are implausible.

(M5)   Hence, there is no plausible ground for the difference between complexes and sums.

(M6)   Hence, there is no plausible difference between the complex aRb and the sum of constituents $a + R + b$ (vs. M1). (M2, M3, M4, M5)

At this point we can do two things: resist or comply. If we resist, can we somehow stop the argument from yielding M6? In other words, can we show that there is something wrong with one of the premises? If instead we comply, is the outcome of the argument philosophically acceptable? Is it plausible that there is no difference in the world between relations and relating relations?

In the following I will consider two further options, one that complies and one that resists, and explore whether they fare better than option D. As we shall see, the first option (*Comply*) rejects M1. The second option defends a version of option B and thus rejects M4 (*Resist*). Both options take issue with one tacit assumption in the master argument: the assumption that that all relations are *relata-unspecific*. In section 3.1, I will analyze both *Comply* and *Resist*, take issue with three feature-pairs of relations that I have left undiscussed so far, and conclude that *Comply* should be preferred because it is the least ad hoc option on offer. In section 3.2 I explain what I mean by this by pushing my analyses a bit further, coming back to the methodological criteria of theory choice in metaphysics based on ad hocness that have guided my arguments so far and that support my conclusion that *Comply* should be preferred. I conclude that *if* we want an ontology including relations relating their relata (a *desideratum* that might or might not be nonnegotiable), especially if we also want a necessitation variant of the truthmaker theory of truth, then we should favor a world of mereological complexes where all relations are relata-specific above a world of (Armstrongian) facts. I show that no matter what our subjective preferences in metaphysics, and no matter what we think of the methodological criterion of avoiding ad hoc entities, *Comply* has clear metametaphysical advantages over facts once costs and benefits are weighed. These considerations conclude the first part of the book. On this basis, I bid farewell to compositional facts.

3.1   Step 2: A Fact-Free Dissolution of the Unity Problem

Let's look at the two new options we have with respect to A, B, C, and D in the master argument above.

First option: *Comply.* Consider premises M3 and M2. Against M3, one might try to come up with some other option. But the list seems complete: that which grounds the relating of relations either lies inside the complex (in the constituents or in some extra constituent), is the complex itself, or lies outside the complex. As to M2, the assumption reflects the dictum "No difference without a difference maker" and does not seem to be objectionable *if M1 is accepted.* But the question is: why should we accept M1?

Against M1, we may indeed hold that there is in the first place no difference between aRb and $a + R + b$, and so that the unity problem lies exactly in asking for a difference where there is none. The argument as it stands makes it quite clear. Dropping M1, and thus complying, may mean several things. One thing it might mean is that we do not need to account for unity in the world at all. However, in the rest of this section, I am going to discuss only the case that dropping M1 means that we need to account for unity in the world, and that R relates its relata already in the sum $a + R + b$. Mutatis mutandis, the same thing can of course be said about properties and their bearers. This view seems immediately attractive, because it means that the extensionality of parthood—the principle according to which if x and y are composed of the same things, $x = y$—*would apply to complexes as well.* For, applying this principle, if aRb and $a + R + b$ are composite objects with the same proper parts, namely a, R, and b, then $aRb = a + R + b$. If one were to succeed in showing convincingly how this could be accomplished, the unity problem would be solved—or in fact *diss*olved. The master argument is then fine, and it is perfectly understandable why things go awry if we look for the reasons for a difference where there is none. I follow this line of argument below.

Second option: *Resist.* We saw while discussing option B that adding a constituent such as *EX* to the sum creates trouble. But why is it structurally impossible to add a relation *EX* to $a + R + b$ that can ground the relating of R? Bradley's relation regress contributes to the idea that this would not work: if *EX* is added, the question returns on what grounds *EX* is related to $a + R + b$, and so on. And the regress is vicious as it stands. But the question remains: what is it, exactly, that makes *EX* fail to unify $a + R + b$ by itself?

Which feature of *EX* is at stake? As long as this is not clarified, one might still hold that the relation regress stops at S1:

(T)   *R* relates in *aRb*, but not in *a* + *R* + *b*.

(S1)   In virtue of what does *R* relate the relata *a* and *b*? In virtue of relation *EX*, which unifies *R* with *a* and *b*.

In the rest of this section I will also discuss EX. For now, we may sum up the situation above as follows. We have two possible ways to deal with the master argument:

Comply   We hold that *R* is able to do the relating work by itself (and so reject M1).

Resist   We hold that some extra binding relation *EX* is able to take over the relating work of *R* (i.e., we defend a version of option B, additional constituent; and so we reject M4).

In the rest of this section and the next I investigate why both *R* and *EX* fail to do any relating work in the complexes according to the master argument. On this basis I make a case for *Comply* and *Resist*, and say why I think the former should be preferred to the latter.

We come now to the crucial question I have ignored so far: what kind of relations are we talking about? We shall see that a particular assumption about the nature of relations motivates Russell's claim that there is a difference between relations and relating relations, and that once this assumption is removed, the thought that the world is a world without facts—one in which there is no difference between facts and sums—is shown to be perfectly sensible.

3.1.1   Relations: Internal versus External, Universal versus Particular, Relata-Specific versus Relata-Unspecific

What are the features of relations that underlie the master argument? In this section, I define three distinct feature-pairs of relations before returning in the next subsection to the understanding of them that seems assumed in the reasoning reconstructed in the master argument. I distinguish among three feature-pairs of relations: internality versus externality, universality versus particularity, and relata-specificity versus relata-unspecificity. The definitions I consider below are not beyond controversy. The main thing I want to show, however, is just that there are three different pairs of features of relations. Without the strict distinction among the three pairs, no good evaluation of the master argument can emerge. Furthermore, without such a strict distinction, no adequate understanding of the ontological category of relations is possible.[1]

We have already seen the first feature-pair in chapter 1:

Universal relations   A relation is universal if and only if exactly similar relations are numerically identical with it.

Particular relations   A relation is particular if and only if exactly similar relations are numerically different from it.

Here's the second feature-pair:

Internal relations   A relation is internal if and only if it is wholly grounded in corresponding properties of its relata, that is, it is not an entity over and above the properties of its relata.

External relations   A relation is external if and only if it is not grounded in corresponding properties of its relata, that is, it is an entity over and above its relata.[2]

Consider the situation that Argle and Hargle have lunch, and that Argle eats as much as Hargle. In this case we would expect that Argle has the property of eating, say, seven apples, and that Hargle has the same property. If this is so, then the relation *eating as much as* between Argle and Hargle is wholly grounded in corresponding properties of Argle and Hargle, namely their *eating* properties. What does it mean that an internal relation is wholly grounded in the properties of its relata? It means that an internal relation is nothing over and above the properties of its relata, that is, that it is not itself an entity falling under the predicate 'eats as much as'.[3] Thus, if *eating as much as* is an internal relation, there is no such entity in the world, but only Argle's property of eating seven apples and Hargle's property of eating seven apples *taken together*. Consequently, only external relations, those not grounded in their relata, are (genuine) entities. Of internal relations, we have only mere (meaningful) names.

Spatial relations, such as standing at two feet's distance, are classical examples of external relations. This is so because it is commonly thought that there are no spatial properties that can function as grounds in this case. Determining which relations are external, however, is not my concern. I just assume that there is at least one such relation for which the question arises of how it does its relating work. This suffices to establish that an external relation is a third thing between the relata—an entity over and above them.[4]

And here is the third feature-pair:

Relata-specific relations   A relation is relata-specific if and only if it is in its nature to relate specific relata.

Relata-unspecific relations   A relation is relata-unspecific if and only if it is not in its nature to relate specific relata.

The feature of relata-specificity is in a certain way the opposite of internality. If a relation is internal, it is in the nature of its *relata* to hold the relation (or better: to be in that relation—as there is actually no such thing as that relation, but just a predicate in language or thought). But if a relation is relata-specific, it is in the nature of the *relation* to relate specific relata. What does this mean? Suppose, again, that the relation of standing two feet away (*R*) holds between *a* and *b*. Then, if *R* is relata-specific, it relates *a* and *b* as soon as it exists, and consequently *R* could not have existed while failing to relate *a* and *b*. But if *R* between *a* and *b* is relata-unspecific, then *R* could have existed while failing to relate *a* and *b*: it could have related other relata, or perhaps could have failed to relate anything at all.

It should be stressed that the features of externality and relata-unspecificity are quite different. More specifically, an external relation may still be relata-specific. In such a case, it is not in the nature of the *relata* to be related, but it is in the nature of the *relation itself* to relate specific relata. Exactly this combination of features proves useful for proposing a fact-free scenario.

The notion of relata-specificity highlighted above is similar to the notion of bearer-specificity or nontransferability in the literature on tropes. But in what sense exactly? Let's see first that we can have corresponding feature-pairs also for properties.

Bearer-specific properties   A property is bearer-specific if and only if it is in its nature to be had by specific bearers.

Bearer-unspecific properties   A property is bearer-unspecific if and only if it is not in its nature to be had by specific bearers.

As mentioned, bearer-specificity of properties and relata-specificity of relations comes close to the nontransferability of tropes as discussed in the literature. Cameron (2006, 99–100) distinguishes three versions of the feature of nontransferability: temporal nontransferability (TNT), weak nontransferability (WNT), and strong nontransferability (SNT). A fourth possible version can be added that is still stronger (SNT+):

(TNT)   If a trope *G* is temporally nontransferable, then if it so happens that *a* has *G* in the actual world at some time, no other bearer can have (i.e., take over) *G* in that world at some other time.

(WNT)   If a trope *G* is weakly nontransferable, then it can belong only to one bearer, say, *a*. Here, *G* is such that it might be had by *a* sooner or later, but no other bearer can have *G* in any possible world whatever.

(SNT) If a trope G is strongly nontransferable, then if a has G in the actual world, a has G in all possible worlds in which G exists. Here, G is such that it is necessarily had by a as soon as G exists.

(SNT+) If a trope G is strongly+ nontransferable, then if a has G in the actual world, a has G in all possible worlds in which a exists. Here, G is such that it is necessarily had by a as soon as a exists.

If we now return to relata-specificity, we can note that only SNT captures the construal of relata-specificity I have put forward. Let us formulate the characterization in terms of properties: a property is nontransferable if and only if it is in its nature to be had by a specific bearer. Suppose that property G is nontransferable in this sense, and it is in its nature to be had by a. On the one hand, TNT and WNT are weaker than this, for under them G could have failed to be had by a. On the other hand, SNT+ is stronger than this, because in those cases a can never fail in having G. SNT is a kind of middle way: it is had necessarily by the bearers it is had by, *but only if it exists*. One can put it in terms of relations: if a relation is relata-specific, it necessarily relates its relata, *but only if it exists*. To put this in possible-worlds terminology: if R holds between a and b in the actual world, it holds between a and b in all possible worlds in which R exists (and not in any possible world in which a and b exist, or in any possible world whatsoever).

Despite the fact that the discussion of relata-specificity offered above is presented within a trope-theoretical framework, there is no reason to restrict it to tropes, and thus to let particularity and relata-specificity collapse. In other words, relata-specific relations can still be universals. In such a case, it is in the nature of relations to relate many different pairs (or triples, quadruples, etc.) of relata at once. The universal variant is complicated, and I will not expound upon it here. But it is important to keep this variant in mind, because there are theories that acknowledge only universals: the solution to the unity problem I will present is open to these theories as well. The remainder of this section can be read as being neutral on the universals/tropes dispute. Whatever the arguments for or against tropes or universals in this context, if the tropes solution is indeed less complicated than the universals solution, intuitively it should be favored.[5] But here I wish to stay neutral on this issue.

The main benefit of distinguishing strictly between the three feature-pairs is that this enables us to combine the six features in a variety of ways—precisely, in eight. Yet, as we have seen, only external relations, not internal ones, are entities (over and above their relata) that can possess other features. Therefore, the number of possible combinations of features (of external relations) reduces to four:

Externality + relata-specificity + universality
Externality + relata-specificity + particularity
Externality + relata-unspecificity + universality
Externality + relata-unspecificity + particularity

3.1.2 The Unity Problem: A Dissolution

We're now able to work toward a dissolution of the unity problem. Our question is: what makes R and EX fail in their relating work? The answer is: only the assumption that relations must be relata-unspecific, that is, that it is not in the nature of relations to relate specific relata. It is because the master argument assumes R to be relata-unspecific in M1 that there must be an account of how R does its relating work (in M2).

Consider *Comply*. As we saw, this involves denying that R is unable to do the relating work by itself and thus complying, because we reject *Russell's claim* at M1, that is, the assumption that there is a difference between the complex aRb (relating relations) and the sum of constituents $a + R + b$ (relations). If R is relata-specific, and thus it is in the nature of R to relate a and b, then aRb exists as soon as R exists. So, there is simply no difference between $a + R + b$ and aRb. Russell's claim is denied, and the unity problem at M2 is dissolved.

Consider *Resist*. If not R but EX is relata-specific, and it is in the nature of EX to relate R to a and b, then aRb exists as soon as EX exists. Then there is a difference between aRb and $a + R + b$, but no difference between $a + R + EX + b$ and aRb. Russell's claim at M1 is maintained, and the unity problem at M2 is solved (rejecting M4). This makes *Resist* a variant of option B (note that in both cases, *Comply* and *Resist*, Bradley's vicious relation regress is blocked).[6]

Can it be so easy? If so, then why are these relata-specific options usually ignored? They do not seem overtly magical and they are not question begging. The reason these options are commonly overlooked in the literature is because the threefold distinction presented in the previous section is confused, such that no proper understanding of relata-specificity can emerge. In particular, if a relation is relata-unspecific in the sense fixed above, then first it is not in its nature to relate specific relata, so that it could have related other relata, and second it is also not exhausted in relating only one pair (or triple, etc.) of relata. Now, both these characteristics happen to be attributed to *externality* instead. Here, for instance, is Vallicella:

(V1) A relation is external if and only if it could have related another pair (or triple, quadruple, etc.) of relata.[7]

(V2) A relation is universal if and only if it is repeatable and not exhausted in relating one pair (or triple, quadruple, etc.) of relata. (Vallicella, 2002, 14–15, 31; 2004, 164)

As we can see, both characterizations come close to relata-unspecificity as defined above. If a relation is relata-unspecific in the sense I indicate, it is not in its nature to relate specific relata; it could have related other relata (as in V1), and also it is not exhausted in relating only one pair (or triple, etc.) of relata (as in V2). The definitions above do not allow a strict distinction between the three feature-pairs. But this is unsatisfactory: if externality and relata-unspecificity are conflated, then some combinations are made impossible, to wit the crucial combination of relata-specificity and externality.[8]

How should we conceive of relata-specific relations? Although it is unclear what the nonmetaphorical content of unsaturatedness would be, a relata-specific relation might perhaps be conceived of as an unsaturated entity that possesses slots in which *specific objects* fit. In the case of the complex *aRb*, the relation in it would have one slot for the particular *a* and one slot for the particular *b*, like this: $_aR\_{_b}$.[9] Note that, in contrast with the Frege-like unsaturatedness mentioned above, the unsaturatedness at issue here is a form of *specific dependence* and not *generic dependence*. That relations be unsaturated or incomplete entities fits well with the intuition that it is hard to see what relations are unless they hold between some pair of objects. If those slots are also relata-specific, the unity problem can be (dis)-solved. More specifically, then, $_aR\_{_b}$ relates *a* and *b* once it exists. A similar observation can be made about properties. A bearer-specific property $F\_{_a}$ is had by its bearer once they exist, but it is not the case that *a* must have *F* once *a* exists.

An important consequence of both *Comply* and *Resist* is that the composite object *aRb* is *identical with a sum of constituents*: $a +_a R\_{_b} + b$ in the case of *Comply* and with $a + R + b + EX_{aRb}$ in the case of *Resist*. That is, in both options the extensionality of parthood suffices: no complexes violate it. Composite objects of this kind, understood as unities of relations with their relata, are then identical with mereological sums, albeit *only* with those sums that contain (i) a relata-specific relation as a constituent (or a certain object-specific EX_{aRb} in addition to *R*), and also (ii) the specific relata of the relation. Henceforth I call these objects *mereological complexes*, or, for short, *complexes*. So, in *Comply*, the complex *aRb* is identical with the sum $a +_a R\_{_b} + b$ (and $b +_a R\_{_b} + a$) but not, for instance, with the sum $a +_a R\_{_b} + c$ or the sum $a+_c\_R\__b+b$. Recall our image of all objects in the world as points on a circle in the previous chapter: the cuts that we can call 'complexes' in the sense just specified are not just any cuts. They must be cuts of the right kind, namely, cuts that include exactly a relation and its relata or a property and its bearer. This answers the question: which sums form a unity? And it does so without assuming nonmereological composition.

Do defenders of facts consider the alternative option I put forward in terms of relata-specific relations (or bearer-specific properties), and if so why do they not embrace it? In the literature on tropes we find one objection to the feature of nontransferability of trope-properties that may easily serve as an objection to the relata-specificity of relations. As a matter of fact, Armstrong himself considers *Comply* at one point, but, as he puts it in response to Martin's adherence to nontransferable tropes, the problem is that the nontransferability of tropes entails "a rather mysterious necessity in the world" (Armstrong, 1989, 117–118; cf. Lewis, 1998). Put in terms of relata-specificity, Armstrong's question becomes: is there not something modally very mysterious in relations that by their nature cannot but relate specific relata?

Not really, no. First, to claim that relations are relata-specific is to claim neither that they exist necessarily, that is, that they could not have failed to exist, nor that relata, like Argle, Bargle, and the plate of crackers, could not have been related by other relations. Whoever claims that relations are relata-specific claims only that *if* a relation exists, it necessarily relates specific relata and could not have failed to do so. As Maurin (2002, 165) points out, there is no necessary connection *simpliciter*: the necessity is only one-way, from relations to relata.

Actually, in light of the previous chapter, those who put "too much necessity in the world" seem rather to be the defenders of option D. Armstrongian facts are the quintessence of too much necessity in the world. Recall that the only difference we were able to find between a fact and the sum of its constituents was the modal difference according to which the constituents a, R, b can form a unity in the sum, but *do* form a unity in the fact. This modal difference is *created* by assuming that relations and properties are unspecific, so that a mereological sum including a relation or a property and their relata or bearers differs modally by definition from a real unity of that relation or property with their relata or bearers. If we introduce facts to solve the unity problem, we introduce entities in our ontology that are over and above their constituents and are *necessarily* such that they are a unity of those constituents; the *only* and *essential* nature of facts is to be unities of their constituents. Yet what this accomplishes, as we've just seen, is to answer a problem raised by one's own assumptions about the nature of relations by inventing a new category of objects, namely, facts. But what compels us to assume that relations must be relata-unspecific (and properties bearer-unspecific), thus landing ourselves in a modal problem of unity, which we then try to solve by assuming special objects that have, indeed, certain very convenient modal properties? There does not seem to be a satisfactory answer to that.

Let's take stock. In the previous chapter we saw that there are no good arguments in favor of the kind of nonmereological composition specific to (Armstrongian) facts (option D). We saw in what sense this makes facts ad hoc entities for the solution of the unity problem (step 1). We just saw in this section that (dis)solutions of the problem are available that do not require nonmereological composition (*Comply* and *Resist*). For if at least some relations are relata-specific, then mereological composition is all we need to ensure that relations form a unity with their objects. We don't need to assume that *aRb* is a nonmereologically composed fact existing on top of the mereological sums of its constituents *a+R+b*. Therefore, if we allow relata-specific relations, then both *Comply* and *Resist* seem to be good options. And both allow us to abandon facts.

One question remains. Which of them is to be adopted, *Comply* or *Resist*? There is an important difference between the two. In *Comply*, *R* is relata-specific, and therefore *R* takes care of its own relating work. In *Resist*, not *R* but an extra binding relation *EX* is to be relata-specific: *EX* unifies a relata-unspecific *R* to its relata. *Resist* could still be more appealing to those who prefer relations not to carry the burden of relating relata by necessity, insofar as it is not *R* but *EX* that carries it (see Meinertsen, 2008; see also Maurin's 2010a). But a moment's reflection will reveal that it is, again, ad hoc to let *EX* rather than *R* carry the burden, because *EX* is a special entity, an entity, again, introduced in a move for which there are no independent arguments except the need to solve the unity problem. Obviously, if *R* itself can be relata-specific and relate its relata, then it is strange and superfluous to add some entity *EX* that has to take over the relating work of *R*. The point is: why should we be prepared to accept relata-specific *binding* relations when we are not prepared to accept relata-specific *ordinary* relations in the first place? Therefore, *Comply* is the most attractive solution and should be preferred. Under *Comply*, the distinction collapses between relations that relate relata and relations that do not: *all* relations relate relata and carry out their own unifying work. So we comply, and endorse M6, which is a rejection of M1: there is no difference between relations and relating relations. The unity problem disappears. So, step 2 is accomplished: facts should be rejected.

One might still think that relata-specific relations as I have characterized them are implausible objects. But why should we take them to be more controversial than either facts or any of the other entities mentioned in this book: plates of crackers, Argle, Bargle, Hargle, the sum of all four, and any relation whatsoever (not to mention All-Purpose Big Bargle)? Actually, *if* you want a world where (external) relations in the world relate their constituents and properties attach to their bearers, then your best option is to acknowledge relata-specific ones, for these are the least improbable, or at least present the fewest costs and most benefits. What if you don't want such a world? We shall see this in the next section.

3.2   What Problem? Relational Unity, the Unity Problem, and Truthmaking

At this point, one could raise the following question: Should we really prefer the relata-specific *EX* at *Resist* to facts at option D, if it's true that, as I said, they are both ad hoc solutions? Yes, *Resist* is still better than option D, though *Comply*, as I said, is the best option.

To see why, let's first of all go back to ad hoc avoidance, that is, avoiding introducing special entities for the sole purpose of solving a problem. In this and the previous chapter I have made heavy use of criteria of theory choice based on ad hoc avoidance. I side with Gonzalo Rodríguez-Pereyra in holding that avoidance of ad hoc metaphysics is the highest constraint we should put on our metaphysical theories. There are profound reasons one can give for this, first and foremost our preference for theories with the greatest explanatory power, which ad hoc solutions can be shown to jeopardize. Yet while some philosophers might be convinced by the weight I lay on ad hoc avoidance, others might tend to prefer other meta-metaphysical criteria such as ontological and ideological (or theoretical) economy. It is, however, not difficult to see that ad hoc avoidance tends to yield an increase in generality and economy (perhaps, in general, simplicity). Two observations might be useful in that respect. First, what are *special* entities, after all? They are entities whose introduction represents a breach in generality somewhere in the ontology of the theory. In the case of facts at option D, a new category of entities is introduced; in the case of special binding relata-specific relations *EXs* at *Resist* a new subcategory of relations is introduced alongside non-relata-specific relations (or: the category of relations is split in two), so that we have special binding relations alongside ordinary relations. Second, why is it desirable to avoid introducing special entities for the sole purpose of solving a problem? One way to reply is this: because theories that solve a metaphysical problem by postulating no (or fewer) special entities (with respect to what is already present in the theory) will explain *more with less*. They will have *higher generality and economy* with respect to theories that explain the same problem by postulating (more) special entities. And since generality and economy with respect to explanatory power are generally considered valuable meta-metaphysical traits of theories, we should eschew ad hoc entities.

It should be said, however, that the precise dependence among meta-metaphysical criteria such as ad hoc avoidance, generality, economy, simplicity and explanatory power has not been extensively investigated.[10] Therefore, it is legitimate to hold criteria other than ad hoc avoidance in higher regard, and to compare theories in terms of those criteria rather than relying on ad hoc avoidance. It should also be said that alternative or adjunctive criteria are important when we have to choose between theories we suspect to be equally ad hoc with respect to a certain problem (which is, possibly, our case with *Resist* and option D), especially when solving that problem appears to be a nonnegotiable issue (which is not the case here, but might be the case in some other situation).

Let's see now whether the above can help us evaluate more precisely the options we've seen so far. I'll put things in terms of problems and solutions. We'll make the following assumption (note that this applies to properties as well).

The Two-Problem Schema

Relations: Our catalog of the world includes (a category of) relations.

The following problem arises:

Problem 1: Under what conditions do relations relate, that is, attach to (form a unity with) their relata?

(I)   As soon as they exist: all relations are relata-specific (*Comply*).
(II)   Not as soon as they exist: it is not the case that all relations are relata-specific (*Resist, Option D*).

If (I), then it's the end of story. If (II), then the following problem arises:

Problem 2 (M1: *Russell's claim*): There is a difference between the complex *aRb* and the sum of constituents $a + R + b$ (M2: *Unity Problem*). Something—an ontological ground—must account for this difference. What is it?

(*Resist*, variant of *option B*)   It is a difference in a part. The complex *aRb* includes a special entity, a relata-specific relation *EX* binding the non-relata-specific *R* to *a* and *b*. The complex is identical to the mereological sum $a + R + b$ plus a part: $aRb = a + R + b + EX_{aRb}$.

(*Option D*)   It is not a difference in a part. We have two distinct colocated entities, the fact *aRb* and the sum *a* + *R* + *b* such that *aRb* ≠ *a* + *R* + *b*, because *aRb* has a special nonmereological composition (reticulating *a*, *R*, and *b* in a special unifying blend), while the sum *a* + *R* + *b* has a mereological composition (and it is just a heap of *a*, *R*, and *b*).

As we see, by choosing *Comply* we solve Problem 1 by assuming that all relations are relata-specific (I), and Problem 2 (the unity problem) does not arise. Problem 1 corresponds to replying *Yes* to the first question in the flowchart in the conclusion of this chapter and the introduction to the book. Let us for the moment forget Problem 1 and concentrate on Problem 2. Problem 2 corresponds to replying *No* to the second question in the flowchart in the conclusion of this chapter and the introduction to the book. It is clear from the above that on the theory assuming a homogeneous category of relations (relations that are all relata-specific, *Comply*), Problem 2—the problem both *Resist* and option D solve in an ad hoc way—turns out to be nongenuine. A fortiori, *Comply* is not ad hoc with respect to Problem 2, and we are thus not compelled to choose between two ad hoc theories to solve it. The theories accepting facts and *EX*s are both ad hoc because they accept special entities that are not justifiable independently of the need to solve Problem 2. The interesting question now is: is *Resist* ad hoc to the same degree as option D with respect to that problem? It seems that one can conclude two things about *Resist:* that *EX*s are less ad hoc than facts (though ad hoc nonetheless) or else that *EX*s are as ad hoc as facts, but accepting *EX*s is still a more economical and general option than accepting facts. In any case, *Resist* should be still preferred to option D because it simply postulates *less*. Contrary to *Comply*, and similarly to option D, *Resist* maintains a difference between relations and relating relations (which is the difference that makes Problem 2 arise), and accepts special entities with respect to the rest of its ontology. But, similarly to *Comply*, and contrary to option D, *Resist* does not require a special kind of nonmereological composition to do so; it also does not maintain a conceptual difference between parts and these parts in a nonmereological unity ('constituents') nor does it entail a world of additional coincident entities over and above other entities.[11] Because of these elements, *Resist* fares better than option D, even though it is still ad hoc because it also assumes special entities. Note that the mereological complexes assumed by both *Comply* and *Resist* are not special objects in any appreciable sense, because they are plain mereological sums. *They* are not assumed for the special purpose of solving the unity problem. What is assumed for the special purpose of solving the unity problem in *Resist* is a special, additional *part* included in those mereological complexes that form a unity. (No such part is assumed in *Comply*.)

Let's turn to Problem 1. Putting things in terms of two problems as in the two-problem schema above helps to clarify my suggestion at the beginning of section 3.1 that dropping M1 in the master argument can mean different things. Two things it might mean (though not the only two) are that we must reject either Problem 1 or Problem 2 as nongenuine. The scenario I considered above includes only the option of rejecting Problem 2 as nongenuine. Could we also reject Problem 1 as nongenuine, a fortiori eschewing Problem 2 as well? Yes, we could. One way to make sense of this option (though arguably not the only way) is to see it as a scenario in which we reject *Relations* in the schema above. For one might think that Problem 1 sensibly arises because we accept *Relations*, and we accept it for a reason, namely, indeed, because we want relations to (be what) *relate*(s). What else would we accept *Relations* for? In a scenario including *Relations*, Problem 1 immediately arises and needs an answer. If we reject *Relations*, both Problem 1 and Problem 2 disappear, and other scenarios open up. Although I am not considering it to any extent in this book, this is an important option, certainly from the metatheoretical perspective we are considering in this section. For consider the following. If we accept *Relations* as a nonnegotiable assumption, and Problem 1 as a genuine one, as I have done so far, *Comply* is, of the solutions we saw, the most attractive solution with respect to both option D and *Resist*: there is no *further* Problem 2, so we need no solution to that, a fortiori none based on special entities. We are then justified in claiming that *Comply* is not ad hoc with respect to Problem 2, that it should be preferred to *Resist*, and that *Resist* should in turn be preferred to option D because it is less ad hoc. (Alternatively, we can say that *Resist* should be preferred to option D because, although it is equally ad hoc, it still fares better with respect to other meta-metaphysical criteria.) Now, though, could we not say, against *Comply*, that this option solves Problem 1 in an ad hoc way, similarly to what I have argued is the case with *Resist* or option D and Problem 2? Could we not, for example, say that assuming only relata-specific relations to solve Problem 1 is a move similar to assuming facts to solve Problem 2? The only reason that *Comply* is able to solve Problem 1 while still guaranteeing relational unity in the world in such a way that Problem 2 does not arise is because *Comply* stipulates that all relations relate their relata *by necessity*. This critical observation could very well be made by someone who rejects Problem 1 as nongenuine, for instance on the account that there are no relations and therefore no need for a metaphysical account of relational unity in the world. This reasoning could be endorsed by a resemblance nominalist, and that reasoning would be correct: all solutions we saw (option D, *Resist*, and *Comply*) are marked by a stipulation of *some* degree of ontological necessity—and that, in these options, is what solves Problem 1. In this case, relata-specific relations have no place in the universe. But, even in this scenario, *Comply* (and, respectively, *Resist*) would be preferable for reasons of economy, generality, and explanatory power. It's altogether more elegant, if you will.[12] So, even if in the eyes of our resemblance nominalist Problem 1 would not be genuine, and *Comply* an ad hoc solution to it, one could still observe that *Comply* brings advantages in ontological economy, namely, generality and theoretical simplicity with respect to the rival theories. The degree of necessity in the world required by assuming that all relations are relata-specific is such that no additional (category of) entities is included in the catalog of the world; we have no additional kind of composition and no reduplication of entities. In addition, we have one problem fewer (Problem 2). This means that generally we will be able to rank some solutions as less ad hoc than others (or, depending on our conceptual framework, equally ad hoc but still preferable) by relying on alternative criteria. One could even avoid resorting to ad hoc avoidance criteria altogether and still show that *Comply* is the most attractive option.

Note that I don't want to defend any specific metaphysics here, so I am not making the strong claim that an ontology of mereological complexes including relata-specific relations is (the ontology of) our world. I am making the weaker claim that *if* we want an ontology including relations relating their relata (i.e., if we want to solve Problem 1) then we should favor a world of mereological complexes where all relations are relata-specific above a world of (Armstrongian) facts. The point is that no matter what we think of relata-specific relations (and bearer-specific properties)—that is, no matter what our subjective preferences—and no matter what we think of ad hoc avoidance, *Comply* has clear meta-metaphysical advantages over facts once costs and benefits are weighed.

In the light of the above, it is interesting to note the following. There may be a large consensus concerning certain specific metaphysical problems that they must be solved no matter what. Yet it might happen that all our solutions to such problems are all in some sense ad hoc. For since ad hoc avoidance is always relative to a problem, in many cases there will be room to consider certain solutions that are apparently not ad hoc from a certain point of view as ad hoc solutions from another point of view. In such cases, one option is to reconsider the theoretical assumptions we are making in our theories, to see to what extent the problem is genuine.

Another option is to simply accept the situation, perhaps as a provisory solution, or for the sake of the argument; we will still be able to rank solutions. The latter is what I did with Problem 1. A similar example of a problem that might not be genuine, as we shall see immediately, is the problem of finding truthmakers.

Suppose that we consider truthmaking to be nonnegotiable. Can the mereological complexes of *Comply* be truthmakers? Yes, and this is fairly easy to show.[13] It is important, however, to get clear on exactly what kind of truthmaking we want. As we saw in chapter 1, there are two conceptions of (ontological) truthmaking: as *necessitation* and as *explanation*. Both find their core in the idea that truths need an *ontological ground*. That is, there must be an answer to the question: *why* is

(1)   Hargle is happy

true?

The basic idea of necessitation is this: for truth (1) to be made true by truthmaking as necessitation, we need some object x that, whenever it exists, necessarily, (1) is true. Now as we have seen, most defenders of facts assume Russell's claim and thus (at least a subcategory of) relata-unspecific relations. In this scenario, the truthmaking entity in question cannot be the mereological sum of Hargle and happiness, because Hargle and happiness may exist and yet (1) may be false. That is, the sum does not *necessitate* the truth (1). The defenders of facts per option D solve this by introducing facts as entities that *are* the being together of Hargle and happiness, and the existence of which in a world necessitates the truth of (1) in the sense outlined (see Armstrong, 1997, 115). A fact is thus the truthmaker for (1). This is what we read in premises (4) and (7) in Armstrong's truthmaker argument. Something similar can be said of *Comply*'s mereological complexes. In this case, however, we do not need to take as truthmaker for (1) the *whole complex* of Hargle and $_H$happiness (that is, Hargle's happiness), but only *a part of* it, that is, only $_H$happiness. Yet truth (1) as a whole *projects onto* a portion of the world that contains as a mereological part $_H$happiness, and the latter is the ('minimal') truthmaker for (1) (Smith, 1999). So, mereological complexes are viable as truthmakers: facts are not needed for the role.

At this point one could object that, exactly as in the case of Problem 1, *Comply*'s ontology of relata-specific relations (and bearer-specific properties) answers the problem of finding necessitation based-truthmakers just because it puts *some* necessity in the world. And so one might think, again, that *Comply* is an ad hoc answer to the requirement of truthmaking as necessitation. This is perfectly true, but, I think, simply unavoidable, *if we find truthmaking as necessitation nonnegotiable.* For how otherwise can we get truthmaking as necessitation? To see this, recall first that, if we follow Russell, then *lying on* is a relation but not *necessarily* a relating relation between Hargle and Argle's lap. If we think of truthmaking as a relation between language and reality such that a certain portion of reality *makes* a certain portion of language *true*, and in such a way that there is no possible world in which such a portion of reality exists *and yet* the portion of language in question is not true, then there is no question that we need to put some amount of necessity in the world. This is a typical case, I'd say, of having to put the rabbit in the hat ourselves if we want to take it out. The point is that we need some amount of ontological necessity somewhere if we want to hold on to truthmaking as necessitation as a nonnegotiable option. In this case we should go for the best truthmaker candidates from a meta-metaphysical point of view, and these, again, will not be facts, for the reasons already given.

One alternative is to retain the nonnegotiability of truthmaking, but abandon truthmaking as necessitation and opt instead for truthmaking as explanation. One important thing we will need to show if we choose this option, however, is that there is a sensible notion of ontological explanation that makes it acceptable to say that *entities* in the world *explain* truths. This is no simple task.[14] (Also, note that going for truthmaking as explanation does not seem to lessen the fundamental dependence of truthmaking on solving the unity problem.[15])

A more radical solution is to take truthmaking to be negotiable, and abandon it for a weak form of the correspondence theory of truth. This option is interesting. It is far less costly, and indeed, in effect, many throughout history have gone this way (to put it anachronistically). The real advantages of truthmaking are not exactly obvious. Truthmaking is a correspondence theory of truth the strength of which is dependent simply on the strength of the assumptions we make about reality, namely that there are bearer-specific properties and relata-specific relations that *explain* or *ground* empirical truths. This is far more difficult to defend than would be an appeal to a notion of *correlation* between truths and things in the world according to which whenever there is a truth there is something in the world, and vice versa.[16] Although I do not see why the role of truthmaker should be played at all, I don't want to question truthmaking here. I want only to say that *if* we want entities to play the role of truthmaker, then we should choose *Comply*'s mereological complexes. But it is certainly interesting to note that abandoning truthmaking as necessitation for weak correspondentism (or perhaps even for truthmaking as explanation) could reveal interesting hidden assumptions behind the solutions to Problem 1 we saw above. I'll very roughly sketch the point in the trope-theoretical variant. If we let go of truthmaking as necessitation, we can remain neutral on whether tropes are transferable or nontransferable. This distinction between versions of trope theories has started to be emphasized in the literature only recently, and seems in fact needed only in a context in which modal notions such as truthmaking as necessitation are at play. The distinction leads naturally to possible-worlds-talk, which I also employed in my discussion of relata-specificity in the previous section. But if no modal notion is involved in truth, then I do not see why we need to distinguish between worlds in which tropes attach *by necessity* to other tropes as soon as they exist, and worlds in which they do not. A possible-world-free scenario of *just tropes* as abstract simple particulars with a weak correspondence theory of truth could be, I would argue, a very appealing scenario for a correspondentist-cum-trope theorist. But I leave this issue unaddressed here.

What we can say on the basis of the above, is that it is not difficult to see that Armstrong's truthmaking argument is not a successful argument in favor of facts. It might be considered, at most, as an elucidation of a scenario in which we make explicit what constraints we want to put on truth (namely truthmaking), and what we think our metaphysics should look like once these constraints are in place: all the argument says is that we need ontological truth-necessitators. But this role can be played by mereological complexes of relata-specific relations and their relata. The argument cannot show that we need facts as truthmakers unless we simply assume that there are facts as unifiers in the universe (or that we need them in that role). But this, I say on the basis of this and the previous chapter, cannot be plausibly assumed.

3.3 Conclusion

What we've seen in this and the previous chapter is summarized in the flowchart in figure 3.1, which ranks solutions from most plausible (top) to least (bottom).

If our universe contains relations and properties that are relata-unspecific and bearer-unspecific, then there is a difference between (a mereological sum of) relata and (suitable) relations and bearers and (suitable) properties and the actual reticulation of these objects in a unity (black box in figure 3.1). It is commonly accepted that this difference cannot be brute and requires an ontological ground. However, we have seen that all proposals as

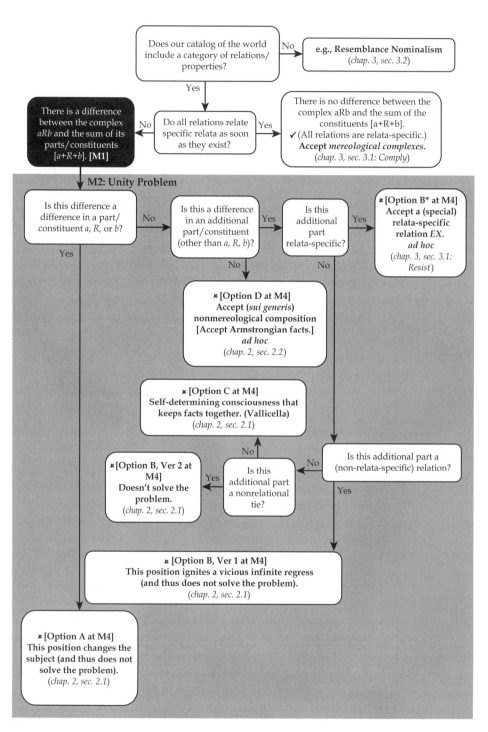

Figure 3.1

to how to account for the ground are implausible (all proposals in the large gray box). As shown, some answers ignite Bradley's relation regress (Bradley, 1893, 27–28; see this vol., chap. 2, sec. 2.1). Others don't ignite the regress, but don't solve the unity problem in a satisfactory way. In fact, following Vallicella (2000), we can say that the unity problem is nothing but the very disease of which Bradley's relation regress is the symptom. The best solution available in this second scenario, at least among those accepting that *all* relations are relata-unspecific, is the primitivist solution offered by Armstrongian facts (chap. 2, sec. 2.1). Still, although Armstrongian facts are not incoherent objects as some say, they are ad hoc entities (chap. 2, sec. 2.2). There are no good arguments in favor of their specific nonmereological composition, and therefore they should be rejected if we can find a better solution. The reasoning I follow here concedes that in option D the idea of "No difference without a difference maker" is maintained without assuming either that the difference maker must be a (proper) part in either the sum or the complex, or that there is only mereological composition. But one can accept that there is nonmereological composition, yet show that this is no argument to accept facts, because the unmereological composition of facts is quite a special one and so facts turn out to be ad hoc entities: entities that serve the sole purpose of solving the unity problem.

In section 3.1 of this chapter, I presented a dissolution of the unity problem that turns on dumping the main assumption that creates the trouble that facts cannot acceptably solve: namely, the claim that there is a difference between relations and relating relations, which I called *Russell's claim*. On this view, the universe contains relations that relate their relata and properties that are had by their bearers directly, because the relations and the properties in question are all relata-specific and bearer-specific. I made clear that having relations R of this kind in the universe does not mean that objects are *necessarily* related in just the way they are. Objects may exist without being related by R, although R relates its relata once it exists. It is in the nature of R to relate specific objects as soon as it exists, but not in the nature of these specific objects to be related. A similar consideration holds for properties. A world of this kind contains not unmereological facts, but mereological complexes composed of relata-specific relations and bearer-specific properties, and their specific relata and specific bearers. Mereological complexes obey the extensionality of parthood insofar as they are identical to the mereological sum of the things of which they are composed. This shows that this solution is a radical dissolution of the problem because the unity problem in this framework simply does not arise.

Put in other words, the following thesis

Russell's claim   There is a difference between relations and relating relations

depends on the further thesis

Relata-unspecific relations   Relations are relata-unspecific,

which is acknowledged by the defenders of facts but rejected in my proposed dissolution of the problem (notice that in my preferred solution, all relations are relata-specific, while in the second best solution *Resist*, i.e., Option B*, only some are). Consequently, the following thesis is also rejected *for complexes of relata-specific relations and their relata*:

The unity versus aggregate assumption   There is a difference between real *unities* and mere *aggregates*.

(Note that similar reasoning can be applied to properties and bearer-specific properties.) An important outcome of this discussion is that since facts as unifiers of the world are simply assumed without good grounds in Armstrong's truthmaker argument for facts as truthmakers, we may conclude that the argument is unsound. My conclusion agrees at bottom with that of Dodd, who in the following passage accepts *instantiation* (a perhaps "hopelessly obscure" notion, he says) for the sake of the reasoning:

This argument is simply unsound. To accept that *a* instantiates *F* is not necessarily to accept that there exists an entity in addition to *a* and *F*: *a's being F*. No reason has been given as to why we should treat the instantiation of a universal by a particular as itself an entity. (Dodd, 1999, 154)

I also wondered, if we consider truthmaking nonnegotiable, whether mereological complexes could be used as truthmakers, and the answer was yes. But I also observed that it is an open question whether truthmaking is after all nonnegotiable, as it is also an open question whether we need an account of (relational) unity in the world (chap. 3, sec. 3.2).

The upshot of all this is that compositional facts must be abandoned. One might wonder at this point whether there is some other, more defensible kind of fact; as I show in the next three chapters, there isn't.

II Propositional Facts

If I am right that compositional facts do not exist, or at least that we have no reason to accept them, why is it, one might ask, that we seem so successfully able to *talk about them*? We can say truly: it is a fact that you are reading this book. In the sentence you have just read, there is reference of some sort to facts, right? So you might think that facts are there after all, and that linguistic arguments can be found to support them.

In the following three chapters, I show that the only kind of facts that can be established by pointing to how we use expressions such as 'the fact that you are reading this book' are so-called propositional facts, not the compositional facts we have seen in previous chapters. So, in any case, arguments from language cannot support compositional facts. But can they support other kinds of facts? And are they successful in this?

In chapter 4, I argue that linguistic arguments for propositional facts aren't successful: they require that propositional facts be referred to by that-clause constructions, but this requirement is unfulfilled because that-clauses do not refer at all. In chapters 5 and 6, I argue, among other things, on the basis of the conceptual toolbox introduced in chapter 1, that even if that-clauses were referential, linguistic evidence would be unable to support an acceptance of propositional facts alongside propositions.

In this part of the book my argumentative strategy, by contrast with the first part, is a *reductio*: I am accepting a methodological attitude known as *descriptive metaphysics* in order to show the intrinsic failure of the linguistic arguments I present. I conclude by reconsidering this methodological attitude, and offering a criticism of linguistic arguments in metaphysics: even if the linguistic arguments I discuss in chapters 4 through 6 were successful, I submit, they would not be able to establish what they seek to establish, because they need to presuppose the very thing they want to show: that there are propositional facts. Besides, they also fail as arguments to the best explanation because there is no genuine metaphysical phenomenon requiring explanation by propositional facts.

My conclusion is that we not only don't need compositional facts, we also don't need propositional facts.

I'm sick and tired of facts! You can twist 'em anyway you like, you know what I mean?
—Juror no. 10, *Twelve Angry Men* (Sydney Lumet, 1957)

We often speak of facts: of facts of the matter, of facts of history, of facts as opposed to opinions. A number of arguments given by philosophers in favor of facts rely on the linguistic evidence given by this everyday parlance. In particular, some observe, that parlance includes *nominal reference* to facts: we can truly say things like 'That Bargle is choppier than Argle is a fact', 'The fact that Bargle is choppier than Argle does not surprise me', and so on. For doesn't '(The fact) that Bargle is choppier than Argle' in such occasions refer to a fact? I argue in this part that it does not.[1] No expression of the form '(the fact) that p' refers to a fact, and if you ask: What *does*, then? I reply: Nothing.

Explaining this claim properly will take about 55,000 words. In a nutshell—or better, squeezed into a couple of pages—the idea is this. Roughly put, some philosophers think that the best method for deciding whether there are, say, hurricanes, is to look at some specific uses of the word 'hurricane' in language. Although at first this may seem incredible and frankly a bit naive, the reasoning behind this approach is technical and sophisticated. The basic idea comes from W. V. O. Quine. In 1953, Quine introduced a method for addressing in a philosophically responsible way questions of the form "do hurricanes exist?" He tells us:

(Step 1) Take a claim *s* in which the word 'hurricane(s)' appears, and translate it into (classical) first-order predicate logic with identity.

(Step 2) Does *s* thus translated (call it *s**) imply a (first-order) statement of the form $\exists x U x$ where 'U' stands for 'is a hurricane' and $\exists x$ is the existential quantifier of first-order predicate calculus?

(Step 3) Is this statement ineliminable from the (formal) language of our best scientific theories?

(Step 4) Is this statement true?

(Step 5) Are (good) identity conditions given for hurricanes, that is, when is it the case that, for U*x* and U*y*, $x = y$?

If the answers to steps 2 through 5 are all *yes*, then language commits us ontologically to hurricanes—to the existence of hurricanes—and we have reached our aim. If some of these answers are *no*, then there's still work to do.

As is clear, this is hardly just a cheap way of showing that objects exist simply because you give them a name. To be sure, these Quinean steps tell you *when* you are entitled to regard expressions as seriously committal, that is, as expressions that purport to refer to objects (steps 1 and 2). But this involves first of all translating natural language expressions into first-order (classical) predicate calculus, and not all expressions of natural language will pass this translation test. Furthermore, this five-step criterion tells you when expressions that pass the test, and which therefore *purport* to refer to objects, actually *do* refer to objects (steps 3–5). This is the case when 'There is an *x* such that *x* is a hurricane' is both ineliminable from the language of our best scientific theories (step 3) and true (step 4). Finally, we must be able to agree upon criteria of identity for hurricanes, that is, when is it that we have two hurricanes and not just one (step 5). What this all means is that once your language is made adequate to talk about hurricanes (i.e., once we regiment it via classical first-order predicate logic), then you still have to show *that* there are hurricanes and *what* hurricanes are.

Far from being incredible and naive, the approach suggested by Quine launches a very difficult enterprise that involves both deductive methods—typical of armchair philosophy—and sometimes, as in the case of hurricanes, empirical observations as well. One important thing about Quine's criterion, at least as he intended it, is that it is not geared toward natural language and finding out what there *really* is, but rather toward giving a way to phrase the question "What is there?" for regimented languages, that is, for formal first-order predicate languages in which science has to be formulated (step 3; see Quine, 1953a, 106–107). And this involves understanding what the formal language of a scientific theory commits us to in an essential way. Suppose you believe that there are hurricanes: if you have a good scientific theory of what hurricanes are, then you'll be rightly pleased to be able to adopt a language for that theory that commits you to hurricanes. The two—your ontological convictions and your language—will harmonize. That's all. And that's already quite a lot.

Now forget about hurricanes and suppose you want to ask whether there are facts. In this case the difficulties are all internal to philosophy, because facts are theoretical entities in the philosopher's toolbox. It is certainly dubious that the entities to which the predicate 'is a fact' are purported to apply to allow for empirical observation. Armchair philosophy here seems entirely unbounded. So if we do find ourselves faced with what looks like a true proposition of the form 'There is an x such that x is a fact', we need to show by philosophical means what facts are, an endeavor that requires in turn that it is agreed when it is that we have two facts and not just one. Is the fact that Oedipus marries Jocasta the same fact as the fact that Oedipus marries his mother? If so, why? If not, why not? Answering these questions requires a well-worked-out philosophical theory of facts.

In the three chapters of this part, I criticize theories of facts that are supposedly not only streamlined or systematized, but allegedly established by a criterion similar to Quine's—*similar*. For a number of reasons that I am not going to discuss in detail, post-Quinean philosophy of language uses a significantly modified criterion that mixes Quine's original criterion of ontological commitment with some quite different ideas. In particular, the modified criterion includes ideas about reference originally due to Bertrand Russell. As a result, when discussing reference, mainstream philosophers of language tend to lay particular emphasis on the workings of so-called *singular terms*, which are absent in Quine's approach.[2] Singular terms are special noun phrases (NPs, or nominal phrases in linguistics) of which paradigmatic examples are proper names like 'Argle', 'Bargle', and 'Hargle', though on the most inclusive list you will find, next to proper names, indexicals ('he'), simple and complex demonstratives ('this', 'that hedgehog'), definite descriptions ('Argle's cutest pet'), and appositive descriptions ('the hedgehog Hargle'). Basically, the idea is that singular terms, if they *really* are such, refer to objects *successfully*: the use of a singular term for something guarantees its existence. This is not magic; it's a definition. Or, at least, it is what should *follow* from any definition of singular term. No one knows how to define the notion of singular term, but given that its referent is singular and that it exists, this is what the definition of singular term should imply. No wonder Russell thought there was only one kind of singular term, namely, demonstratives such as *this* (while pointing). Others are less discriminating than Russell.

In the kind of philosophy of language I will take issue with, the idea is widespread that if there are singular terms in natural language for facts, then facts exist.[3] Notice that in this framework the relation between natural language and its regimentation in first-order predicate logic is seen in a quite different way from how Quine sees it (see Quine 1960, §33, esp. p. 159). Philosophers of language who operate with the conception of singular terms sketched in the previous paragraph take the workings of natural language very seriously. Rather than moving straight from natural language to theories couched in formal languages geared to the aims of science, and paired off with whatever ontologies we might want to defend, these philosophers instead merely move back and forth from natural language to formal language. And in general they pay little attention to the divergences between natural and formal language: their goals are concerned exclusively with natural language and with the absolute reference of its terms to the world. This absolute reference is investigated with the aid of formal tools borrowed from Quine, among others, but then adjusted in such a way that, unlike Quine, advocates of this view tend to neglect the complicated issues raised by regimentation. Step 3 looks quite different in such a modified criterion, and more often than not step 5 gets forgotten or is all too quickly resolved.

Singular terms are thus important in present-day mainstream philosophy of language because they are understood to be our hook on the world. The mainstream reasoning, as manifested in the practice of philosophers in this tradition, usually proceeds as follows. We begin with a question: do we have singular terms for facts? Singular terms are formalized in first-order predicate calculus as constants, and appear in statements of the form *Fa*. So to answer our question, we look for natural language expressions that seem like good candidates to serve as singular terms for facts and that we can translate as *a* in *Fa*. If we find such expressions, then we have nominal reference to facts, at least so long as *Fa* is true. But can we really find such expressions and such true sentences? Yes: a paradigmatic example is the expression 'the fact that ...' as in 'the fact that Dargle is a liar is a surprise'. Derivatively, we also say 'that fact (that Dargle is a liar) is a surprise'. Another paradigmatic example is that-clauses, as in: 'That Dargle is a liar is a fact'. The form of this sentence, so goes the argument, is *Fa*, where 'that Dargle is a liar' takes the place of *a* and 'is a fact' of *F*. And there are, uncontroversially, truths of this form in natural language. So all we need to show is that the sort of expression in question, that is, of the form 'that *p*' (or 'the fact that *p*'), are singular terms.

But are these expressions, that-clauses, really singular terms? Well, usually to check this kind of claim philosophers recur, in part, to step 2 of Quine's criterion. If *a* is a singular term, then it is always possible to go from *Fa* to ∃*xFx* (from 'That *p* is a fact' to 'Something is a fact'). Now, if it is possible to get ∃*xFx* from *Fa* when *Fa* is 'That *p* is a fact', then this is an indication that the *Fa* we started with was a good one: that *a* was a good singular term for a fact.[4] So that-clauses are good singular terms for facts, and in ∃*xFx* the variables range over facts: we're half done. The other half of the work is done by making sure that quantification over facts in natural language is ineliminable, and by setting up identity conditions for facts (though often, as I've said, philosophers tend to stop halfway). In other words, first we check our work by forcing translations of 'That *p* is a fact' into 'Something is a fact' in first-order predicate logic; then we check the ineliminability of expressions such as 'That *p* is a fact' from natural language; then, finally, we set up plausible identity criteria for facts. If this procedure is successful, then we can be sure that facts exist, since natural language—the language we speak every day—commits us to them. Note again, importantly, that philosophers who endorse the latter claim think that the commitment of *natural language* to facts, hurricanes, or what have you is enough to support the metaphysical claim that these things exist and, what's more, to support an assertion of such claims as absolute, true once and for all and for everybody. This is far distant from Quine's emphasis on the *formal language of our best scientific theories*. (This reasoning is, besides, often restricted to English; whether this should mean that Chinese, for instance, might not have facts according to this reasoning is not always a matter included in the discussion.)

Let's take stock. I started above by saying that, roughly, some philosophers think that the best method for deciding whether there are hurricanes is to look at some specific uses of the word 'hurricane' in language. Since then we have acquired some more detail about the current methodology in present-day philosophy of language that embodies this rough idea, and have learned something about its historical roots. Historically speaking, this methodology draws upon Quine's seminal idea of ontological commitment, but with three major modifications in its aim and tools: first, the language that matters now is natural language (not the formal language of

Quine); second, the translation from natural language goes *to* first-order predicate logic *and back again*—that is, it serves as a test to see whether we've gotten things right in natural language rather than, as for Quine, a way to set up a formal language within the bounds of which we can responsibly do science; third, singular terms in natural language are privileged expressions (again against Quine, who set out to *eliminate* singular terms in the passage to formal language).

The current methodology in philosophy of language I have just briefly outlined is the one I will endorse by way of reductio (and thus not dispute for the sake of the argument) in the following three chapters. What will concern me in these chapters is the *specific application* of this methodology to facts. Do mainstream arguments following this methodology manage to establish convincingly that there are facts? No.

Within this methodology, I maintain that the reasoning sketched in the previous paragraphs in favor of facts is ill conceived. First of all, that-clauses cannot function as singular terms for facts. Nor can any other expression. Moreover, the translation of 'Something is a fact' into the language of first-order logic is only apparently successful. Even if singular terms for facts were available, an examination of the conception of facts that such terms commit us to shows that these terms would be able to refer not to facts, but to something else.

In saying all this, I am pitting myself against a position defended by philosophers such as Kit Fine. In Fine (1982), he makes three points:

The first point is that there is singular or nominal reference to facts; the second is that facts are not true propositions, but a distinctive kind of entity; and the last is that the obtaining of a fact is merely a form of existence. (Fine, 1982, 44)

In chapters 4 through 6 I show first of all that these three claims are mutually incompatible. Second, I argue that each is on its own either false or arbitrary. I argue in chapter 4 that the first claim is false. In chapters 5 and 6 I argue that the first claim is incompatible with the second and third claims. If there were nominal reference to facts, facts would be true propositions; and if facts were true propositions, they would *not* be a distinctive kind of entity. Therefore Fine's second claim is false and consequently so is the third, since the obtaining of a fact would be identical with the truth of a proposition, and thus not a form of existence of something else (on both conceptions of proposition I elucidated in chapter 1, the Fregean and the Aristotelian).

The arguments for facts I discuss in chapter 4, based on the assumption that that-clauses are singular terms, are disproved on the very same linguistic grounds upon which they rely. The linguistic theories often invoked by philosophers who endorse such arguments are at best controversial from the point of view of language data and linguistics itself. There exist alternative and independent accounts of that-clauses, both in different areas of philosophy and in linguistics, that reject the referential role of that-clauses and which seem to do better justice to the deep scientific insight that 'that-clauses are a mess' (Fara, 2000). It is on the basis of these accounts that I demonstrate, in the remainder of chapter 4, that arguments for facts based on the modified, Quine-like criterion of ontological commitment invariably fail.

In chapters 5 and 6 I offer a fallback position for defenders of facts. This position assumes the opposite of what I argue in chapter 4, that is, it assumes that that-clauses *are* referential parts of speech. I show that even if that-clauses were referential parts of speech, still the arguments usually invoked in philosophy of language based on the workings of that-clauses in natural language would be unable to support the existence of facts as items in their own right, distinct from true propositions.

An important outcome of chapters 5 and 6 is that, independently of whether they succeed, the language-based arguments for facts I'll review cannot support the items I called 'facts' in the previous part of this book—that is, the compositional, worldly kind of facts à la Armstrong with objects 'in' them. At most, the objects that the arguments I here consider can aim to establish are so-called *propositional facts*, items whose nature seems rather mysterious even to their supporters. About these creatures we know little: they are parasitic on propositions, and appear in some strong correspondence theories of truth like that championed in the 1950s by G. E. Moore. These ghostly critters, though less popular in some quarters than their down-to-earth compositional cousins, are still to be found in the work of both correspondentists and noncorrespondentists such as John Searle and Wolfgang Künne.

It is interesting to ask what the discussions of chapters 4 through 6 imply for the methodology of metaphysics. Arguing on the basis of what natural language commits us to with the aim of deciding what we should admit in the catalog of the world is not my preferred metaphysical method, nor do I think that this is actually how things go in practice. If I follow this method in this part, it is because my criticism here can be conducted fully without stepping outside the language-based framework common in philosophy of language and in some metaphysics. There is no need to invoke other, more or less radically different points of view.

The Argument for Facts from Nominal Reference

A prima facie reason often given when making a case for believing in facts—
to take them to be part of the catalog of the world—is that we appear to
make reference to them, either by devices of *nominal* reference or by devices
of *sentential* reference. In an influential paper, for instance, Kit Fine writes:

> Surely when we say that not all of the relevant facts have been considered or that the
> recently discovered fact will prove critical, there is reference of some sort to facts, a
> reference that will show up either in the use of nominal or sentential variables. (Fine,
> 1982, 45)

So, according to Fine there is either nominal or sentential reference to facts
(or, perhaps, both). Suppose these are the only options (I have no reason to
think they are not). It follows that, should neither nominal nor sentential
reference be shown to work convincingly, the view that we are committed
to facts via language (or, as we shall say, that language commits us to facts)
is left unsupported by arguments. This is indeed the main conclusion
toward which I shall be building in chapters 4 through 6.

One might wonder whether by 'reference' both Fine and I here mean
successful reference. Indeed, 'successful reference' is what I mean now by
'reference', and it can easily be shown that Fine does too. The point is connected with a version of Quine's criterion of ontological commitment
(Quine, 1953b, 1969). As mentioned in the previous section, according to
this version of the criterion, which actually differs considerably from
Quine's original one, facts, hedgehogs, bucatini, smiles, flowers, and so on
exist whenever there are *true* statements of (natural) language ontologically
committed to facts, hedgehogs, bucatini, smiles, and so on—which means,
in turn, that (natural) language is such as to imply first-order statements of
the form $\exists x Fx$ ([there is] something [that] is a fact, a hedgehog, a bucatino,
etc.). Note that since statements of the form $\exists x Fx$ are always derivable from
statements of the form Fa (where a is a singular term), showing that natural
language has singular terms for facts is sufficient to show that natural language is ontologically committed to facts. An important requirement in
this version of the criterion, and one that has proved amazingly rich in its
philosophical consequences, is that the quantified statements at issue must
be *ineliminable* from (natural) language; they cannot be *paraphrased away*.
(But I will leave this issue aside here.[5]) To sum up: yes, when Fine says that
"the phrase 'that p' does indeed refer to a fact when the whole statement
['that p is a fact'] is true," he is accepting both the criterion above and the

implication that there are facts on the basis of that criterion. We have, he says, *successful* reference to facts in natural language.

That language carries *sentential* reference to facts can mean, following Fine, two things: that reference is carried by expressions in sentential position or that it is carried by sentential variables (Fine, 1982, 45). In the first case, Fine thinks of sentences themselves as 'carrying reference' to facts (*definite* sentential reference); in the second case, he has probably something in mind like 'Bargle remembers whatever Argle says' (*indefinite* sentential reference). Note that in speaking of sentential reference we should be wary of taking it to be unproblematically a kind of *naming*. To be sure, the idea that sentences or propositions denote or designate facts just as terms denote things has been defended,[6] but it is not very popular, and was famously attacked by both Russell and Wittgenstein. According to Russell, for instance, facts exist, but are not items that can be *named* by sentences or propositions. It's not that the whole sentence, say, 'Bargle is choppy' (if true) *names* a fact (Russell, 1918–1919, 504). Facts can be represented in language by sentences, which are their adequate 'symbols', but a sentence is not a fact's *name* (Russell, 1924, 335).[7] In general, sentences may very well be said to have facts as ontological *counterparts* in the world, but this is not the same as saying that the former *name* the latter. Sentences do not name anything. In other words, names and sentences fall into different categories—and never the twain shall meet.

The difference between these two positions—sentences as special referring names versus sentences as not names at all (though having ontological counterparts)—is arguably significant, since it has bearing on the theory of truth one will be inclined to accept. Neither position, however, can be taken as offering prima facie evidence for facts. Indeed it would be difficult to argue that any form of definite sentential reference to facts, especially in the latter, no-name version, can function as a prima facie language-based argument for the existence of facts, because in sentences such as 'Bargle is choppy' there is no mention of any fact, nor is there any part that can be identified as serving that mentioning role. Sentences don't wear reference to facts on their sleeves, so to speak. At most a (true) sentence such as 'Bargle is choppy' can be taken to carry commitment prima facie to Bargle and (eventually) to choppiness, but what argument could possibly establish that here we have prima facie sentential reference to a fact? The same holds a fortiori for indefinite sentential reference. Indeed, complete sentences aren't usually taken to carry ontological commitment to anything. There is no agreed upon criterion of ontological commitment that relies on the referential role of sentences in this sense.

One could object that the prima facie evidence we have in the sentential case is structural, that is, that sentences have a complex grammatical structure and refer to items that mirror that structure, namely facts. But the complexity of the grammatical structure of sentences cannot serve as prima facie evidence, because the degree of grammatical complexity of linguistic entities says nothing about the degree of ontological complexity of the referents (if any).[8] So, one can defend the idea that facts are structural counterparts of truths, but it would be difficult to use this as prima facie evidence for facts, which is what counts here.[9]

Since, as we saw, there is little support for the idea that the grammatical structure of sentences can be used as prima facie linguistic evidence for facts, we may part from sentential reference at this point and turn to nominal reference.

Claiming that natural language shows nominal reference to facts means claiming that there are expressions in nominal position that refer to facts. This is guaranteed whenever, roughly put, there are singular terms for facts. Unlike in the sentential case, here we do have widely shared criteria of ontological commitments that rely on nominal reference, so this aspect of language would indeed seem to give us a prima facie reason to believe that there are facts. Which expressions serve the purpose? The most obvious (type of) candidate is *the fact that p*, but it's not the only one. Here's Fine again:

[A] Nominal reference is reference by means of an expression in nominal position. It is either definite, with a name referring to a particular object, or indefinite, with a variable ranging over a class of objects. Now on the face of it, there is nominal reference to facts of both varieties in ordinary usage. When we say 'the fact that the Watergate bugging took place is disgraceful' or 'whatever fact he uncovers is unlikely to help,' we seem to be using 'the fact that the Watergate incident took place' as a name for a particular fact and the phrase 'whatever fact' as part of the nominal quantificational apparatus for referring to facts; ...

[B] Even locutions that might appear to suggest an alternative view conform readily [to this one]. With the construction 'it is a fact that *p*' for example, it seems most natural to follow the transformational grammarians and to take it as a transform of 'that *p* is a fact', and then to suppose, not too recklessly one hopes, that the phrase 'that *p*' does indeed refer to a fact when the whole statement is true. (Fine, 1982, 44)

The point at [B] perhaps needs some further elucidation. Although it might seem that with 'it is a fact that *p*' we do *not* have nominal reference to facts, Fine says it turns out that we do. The reason, he continues, is that a sentence like

(i)   It is a fact that Bargle eats more than Argle

is, according to transformational grammarians, a *transform* from

(ii)   That Bargle eats more than Argle is a fact.

This means that (ii) is syntactically basic while (i) results from it by *extraposition*, that is, by moving 'that *p*' to the end of the sentence and inserting a dummy or anticipatory pronoun ('it') at the beginning.[10] And in the syntactically basic form (ii) we do have nominal reference to a fact because 'that *p*' ('that Bargle eats more than Argle') occurs in nominal position. Therefore, Fine concludes, we can take 'that Bargle eats more than Argle' in this sentence to refer to the fact that Bargle eats more than Argle (assuming that (ii) is true). It is important to see that what Fine takes to be committal to facts here is not the occurrence of 'is a fact' in (ii) in predicate position, but the occurrence of a referential that-clause in subject position, which functions like a singular term referring to a fact. If the clause were not referring to a fact, 'is a fact' could not be *truly* predicated of it. The occurrence of 'truly' in the last sentence calls for comment.

Fine's whole argument is this: language puts at our disposal expressions such as 'the fact that *p*' and 'whatever fact' that, on their face, commit us to facts by definite and indefinite nominal reference ([A]). Moreover, arguably, some expressions of the form 'that *p*' (that-clauses) also commit us to facts by nominal definite reference (i.e., by functioning as singular terms). The constructions 'That *p* is a fact' and 'It is a fact that *p*' are widely available and widely used, and also intimately related. Their mere existence and their intimate relationship, fixed by a view borrowed from some parts of linguistics,[11] seem to suggest that 'that *p*' in sentences of the form 'That *p* is a fact' refers to a fact when the whole sentence is true ([B]).

There is one additional conjecture suggested by [B]: since what is committal in 'That *p* is a fact' is the that-clause in subject position, not the predicate 'is a fact',[12] we may generalize the point and assume that that-clauses refer to facts not only in constructions of the form 'That *p* is a fact' but also in other constructions of the form 'That *p* f*s*', in which something is predicated of a fact that is referred to via a that-clause, as for instance is the case in 'That Bargle eats more than Argle does not surprise me'. That some (kinds of) that-clauses refer to facts, as we shall see shortly, seems to find support in literature at the interface of linguistics and philosophy. The situation with

(ii)   That Bargle eats more than Argle is a fact

and

(1)   That Bargle eats more than Argle does not surprise me

is seen, if we can put it this way, as pretty much the same as the situation in which we truly say

(iii)   Hargle is a hedgehog

and

(iv)   Hargle likes apples.

Sentence (iii) is a so-called substantial predication of form *Fa*, where we say what kind of thing Hargle is. Sentence (iv) is a predication in which we ascribe to Hargle the property of liking apples. Yet 'Hargle' refers to a hedgehog in both. The same thing allegedly applies to (ii) and (1).

Let's call Fine's argument thus enlarged with the additional conjecture just elucidated the *argument from nominal reference*. An important presupposition in this argument is the modified, Quine-like criterion of ontological commitment discussed above. So here are the relevant parts of the argument for the claim that facts exist insofar as certain expressions of natural language in nominal position (successfully) refer (see the end of the introduction to chap. 4 for the argument):

(*Quine-Like*) Facts exist if and only if statements of natural language are true that are ontologically committed to facts.

A statement *s* of natural language is true that is ontologically committed to facts if and only if

> (*First Conjunct*) *s* implies a true first-order statement of the form $\exists x F x$ (indefinite reference) where 'F' is 'is a fact'.
>
>> (*SuffFirstConjunct*) A sufficient condition for *First Conjunct* is that *s* contains singular terms for facts in natural language (definite reference).
>>
>> Sufficient conditions for *SuffFirstConjunct* are
>>
>>> (*SuffSuffFirstConjunct 1*) Some (kinds of) that-clauses are singular terms referring to facts; (B, additional conjecture)
>>>
>>> (*SuffSuffFirstConjunct 2*) 'The fact that *p*' is a singular term referring to the fact that p; (A)
>>>
>>> (*NecFirstConjunct*) A necessary condition for *FirstConjunct* is that 'is a fact' functions genuinely as a predicate in predications of the form '*x* is a fact'. (B, additional conjecture)
>
> (*Second Conjunct*) We have identity criteria for facts.
>
> (*Third Conjunct*) The quantification over facts in natural language is ineliminable. (A)

The Quine-like criterion is an assumption that underlies much philosophy that believes that language-based arguments can establish metaphysical results. I accept it for the moment for the sake of the argument, but it is not a conviction I share about reference and existence.[13] I think that we cannot discover much about what is in the catalog of the world by looking at everyday speech and its reference devices, because we cannot take language to refer to anything unless we have already set our mind on what there is (see Betti, 2014). In these next chapters I work inside assumption *Quine-Like* in a reductio mode. I think it is important to stress once again, however, that Quine's original criterion was not meant to apply to natural language directly, but rather to its regimentation in first-order logic. I stress this point of difference because difficulties linked to it will turn out to be important to our rejection of *NecFirstConjunct*, which is, in turn, crucial to our rejection of *First Conjunct* and thus to our rejection of the claim that facts exist according to this argument. According to Quine, the question 'What is there?' can be raised only after this process of regimentation, and in particular can be raised only about a formal language equipped with a device of objectual quantification and in the context of scientific theories, not in the context of daily speech or of so-called commonsense ontology. Contemporary philosophers of language such as Fine forget this scientific context completely, skip the preliminary regimentation step altogether, and apply the criterion to natural language directly, as in *Quine-Like*. Some do this because they take up Quine's criterion only partially, that is, only insofar as they are convinced that ordinary language is superior to any formal regimentation; others may do it because they take for granted that regimentation is possible; most often it is not quite clear why. Whatever the reason, the difference between *Quine-Like* and Quine's criterion is by no means innocuous; this is why I speak of *Quine-Like* as a *version* of Quine's criterion. The path from natural language to the target formal language via regimentation and back is fraught with difficulties, and the issues that might be raised in this connection are complicated. I will not address the issue in any depth in these three chapters to come, but will mention it whenever it is relevant to my account.[14]

Once we agree on *Quine-Like*, the strength of the argument rests on whether we can show convincingly *First Conjunct* (never mind *Second* and *Third Conjunct* for now). Two things are worth mentioning about these claims. First, note that although I keep them separate to ensure a more transparent analysis, *SuffSuffFirstConjunct 1* and *SuffSuffFirstConjunct 2* are not necessarily independent. For instance, we might think that there is only one expression—a privileged expression—that commits us to facts prima facie, namely 'the fact that *p*'. In this case all one needs to show is *SuffSuffFirstConjunct 2*. But, on the other hand, we may think instead that 'the fact that *p*' carries definite nominal reference to facts only by virtue of the expressions it embeds, that is, thanks to, first of all, 'that p'; in that case, *SuffSuffFirstConjunct 1* would be primary. I see no reason not take *SuffSuff-FirstConjunct 1* to be primary and not to take *SuffSuffFirstConjunct 2* to depend on it: 'the fact that p' is not a nondecomposable *idiom*, that is, a complex linguistic unit that is completely frozen, like 'kick the bucket' (Tabossi, 2006), but a complex expression composed of 'the', 'fact', 'that', and 'p' (or more precisely, since I take 'that p' to be a syntactic unit, of 'the', 'fact', and 'that p').

By the end of chapter 4, *First Conjunct* will have been rejected. Sections 4.1 and 4.2 criticize *SuffFirstConjunct* 1 and 2: section 4.1 criticizes *SuffSuff-FirstConjunct 1* insofar as, I argue, that-clauses are not singular terms; section 4.2 criticizes *SuffSuffFirstConjunct 2*: 'the fact that p' is not a singular term—a conclusion that relies in part on the finding that 'that p' is not a singular term either. Section 4.3 criticizes the claim that 'is a fact' is a predicate, namely of the claim *NecFirstConjunct*. *NecFirstConjunct* is a necessary condition for *First Conjunct*—which is crucial to get to *Quine-Like* and therefore to claim that facts exist. Notice, however, that although the claim that that-clauses are singular terms for facts is only a sufficient condition to derive $\exists xFx$, this claim is a *necessary* condition for *NecFirstConjunct*, which in turn is necessary to *First Conjunct*: for the expression 'is a fact' to function as a predicate in 'That p is a fact', 'that p' must be a singular term. Therefore, by rejecting the claim that that-clauses are singular terms, we do something more than merely rejecting a sufficient condition to get to $\exists xFx$ in natural language. By rejecting the first sufficient condition we have also rejected the necessary condition for deriving $\exists xFx$. By this reasoning, anyone sharing the methodology set out in the argument for facts from nominal reference will have to conclude that facts do not exist.

In chapters 5 and 6, I present a fallback position: I show that even if that-clauses were singular terms, *SuffSuffFirstConjunct 1* would hardly hold, or at least it would not hold in the sense intended, since that-clauses would refer to facts only if we identify them with true propositions.

4   Reductio

As we saw in the previous section, a fundamental assumption in the argument for facts from nominal reference is the claim that facts are picked out by a certain class of that-clauses functioning as singular terms (see *SuffSuffFirstConjunct 1* on p. 119). This assumption is widespread, but controversial.

Let us first of all push the analysis of this claim a bit further. The claim that that-clauses of a certain class function as singular terms referring to facts can be articulated in the following subclaims:

Syntactic Units   That-clauses are *syntactic units* (that-p).
Singular Terms   That-clauses are *singular terms*.[1]
Fact Reference   Whereas some (kinds of) that-clauses (are singular terms) *refer(ring) to propositions*, some (kinds of) that-clauses (are singular terms) *refer(ring) to facts*.

I will argue that *Fact Reference* and *Singular Terms* are false. I am not sure what to think about *Syntactic Units*, but this doesn't matter much here.[2] We can grant that that-clauses need to be syntactic units to be singular terms, but once we do we still have a long way to go to show that that-clauses are singular terms like 'you' and 'me'. But let us proceed in order.

Each of these three claims entails the previous one: *Fact Reference* entails *Singular Terms*, which entails *Syntactic Units*. Let's try to understand this. Those who defend that some that-clauses refer to facts usually maintain that whereas some (kinds of) that-clauses refer to facts, other (kinds of) that-clauses refer to propositions as in *Fact Reference*.[3] In *Singular Terms* the notion of *singular term* appears; in *Fact Reference* that of *reference* is added. Although there is no uncontroversial definition of what a singular term is, for now it will suffice to say that a singular term is any expression that purports to picks out—to refer to—exactly one object.[4] This means that unless we allow for plural reference, 'referring' and 'being a singular term' will be synonymous, and *Fact Reference* will entail *Singular Terms*.[5] Although I am sympathetic to plural reference (and I am not alone in this; see Ben-Yami, 2004), plural reference won't play any role in the following, so I shall keep matters simple concerning this point and accept that *Fact Reference* entails *Singular Terms*. By this I do not mean that matters of reference in general are simple; they aren't simple at all. I shall come back to singular terms again in the next sections. One thing I need to make clear, though, is the following. Recall the Quine-like criterion of the argument from nominal reference:

(*Quine-Like*) Facts exist if and only if statements of natural language are true that are ontologically committed to facts.

A statement s of natural language is true that is ontologically committed to facts if and only if

(*First Conjunct*) s implies a true first-order statement of the form $\exists x F x$ (indefinite reference) where 'F' is 'is a fact';

(*SuffFirstConjunct*) A sufficient condition for *First Conjunct* is that s contains singular terms for facts in natural language (definite reference).

Once we have agreed on this step (and agreed both to provide identity criteria for facts, and to show that quantification over facts is ineliminable) it does not yet matter whether that-clauses are *successfully* referential singular terms or not.

Successful reference of 'that p' in sentences such as 'that p is a fact' follows, according to the above, from the *truth* of sentences in which existentially quantified statements of the form 'There is an x such that x is fact' appear. But a necessary condition for any such statement to follow from 'That p is a fact' is that 'that p' is *logico-grammatically* a singular term. That's what *Singular Terms* is about.

Singular Terms requires *Syntactic Units*, and their conjunction is often called the *standard view* on that-clauses. Both these claims have been challenged, but while the view that that-clauses form a syntactic unit is hardly controversial and to my knowledge meets with unanimous consent among linguists, the view that that-clauses are singular terms has recently been put seriously into question.

With an eye to the upcoming sections, the following, much weaker claim deserves a word of comment:

Semantic Value   at least some (kinds of) that-clauses have facts as their *semantic value.*

Here we meet the notion of *semantic value*, which is different from the notions of referring and of being a singular term. Singular terms enjoy a privileged status in contemporary philosophy of language: if an expression of natural language qualifies as a singular term, it can be bound by a quantifier in nominal position, and it is taken to carry ontological commitment to its referent when the sentence in which it appears is true. No other expression is taken to carry such commitment. Still, expressions that turn out to be nonreferring in this sense—that is, they turn out not to be singular terms—can be taken to have a semantic value in the sense that they can be set-theoretically *modeled* in order to take such values in Montague grammar or in some other formal semantics.[6] *Semantic Value* does not entail *Fact Reference*. One can thus reject both *Singular Terms* and *Fact Reference* while accepting *Semantic Value*. This would be the case if, for instance, someone defended facts on the basis of evidence that does not depend on the logico-grammatical role of that-clauses. For in this case that-clauses would not refer to facts, but facts could still be their semantic value by technical stipulation. *Semantic Value* is not what the argument from nominal reference aims to establish; it aims, rather, to establish something much stronger. What is at issue has been worded quite effectively in another context by Stephen Yablo:

Now in asking, "Are they referential?" I mean not, "Are there Montague grammarians or other formal semanticists who have cooked up super-duper semantical values for them, say, functions from worlds to functions from worlds and n-tuples of objects to truth-values?" ... The answer to that is going to be *yes* almost no matter what part of speech you're talking about—connectives, prepositions, and apostrophes 's' not excluded. I mean: Are they referential in the way that singular terms are, so that someone ... could reasonably be said to be *talking about* its referent, or purporting to talk about its purported referent? (Yablo, 1996, 260)

To sum up: following *Quine-Like*, ontological commitment to facts in natural language is ensured by the availability of singular terms for facts. This means that if *Singular Terms* is rejected, so will the part of Fine's linguistic argument for facts based on the referential role of that-clauses, that is, *(SuffSuffFirstConjunct 1)*. So if that-clauses are not singular terms (and, a fortiori, if they are not syntactic units), then language-based arguments for the existence of facts based on the assumption that they are singular terms lose all force.[7]

You will find an extended discussion of *Singular Terms* and *Fact Reference* in this chapter, and the following two. As to *Semantic Value*, for one thing defending it successfully requires that you find a convincing argument for including facts in your ontology *other than* the reference of that-clauses (with 'facts' here meaning items other than true propositions, tropes, complexes, special properties of any of those items, and so on). As with sentential reference to facts, I refer to part 1 for a rebuttal of arguments for facts that are not based on language. I will come back to some aspects of *Semantic Value* in my conclusion.

We can now state the argument from nominal reference in a more analytic fashion (the additions are indicated in boldface; I have also indicated the sections to come where the corresponding points are discussed):

Argument for Facts from Nominal Reference for Facts

(*Quine-Like*) Facts exist if and only if statements of natural language are true that are ontologically committed to facts.

A statement *s* of natural language is true that is ontologically committed to facts if and only if

(*First Conjunct*) *s* implies a true first-order statement of the form $\exists x Fx$ (indefinite reference) where 'F' is 'is a fact'.

(*SuffFirstConjunct*) A sufficient condition for *First Conjunct* is that *s* contains singular terms for facts in natural language (definite reference).

Sufficient conditions for *SuffFirstConjunct* are

(*SuffSuffFirstConjunct 1*) Some (kinds of) that-clauses are singular terms referring to facts (part of **Fact Reference**). (sec. 4.1)

(*SuffSuffFirstConjunct 2*) 'The fact that *p*' is a singular term referring to the fact that *p*. (sec. 4.2)

Necessary condition for *SuffSuffFirstConjunct 1* and *SuffSuffFirstConjunct 2* (sec. 4.2) is

(*NecSuffSuffFirstConjunct 1 and 2 = Singular Terms*) That-clauses *are singular terms* (**Singular Terms**). (sec. 4.1)

(*NecFirstConjunct*) A necessary condition for *First Conjunct* is that 'is a fact' functions genuinely as a predicate in predications of the form '*x* is a fact'. (sec. 4.3)

(*Second Conjunct*) We have identity criteria for facts.

(*Third Conjunct*) The quantification over facts is ineliminable.

(*Conclusion*) Under *Quine-Like*, facts exist because of *First Conjunct* (*SuffSuffFirstConjunct 1*), *Second Conjunct, Third Conjunct,* or because of *First Conjunct* (*SuffSuffFirstConjunct 2*), *Second Conjunct, Third Conjunct,* or because of *First Conjunct* (with the proviso *NecFirstConjunct* holds), *Second Conjunct, Third Conjunct.*

The rest of this book is a sustained argument against *First Conjunct*, or rather *for* the claim that *there is no genuine true (first-order) quantification on facts*.

I will proceed as follows. In the following two sections, I will argue against *First Conjunct*, both against the sufficient condition (*SuffFirstConjunct*) and the necessary condition (*NecFirstConjunct*). More precisely, I argue against *SuffSuffFirstConjunct 1* in section 4.1, against *SuffSuffFirstConjunct 2* in section 4.2, and against *NecFirstConjunct* in section 4.3. But note that these claims are by no means independent. For actually, as I will show, both the second sufficient condition for the claim that there is genuine true first-order quantification on facts, namely *SuffSuffFirstConjunct 2*, and the necessary condition for that claim, namely *NecFirstConjunct*, depend crucially on *SuffSuffFirstConjunct 1*, the claim that that-clauses are singular terms (for facts), although the latter is only a sufficient condition for showing that there is genuine true first-order quantification on facts (i.e., *First Conjunct*). Given its importance, I will devote considerable space to disproving the claim that that-clauses are singular terms, that is, *Singular Terms* (which is the necessary condition for *SuffSuffFirstConjunct 1* and *2*) A possible doubt concerning my claim that *NecFirstConjunct* depends crucially on *SuffSuffFirstConjunct 1* will be discussed in section 4.3.

The first and most crucial step, then, is to disprove *SuffSuffFirstConjunct 1*. To do so it is sufficient to show that *Singular Terms* is false. To this end I will offer a yet more detailed articulation of the argument for facts from nominal reference: one that brings the analysis of *Singular Terms* to a deeper level. The next section is devoted to this analysis and, on its basis, to the rebuttal of *SuffSuffFirstConjunct 1*.

4.1   Against *SuffSuffFirstConjunct 1*: That-Clauses Are Not Singular Terms

A growing body of literature challenges the claim that that-clauses are singular terms (Fara, 2000; Moltmann, 2003, 2004; Hinzen, 2007, 173; Pryor, 2007; Rosefeldt, 2008; see also the discussion in Harman, 2003, 172–173). In this section, I draw from and expand upon this literature, adding some results from linguistics in support of the point. The question of whether that-clauses are referential has immediate and important implications for debates in metaphysics, philosophy of language, philosophy of mind, epistemology, and ethics that rely upon the so-called relational theory of propositional attitudes, or that take for granted that 'that p' is the name of a special object, namely a proposition, which we can hope, believe, or desire. Outside philosophy, the point also connects to the debate on sentential subjects in linguistics (see Alrenga, 2005), and in particular to the status of that-clauses as objects of category COMP (complementizer) or OBJ (object) in Lexical Functional Grammar (LFG; see Bodomo & Lee, 2003). The important point for us is this: if that-clauses are not singular terms—that is, if *Singular Terms* is false—then *Fact Reference* is also false, since the latter (as we have assumed) requires the former. More specifically, if *Singular Terms* is false then *Fact Reference* will be false, not because that-clauses refer univocally to propositions and never to facts, but because that-clauses just *do not refer to anything*. Call this the *No Singular Term theory* as opposed to the *Singular Term theory*, which holds that that-clauses are singular terms.

Are that-clauses singular terms? Grammatically, that-clauses are sentential complements (CPs, complementizer phrases in linguistics) that, from the logical point of view, behave apparently like singular terms, that is, like some special noun phrases (NPs, in linguistics, or nominal phrases) of which paradigmatic examples are proper names like 'Argle'. And because of the similarity between sentences like (a.i)–(a.ii) and sentences like (b.i)–(b.ii), that-clauses are often taken to *be* singular terms (cf. Moltmann, 2003, 77, 79):

(a.i)   Cargle believes that Argle stole the colander.
(a.ii) Cargle likes Argle.
(b.i)   Cargle believes something.
(b.ii) Cargle likes something.

This similarity is taken quite seriously by relational views of propositional attitudes (Stalnaker, 1985, 140–141; Parsons, 1993; Bealer, 1993, 18; Schiffer, 1992, 500; 2003, 12–13; Künne, 2003, 4–5, 154–155, 254; for a criticism, see Tye, 1989, 163, and Matthews, 2007, chap. 4), and in philosophy such a view is commonly regarded as standard. According to this standard view, the verb *believes* in (a.i) behaves transitively, exactly as *likes* does in (a.ii). Logically speaking, *believes* is a two-place predicate taking two singular term arguments, and it expresses a relation between two things, here between Cargle and a proposition, namely that Argle stole the colander. *Singular Terms* is a fundamental assumption in this view: a relational view of propositional attitudes is a Singular Term Theory because to be able to slot a that-clause in argument position in (a.i) we need the that-clause to be a singular term.

So far, the view rests on no more than a linguistic analogy, but this analogy could well be superficial. What's the case for it? Here it is. Consider the following inferences:

(c)   Cargle believes everything Dargle says.
       Dargle says that Argle stole the colander.
       _____

       So, Cargle believes that Argle stole the colander.

(d)   Cargle believes that Argle stole the colander and so does Dargle.
       _____

       So, there is something Cargle and Dargle both believe.

These do seem like logically valid inferences. Singular Term theorists say: if that-clauses weren't singular terms, the validity of (c) and (d) would be a mystery (Parsons, 1993, 443–444). At the very least, Singular Term theorists adduce the view that that-clauses are singular terms as the "most straightforward" way to account for the validity of inferences of this kind—thus as an inference to the best explanation (Schiffer, 1992, 504; 2003, 12–13; Soames, 1988, 105–106). So, that-clauses are singular terms. No Singular Term theorists counter that this reasoning—from the validity of (c) and (d) to the claim that that-clauses are singular terms—is inconclusive (Moltmann, 2003, 80–81, Rosefeldt 2008: 315). It is not because that-clauses are singular terms that (c) and (d) are valid, they argue, but because the quantifiers 'everything' and 'something' in such cases function *nonnominally* (as in 'There is something both Argle and Bargle are, namely nice').[8] That-clauses are not singular terms: and since the validity of cases such as (c) and (d) is just about the only evidence offered in support of it, the Singular Term theory is wrong.

Who is right? The issue could be settled by looking at some uncontroversial definition of singular term, but unfortunately there is none. What we can do, developing Rosefeldt's strategy, is to appeal to plausible characterizations that give jointly necessary conditions to be a singular term, upon which Singular Term theorists can be said to agree (Rosefeldt, 2008, 302–303). We can then make these explicit by spelling out counterarguments in some detail. Next, we can look at whether that-clauses satisfy all those necessary conditions; if they don't, that-clauses are not singular terms. To show that the Singular Term theory is false, the No Singular Term theory builds an argument in which the crucial step is this: if that-clauses were singular terms referring to propositions (or, I add, referring to facts), then we would always be able to substitute the coreferential expressions *the proposition that p* (or *the fact that p*) for the appropriate that-clauses with no consequence for the truth-value or the grammaticality of the sentences embedding them. But this is not the case; therefore, that-clauses are not singular terms. Substitutivity salva veritate and congruitate is thus a key characterization of singular terms in the counterargument (see *NecSingularTerms 1* below).

I am sympathetic both to the No Singular Term theory and to the reasoning just sketched. In this section I shall present a counterargument against the Singular Term view that goes beyond existing literature with respect to the necessary conditions taken into account for an expression to be a singular term. This is particularly the case with respect to *NecSingularTerms 2*, and also with respect to the additional considerations from linguistics in *NecSingularTerms 4* below. Besides, I make sure to offer enough evidence that condition *NecSingularTerms 1* can be interpreted in a way broad enough to hold beyond the framework of assumptions with which Rosefeldt and other No Singular Term theorists work. Basically, my counterargument will go as follows:

That-clauses are not singular terms (*against SuffSuffFirstConjunct 1*)
(I)   Necessary conditions for an expression x to be a singular term (that is, an expression purporting to picking out exactly one object) are

> (*NecSingularTerms 1*) x is substitutable by a coreferential singular term salva veritate and congruitate;
> (*NecSingularTerms 2*) x is able to replace an individual variable in an open sentence in a first-order logical theory (i.e., a variable that can be bound by a nominal quantifier);
> (*NecSingularTerms 3*) x is substitutable by a kind-restricted natural language particular quantifier;
> (*NecSingularTerms 4*) x is able to function as structural subject of natural language sentences (NP in Spec, IP).

(II)   That-clauses are

> ($\overline{NecSingularTerms\,1}$) not substitutable as *NecSingularTerms 1* says,
> ($\overline{NecSingularTerms\,2}$) not replaceable like *NecSingularTerms 2* says,
> ($\overline{NecSingularTerms\,3}$) not substitutable as *NecSingularTerms 3* says,
> ($\overline{NecSingularTerms\,4}$) not able to function as *NecSingularTerms 4* says.

(III)   Hence, that-clauses aren't singular terms.

It is worth mentioning that I endorse this counterargument in a descriptive, reductio mode. I assume that Singular Term theorists accept *NecSingularTerms 1–4* as necessary conditions for an expression to be a singular term, but I do not defend any philosophical position myself as to what singular terms are, if indeed there are any at all. Nor do I commit myself to the view that analyses of this kind let us discover what is in the world. All I say is that if anything is a singular term in the sense of *NecSingularTerms 1–4*, then that-clauses aren't. What is important to the argument is the Singular Term theorist's acceptance, explicitly or implicitly, of at least one of these conditions; maybe all of them are needed. In any case, I shall argue that *these conditions are all violated by* that-clauses. If these conditions are violated, the argument for that-clauses being singular terms is rejected. Hence, the question becomes whether Singular Term theorists are prepared to accept *NecSingularTerms 1*, *NecSingularTerms 2*, *NecSingularTerms 3*, and *NecSingularTerms 4*. Let's check.

The Singular Term theory accepts *NecSingularTerms 2*: this is obvious from the fact that the case offered for this view, namely the validity of inferences such as (c) and (d), is based on it.[9] An alternative way to put *NecSingularTerms 2* is to say that singular terms can appear only as subjects/arguments (of the lowest type), not as predicates/functors of sentences (Stirton, 2000, 196). Things seem slightly more complicated with *NecSingularTerms 1* and *NecSingularTerms 3*, but there seems to be no reason why Singular Term theorists would not accept them as well: the substitutability of coreferentials is taken to be the core requirement of singular terms as a matter of course (Davidson, 1968, 130). As to *NecSingularTerms 4*, from a *logical* point of view it is just entailed by *NecSingularTerms 2*, and so whoever accepts *NecSingularTerms 2* should find *NecSingularTerms 4* uncontroversial. We can quite safely assume that Singular Term theorists accept it. The reason to list *NecSingularTerms 4* as a separate requirement is that it makes a *linguistic* point rather than a logical one: of course we would like to know when a failure is due to subtle linguistic behavior rather than to logical behavior, and since we might fail to detect this by using the wrong device of analysis—that is, notions from standard first-order logic—we'd better be cautious and keep linguistic and logical uses apart. Indeed, an additional reason why I discuss *four* necessary conditions is the fact that they come from at least three unrelated discussions in different areas (philosophy of language, metaphysics, and linguistics), and have never been discussed at once before. By considering all four conditions, the No Singular Term theory becomes particularly convincing as the position that offers the best explanation for the behavior of that-clauses.[10]

4.1.1   First Necessary Condition for That-Clauses Being Singular Terms (*NecSingularTerms 1*)

Let's start by reviewing the evidence (for the first part of (II)).

(*NecSingularTerms 1*)   If x is a singular term, it is substitutable by a coreferential singular term salva veritate and congruitate.

(*NecSingularTerms 1*)   That-clauses are not substitutable as *NecSingularTerms 1* says.

To discuss coreferentiality, we must specify what exactly that-clauses are taken to refer to, supposing they refer at all. In keeping with *Fact Reference* I assume, first, that some (kind of) that-clauses refer(s) to propositions and some (other kind of) that-clauses refer(s) to facts; second, anticipating an issue that I will discuss extensively in section 5.1 of chapter 5, I assume that we have a criterion to decide, allegedly, which (kind of) that-clauses refer(s) to facts (i.e., which are *factive* that-clauses), and which (kind of) that-clauses refer(s) to propositions (i.e., which are *non-factive* ones) according to that criterion. As to the criterion in question, you will find it discussed in chapter 5, section 5.1: feel free to check before going on reading. Rest assured, however, that the two assumptions I am making are not only harmless to the point, but even strengthen the position I criticize in this section and make the discussion itself as transparent as possible. To explain this point a bit more: the majority of both Singular Term theorists and No Singular Term theorists (the exception being Friederike Moltmann) do not distinguish between propositions and facts, and in the debate on *NecSingularTerms 1* the factive/nonfactive distinction just mentioned hardly plays a role. The reason for this, I presume, is that the parties involved are most often either direct reference theorists, for whom propositions are Russellian hybrids of propositions and states of affairs (and to whom the proposition/ fact distinction is thus irrelevant), or else philosophers who adhere to the Singular Term theory because they take it to provide an argument in favor of *propositions* rather than one in favor of facts. Another possible reason is that the philosophers involved in this debate do not link the factive/ nonfactive distinction to reference, and take it to be a matter of truth-entailment or presuppositions of the clause following a predicate (as I will point out at the end of chapter 6, this is, said *en passant*, a welcome 'mini-malist' position on factivity). Consequently, the examples given in the debate frequently mismatch the factive/nonfactive distinction.[11] Since my discussion here takes care of cases in which that distinction is accepted, objections that allege carelessness on this point are not supposed to arise here. A third assumption I will make for the sake of the argument is that the expression 'the proposition that p' is a singular term (successfully) referring to the proposition that p, and that 'the fact that p' is a singular term (successfully) referring to the fact that p (at least when the statements at issue are true which contain that expression). In section 4.2 I am going to retract this claim: in particular, I will argue that 'the fact that p' is not a singular term from the logical point of view, although it is, grammatically, a noun phrase (NP) (while 'that p'—as I argue in this section—is not even an NP). A last remark: the failure of substitutability of singular terms salva veritate in (hyper)intensional contexts (as in 'Cargle knows that Hargle is cute' and 'Cargle knows that Argle's favorite pet is cute') is a known phenomenon. So one might be puzzled by *NecSingularTerms 1*, namely my taking singular terms to be such that their substitutability by coreferentials salva veritate is a necessary condition to be a singular terms, since strictly speaking this would mean that very few expressions are singular terms. This is a legitimate observation, but here two things should be said. First, the parties in the debate that form the framework of the discussion on that-clauses whom I consider here are, as I said, direct reference theorists. For direct reference theorists, the substitutability problem is indeed pressing, but its solution does not pass through dropping substitutability salva veritate as a necessary condition, at least not as a matter of course. Those uncomfortable with the direct reference framework can drop the part of the necessary condition *NecSingularTerms 1* that requires substitutability salva veritate for the sake of the argument, and retain only the part that requires substitutability salva congruitate; this would amount to accepting a weaker, minimal condition. Second, there is broad consensus that substitutability salva veritate in extensional contexts is a *basic* feature of singular terms; that is, if the context is extensional, then substitutability salva veritate must hold. So, alternatively, one can read *NecSingularTerms 1* as restricted to extensional contexts (this would require adjustments of some of the examples I use, but that would be unproblematic). No cases of (hyper)intensional contexts that are similar to the problematic ones and *within which* that-clauses are substituted will appear in what follows. Substituting 'the proposition that p/the fact that p' for 'that p' in 'Cargle believes/knows/fears that p' is not a case similar to substituting 'Hargle'/'Argle's favorite pet' *within the that-clause in* 'Cargle knows that Hargle is cute' and 'Cargle knows that Argle's favorite pet is cute'. I will consider a possible doubt in this sense below, and show that it is misplaced. Some might still be unconvinced by my reasoning in this case: for the sake of the argument these readers can, again, drop the requirement of substitutability salva veritate and retain only the part that requires substitutability salva congruitate. Besides, as I said, not only

NecSingularTerms 1 fails, but all of *NecSingularTerms 2*, *NecSingularTerms 3*, and *NecSingularTerms 4*, so if one really does not want to adhere to *NecSingularTerms 1*, she may still want to accept one or more of the other necessary conditions for being a singular term.

With this in place, let's observe that *NecSingularTerms 1* involves a substitution rule that can be formulated more precisely as follows:

(Rule 1)   A singular term t referring to an object o occurring in a grammatically well-formed sentence s of the form $F(t)$ can be substituted by any other singular term t^* referring to o salva veritate and salva congruitate—unless t^* becomes part of an ill-formed complex singular term.[12]

Some comments on Rule 1 are in order, especially concerning the restriction placed at the end. But first let's check whether the rule is obeyed by (expressions that are normally given as examples of) singular terms, that is (on the most inclusive list available) by proper names ('Hargle'), indexicals ('he'), simple and complex demonstratives ('this', 'that hedgehog'), definite descriptions ('Argle's cutest pet'), and appositive descriptions ('the hedgehog Hargle'). Consider:

(e.i)   Bargle hears Hargle in the kitchen.
(e.ii)   Bargle hears *Argle's cutest pet* in the kitchen.

(e.iii) Bargle fears that hedgehog.
(e.iv)   *He* fears that hedgehog.
(e.v)   Bargle fears *this (pointing at Hargle)*.

Let us suppose that the singular terms 'Bargle'/'*He*', 'Hargle'/'*Argle's cutest pet*', and 'that hedgehog'/ '*this*' are all coreferential; then, all would obey the rule since all would be substitutable salva veritate and congruitate: (e.i) and (e.iii) on the one hand are as true and grammatical as (e.ii), (e.iv), and (e.v) on the other. The reason why the restriction 'unless t^* becomes part of an ill-formed complex singular term' is part of Rule 1 is this: there are cases in which singular terms that are parts of appositions would violate Rule 1 if we didn't restrict it like that. In these cases the substitution of coreferentials turns perfectly well-formed sentences into nonsense:

(f.i)   The small hedgehog Hargle hates milk.
(f.ii)   *The small hedgehog *Argle's cutest pet* hates milk.

This case shows that some singular terms ('Argle's cutest pet': *The G*) cannot always be part of coreferential complex singular terms (*The Fa*) without sacrificing grammaticality (**The F The G*), while other singular terms ('Hargle': *a*) can do so, which means that the former cannot be substituted for the latter salva congruitate: a singular term in apposition is a bad candidate for substitution by a coreferential singular term.

Now, if that-clauses were singular terms, they would work in the same way as coreferential singular terms like 'Hargle', 'he', 'this', 'that hedgehog', and 'Argle's cutest pet' do. But they don't. To show this, let us first of all suppose that 'that p' is a singular term. By Rule 1, it must be substitutable in similar contexts by a coreferential term. What would be a good candidate for a coreferential term here? With what could 'that p' be substitutable? The perfect candidates are 'the fact that p' (if the clause is factive) and 'the proposition that p' (if the clause is nonfactive). A Singular Term theorist would accept this: since she assumes that 'that p' is a singular term referring to a fact (as I have granted for the sake of the argument to be the case for factive clauses) or to a proposition (same point granted for nonfactive clauses), then 'that p' is coreferential with 'the fact that p' if the clause is factive, and with 'the proposition that p' if the clause is nonfactive. From now on I shall sometimes appose '$_p$' and '$_f$' to nonfactive and factive verbs respectively, and designate factive that-clauses with <that-p>$_f$ and nonfactive that-clauses with [that-p]$_p$.

With this in place, we can now show the substitution-failure. Here it is. Consider the following sentences:

(g.i)   Bargle hears$_f$ <that Dargle is talking to Cargle>$_f$.

(g.ii) *Bargle hears$_f$ the fact that Dargle is talking to Cargle.

(h.i)   Bargle fears$_p$ [that Argle does not like bucatini]$_p$.

(h.ii) *Bargle fears$_p$ the proposition that Argle does not like bucatini.

(g.i) and (h.i) are grammatical and true, but (g.ii) is ungrammatical and (h.ii) either just false or (false because) ungrammatical (I'd say it's ungrammatical for everyone except philosophers; see Künne, 2003, 260). Note also that

(i.iii) *Bargle fears$_p$ the fact that Argle does not like bucatini

does not work either (one would perhaps rather say 'Bargle fears$_p$ *the possibility that* Argle does not like bucatini'). Another interesting case is this one:

(j)   Argle felt$_p$ [that Bargle was defending him]$_p$.

In this case, neither

(k.i)   *Argle felt$_p$ the proposition that Bargle was defending him

nor

(k.ii) *Argle felt the fact that Bargle was defending him

nor *any other* definite description ('the possibility that *p*', 'the belief that *p*', 'the desire that *p*' ...) works when substituted for 'that *p*' (King, 2002, 354). Note also that we have *never* substituted 'the fact that'/'the proposition that *p*' for 'that *p*' within a complex singular term, so Rule 1's restriction 'unless *t** becomes part of an ill-formed complex singular term' cannot account for the failure, since expressions like 'the proposition that Argle does not like bucatini' are not ill formed, unlike expressions like 'the small hedgehog *Argle's cutest pet*', which are. So, that-clauses violate Rule 1, and therefore are not singular terms—at least according to this rule.[13]

What is the Singular Term theorist to do? Well, perhaps she could invoke plausible exceptions to Rule 1 to restrict it further. What we have with *hear*, *feel*, and *fear*, she could say, is a case of (what Moltmann calls) the *objectivization effect*, in which the substitution shifts the reference from the *content* of an attitude to its *object* (Moltmann, 2003, 85; see also Rosefeldt, 2008, 305; Künne, 2003, 258–263). So the Singular Term theorist could request that we do not allow substitution of 'that *p*' in '*x f*s that *p*' for 'the fact that *p*'/'the proposition that *p*' *if this changes the reading of f*. In this case Rule 1 would be modified as follows:

(Modified Rule 1)   A singular term *t* referring to an object *o* occurring in a grammatically well-formed sentence *s* of the form *F*(*t*) can be substituted by any other singular term *t** referring to *o* salva veritate and salva congruitate—unless the substitution changes the reading of *F*( ) in *s*.[14]

Certainly one is free to modify the rule like this. But the question is: Why should we? Why should we want to avoid the substitution failure by restricting the rule in this way? At this point we have no independent support for the claim that that-clauses are singular terms, and stipulating an exception to a general rule that no other singular term violates in the absence of independent support looks like an ad hoc move to save the claim that that-clauses are singular terms. Ad hoc moves give us poor explanations (if any at all), and were the Singular Term theorist indeed to take this way out, we would start suspecting that her pet view begs the question. But perhaps we should not want to say that she is already begging the question at this point, or that ad hoc modifications are always unacceptable; after all, it would not be the only case of exceptions to rules in philosophy of language (one easy example is that mentioned above, namely the substitutivity failure of coreferentials in [hyper]intensional contexts). However bad this kind of move may seem to us, it does happen, and one could argue that in some cases it's difficult to decide whether we can do any better than assuming ad hoc rules, at least provisorily.[15] So, let's say this ad hoc move is not the problem and let it pass. The real problem is that it quickly becomes clear that modifying the rule in this way would not get us very far, since these cases would not be blocked after all. Consider these examples:

(l.i)   Dargle complained that the colander was expensive.
(l.ii)   *Dargle complained the fact that the colander was expensive.
(l.iii) *Dargle complained the proposition that the colander was expensive.

(m.i)   Dargle bemoaned the fact that the colander was expensive.
(m.ii) *Dargle bemoaned that the colander was expensive.

(n.i)   Argle is happy that Bargle is a real friend.
(n.ii) *Argle is happy the fact that Bargle is a real friend.
(n.iii) *Argle is happy the proposition that Bargle is a real friend.

(o.i)   Cargle believes the proposition that Argle stole the colander to be true.
(o.ii) *Cargle believes$_p$ [that Argle stole the colander]$_p$ to be true.

(p.i)   Cargle, the fact that Argle bought the colander should not have bothered.
(p.ii) *Cargle, [that Argle bought the colander]$_f$ should not have bothered$_f$.

(q.i)   It's true$_p$ [that the colander was expensive]$_p$.
(q.ii) *It's true the proposition that the colander was expensive.[16]

The ungrammatical examples ((l)–(o) and (q)) and the 'significant improvement' of (p.i) on (p.ii) (see Alrenga 2005, 177, n. 3) just quoted are all ungrammatical in a manner that cannot be explained away by the objectivization effect or a switch in meaning.[17] Therefore, the modified rule would be violated. One could observe that 'Dargle complained *about* the fact that the colander was expensive' does work. That's right, but now 'Dargle complained about that the colander was expensive' is gibberish. If 'that the colander was expensive' were functioning as a singular term in 'Dargle complained that the colander was expensive' (l.i), then the interpolation of either 'the fact that' (e.ii) or 'the proposition that' (e.iii) or *some* other case with similar head interpolation would be grammatical. But none is, because *complain* is intransitive. If the Singular Term theorist insisted that that-clauses are direct objects of *complain* or that they are the *only* objects that the intransitive *complain* can govern, she would make appeal to a situation "which is anomalous, to say the least" (Rundle, 1979, 283).[18] The same is true of the transitive *bemoaned*.

Indeed, to block cases (l)–(q) one would have to modify Rule 1 in such a way that maximally ad hoc restrictions are assumed to excise exactly these specific cases. Then that-clauses would count as singular terms and the Singular Term view would be safe. But there would be little theoretical worth in this. For it would mean that in fact that-clauses *do* violate the rule—we just save them arbitrarily in a some-are-more-equal-than-others kind of way. So modified Rule 1 is a poor cover-up. Yet there must be some explanation for the substitution failure we saw. What's on offer is this: the problem arises simply because *that-clauses are not singular terms*. The ready availability of this plain and simple explanation makes it clear that insisting on the claim that that-clauses are singular terms, and then considering this claim itself as the reason for modifying the rule in order to save that claim on the face of (l)–(q), is nothing short of question begging. So, on the face of the evidence given above, the Singular Term theorist begs the question; unless, of course, she can come up with independent arguments.

Are there such independent arguments?

4.1.2   Second Necessary Condition for That-Clauses Being Singular Terms (*NecSingularTerms 2*)

(*NecSingularTerms 2*)   If x is a singular term, then x is able to replace an individual variable in an open sentence in a first-order logical theory (i.e., a variable that can be bound by a nominal quantifier).
(*NecSingularTerms 2*)   That-clauses are not replaceable as *NecSingularTerms 2* says.

It could appear that when the Singular Term theorist points to the validity of the inferences *ad* (c) and (d) which we saw above (and which I reproduce here below for convenience), she could be taken as providing such an independent argument. But appearances are deceitful. Let's see this. Recall:

(c)   Cargle believes everything Dargle says.
        Dargle says that Argle stole the colander.

        So, Cargle believes that Argle stole the colander.

(d)   Cargle believes that Argle stole the colander and so does Dargle.

        So, there is something Cargle and Dargle both believe.

The defender of Singular Terms sees (c) and (d) as instances of the following schemas:

(c′) $\forall x(Sdx \rightarrow Bcx)$

$\dfrac{Sda}{Bca}$

(d′) $\dfrac{Bca \wedge Bda}{\exists x(Bcx \wedge Bdx)}$

When she makes the claim that that-clauses are singular terms on the basis of this evidence, the defender of the Singular Term view hangs on to *NecSingularTerms 2*: that that-clauses are singular terms because they are able to replace an individual variable in an open sentence in a first-order theory, that is, a variable that can be bound by a nominal quantifier. So the question now becomes whether ($\overline{NecSingularTerms\,2}$) holds, that is, whether that-clauses fall under the characterization of singular term *ad NecSingularTerms 2* or not. According to the Singular Term theorist, it's a matter of course that that-clauses are singular terms in the sense of *NecSingularTerms 2*. For don't these cases show precisely that that-clauses are singular terms insofar as they take the place of a bound nominal variable? If that-clauses were *not* singular terms, how could these inferences be valid?

Can the rival, the No Singular Term theory, offer a plausible explanation of why (c) and (d) do in fact go through, if indeed that-clauses are not singular terms? Yes. These inferences are similar to

(r) Cargle does everything Dargle does.

Dargle eats bucatini every day.

So, Cargle eats bucatini every day.

(s) Argle is nice, and so is Bargle.

So, there's something Argle and Bargle both are (namely nice).

How do (r) and (s) function? In these inferences we quantify into the position of 'eats bucatini every day' and '(is) nice'; that is, into *general*, not singular, term position.[19] These examples show that natural language has not only nominal quantifiers, but also nonnominal ones. In natural language 'something', 'everything', and 'nothing' can all be used as both nominal quantifiers (as in (b.ii), 'Cargle likes something') and nonnominal quantifiers (as in (b.i), 'Cargle believes something').[20] Therefore, the circumstance that in natural language a that-clause can take the position of 'everything' in 'Cargle believes everything Dargle says' is no evidence that that-clauses are singular terms. Put otherwise, the Singular Term theorist is wrong to treat the logical form of (c) and (d) as an instance of a first-order schema.

It's not hard to see that the claim that that-clauses can be treated as first-order individual variables, as *NecSingularTerms 2* requires singular terms to be, is ill conceived. If this were the case, that-clauses would be able to flank the identity sign. But they can't (Mulligan & Correia, 2008):

(t.i) $x = x$

(t.ii)   *That Argle is nice is identical with that Argle is nice.

The following, on the contrary, is fine:

(t.iii)   The proposition that Argle is nice is identical with the proposition that Argle is nice.

(t.iv)   The fact that Argle is nice is identical with the fact that Argle is nice.

Therefore, (t.ii) cannot be an instance of (t.i); that-clauses cannot be replaced by individual variables in an open sentence in a first-order theory. The translation to first-order logic must be conservative in both directions: if the translation of certain expressions from natural language to the language of first-order logic is fine, then movement in the opposite direction must be fine as well—one cannot just forget the first-order logic test whenever it is convenient. (Note that this is one of the cases in which it pays to remember that natural language and formal language—i.e., the a fortiori formal language of first-order classical predicate calculus—are not the same thing.) But here the translation does not work both ways, and so that-clauses do violate *NecSingularTerms 2* and therefore are not singular terms according to this characterization. Our conclusion: ($\overline{\text{NecSingularTerms 2}}$) holds.

4.1.3   Third Necessary Condition for That-Clauses Being Singular Terms (*NecSingularTerms 3*)

(*NecSingularTerms 3*)   If x is a singular term, then x *is substitutable by a kind-restricted natural language existential quantifier.*

($\overline{\text{NecSingularTerms 3}}$)   That-clauses are not substitutable as *NecSingularTerms 3* says.

The point made above about nonnominal quantification connects immediately to the reason why that-clauses fail to be singular terms also according to the characterization *ad NecSingularTerms 3*. Let's look at the characterization at issue in greater detail. First of all, consider

(u.i)   Argle likes Hargle.

(u.ii)   There is some hedgehog that Argle likes.

(v.i)   Bargle fears Argle's cutest pet.

(v.ii)   There is at least one hedgehog that Bargle fears.

These inferences are all perfectly fine. The rule according to which they go through could be put like this:

(Rule 2)   A singular term t referring to an object o of kind F occurring in a grammatically well-formed sentence s can be substituted by a natural language quantifier that is restricted to Fs (i.e., by an expression of the form 'some F' or 'there is at least one F which') (modified from Rosefeldt, 2008, 309).

Do that-clauses obey Rule 2? No.

(w.i)   Dargle says that Argle stole the colander.

(w.ii)   *There is some proposition that Dargle says (Rosefeldt, 2008, 310).

(w.iii)   *There is some fact which Dargle says.

Yet this, as we know, is fine:

(w.iv)   There is something that Dargle says.

Syntactically speaking, 'something' here is not a nominal phrase; and the substitution of (w.iv) in (w.ii) and (w.iii) fails because it forces a kind-restricted *nominal* quantifier ('some proposition', 'some facts') in *nonnominal* position, that of 'something'.[21] This shows that ($\overline{NecSingularTerms\,3}$) holds.[22]

4.1.4   Fourth Necessary Condition for That-Clauses Being Singular Terms (*NecSingularTerms 4*)

(*NecSingularTerms 4*)   If x is a singular term, then x is able to function as the structural subject of a natural language sentence (NP in Spec, IP).

($\overline{NecSingularTerms\,4}$)   That-clauses are not able to function as *NecSingularTerms 4* says.

At this point we have reached the last step of the argument, with regard to which we need to discuss the characterization *ad NecSingularTerms 4*. In this case issues such as the relationship between natural and formal languages are not relevant. Suppose, then, that we disregard all questions of logical analysis. From a purely linguistic point of view, it seems at first difficult to deny that at least in some cases that-clauses are (what philosophers call) singular terms insofar as they can function as the structural subject of a sentence (or as the *genuine* or *real* subject). These examples seem uncontroversial:

(y.i)   That Argle stole the colander is very unlikely.

(y.ii) That Bargle eats more than Argle does not surprise me.

And here the substitution is no problem:

(z.i)   The fact that Argle stole the colander is very unlikely.

(z.ii) The fact that Bargle eats more than Argle does not surprise me.

Is it possible, then, 'the fact/proposition that'/'that' substitution failure we saw above while discussing *NecSingularTerms 1* depended on the specific choice of examples we made, or on their structure? To be sure, almost all the problematic examples we saw had, first, the relational form *Rab* ('*a R* that-*p*'), and, second, they were quite specific examples of an *R* expressing an *attitude*. They almost all had the form: *x f*s that *p*, where *x* was a place-holder for a singular term for an *agent*, and *f*s was an attitude predicate. So perhaps there is something funny about the *specific f* we chose? The only example of substitution failure that did *not* have this form was

(ab.i) It's true$_p$ [that the colander was expensive]$_p$.

(ab.ii) *It's true the proposition that the colander was expensive.

Although (ab.ii) is bad, the following, if we look more closely, are all fine:

(ab.iii) [That the colander was expensive]$_p$ is true$_p$.

(ab.iv) The proposition that the colander was expensive is true.

Both (y.ii) and (ab.iii), that is,

(ab.iii) [That the colander was expensive]$_p$ is true$_p$

(y.ii) That Bargle eats more than Argle does not surprise me

seem like perfectly fine ways of speaking, and the that-clauses they contain look like nothing other than sentence *subjects*: the forms of (y.ii) and (ab.iii) seem to be no other than *Fa* and *Rab*, where *a*, the that-clause, is a subject. To put it in the linguistic terms of X-bar theory, the that-clause here seems to be an NP, a noun phrase, occupying Spec, IP position (the position of the 'specifier of the inflectional phrase', i.e., the position of the subject of the sentence). More plainly put, since talk of a 'subject' is not always unam-biguous (see Alrenga, 2005, 175, n. 1), one could contend not only that (y.ii) and (ab.iii) *appear* to have a sentential subject in a pretheoretical sense, that is, in the sense in which, on a superficial analysis, 'That the colander was expensive is true' looks the same as 'John is tall'; more than this, at a deeper structural level, one could contend that these sentences really *do* function like 'John is tall': they really do turn out to have a real, structural position filled by an NP, namely the that-clause. So perhaps we could fix:

Structural Subject Rule   That-clauses are singular terms just in case they are structural subjects (NP in Spec, IP).

This would mean that that-clauses that occupy position b in cases of form aRb, including those following an attitude verb, will be singular terms (they would be NPs in object position) only insofar as it can be shown that they undergo the Structural Subject Rule; they might obey it, they might not. In other words, we could reason like this: we accept the Structural Subject Rule, assume that that-clauses are NP that change position from subject to object, and on this basis we decide that the following that-clause

(ab.i)   It's true$_p$ [that the colander was expensive]$_p$

is a singular term *because* the that-clause is NP in Spec, IP in

(ab.iii)   [That the colander was expensive]$_p$ is true$_p$.

Similarly, we would say that the that-clause in

(#)   It does not surprise me that Bargle eats more than Argle

is a singular term *because* the that-clause is NP in Spec, IP in

(y.ii)   That Bargle eats more than Argle does not surprise me.

But can we deny the *evidence* on the basis of which it is claimed that sentences such as (y.ii) and (ab.iii) have that-clauses as their structural subject and that therefore they undergo the Structural Subject Rule? Yes, we can. Once again, the surface evidence that backs up the reasoning we just saw from the cases above proves dubious upon closer scrutiny. Let us turn the question around and ask: are that-clauses in such cases really structural subjects obeying the rule? What is the argument for this claim? It's an argument from linguistics. We saw that, when faced with examples like

(A)   It is a fact that Bargle eats more than Argle

which are similar to (ab.1) and do not have the prima facie form *Fa*, Fine invokes an account from generative grammar (TGG) according to which (i) is a transform by extraposition from a sentence that does have that form, such as

(ii)   That Bargle eats more than Argle is a fact,

and which is similar to (ab.iii), that is,

(ab.iii)   [That the colander was expensive]$_p$ is true$_p$.

Let's hear Fine again:

[A] Nominal reference is reference by means of an expression in nominal position. It is either definite, with a name referring to a particular object, or indefinite, with a variable ranging over a class of objects. Now on the face of it, there is nominal reference to facts of both varieties in ordinary usage. When we say 'the fact that the Watergate bugging took place is disgraceful' or 'whatever fact he uncovers is unlikely to help,' we seem to be using 'the fact that the Watergate incident took place' as a name for a particular fact and the phrase 'whatever fact' as part of the nominal quantificational apparatus for referring to facts. ...

[B] Even locutions that might appear to suggest an alternative view conform readily [to this one]. With the construction 'it is a fact that p' for example, it seems most natural to follow the transformational grammarians and to take it as a transform of 'that p is a fact', and then to suppose, not too recklessly one hopes, that the phrase 'that p' does indeed refer to a fact when the whole statement is true. (Fine, 1982, 44)

This (especially [B]) means that sentences like (i) are *basic*, and that sentences like (ii) are *transforms* from them by *extraposition*. Extraposition is the moving of an element from its normal place to a place at the end or near the end of a sentence, as in

(#)   The cook arrived *whom we had called earlier.*

In (#), *whom we had called earlier* has been moved or *extraposed* from its normal position after *cook*. In the case under discussion, (i) *that Bargle eats more than Argle* has been, according to Fine, extraposed from (ii), where it was in subject position—which, according to the extraposition account, is the normal and ruling case. The extraposition account assumes that that-clauses behave like NPs. It was first proposed in the 1960s by Rosenbaum, an exponent of the abstract syntax/generative semantics movement in transformational grammar (Rosenbaum, 1967).

Today, however, over thirty years after Fine and fifty after Rosenbaum, the standard approach is no longer the extraposition analysis of (i) and (ii) but rather the rival account, the *intraposition* analysis, presented by Emonds (1972). Roughly put, according to this account, the opposite of what Fine says is the case:

(i)   It is a fact that Bargle eats more than Argle

does not result from the basic

(ii)   That Bargle eats more than Argle is a fact,

by extraposition. The basic form is that of (ii): 'It is a fact that p', not that of (i): 'That p is a fact'; (i) results by intraposition and is, according to Koster (1978), a form of topicalization ((p.i) and (p.ii) above are topicalizations;

Cargle there is in topic position. See Harman, 2003). The complementizer phrase (CP) 'that *p*' in (ii) is not a noun phrase in subject position (NP in Spec, IP), but a sentential complement in topic position. These results by Koster are standardly exploited.[23]

It is commonly assumed ... that *that* clause complements in English do not them-selves occupy NP positions, but have a special XP-final complement position(Emonds 1972, Koster 1978, Grimshaw 1982, Webelhuth 1992: 108–10). (Bresnan, 1995, 37)

The intraposition analysis is a line of analysis from linguistics that has been variously corroborated,[24] and that is independent of the philosophical dis-pute about singular terms we have seen so far; no semantic issues such as the reference of that-clauses are addressed in this literature, and no onto-logical assumptions are made regarding propositions and facts as referents. This should be considered strong evidence for trusting the intraposition analysis in the present context.

The above means that, although there is nothing wrong with the rule we considered,

Structural Subject Rule   That-clauses are singular terms just in case they are structural subjects (NP in Spec, IP),

it operates in the void in the case of that-clauses because that-clauses are *never* structural subjects.

Let us now come back to Fine to see where exactly things go wrong. If we embed the extraposition account in it, Fine's argument can be represented like this:

1.   Whatever can occupy the place of the structural subject of a sentence (Spec, IP) is a singular term. (*NecSingularTerms 4*)
2.   The grammatical structure, the logical form, and the meaning of a TGG-transform are the same as (the one revealed by) those of the TGG-basic sentence (Assumption 1)
3.   A sentence like

(i)   It is a fact that Bargle eats more than Argle

is a TGG-transform by extraposition from the basic form

(ii)   That Bargle eats more than Argle is a fact. (Rosenbaum's hypothesis)

4.   The structural subject of (ii) is a that-clause. (2, 3)
5.   That-clauses are singular terms. (1, 4)

NecSingularTerms 4 regarding (1) is what we have assumed. There is nothing wrong with it. Assumption 1 in 2. is a formulation of a strong principle once considered fundamental to generative semantics known as the *Katz–Postal principle*: "Transformations don't change meaning." It is also Fine's main methodological assumption here. I accept Assumption 1 for the sake of my reductio argument just as I have accepted several other assumptions here in part 2, that us, chapters 4–6 (though I do not see why we should assume it: it is controversial and not widely assumed in linguistics since the 1970s).[25] Rosenbaum's hypothesis in (3i) is the linguistic hypothesis on which the whole argument is based, and thanks to it Fine can conclude—put in our terms—that although

(i)   It is a fact that Bargle eats more than Argle

does not seem to have the form *Fa*, it actually does; therefore, that-clauses are singular terms. But, as we saw, given the intraposition analysis, this isn't right. The argument isn't straightforwardly sound, since at the very minimum (3) is far from uncontroversial. (Again, my reasoning is a reductio; I do not see *this* as the big problem with Fine's argument. This is how I see things: *if* it is a linguistic game, no ontological prize can be won by playing it.) It goes without saying that if Fine is allowed to point to an analysis from the linguistics of the 1960s to support his philosophical point, we can do the same: we can point to a more recent, opposite analysis, and reject his argument as unsound on similar grounds.

The upshot of this is that the No Singular Term theory is well supported by the intraposition analysis, which has been considered the standard analysis of complement clauses *for English* in generative grammar since Emonds's work in the 1970s. And so we find that the conclusion that that-clauses are not singular terms, aside from being supported by the specifically philosophical arguments we saw so far in *NecSingularTerms 1–3*, is also supported by a group of independent arguments from linguistics. We can thus rely on these linguistic results to accept the fourth step of the argument against the claim that that-clauses are singular terms: $\overline{NecSingularTerms\,4}$ holds, because the claim that that-clauses are NPs behaving as structural subjects is disproved by linguistics.[26]

At this point we have reviewed all the steps of the argument against the view that that-clauses are singular terms. Is it the case, as Fine claims, that in 'That Bargle eats more than Argle is a fact' there is nominal reference to a fact via the subject 'that Bargle eats more than Argle'? If this depends on that-clauses being singular terms, as the assumption goes, the answer is *No*. That-clauses are not singular terms. (They are not even NPs, unlike expressions such as 'the proposition that *p*' and 'the fact that p'.) And since we have supposed that there is no other reference than singular terms reference, that-clauses cannot thus refer to facts because they do not refer *at all*.

4.2   Against *SuffSuffFirstConjunct 2*: 'The Fact That p' Is Not a Singular Term, in Particular Neither a Definite Nor an Appositive Description

In my discussion in section 4.1 of the substitution problem of a factive *that p* with 'the fact that p', I did not settle the question of what expressions of the form 'the fact that p' are. I will argue here that although 'the fact that p' is grammatically a noun phrase, it is not a singular term, and in particular it is neither a definite description nor an *appositive description*—that is, an expression such as 'the poet Burns'.[27]

Grammatically, 'the fact that p' is a noun phrase—unlike that-clauses, which, as I argued in section 4.1 ad *NecSingularTerms 4*, are not even noun phrases. But being grammatically a noun phrase is not enough to make an expression a singular term. In section 4.1 I argued that that-clauses are not singular terms because they violate all the necessary conditions to be a singular term. We cannot argue here that 'the fact that p' is a singular term because it does *not* violate those conditions, since the latter are not jointly sufficient (we saw that no definition of a singular term is available). Still, one can follow a rather common methodology and reason by analogy: an expression x, if complex, can be shown to be a singular term by drawing structural analogies with other classes of expressions whose status as singular terms is minimally controversial. One can then consider the most inclusive list of (kinds of) singular terms, and test whether x is structurally similar to any item listed. Recall our most inclusive list available of (kinds of) singular terms: proper names ('Hargle'), indexicals ('he'), simple or complex demonstratives ('this', 'that hedgehog'), definite descriptions ('Argle's cutest pet'), and descriptive appositions ('the hedgehog Hargle').[28]

If expressions of the form 'the fact that p' are to be singular terms by virtue of being similar to any of the items on this list, then, arguably, they would also be definite descriptions, for they look very much like that:[29]

(1)   the fact that p
(2)   the movie legend who coinvented spread-spectrum broadcast communications technologies.

Despite appearances, however, expressions of the form 'the fact that p' can hardly be definite descriptions because, as Lowe and Künne have pointed out, they lack at least one (if not two) of the necessary conditions for being one. Definite descriptions are expressions that contain a part which signifies a condition that can be met by exactly one object (Künne, 2003, 10, n. 23, 255; see also Lowe, 1998b, 231). Indeed, to be *the F* one must also be *an F*: to be *the* movie legend who coinvented spread-spectrum broadcast communications technologies, you must also be *a* movie legend who coinvented such a thing; to be *the* hedgehog that Argle loves most you must also be *a* hedgehog. But in the case of 'the fact that *p*' there is no such '*an F*'-expression. Consider the following:

(3)   The fact that Hargle doesn't like milk.

An analysis of (3) in terms of definite descriptions would go like this:

(4)   For some *x*, *$*x$ is *a* fact that Hargle doesn't like milk, and for all *y*, if *$*y$ is *a* fact that Hargle doesn't like milk, then *y*=*x*.

But this does not make much sense, because 'is *a* fact that Hargle doesn't like milk' is hardly meaningful (try to make sense of any substitution of '*x* is *a* fact that *p*'—where *x* is placeholder for a singular term). The expression 'is *a* fact that *p*' is not a genuine predicate but a *pseudo-predicate* that can compose sentences of the form

(5)   It is a fact that Hargle doesn't like milk

only by taking dummy subjects. Sentences like (5), as we already in section 4.1.4 of this chapter, do not have a real, structural subject; the presence of the 'it' here is easily explained: languages such as English do not tolerate so-called *phonologically null subjects*. These languages require that something play the subject-role at the surface level in such sentences, and in (3) this role is played by the dummy (pleonastic/expletive) pronoun 'it', as in 'It happens', 'It is Argle whom we like', and 'It's me' (as we might say when starting a phone call). If you translate these sentence into so-called *null subject languages* such as Italian, what one might be prone to call 'the subject' at the surface level disappears: 'succede' ('It happens'), 'è Argle che mi sta simpatico' ('It's Argle whom I like'), 'sono io' ('it's me'), and (5): 'è un fatto che a Hargle non piaccia il latte'.[30] The point is that, despite appearances, 'it' in (5) is not a genuine structural subject since it cannot be replaced by a NP.

    '*A* fact that Hargle doesn't like milk' does *not* stand to '*a* movie legend who coinvented spread-spectrum broadcast communication technologies' as '*the* fact that Hargle doesn't like milk' stands to '*the* movie legend who coinvented spread-spectrum broadcast communication technologies'. Since 'being *a* fact that *p*' is not a predicate, and 'being *a* fact that *p*' in no sense designates a property that something can have, it follows that noun phrases of the form 'the fact that *p*' cannot be definite descriptions.[31] Therefore, if 'the fact that p' is a singular term, this cannot be because it is a definite description—it's not.[32] So what else would make 'the fact that *p*' a singular term?

According to Künne, expressions of the form 'the fact that *p*' are singular terms by virtue of being *appositions*; that is, in

(6)   the fact that Hargle doesn't like milk

the that-clause would be "preceded by an appositive which specifies the kind of thing to which the designatum of the clause belongs" (Künne, 2003, 255; see also Austin, 1961, 114; Delacruz, 1976, 190–191; Hugly & Sayward, 1996, 390; Künne, 2010). The point rests on an analogy between (6) and

(7)   the hedgehog Hargle

(8)   the number eight.

So, 'fact' would stand to 'hedgehog' and 'number' as 'that Hargle doesn't like milk' would stand to 'Hargle' and 'eight'. But this cannot be right.

An apposition is a construct in which two noun phrases are placed side by side, and thus said to be *in apposition*; in (7) 'Hargle' is in apposition to 'hedgehog'. Although appositions come in various kinds, those relevant to us (i.e., the sort involved in Künne's analogy), called by Schnieder *appositive descriptions* and represented as 'the *Fa*', are a combination of a general term and a singular term that has the same reference as the whole phrase (Schnieder, 2006, sec. 2b). This means that in order for 'the fact that Hargle doesn't like milk' to be an appositive description, 'fact' must be a general term and 'that Hargle doesn't like milk' must be a singular term that stands for the whole of (6). While there's no apparent problem with the former condition, the latter is problematic because, as we amply saw in section 4.1, that-clauses are not singular terms. (So this argument also depends on the argument against Singular Terms). And, indeed, if we try to apply Schnieder's analysis to 'the *Fa*' we'll see this easily. The analysis goes as follows:

(9)   For some x, x is an F, and, for all y, if y is F then $y = x$, and $x = a$.

This works for 'the hedgehog Hargle': that is, the only hedgehog identical with Hargle:

(10)   For some x, x is a hedgehog and, for all y, if y is a hedgehog then $y = x$ and $x = $ Hargle.[33]

But now look what happens when we apply this analysis to any expression of the form 'the fact that *p*':

(11)   For some x, x is a fact and, for all y, if y is a fact then $y = x$, and $*x =$ *that p*.

This does not work because, as we saw in section 4.2.1 *ad NecSingular-Terms 2* following Mulligan and Correia (2008), 'that p' cannot flank the identity sign. Therefore, 'the fact that p' is not an appositive description, either.[34] If 'the fact that p' is neither a definite nor an appositive description, on which grounds can we take it to be a singular term? What could make it such? If x does not look like any item on our most extensive catalog of singular terms, x might, strictly speaking, still be a new kind of singular term or a singular term sui generis; but we cannot accept any new item for inclusion *without good reasons to do so*. It is commonly maintained, and rightly so, that in order for a complex x to be added to our list we must be able, at a minimum, to give a satisfactory *structural analysis* of it. Now, since 'the fact that p' is not a case of anything already on that list, and no convincing suggestion is available as to how we should construe it in natural language, I see no reason to agree to take 'the fact that p' to be a singular term. A still unknown, mysterious kind of complex singular term, for which no analysis is offered, is as much a singular term as kryptonite is a chemical compound.

From a methodological point of view, one could insist that what I just showed is that the claim that 'the fact that p' is a singular term is *unmotivated*, or, as I prefer to say, ad hoc; it does not show that it is *false*, and one could insist that one should be agnostic on the matter. Again, whether this reasoning is correct depends on shared methodological criteria to assess questions such as 'when is x a singular term?'. If we agree that our only shared criterion is that 'the fact that p' must either fit a definition of singular term or function analogously to a singular term, it follows that it is not only unmotivated, but false that 'the fact that p' is a singular term. If we agree on other criteria, the conclusion offered here might be weaker.[35] However, it is unclear what criteria alternative to these might be; in any case, a satisfactory analysis of 'the fact that p' that advances the account I just gave has still to be found, and the onus is on those who claim that 'the fact that p' is a singular term.

4.3   Against *NecFirstConjunct*: 'Is a Fact' Is Not a Predicate

In the previous sections I have discussed *definite* nominal reference to facts. I showed that neither 'that p' nor 'the fact that p' are singular terms, against claims *SuffSuffFirstConjunct 1* and *2* of the argument from nominal reference. But having singular terms for facts is only a *sufficient* condition for the argument from nominal reference: there might be no singular terms for facts, but if there is *indefinite* reference to facts, then the argument from nominal reference goes through anyway. For, as we saw in section 4.1, the *necessary* condition is that the expression 'is a fact' is a genuine predicate (*NecFirstConjunct*). This is necessary for the Quine-like criterion adopted in the argument to be able to show that we are able to quantify over facts. Indefinite reference to facts and the supposition that 'is a fact' is a genuine predicate are strictly related. In this section, I show that we have no indefinite reference to facts either: 'is a fact' is not a genuine predicate applying to the objects falling under 'something' in 'something is a fact'.

Put in first-order logic, a sentence such as 'Not all relevant facts have been considered' would read (read F for 'is a fact' and C for 'has been considered')

(2) $\neg\forall x\ (Fx \to Cx)$

or

(2') $\exists x\ (Fx \wedge \neg Cx)$

Apparently, here we have indefinite nominal quantification over facts ($\exists x$ (Fx …)): so the necessary condition for the argument from nominal reference seems fulfilled. But is it really? If we want to take (2) to include a *genuine* quantification over facts, we need to show that 'is a fact' here is a *genuine* predicate of natural language (i.e., a genuinely referring one). If showing this were not needed, then, for instance, the mere analysis of

(3)   Not all the invaders from Mars (M) have been captured by the police (P).

as

(3') $\exists x\ (Mx \wedge \neg Px)$

would be sufficient to show that 'is an invader from Mars' is a genuine predicate of natural language—that is, a predicate that *truly* applies to some objects, and which *therefore* shows that there are invaders from Mars. This is obviously not the case. How do we show that 'is a fact' is a genuine predicate? One can very well claim that showing this depends on having good reasons to assume that facts exist. But now, this is exactly what we are discussing. What we can agree on, at this point, is that in any case we need to show something even more basic about the purely linguistic characteristics of 'is a fact', namely that 'is a fact' in 'x is a fact' works like 'is a hedgehog' in 'x is a hedgehog'.

Recall now the example of a seemingly predicative use of 'is a fact' which we just saw in section 4.1 in discussing the status of that-clauses as genuine structural subjects:

(1)   That Bargle eats more than Argle is a fact.

We saw that 'that Bargle eats more than Argle' here is not a structural subject: that-clauses are not singular terms that can occupy that role. But if so, (1) is not a substantial predication and its structure is not *Fa*. (From the point of view of our schematic argument from nominal reference, disproving (1, a) depends on the argument against singular terms). Therefore, despite appearances, there is little similarity between (1) and

(2)   Hargle is a hedgehog.

Sentence (1), however, is an example of expression in natural language of the form *Fa*, that is, embedding a singular term, and therefore an (alleged) example of definite reference. What we need to examine are cases of indefinite reference to facts, cases that involve expressions in natural language that translate the form '*x* is a fact'. Examples in natural language are important because the argument from nominal reference itself is formulated for natural language. The quantified expression 'For some *x*, *x* is a fact' belongs to a formal or regimented language: if we want such analyses to tell us something informative about natural language, we need some way to express the same in natural language. The closest equivalent to 'For some *x*, *x* is a fact' in natural language would be '*Something* is a fact'.[36] Now, for 'is a fact' to be able to function as a genuine predicate, here 'something' has to be a nominal quantifier. But if it is, then we're stuck again. For what evidence do we have that 'something' here is a nominal quantifier? The analysis of section 4.1 gives us enough evidence to answer: 'something', here, does *not* work like 'he', 'this', and so on. Trying to substitute 'this' or 'that' for 'something' in 'something is a fact' does not bring us very far:

When we use 'this' or 'that' in referring to facts, these terms never function as proper referring expressions. When I say 'this fact' I do not add a gesture of pointing, as I might do when I say 'this tree' or 'this sentence'. (Tillman, 1966, 123)[37]

'Something is a fact'—full stop—in natural language sounds like nonsense. Of course you do have uses such as 'Something is a fact when …', or 'How do you know when something is a fact and not an opinion?' But compare cases such as asking: 'When do you know if something is a real Caravaggio?' In this case you can reply 'A *painting* is a Caravaggio when …' Or consider this case:

'Something is wrong with my hedgehog', said Argle, to which Bargle asked, 'Hargle? What's wrong with her then?' 'I don't know', replies Argle, 'her digestion, I think'.

There are wrong things with hedgehogs that are bad digestions and there are paintings that are real Caravaggios, but what are the things that are facts? The only good natural language candidate to substitute for x in 'x is a fact', in uses that could match the other uses we just saw (involving digestion and paintings), are expressions of the form 'that p'. But if so, again, we have gained nothing: as I have shown in the previous sections, that-clauses are nonreferential. The expression 'is a fact' is thus not a genuine predicate, it does not work like 'is a hedgehog' in 'Hargle is a hedgehog'. But if 'is a fact' is not a genuine predicate, then there is no indefinite reference to facts either.[38]

What the above shows is that demonstrating that in natural language there is indefinite reference to some object A seems to depend very much on showing that there is definite reference to A. So, although definite reference—that is, having singular terms for facts—is only a sufficient condition for the argument from nominal reference, while indefinite reference is necessary, if you look at natural language indefinite reference seems rather to depend on definite reference. So, since there is no definite reference to facts, there is no indefinite reference either. This concludes my rebuttal of the argument from nominal reference.

One might want to ask the following. If (1) is not a predication where the predicate is 'is a fact', what is it? How should we construe similar statements? One possibility is to construe 'is a fact' in such cases as functioning *adverbially*. So, '(That ...) is a fact' would function like 'in fact'.[39] Consequently, (3)–(3.3) below all say the same thing (although we might want to say that (3) says it in the most illuminating way and (3.3) in the least):

(3)   Smoking in fact causes cancer.
(3.1)   It is a fact: smoking causes cancer.
(3.2)   It is a fact that smoking causes cancer.
(3.3)   That smoking causes cancer is a fact (Rundle, 1979, 324).

In (3.1)–(3.2), 'it' is not a pronoun, but functions, roughly, similarly to 'it' in

(4)   'It's cold in here',

where 'it' is not an expression with a referential role, for it is not the case that we are characterizing as cold some item referred to by 'it'. The expressions 'is a fact' in (3.3) and 'in fact' in (3) function just as 'is obvious' and adverbs like 'obviously' do:

(5)   Obviously, Bargle eats more than Argle.

(5.1) It is obvious: Bargle eats more than Argle.

(5.2) It is obvious that Bargle eats more than Argle.

(5.3) That Bargle eats more than Argle is obvious.[40]

Similarly,

'Caesar's dying was protracted' is to say no more, perhaps, than that Caesar died slowly. (Clark, 1975, 6)

On this basis, some suggest we should think of 'is a fact' as having a role comparable to that of the assertion sign:

'Fact' is not a general name; it is an authority-giving device applicable to assertions. (Tillman, 1966, 129)

In adding 'it is a fact (that)' to an assertion, we are saying that we take ourselves to be fully warranted in speaking in the terms that follow, that we are not speaking merely conjecturally. It compares, if you wish, with the assertion sign. (Rundle 1979: 332)

E.g. 'On account of the fact that no trams are running we shall be forced to walk' ≡ 'No trams are running; we shall therefore be forced to walk.' The part played by the phrase 'the fact that' in such sentences is simply to indicate that the truth of the statement 'No trams are running' is meant to be taken for granted. Thus the phrase 'the fact that' occurs in practice whenever it is useful to slide over the *assertion* of the truth of some statement by concealing that assertion in the implications of another, actually asserted, statement: e.g. as a rhetorical device for begging the question or when the truth of the statement in question has already be conceded. (Black, 1934, 40)

By acknowledging the above, one commits oneself neither to saying that '(That ...) is a fact' can *only* be substituted by 'in fact' or 'actually', nor to denying that there are any uses in which 'is a fact' could be considered predicative. Consider, for instance:

(6)   The victory of the Labour party is a fact (Künne 2003: 10).[41]

(7)   Georgia Evolution Lawsuit Is a Fact (*Los Angeles Times*, November 9, 2004).[42]

Examples like (6) and (7) show that 'is fact' can also be substituted by 'has happened' or 'occurred' or 'taken place', which we say of events, or by 'has been passed, proved, approved, ratified', which we say of decisions, declarations, bills, statements, and lawsuits when describing these as the result of certain processes. The use of 'is a fact' in these examples (to mean something like 'it's done', 'it has been accomplished') is more perspicuously related to the original meaning of the word 'fact', namely *deed*.[43] But what uses like (6) and (7) have in common with the one we saw above (3.3) is this: when we say that it is a fact that smoking causes cancer, that the victory of the Labour Party is a fact, and that the Georgia Evolution Lawsuit is a fact, all we are saying, with regard to its semantic content, is that smoking causes cancer, that the Labour Party won, and that the Georgia Evolution Lawsuit has been initiated. I don't say there is no difference whatsoever between all these expressions; I say that whatever difference there is is just one of emphasis or coloring or, as in cases (6) and (7), perhaps due to a definite exclusion of alternative possibilities by the actualization of a particular one ('there is no way back').[44] An analysis in terms of the assertion sign or alternative analyses to similar effect seem to have the advantage of providing a general way to handle all occurrences of 'is a fact'. What I am gesturing at is, clearly, an analysis similar to the one that Frege thought appropriate for 'is true'. For, let us note *en passant*, the two expressions—'is a fact' and 'is true'—appear synonymous in many contexts.[45] Both Frege and the similarities between truth(-talk) and fact(-talk) will appear again in chapter 6.

4.4 Conclusion

The upshot of this chapter is the following. Sections 4.1, 4.2, and 4.3 have shown that the argument for facts from nominal reference (which we saw on pp. 119, 126–127) has lost its *First Conjunct*, which also means that its *Third Conjunct* is also lost. Now the argument looks like this:

✓   (*Quine-Like*) Facts exist if and only if statements of natural language are true that are ontologically committed to facts.

    A statement *s* of natural language is true which is ontologically committed to facts if and only if

✓   (*First Conjunct*) *s* implies a true first-order statement of the form $\exists x Fx$ (indefinite reference) where 'F' is 'is a fact'.

✓   (*SuffFirstConjunct*) A sufficient condition for *First Conjunct* is that *s* contains singular terms for facts in natural language (definite reference).

✗   Sufficient conditions for *SuffFirstConjunct* are

✗   (*SuffSuffFirstConjunct 1*) Some (kinds of) that-clauses are singular terms referring to facts. (sec. 4.1)

✗   (*SuffSuffFirstConjunct 2*) 'The fact that *p*' is a singular term referring to the fact that *p*. (sec. 4.2]

✗   Necessary condition for *SuffSuffFirstConjunct 1* and *SuffSuffFirstConjunct 2* (sec. 4.2) is that

✗   (*NecSuffSuffFirstConjunct 1 and 2 = Singular Terms*) That-clauses
           are singular terms. (sec. 4.1)

✗   (*NecFirstConjunct*) A necessary condition for *FirstConjunct* is that 'is a
           fact' functions genuinely as a predicate in predications of the form '*x*
           is a fact'. (sec. 4.3)

✗   (*Second Conjunct*) We have identity criteria for facts.

✗   (*Third Conjunct*) The quantification over facts in natural language is
           ineliminable.

(Conclusion) Under *Quine-Like*, facts exist because of *First Conjunct*
(*SuffFirstConjunct, SuffSuffFirstConjunct 1, NecSuffSuffFirstConjunct 1 and 2 = Singular
Terms*), *Second Conjunct, Third Conjunct*, or because of *First Conjunct*
(*SuffFirstConjunct, SuffSuffFirstConjunct 2, NecSuffSuffFirstConjunct 1 & 2 = Singular
Terms*) *Second Conjunct, Third Conjunct*, or because of *First Conjunct* (with the
proviso *NecFirstConjunct* holds), *Second Conjunct, Third Conjunct*.

Since First Conjunct is false (because (a) *SuffSuffFirstConjunct 1* and *SuffSuffFirstConjunct 2* are both false, in turn due to failure of *NecSuffSuffFirstConjunct 1 and 2 = Singular Terms* in both cases, and because (b) *NecFirstConjunct*
is also false), there are no true statements of natural language that are committed to facts, and therefore, in the light of *Quine-Like*, facts don't exist.
There is no genuine quantification over facts (the latter can count as a
weaker conclusion on the existence of facts if you do not accept the Quine-
like criterion and the equation of the existence of something in a transcen-
dental ontology with genuine quantification over it in natural language).
Note that these findings mean that the Third Conjunct is a fortiori false:
since there is no such a thing as quantification over facts, there cannot be
ineliminable quantification over facts. I take the case with *Fact Reference* to
be closed at this point, and defenders of a metaphysics of facts based on this
argument have to grant this much. (Don't forget that for me, however, the
reasoning in this chapter is a reductio, so from my point of view all that has
been said is that this argument, which aims at establishing that facts
exist on the basis of natural language possessing singular terms for them, is
unsound.)

It's interesting to note that although here I am only interested in reference to *facts*, the problems I surveyed in this chapter, insofar as they are
problems for singular terms, are problems for any argument resting on the
referential role of that-clauses, and thus a problem also, for instance, for
whoever would defend *propositions* (partly or fully) on the same basis (see
McGrath, 2012, sec. 5).

In the next two chapters I review a fallback position. Suppose that for some reason the case is not closed. Suppose that *Fact Reference* still stands: then, I argue, it faces insurmountable problems. It cannot account for all counter-examples, and even if it could, *Fact Reference* would be self-defeating since it would entail the collapse of (true) propositions into facts even though the distinction between facts and propositions is at its very core. This comes down to showing that the Second Conjunct is also false.

5 A Fallback Position (1)

In this and the next chapter I present a fallback position with respect to my criticism above of the referential role of that-clauses, that is, my rebuttal in chapter 4 of the first conjunct of the argument from nominal reference. There I argued that that-clauses are not singular terms. That-clauses do not refer to facts, because that-clauses simply don't refer to anything.

The arguments I provide in this chapter and the next do not depend on these previous arguments, for in what follows I argue that *even if* that-clauses were (shown to be) singular terms, still they would not refer to facts: in the best hypothesis, all that-clauses would refer to propositions. There would not be two kinds of that-clauses referring to items of two different categories of entities, facts and propositions.

To show this, I proceed as follows. In section 5.1, I introduce and discuss a thesis that is a refinement-cum-strengthening of Fact Reference (the thesis that some that-clauses refer to facts), and which I call Fact Reference*Power!*.

This thesis says that *factive* that-clauses refer to facts while *nonfactive* that-clauses refer to propositions. In sections 5.2 and 5.3, I show that the only kind of facts that Fact Reference*Power!* (if true) can be taken to involve are so-called *propositional facts*. In section 5.4 I argue that propositional facts are identical to true (Fregean) propositions, and I reject five attempts to block that identification. In the next chapter I move on to investigate whether certain linguistic evidence, often seen to support Fact Reference*Power!*, can indeed be used in the way that advocates of this position would like—that is, to reject the identification of propositional facts and propositions and support an acknowledgment of propositional facts as distinct entities. On the basis of counterexamples that disprove the linguistic evidence in question and that defenders of Fact Reference*Power!* cannot explain—not even on pains of great contortion—I conclude that this evidence cannot be used to make a convincing case for propositional facts, and so that this sixth and final attempt to make that case is a failure. On this basis I further conclude that language alone cannot establish a difference between facts and propositions, and that therefore it is false that some (kinds of) that-clauses refer to propositional facts while other (kinds of) that-clauses refer to propositions. The thesis that factive that-clauses refer to facts and nonfactive that-clauses to propositions is, I argue, so problematic as to be indefensible: *even if* that-clauses were Singular Terms, it would still not be the case that there are two kinds of that-clauses, one referring to facts and another referring to propositions. I contend that the only defensible position, should that-clauses turn out to be Singular Terms, is the position that takes them to refer to propositions and *only* to propositions, to the effect that factive that-clauses refer to *true* propositions.

Fact Reference at its best—that is, in the version I call Fact Reference*Power!*—is thus false: there is no category of facts alongside true propositions to which that-clauses refer. This said, however, the conclusion of the previous chapter still stands: the most attractive position at the moment remains that of taking that-clauses to be nonreferential. The last section of the next chapter is devoted to making sure that the argument against Singular Terms I offered in chapter 4 is also effective against the somewhat different kind of literature I use in chapter 5 and 6.

Methodologically speaking, some of the points I make in this chapter are of a somewhat different nature from the points I made in the previous chapter. My strategy in chapter 4 was a reductio: I sought to disprove linguistic arguments, that is, arguments based on the use of language, on the very same linguistic grounds those arguments invoke, including findings from linguistics. As I already mentioned, I consider linguistic arguments in general bad tools for doing real work in metaphysics. This undermines linguistic strategies as a whole, of course, though for my purpose here—of showing that that-clauses do not refer to facts because they don't refer at all—this is not necessary; there is no need to invoke such a principled revisionary position that refuses linguistic arguments altogether. It suffices to turn the linguistic, *descriptive* strategy (as it is normally called) against its proponents.

In this and the next chapter I shall again go along with the linguistic strategy to a certain extent, for it can be shown that Fact Reference$_{Power!}$ is disproved directly on the very linguistic grounds that are invoked by its proponents. My critical account of the linguistic evidence for Fact Reference$_{Power!}$ in chapter 6 is prepared in the present chapter, however, by a discussion of five attempts to block the identification of facts and true propositions that rely on nonlinguistic, that is, metaphysical considerations as well.

5.1   Fact Reference Refined and Strengthened: Fact Reference$_{Power!}$

Suppose it is true that that-clauses are singular terms. Is it also true, then, that some that-clauses refer to facts? On what grounds can we say this? In chapter 4, I said that the expression 'that p' is systematically ambiguous insofar as philosophers use it to refer either to a proposition or to a fact. But according to an influential view put forward by Zeno Vendler, 'that p' is not ambiguous at all, or at least the ambiguity is not in language itself. According to Vendler, it can be shown that language does discriminate between contexts in which *propositions* are referred to on the one hand, and contexts in which *facts* are referred to on the other. This makes the identity of that-clauses only superficial and suggests a criterion to disambiguate that-clauses, namely the context in which they are embedded (Vendler, 1972, 89). I have already mentioned a certain criterion to disambiguate that-clauses while discussing the substitution problem in section 4.1 of chapter 4; now I will explain in more detail how it works.

The criterion I shall consider has been proposed by Philip L. Peterson who, by combining Vendler's ideas with independent and roughly coeval work by Paul and Carol Kiparsky, has introduced into linguistics another idea related to the behavior of that-clauses: factivity (Kiparsky & Kiparsky, 1971; Peterson, 1997). Both Vendler and the Kiparskys are classical references among philosophers and linguists working in this area, but they are seldom discussed in a unified critical assessment. In combining both clusters of results Peterson offers, to my knowledge, the most extensive and most recent analysis available of the distinction between factive and nonfactive predicates in natural languages relevant to our project here—where 'predicates' includes verbs ('realizes'), verb phrases ('must have been discovered'), predicate adjectives ('is a mystery'), and predicate nominatives ('is significant', 'is unlikely'). Put in our terms, Peterson develops a refinement of Fact Reference by characterizing certain that-clauses as *factive*, and taking these to refer to facts, and certain others as *nonfactive*, and taking those to refer to propositions.[1] I shall call this refinement Fact Reference$_{Power!}$.

It is important to stress that the claim that *factive* that-clauses refer to facts (Fact Reference$_{Power!}$) is methodologically more convincing than the claim that *some* or *some kinds of* that-clauses refer to facts (Fact Reference), insofar as the latter is just a vague stipulation while the former identifies precisely *which* that-clauses refer to facts with the aid of results from linguistics. This is why I shall take issue with Fact Reference$_{Power!}$, rather than with Fact Reference: it is the best version of the theory I want to challenge. My conclusion, for which I will need some time and a couple of detours, will be that Fact Reference$_{Power!}$ is deeply problematic, and that these problems carry over directly into Fact Reference.

In the following I will mainly take Peterson's work as a starting point. On the basis of semantic and syntactic tests, Peterson puts forward a thesis that we can analyze as consisting of two related but different theses:

Factivity Language exhibits a phenomenon called factivity; this phenomenon is linked to the implication or presupposition of truth of certain embedded clauses.[2]

Fact Reference$_{Power!}$ Factive that-clauses *refer to facts* whereas nonfactive that-clauses *refer to propositions*.

Factivity is based on the Kiparskys' work; Fact Reference$_{Power!}$ combines the latter with ideas inspired by Vendler. It is important to keep these two fundamental theses, Factivity and Fact Reference$_{Power!}$, distinct. In what follows I discuss them in turn, starting with Factivity.

Consider

(1) Bargle noticed that Argle bought the colander.

(2) Cargle believed that Argle stole the colander.

Suppose that both (1) and (2) are true. A known phenomenon is that in hearing (1), we think that Argle indeed bought the colander, that is, we take the embedded clause 'Argle bought the colander' to be true. In hearing (2), however, we do not take 'Argle stole the colander' to be true: (1) implies that the embedded clause is true, while in (2) no such implication (or presupposition) is present. So, if we see (1) and (2) as together telling a short story, we would conclude that Cargle is wrong rather than that Argle is a thief. The reason given for this phenomenon, put briefly, is that the *verbs* appearing in these sentences are different: 'notice' is *factive*, whereas 'believe' is not.

Can factivity be captured systematically? Peterson characterizes it first of all by providing a semantic test: the predicate f of a sentence s is factive when it takes a complement clause (like that-clauses in English) in such a way that, were we to negate s or to form yes/no questions from s, the truth of the clause taken by f in s would still be presupposed (see Peterson 1997, 7–8).[3] To see this, consider:

(3)   Bargle noticed that Argle bought the colander.

(3.1)   Did Bargle notice that Argle bought the colander? (Yes/No)

(3.2)   Bargle did not notice that Argle bought the colander.

(3.3)   Argle bought the colander.

The clause that is presupposed in (3), namely, (3.3), is still presupposed both when we turn (3) into a yes/no question, as in (3.1), and when we deny it, as in (3.2) (see Peterson, 1997, 68). In other words, the test goes like this: if negation and yes/no questioning of f (in 'x fs that p') are truth-preserving with respect to 'that p', f is factive. Nonfactives make no presupposition of truth, so there is nothing to preserve: in 'Cargle believed that Argle stole the colander', 'believed' carries no presupposition as to the truth of 'Argle stole the colander'.

Peterson considers also a second characteristic of factive predicates, one already proposed by Vendler, which yields instead a syntactic test for factivity: complement clauses of factive predicates can be transformed into *wh*-nominals (clauses introduced by 'when', 'who', 'what', 'why', and 'how'), preserving grammaticality, whereas complement clauses of nonfactives cannot. Consider the following:

(3)   Bargle noticed that Argle bought the colander.

(3.4)   Bargle noticed what Argle bought.

(3.5)   Bargle noticed who bought the colander.

As we see, 'notice' passes the syntactical test. But now consider:

(4)   Cargle believed that Argle stole the colander.

(4.1)   *Cargle believed what Argle stole.

(4.2)   *Cargle believed who stole the colander.

(4.1)* is ungrammatical, (4.2)* grammatical only under a reading that modifies its meaning or, if you prefer, its 'reading' ('Cargle believed the person that stole the colander'). Thus 'believe' fails the test. Let us conclude therefore that there is evidence and two tests available for Factivity:

Factivity   Language exhibits a phenomenon called factivity; this phenomenon is linked to the implication or presupposition of truth of certain embedded clauses.

As is clear, Factivity is a metaphysically innocent thesis: neither the very idea of factivity nor the two factivity tests just mentioned involve anything of metaphysical relevance. The only thing at issue is the presupposition of the *truth* of certain complementizer phrases (CPs), as linguists call 'that *p*'-constructions of the kind we are interested in. So far as Factivity is concerned, truth can be conceived in whichever way: no particular conception of truth is required. Notice that when I say that Factivity is metaphysically harmless, I do not mean that it cannot be disputed.[4] What I mean is that I am not going to investigate whether Factivity is true: as was the case with the question whether that-clauses are syntactic unities or not, I will refrain from arguing against it. My target in the remaining sections of this chapter and the next one is the second fundamental thesis, Fact Reference$_{Power}$.

Recall that Fact Reference$_{Power!}$, introduced by Peterson, again following Vendler,[5] goes as follows (in my reformulation):

Fact Reference$_{Power!}$ Factive that-clauses *refer to facts* whereas nonfactive that-clauses *refer to propositions*.

Unlike Factivity, Fact Reference$_{Power!}$ is not metaphysically innocent. It assumes three things: first, it assumes that facts and propositions are entities right there at our disposal to be referred to by that-clauses (a metaphysical claim); second, it assumes that that-clauses are singular terms, and that there are *two kinds* of that-clauses functioning as singular terms—one referring to facts and one referring to propositions (a claim about reference); third, it tells us exactly *which* that-clauses refer to facts and which to propositions. This is fixed by the tests leading to Factivity: factive clauses refer to facts, nonfactive clauses to propositions. The metaphysical innocence has ended here.

Fact Reference$_{Power!}$ thus takes for granted that facts and propositions are two distinct categories of items. To be sure, questions such as what facts are, how facts are individuated, what their identity conditions are, and how fine-grained facts are with respect to propositions all seem to be left open. Yet Fact Reference$_{Power!}$ eventually determines these issues to considerable extent, as we shall see in section 5.3, by entailing the so-called *propositional* view of facts. This position is characteristic of those who see both facts and (Fregean) propositions as ideal entities, that is, as entities that are 'not in the world' (for the notion of proposition, and that of 'being in the world', see the chapter, section 1.3, condition 3, and section 1.4). What I am going to argue, in particular, is that propositional facts on this view are just as fine-grained as (Fregean) propositions, and that there is no convincing way to show that these items are something *different* from true propositions. So it is that with Fact Reference$_{Power!}$ metaphysics enters the picture. It is this thesis that I will take issue with.

As we saw in chapter 4, the most serious problem with the thesis that some kind of that-clauses refer to facts (Fact Reference) is that that-clauses are not singular terms. If that-clauses are not referring expressions, then Fact Reference is false, because that thesis depends on the referential role of that-clauses. It is easy to see that the problem carries over into Fact Reference$_{Power!}$, and I will devote section 6.3 of the next chapter to the removal of doubts on this point, for example, the doubt that Fact Reference$_{Power!}$ might not be threatened by the nonreferential role of that-clauses after all.

Irrespective of the conclusion of the previous chapter, in the remaining sections of this chapter and in the next I shall take issue with Fact Reference$_{Power!}$ under the hypothesis that that-clauses *are* referential. I have three reasons to devote an extensive discussion to this position, which I consider a fallback one. The first is that one might come up with a rebuttal of my earlier arguments, from which it would follow that that-clauses are singular terms after all (never mind that it is difficult to conceive of what form this could take). If this happens, then what I am about to say in the rest of this book suddenly becomes crucial. The second reason I have to investigate in detail what follows from acknowledging Fact Reference$_{Power!}$ is the reputation that Vendler-like analyses enjoy in contemporary debates, judging from how widely quoted Vendler's work is: this makes it important to show in detail what such analyses really commit one to. The third reason, perhaps the most important, is that the following analysis shows that facts are in trouble anyway. This is why it makes sense to see what happens when Fact Reference$_{Power!}$ is accepted. Kenneth Olson writes:

If facts were "wedded to that-clauses" as closely as Strawson claims, their reality would indeed be suspect. (Olson, 1987, 8)

The rest of this chapter is devoted the substantiation of this claim with arguments.

As noted, I discuss problems with the linguistic evidence invoked to fix Fact Reference*Power!* in the next chapter. As we shall see, serious problems are posed to Fact Reference*Power!* by counterexamples to the analysis of factivity, and by cases of cross-factive/nonfactive anaphora. The first thing I will do, however, is to ask, in the next section, what kind of facts the thesis that factive that-clauses refer to facts commits us to. One important thing that this discussion will show is that the facts with which Fact Reference*Power!* is concerned are not facts of the kind we have seen so far, that is, compositional facts in Armstrong's sense, but facts of another kind: *propositional* facts. Once we have seen what such facts are, the question will arise whether propositional facts are not, after all, identical to propositions. In sections 5.3 and 5.4 I argue that this question must be answered in the affirmative: propositional facts *are* identical to propositions, and attempts to avoid this identification are unsuccessful. This means that Fact Reference*Power!* is false: there aren't two different kinds of that-clauses, one referring to facts (factive that-clauses) and one referring to propositions (nonfactive that-clauses), but at most one kind: all that-clauses, if referential at all, refer to propositions.

5.2   Propositional Facts

Suppose that Fact Reference*Power!* is true, that is, it is true that factive that-clauses *refer to facts* while nonfactive that-clauses *refer to propositions*. What kind of facts does this thesis commit us to? In particular, does it yield a view of facts according to which they are in the world? Vendler, for one, denies that facts are in the world:

> But how can facts be in the world? When they cannot even be in more familiar receptacles like rooms or continents? Certainly facts are *about* things in the world, but this *about* is not the about of *she is working about the house all day*. It is the *about* of *talking about something*. I do not find any justification for the claim that facts are in the world, (Vendler, 1967, 145)

The sense in which Vendler speaks of facts here is the sense of facts on the view called by Kit Fine the "propositional view" of facts, as opposed to the "worldly view" (Fine, 1982, 51–53). The worldly view of facts is the view I dealt with in part 1, the one on which facts have constituents *in* them and on which they are sometimes called 'compositional facts'. Facts in the propositional view, for short 'propositional facts', are not structured objects in Armstrong's compositional fashion. Propositional facts are not characterized as an object's having (or instantiating) a property, or as pieces of the furniture of the world with a special relational reticulation. To say what propositional facts are is difficult, because philosophers have hardly given them any theoretical characterization. What we can say is the following.

Propositional facts are parasitic on propositions, and are often a by-product of some semantic position. They are usually more inspired by considerations from the philosophy of language and the philosophy of logic rather than from metaphysics. Whereas it is on the basis of their constituents that we can characterize worldly, compositional facts, nonworldly propositional facts cannot be characterized other than by recourse to the propositions that 'describe' them or to which they 'correspond' or with which they 'fit'. Propositional facts *are* whatever corresponds to true propositions. This sounds uninformative, but it does tell us one important thing. If propositional facts are whatever corresponds to true propositions, and if their identity depends on the proposition they correspond to, then what Fine calls *the one-one thesis* ensues: for every true proposition, there is one and only one fact to which that proposition corresponds, and for every fact there is one and only one true proposition to which this fact corresponds. According to the propositional view, then, there are no more and no fewer facts than the facts that correspond to true propositions (Fine, 1982, 63).

This ... then *reduces* the question of the identity of facts, within a given world, to the identity of propositions. For under the assumption ... that for each fact there is a proposition to which it corresponds, two facts will be identical iff the propositions to which they correspond are identical. (Fine, 1982, 57)

The one-one thesis states the fundamental characteristic of propositional facts and gives us identity conditions for them. Importantly, the latter are such that the *granularity* of facts, as it is called, is identical to the granularity of propositions they 'fit': propositional facts are as fine-grained as the propositions they depend on for their identity. Fine points out that ordinary language suggests the propositional view.[6]

Can we say something more about the granularity of compositional and propositional facts, and about their identity criteria? For instance, what is their relationship to the propositions they fit? According to Fine, propositional facts on the one hand and compositional facts on the other are best set off by (and each paired off) with two different criteria of identity:

Two distinct categories of fact-type entities can be distinguished, one satisfying an empirical [I] and the other a quasi-structural criterion of identity [II]. (Fine, 1982, 57)

The criteria are the following:

[I] *Quasi-structural identity criterion for facts.* Under the assumption ... that for each fact there is a proposition to which it corresponds, two facts will be identical iff the

propositions to which they correspond are identical. ... On a broadly structural conception of propositions ... their identity is explained in terms of their structure. The
identity of facts might then also be explained in structural terms ...; for the fact will
inherit whatever structure is possessed by the proposition. (Fine, 1982, 57)

[II] *Empirical identity criterion for facts.* Under this account, two facts will be identical when they necessarily co-exist, i.e. when it is necessary that the one exist just in
case the other does. ... The present criterion ... is best seen as arising from the demand that facts be empirical entities. Roughly speaking, we may say that empirical
entities are ones that are empirically distinguishable, where empirical distinctions
are ones that make a possible difference to the world. (Fine, 1982, 60)

These criteria, and their match with the two kinds of facts so far discussed,
suggest a rather sharp distinction between the two kinds of facts as far as
their relation to propositions is concerned. The reasoning beyond this
observation is quite plausible, and I see no reason to reject it. Propositional
facts are ideal (they are 'not in the world'), and they obey a quasi-structural
criterion of identity by virtue of which they enjoy a one-one correspondence to propositions, from which they inherit their structure (if it is at all
possible to speak of structure for ideal facts) and granularity. Compositional
facts are structured entities made up by the objects they reticulate. Two
compositional facts are identical if and only if they have the same constituents arranged in the same way (Armstrong, 1997, 132). Compositional facts
are part of the empirical world and are causally effective in it. They are entities that are perceptible and fit the role of truthmakers for empirical truths;
being empirically indistinguishable for these entities means fulfilling the
same role. So, it makes sense to accept a criterion for compositional facts
that sees a one-many correspondence between facts and propositions,
which means that their granularity will differ. Compositional facts (the
facts we have seen in chapters 1 through 3) are more coarse-grained than
the propositions they make true or fit.

An additional useful observation on the role and structure that compositional facts must have—at least if we want the notion of compositional
fact to be a sensible one—is made by Stephen Neale. In the technical prose
of *Facing Facts*, he writes:

I take it that no fact-theorist who intends to get some metaphysical work out of facts
wants to deny that FIC is +PSST. (Neale, 2001, 221)

Dropping the jargon, this means that whoever wants facts to do some metaphysical work must accept sentences stating fact identities such as the
following

(FIC)   The fact that p is identical with the fact that s

when coreferential singular terms are substituted, such as 'Mary Ann Evans' and 'George Eliot', for p and s, as in the following case:

(#)   The fact that George Eliot wrote *Middlemarch* = the fact that Mary Ann Evans wrote *Middlemarch*.

Now, whereas for compositional facts (#) is true, for propositional facts, which obey a quasi-structural criterion of identity, (#) is false—or at least it is false insofar as, in the theory of propositional facts that's presupposed here, the proposition that George Eliot wrote *Middlemarch* and the proposition that Mary Ann Evans wrote *Middlemarch* are different propositions. We might understand the claim that propositional facts 'do not do any metaphysical work' to mean that facts have to be different *enough* from propositions to take up roles in metaphysics that propositions can only implausibly take up (such as that of truthmaker, or causal relatum): if the only role they can take up is that of the referent of a that-clause, for instance, then they are metaphysically irrelevant.

The plausible reason why (#) holds for compositional facts is due to the empirical criterion of identity: if the facts mentioned in (#) are compositional, then they are empirically indistinguishable. On this view, facts, as suggested above, may be plausibly conceived as truthmaking entities that are in the world (i.e., not ideal) and so placed in time and space. It would be hard to argue, against this background, that facts that obey an empirical criterion are ideal objects. If instead facts obey a quasi-structural criterion, then they are as fine-grained as propositions, there is a one-one match between facts and propositions, and the most plausible position to take with respect to them is that they are ideal. These are propositional facts.

The following important picture of the essential characteristics of compositional and propositional facts emerges at this point:

Compositional facts	*Propositional facts*
do metaphysical work	don't do metaphysical work
are more coarse-grained than propositions	are as fine-grained as propositions
follow the empirical criterion of identity	follow the quasi-structural criterion of identity
are worldly, i.e., real	are not worldly, i.e., ideal

Can we fix the list of characteristics of propositional facts somewhat more precisely? It is not easy to reconstruct an answer to this question based on the scant suggestions offered by those who seem to acknowledge propositional facts. The following is a list of characteristics adapted from Clark (1976) and Fine (1982):

PF1 (*ideal*) Propositional facts are not in the world: they are ideal entities.

PF2 (*not-propositions*) Propositional facts are not statements, or propositions.

PF3 (*aboutness*) Propositional facts are about something.

PF4 (*unstructured*) Propositional facts are not composed of the objects they are about; in this sense, they are unstructured.

PF5 (*fine-grainedness*) Propositional facts are as fine-grained as propositions.

In the following, whenever I speak of propositional facts I will mean entities having all five characteristics. Not every philosopher who accepts propositional facts agrees on all five characteristics, nor accepts them without exception or without further ado.[7] But, as I will argue, the position on facts essentially characterized by PF1–PF5 is the only position compatible with Fact Reference$_{Power!}$, that is, the thesis that factive that-clauses refer to facts. Philosophers who argue that facts exist, on the basis of linguistic evidence concerning the behavior of that-clauses embedded in the modified, Quine-like argument I reconstructed and offered above, must thus adhere to PF1–PF5. Before I show this, I will comment briefly on each of these five characteristics in turn.

PF1 (ideal). Propositional facts are not in the world. This position has been famously defended by Strawson, who likened facts to true statements, against Austin, who likened facts to events (Strawson, 1950, 194–195, 199). Anyone acknowledging facts as ideal objects could adhere to the claim that facts are not in the world, in the sense that facts cannot be considered as entities that *make up* the world or are constitutive of it in the way that hurricanes and their destructive properties are.[8] According to this position, facts are ideal, timeless, and placeless items similar in status to Fregean propositions (Slote, 1974, 93). In this position, next to PF1 (*ideal*), PF4 (*unstructured*) also holds: facts that are not in the world, are not composed or constituted by the objects they are 'about' (PF3, *aboutness*). The objects propositional facts are said to be 'about' are not said to be their 'constituents'.

It should be said that among philosophers who accept ideal facts, there are some who see them (in the simplest case) as the instantiation of an object by a property, an instantiation that, as a whole, is not itself a constituent of the world—and expressible in language as in '*a*'s (not) being *b*'—and yet they hold that *a* and *b* themselves, that is, the 'parts' involved in the instantiation as a whole, *are* constituents of the world (one example is Clark, 1976).[9] This is also, for instance, Meinong's or Chisholm's position. However, Meinong, followed by Chisholm and others, accepts objects (his 'objectives') that have characteristics of both (Fregean) propositions and compositional facts: truths are "subsisting objectives," which are facts (Meinong, 1983, 55, 71–72, see also n. 93; Chisholm, 1976, 115); they are, we would say, obtaining states of affairs. This is a hybrid position that cannot be said to accept propositional facts. In a hybrid position of this kind, that is, in which states of affairs are accepted as a mixture of propositions and facts, it is usually not the case that *two kinds* of entities are accepted, that is, propositional facts *and* (Fregean) propositions: only *one* kind of entities is accepted that subsumes the characteristics of both facts and propositions. In fact we can't say that PF2 (*not-propositions*) is accepted on this view.

But if a philosopher has instead *both* ideal facts and ideal propositions in her universe, and ideal facts are about objects (PF1, 2 and 3), what does that 'aboutness' look like? Several options are available. One is that the relation between facts and the objects they are 'about' is—following Meinong, but with the necessary modifications—a not-further-specified relation of 'foundation'; however, it is rather unclear exactly how we should spell this out.[10] Another option is that facts might look like a kind of ideal replica of the world in a way very similar to that in which propositions are such: facts are then composed of the ideal replicas of the objects they are about. However, since propositional facts are supposed to be unstructured (PF4), they cannot be said to be 'composed' by anything, except in a sense parasitic on that of the propositions they correspond to, or 'fit'. I will return to some of these variants and the problematic notion of 'aboutness' in what follows.[11] For the time being, it suffices to say that if PF2 (*nonpropositions*) holds, in all these variants facts would have to be ideal (not in the world), but still different from propositions. The question that interests us is: how? On what grounds should we acknowledge propositional facts alongside propositions? How do we *motivate* the following claim?

PF2 (nonpropositions). Propositional facts are not statements, or propositions. All philosophers who acknowledge facts alongside propositions, no matter whether they accept propositional or compositional facts, accept PF2, and they all agree that to speak of 'true facts' and 'false facts' is improper—while they think it *is* proper to speak of 'true propositions' and 'false propositions'. Facts, they claim, cannot be *said to be* true or false ("it is not proper to say that," Clark, 1976, 261). But for those who accept propositional facts, it is particularly difficult to argue for the claim that facts are not true propositions.[12] If facts are different from true propositions, then they should be different in *some way*. What is this way? PF3 (*aboutness*) complicates things further. For instance, if we say that the fact that Japan is planning to have a satellite orbiting around the Sun to transmit electricity wirelessly to the Earth is 'about' Japan, the Sun, the Earth, and so on, in what respect is this 'aboutness' different from the aboutness of the proposition that Japan is planning to have a satellite orbiting around the Sun to transmit electricity wirelessly to the Earth?

PF3 (aboutness). Propositional facts are about something (Vendler, 1967, 145; Fine, 1982, 59–61, 65). Far from enabling us to sharpen the boundary between propositional facts and propositions, saying that facts are 'about' objects actually makes facts and propositions more proximate. It is unclear in what way the notion of aboutness that is relevant to facts should relate to the notion of aboutness that is relevant to propositions. Again, in itself the aboutness of facts is not a problem when facts are identified with true propositions, or when entities are accepted with characteristics that subsume both (Malcolm, 1940, 334, 341). For in this case, one could invoke the notion of *reference* or *designation* to account for the aboutness of these entities. But when propositional facts are accepted alongside propositions, what would account for the aboutness of facts? In what *other* sense are facts about objects? How else do they *represent* objects, or, even more modestly, *involve* them?[13] On some views that accept PF3 (*aboutness*), such as those of Clark (1976) and Prior (1948), the aboutness of facts is immediately connected to containment: "a fact contains the objects it is about" (Prior, 1948, 66). This option is open, however, only to those who accept that facts are structured with the aid of the objects they contain—and who in turn reject PF4. But if one holds that facts are ideal (PF1), different from propositions (PF2), and unstructured (PF4), how is the 'aboutness' of a fact to be construed?

PF4 (unstructured). Defenders of propositional facts who accept PF1, PF2, and PF3 tend to agree that *facts are unstructured*, in the sense of not containing or being composed of the objects they are about (Fine, 1982, 62). This seems a fundamental characteristic of propositional facts, yet in the literature defenders of propositional facts recur to containment language remarkably often. The contorted way in which this point is usually brought forward suggests that this is not a minor difficulty, as is apparent in the case of the idea that propositional facts are *about* objects.

Figuratively speaking, Rachel is not 'contained in' the fact that Leah's husband was very fond of Joseph, and a fact that does *not* contain Rachel cannot be identical with a fact that *does* contain her. But notice that the present attack on Davidson's assumption does not depend on taking facts literally to be structured entities somehow containing objects as parts. (Künne, 2003, 137)

Figuratively speaking, the property of being a husband is not 'contained in' the fact that Jacob is the only man that made love to Rachel, and a fact that does *not* contain that property cannot be identical with a fact that *does* contain it. But notice, once again, that the rejection of (L[iberal] T[erm] S[ubstitution]) does not depend on taking facts literally to be structured entities somehow containing properties as parts. (ibid., 140–141)

We can accept that 'containment' here is used figuratively: what is odd is the lack of a *nonfigurative* account of the relation of objects to facts.[14] We could read these passages only as evidence of Künne's adherence to PF3, that is, that facts are about something, but that would not help much. For again, the meaning of this 'aboutness' as different from the aboutness of propositions eludes understanding. I take that elusiveness to be an indication that propositional facts and propositions are, in fact, the same. By this I mean, to be precise, that there is no need or reason to accept propositional facts in one's catalog of the world next to propositions.

It is no coincidence that Künne's first take on the 'aboutness' and 'containment' of facts is in fact entirely parasitic on the 'aboutness' and 'containment' of propositions. For the reason why Rachel is not 'contained' in the fact that Leah's husband is very fond of Joseph, and also why Leah is not 'contained' in the fact that Rachel's husband is very fond of Joseph, is apparently that *in the proposition* that Leah's husband is very fond of Joseph there is no singular term standing for Rachel. The fact that Rachel's husband is very fond of Joseph and the fact that Leah's husband is very fond of Joseph are not the same fact (although Jacob is both Rachel's and Leah's husband) because

At least one of two co-designative singular terms (*Rachel's husband, Leah's husband*) contains a singular term (*Rachel*) that does not designate the same object as the containing term (*Rachel's husband*). (Künne, 2003, 137)

But, again, what is the relation between the containment of some terms in other terms and the 'containment' of objects in facts? The first containment is compositional (in fact, mereological). If we exclude that the second containment is compositional (or quasi-unmereological), then what is it that we have in mind?

PF5. Facts are as fine-grained as propositions. As we saw, this characteristic of propositional facts follows directly from the one-one thesis, and is, like this thesis, related to the identity conditions for facts. However, not everybody that agrees that facts are ideal (PF1), different from propositions (PF2), 'about' objects (PF3), and unstructured (PF4), nor sees the need to agree that propositional facts are as fine-grained as propositions (PF5). For instance, Vendler, Searle (Searle, 1995, 220), and Künne maintain that facts are more coarse-grained than propositions.[15] In particular, as I will show in the next section, Vendler thinks that since facts are 'objective entities' whereas propositions are 'subjective entities', the correspondence between propositions and facts must be many-one. Künne and Searle have different reasons for denying that facts are as fine-grained as propositions, linked to their attempts to block a famous argument that purports to show that there is just one Big Fact: the Slingshot argument. Yet, for whatever reason one might want to hold the view that facts are more coarse-grained than propositions, a view like Searle's or Künne's will harbor a tension. The tension is one between, on the one hand, the desire to take a position on that-clauses that requires us to construe propositional facts as fully parasitic on propositions, inheriting their structure unrestrictedly and thus being as fine-grained as the propositions facts are paired off with (accepting PF5), and, on the other hand, the desire to construe propositional facts as being more coarse-grained than the propositions they are paired off with (rejecting PF5). In the remaining pages of this section and in the next I will argue that this tension is irresolvable, and that one must choose between these two options: (i) if the reference of that-clauses to facts is nonnegotiable, accept *propositional* facts (which obey all of PF1–PF5, and are thus as fine-grained as propositions and, as I will argue, eventually collapse into propositions), or else (ii) if facts being more coarse-grained than propositions is nonnegotiable, accept *compositional* facts (which are problematic for other reasons, as we saw in chap. 2).

The position that denies that propositional facts are as fine-grained as propositions is incompatible with the claim that facts are referred to by that-clauses. The question is thus whether Künne's and Vendler's positions are coherent and, if they're not, how they can be made coherent. To be sure, there are philosophers who reject that facts are as fine-grained as propositions, such as Clark and Prior ("'All mammals are vertebrates' and 'All non-vertebrates are non-mammals' are different ... propositions, and express ... the same fact" [Prior, 1948, 62]), and who consequently reject the one-one thesis. But Clark's and Prior's positions are coherent in this respect because neither accepts that that-clauses are singular terms for facts: Prior rejects even that that-clauses are a syntactic unit; Clark rejects both disjunctive facts and facts about identity (Clark, 1976, 266). The positions of both Künne and Vendler are problematic in this respect.[16] Given the difference between their positions, I examine Vendler's position first and discuss Künne's point only later, and in a rather different guise than that which he originally intended, namely as an attempt to distinguish facts from true propositions.

Now is the time to show that anyone wanting to hold onto the claim that factive that-clauses refer to facts must accept that facts are as fine-grained as propositions. This is what both Peterson and Fine correctly hold (following Slote and Moore).

5.3   Fact Reference$_{Power!}$ Commits Us to Propositional Facts

We know now somewhat better what propositional facts are. They are ideal ('not in the world'), unstructured (or 'quasi-structured') entities that do not make up our empirical world. They are as fine-grained as the propositions they are paired off with (though they are not identical with them), and they have a problematic relationship with the objects they are said to be 'about' and metaphorically to 'contain'. Independently of how problematic they are, it can be shown fairly easily that propositional facts are the only kind of facts that can be accepted by someone who accepts that facts are the referent of factive that-clauses on the basis of Vendler's and Peterson's linguistic considerations.

If facts are referents of *any* factive that-clause, then for whatever proposition that can take the place of p in 'the proposition that p' there is a fact: 'the fact that p'. Two things follow.

The first is this: there are molecular facts of all kinds, disjunctive ones included. However, it can be shown that disjunctive facts cannot plausibly be of the worldly kind.[17] Consider the following case. Suppose we have a (true) disjunctive claim:

(1)   Either Cargle is wrong or Argle is a thief.

There are two disjuncts in this disjunction. Let us say that the first disjunct is true (poor Argle did not steal the colander) and the second disjunct is false. If this is the case, then there is only *one* fact relevant to the truth of (1), and this is the one fact that is relevant to 'Cargle is wrong' (whatever internal structure we take that fact to have). The question now is this. Consider claim (1) as a whole. Is there *also* a disjunctive fact involved in the truth of (1) *as a whole* or not?

As we've seen, worldly facts, first, are built up by constituents and, second, furnish the world; whoever accepts worldly *molecular* facts must find ways to handle them that comply with these two characteristics. Armstrong does it in this way: he argues that molecular conjunctive facts, in the simplest case, aren't facts additional to the atomic facts that are the conjuncts: conjunctive facts are mereological sums of atomic facts.[18] But what about disjunctive cases such as (1)? There are *no* compositional means that could enable us to get a disjunctive fact. Since there is just one fact (the one corresponding or relevant to the true disjunct, i.e., *Cargle's being wrong*), the only thing we can say is that the fact involved in the truth of (1) as a whole is identical with the fact involved in the truth of 'Cargle is wrong'. But this means that we have just *one* atomic fact after all, which is involved both in the truth of the disjunctive proposition (1) and also in the truth of one of its atomic disjuncts. So we have two true propositions, and just one fact involved. This is compatible with the empirical criterion, because on this criterion the facts in question would be empirically indistinguishable. Compositional facts, which obey this criterion, arise from the way in which their constituents are put together. The situation with two propositions—the disjunctive proposition and the true disjunct—but only one fact, corresponding to the true disjunct, is incompatible with the quasi-structural criterion, however, and also with the one-one thesis entailed by it, because according to that criterion facts are fully parasitic on the propositions they are paired off with and depend for their identity on their identity conditions. Therefore, if there are propositional facts fitting disjunctions—and according to the quasi-structural criterion there must be, since 'Cargle is wrong' and 'Cargle is wrong or Argle is a thief' are distinct propositions—then the corresponding facts must be different; different, and also not worldly, because they are ideal and as fine-grained as the propositions whose structure they inherit.[19] We have two facts: the fact that Cargle is wrong, and the fact that Cargle is wrong or Argle is a thief.

Now, obviously we can have a disjunctive that-clause after a factive verb such as 'know':

(2) 'But Dargle', said Bargle, 'what we know is that either Cargle is wrong or Argle is a thief'.

This means, on Peterson's view, that the object of (2) is the fact that either Cargle is wrong or Argle is a thief. The fact that either Cargle is wrong or Argle is a thief is as fine-grained as the proposition that either Cargle is wrong or Argle is a thief, and, like this proposition, is ideal.

The second thing that follows from accepting that, if *p* and *q* are different propositions, then the propositional fact that *p* and the propositional fact that *q* are also different, is that we find ourselves in the following scenario. Suppose

(1)   The proposition that Onassis married Jacqueline Kennedy ≠ the proposition that Onassis married the widow of the late president of the United States.

Then the following is the case:

(2)   The fact that Onassis married Jacqueline Kennedy ≠ the fact that Onassis married the widow of the late president of the United States.

According to Vendler and Peterson, factive that-clauses refer to facts, not to propositions. Suppose that

(3)   Tim knows that Onassis married Jacqueline Kennedy.

(4)   Tom knows that Onassis married the widow of the late president.

It should follow that Tim and Tom do not know the same fact. Surprisingly enough, Vendler *denies* that this is the case. If he is right, then the claim I just made that Fact Reference$_{Power!}$ entails that propositional facts are as fine-grained as propositions is wrong. I will show in what follows that it isn't wrong and that, rather, Vendler is wrong.

According to both Vendler and Peterson, it follows directly from Fact Reference$_{Power!}$ and from the circumstance that 'know' takes factive clauses that what we know are facts, not propositions: knowing that I have two X chromosomes quite literally means knowing a fact in the sense, says Vendler, that the direct object of my knowing attitude is an 'objective reality' (Vendler, 1972, 84). Consider again:

(3′)   Tim knows$_f$ <that Onassis married Jacqueline Kennedy>$_f$.

(4′)   Tom knows$_f$ <that Onassis married the widow of the late President>$_f$.

It is notorious that opacity problems surround the verb 'know'. Tim and Tom in (3′) and (4′) should *not* necessarily know the same fact. According to Vendler, however, they do:

> Without either of them knowing that Jacqueline Kennedy is that widow, [they] know the same fact, namely *whom Onassis married*. ... If [they] know the same fact, what they know ... will be the same thing. (Vendler, 1972, 115; cf. also 83, 117)

This cannot be the case, however, owing to a phenomenon amply noted at least since Frege (or at least since the rediscovery of Frege's puzzle by direct reference theorists such as Donnellan, Kaplan, and Kripke). If it were the case, the following inference would go through:

(5)   Oedipus knew that he married Jocasta.

(6)   Oedipus knew that he married his mother.

But (6) does not follow from (5), unless we interpolate an extra claim, that is

(5.1)   Oedipus knew that Jocasta was his mother.

Since (5.1) isn't true, (6) does not follow from (5); the that-clauses in (5) and (6) thus cannot refer to the same fact and, by the same reasoning, Tim and Tom do not know the same thing in (3′) and (4′), contrary to Vendler's claim. So we are forced either to abandon Fact Reference$_{Power!}$— the thesis that that-clauses following 'know', being factive, refer to facts—or else to assume that facts are at least as fine-grained as propositions. Both block the inference from (5) to (6).

It might be objected that Vendler could still be right, and interestingly so, since on *his* understanding of 'know', Oedipus *did* know that he married his mother.[20] The problem with this is that it turns Vendler's 'know' into a theory-laden term that is at odds with the most common use of 'know': it's this latter common use that requires (5.1) for the inference from (5) to (6) to go through, and which has also given us Greek tragedies. Note that this is no idiosyncratic characteristic of 'know'; it extends to other factive predicates such as 'is a surprise'. As Fine points out,

> But when it comes to truths [propositional facts], ordinary usage seems to favour the quasi-structural criterion. Thus we acknowledge that someone may be surprised at the truth of Gödel's Incompleteness Theorem yet not at some simple arithmetical truth, even though both truths necessarily obtain. (Fine, 1982, 59)

Notice that by 'truth' Fine means here a propositional fact, which he takes to be different from a true proposition. I shall come back to Fine's position in section 5.4.5. There are two problems here. First of all, Vendler does not engage in any serious debate as to what facts are and offers no serious discussion of the criteria of identity that facts should satisfy to be what he calls "an objective reality," or of what this means for the view of language and reality he defends. Second, Vendler seems to think that he is looking purely at how *know* works in language, and that his conclusion rests *solely* on the basis of that inspection. But this cannot be true, and Vendler cannot maintain—as he seems to want to—that the understanding he proposes is the *only* possible understanding of 'know' grounded in natural language, since it is clear that his understanding stems not from purely linguistic considerations about natural language (or even from pragmatic ones) but from a theoretical position on what knowledge is. In this way, Vendler's 'know' becomes part and parcel of a technical language—one that slips in a specific theoretical view of facts as well, as if we were looking the other way. Again, Fine notices that a departure from the quasi-structural criterion of identity of facts might be required in certain philosophical contexts that favor the empirical criterion of necessary coexistence, but, he clarifies:

> If I am right about ordinary usage, then this use of 'fact' is somewhat technical. Thus we have here a case in which a new class of entities is introduced in order to meet a certain theoretical demand—in this case, from ontological inquiry. (Fine, 1982, 60)

In this sense, facts are a philosopher's invention. Now, operating with a theoretical language under a technical understanding of its terms is a perfectly legitimate enterprise, but it is incompatible with Vendler's general strategy of taking language at face value. So I do not see on what methodological grounds he can push this point. (Besides, who wants *Oedipus the King* to be a boring tragedy?)

And so I conclude that Vendler's position is incoherent. It is not surprising, then, that Peterson does not take up Vendler's position in his defense of Fact Reference*Power!*, as we shall see in the next chapter.

To sum up: in this section we have seen arguments for the claim that that-clauses require propositional facts. In the previous section, we saw that if one accepts the propositional view of facts as ideal entities (PF1) and so also the quasi-structural criterion (related to PF4), then one is stuck with the one-one thesis: with each true proposition a fact is paired off; and if one has the one-one thesis, then propositional facts are as fine-grained as propositions (PF5, and related to PF2). The disjunction argument I give in this section shows that compositional facts cannot be disjunctive, and that if you want disjunctive facts you have to accept propositional ones. Since Fact Reference*Power!* requires disjunctive facts, the disjunction argument may be applied to show that the kind of fact that Fact Reference*Power!* requires must be propositional facts, in particular, facts that are as fine-grained as propositions.

The position that facts are as fine-grained as propositions is thus *entailed* by Fact Reference*Power!*. This suffices to establish the conclusion that defending facts on the basis of linguistic claims such as Fact Reference*Power!* entails defending propositional facts, that is, accepting items that are parasitic on propositions. Such facts are as ideal as propositions, as fine-grained as propositions, and as much 'about objects' (PF3) as propositions are. And the question still stands: are there good reasons to accept propositional facts as entities different from true propositions? As I argue below, there aren't. Propositional facts collapse into true propositions.[21]

5.4   The Collapse of Propositional Facts into True Propositions

Fine claims:

It has been suggested (by Ducasse..., Carnap ... and others) that facts are merely true propositions. ... There are, however, compelling arguments against the proposed identification. (Fine, 1982, 46)

I argue here that these compelling arguments fail.[22]

5.4.1   First Attempt

A first attempt to show that (propositional) facts are not identical with true propositions relies on an application of Leibniz's principle of the indiscernibility of identicals. The attempt originates with Moore (1953, 308; see also Sprigge, 1970, 83; Slote, 1974, 99; Fine, 1982, 46–47). In general, reasoning according to this principle means finding a property φ that holds for an x (in this case: true propositions) but not for a y (in this case: facts), from which we conclude that $x \neq y$. In other words, the reasoning goes like this: if something holds of true propositions that does not hold of facts, then true propositions and facts are different things. And now here's that something, namely, our φ—or so the argument goes. Let's call it 'Moore's φ'.

Moore's φ   True propositions have a false counterpart, namely, false propositions. False propositions have the same ontological status as true ones; that is, they *are* as much as true propositions *are*: it is not that false propositions are lesser beings with respect to true ones. Nothing of this kind holds of facts.[23]

So, the argument goes, consider the proposition p that Argle bought the colander and the fact f that Argle bought the colander. If Argle had not bought the colander, p would be in the universe but f would not.

As Richard Cartwright has argued, this first attempt is ineffective (Cartwright, 1987, 77–79; Künne, 2003, 10). On one reading, it does not deliver what it promises; on another reading, it is question begging (for a critical discussion of the general form of such arguments, see Varzi, 2002, 2005).

One can read the argument as question begging because it presupposes what it sets out to prove: we can conclude $f \neq p$ just in case we presuppose $f \neq p$. To see this, consider the following.

(Scenario 0)   Argle bought the colander. The proposition that Argle bought the colander is true. The proposition that Argle bought the colander is present in the universe.

(A)   If Argle had *not* bought the colander, the proposition that Argle bought the colander would be present in the universe, but the fact that Argle bought the colander would not.

(B)   Therefore (?) (in Scenario (0)), the fact that Argle bought the colander is not identical with the true proposition that Argle bought the colander.

On scenario (0), (A) holds, but on its basis we cannot conclude to (B), since (A) holds also in case facts are identical with true propositions. If the fact that Argle bought the colander *is* identical with the true proposition that Argle bought the colander, then (A) holds: had Argle not bought the colander, the proposition that Argle bought the colander would be present in the universe, and the fact that Argle stole the colander would not. But (B) does not follow, that is, it does not follow that the fact and the true proposition in question are not identical. To see this, consider: if Argle had *not* bought the colander, there would be no *true* proposition in the universe identical with the fact that Argle bought the colander. There would be a proposition but it would be false, and so there would be no fact. Yet (B) would not follow. Step (B) follows from (A) *just in case* we assume what we want to prove, namely that facts are not identical with true propositions. Thus the first attempt rests on a fallacious argument.

5.4.2 Second Attempt

The second attempt, reviewed in and endorsed by Wolfgang Künne in his marvelous *Conceptions of Truth*, is again based on Leibniz's principle, but in this case the relevant property by virtue of which facts are taken to be different from true propositions is their degree of granularity (Künne, 2003, 11–12). Facts, says Künne, are less finely individuated than propositions, and therefore cannot be identified with true propositions (this is Künne's φ, say). As an argument to show that true propositions and facts are different entities, this second attempt is question begging just as the first attempt was: to claim that two kinds of entity are different on the basis of a property φ, you must already assume that there *are* two kinds of entities (facts and true propositions) rather than one (true propositions). But this argument is problematic also for another reason. As we saw in the previous section, on the view according to which facts are more coarse-grained than propositions, facts obey the empirical identity criterion. This view is not compatible with the claim that all factive that-clauses refer to facts, since this claim obeys the alternative quasi-structural criterion. From a purely linguistic point of view, 'that' can precede *any p*. If we now want to make exceptions to the quasi-structural criterion—if we want to claim that restrictions must hold according to which, for instance, 'that p' and 'that s' do not name different facts but the same fact, although p and s express different propositions—then good grounds must be given. If we don't give any good grounds for the difference, then the way to an identification of facts and true propositions is arbitrarily blocked—blocked in an ad hoc way. As far as I can see, Künne gives no such grounds, at least not really. It might seem that he does, however, so the point requires some attention. It is important to keep in mind that, as in Vendler's case, Künne cannot *both* adhere to Fact Reference$_{Power!}$ *and* hold that propositional facts are more coarse-grained than propositions. One of the two claims must be abandoned.

The specific restrictions Künne puts on propositional facts to ensure that they are more coarse-grained than propositions arise from his discussion of attempts at blocking the Slingshot. 'The Slingshot' is the name given to a famous argument, best known from Davidson (1969), to the effect that if true propositions correspond to facts, then there is just one fact: the so-called 'Great Fact'. Note that the Slingshot argument does not force the collapse of facts into true propositions, but rather the collapse of facts into each other. Given the way the argument works, however, in the course of discussing it Künne is led to be more specific about which restrictions on granularity he thinks one should put on facts. One element of this discussion is particularly important for us. As we shall see, accepting that facts are as fine-grained as propositions gives a straightforward way to block the argument, so anyone who accepts the one-one thesis is immune to the Slingshot. Künne does not adhere to the one-one thesis, nor is he even a correspondentist about truth. Nevertheless, he accepts facts, he accepts propositions, he denies that facts are true propositions, and he accepts that some that-clauses refer to facts and other that-clauses refer to propositions. I discuss this position at length because Künne's treatment of it goes further than other correspondentist literature on this point (e.g., Searle, see n. 27 below); it is very explicit about its assumptions, and this enables us to make the point in the most clear and useful way (see the end of this section). As we saw, Künne claims that, in the course of a direct attempt to make a convincing case for distinguishing true propositions from facts, facts are more coarse-grained than propositions. Then, when discussing the Slingshot, he describes a plausible correspondentist way out that he himself, were he a correspondentist (though he is not), would approve of: imposing certain restrictions of the granularity of facts while not allowing a fact for each and every proposition. This position, I argue, is indefensible. My conclusion—which holds regardless of whether one is a correspondentist about truth—is that the second attempt to avoid the identification of true propositions with propositional facts on the basis of their difference in granularity fails.

Let's have a quick look at the Slingshot argument. Fundamental to it are certain assumptions about definite descriptions. Once these and other assumptions are in place, one is forced to accept the collapse of different facts into one, so that in the end one is left with just one fact. Mulligan and Correia present the following reconstruction of the argument:

Let 's' and 't' be two true sentences, consider the sentences of following list, and assume they all correspond to facts:

(a) s
(b) $\iota x[x = \text{Socrates and } s] = \iota x[x = \text{Socrates}]$
(c) $\iota x[x = \text{Socrates and } t] = \iota x[x = \text{Socrates}]$
(d) t

Then under certain assumptions about definite descriptions, we can prove that these four sentences correspond to the same fact. So under these assumptions, we can draw the following general conclusion: any two true sentences 'u' and 'v' correspond to the same fact if they correspond to facts at all.

The assumptions are the following:

A. Sentences 'u' and 'v' correspond to the same fact (if they correspond to facts at all) if 'u' and 'v' are logically equivalent;

B. Sentences 'u' and 'v' correspond to the same fact (if they correspond to facts at all) if 'u' can be obtained from 'v' by replacing a definite description by another, co-referential definite description;

C. '$\iota x[x = \text{Socrates and } u] = \iota x[x = \text{Socrates}]$' is logically equivalent to 'u';

D. If sentences 'u' and 'v' are both true, then '$\iota x[x = \text{Socrates and } u]$' and '$\iota x[x = \text{Socrates and } v]$' are co-referential.

(Here we understand 'a' and 'b' are co-referential' as meaning that '$a = b$' is true.) (Mulligan and Correia, 2008)

As Mulligan and Correia (2008) remark, to block the Slingshot, one can reject one or more among A, B, C, and D. Künne chooses (or better, advises the correspondentist) to reject B: he blocks substitution of *some* coreferential definite descriptions. The effect is that

(1)   The fact that Leah's husband is very fond of Joseph ≠ the fact that Rachel's husband is very fond of Joseph

but

(2)   The fact that George Eliot wrote *Middlemarch* = The fact that Mary Ann Evans wrote *Middlemarch*.

(3)   The fact that George Henry Lewes is Mary Ann Evans's lover = The fact that George Henry Lewes is George Eliot's lover.[24]

One needn't face this situation in order to block the Slingshot. One could just as well argue that all those facts are different *because* all the propositions involved are different (this would be a very strong take on rejecting A). If that were assumed, this would follow:

(2′)   The fact that George Eliot wrote *Middlemarch* ≠ The fact that Mary Ann Evans wrote *Middlemarch*.

(3′)   The fact that George Henry Lewes is Mary Ann Evans's lover ≠ The fact that George Henry Lewes is George Eliot's lover.

What are the reasons for rejecting the alternative situation just sketched? Why would someone, for having (1), choose to reject *B* in favor of (a version of) A, and prefer (2) to (2′) and (3) to (3′)? In support of (1) Künne says, as part of his correspondentist suggestion, that the two subpropositions "intuitively ... do not state the same fact" (Künne, 2003, 140). In support of (2) he says that it "is in agreement with our everyday use of 'fact'" (ibid., n. 158). Arguably, he would say the same about (3).

   These reasons are mutually incompatible. It can be derived from (1)–(3) that the identity criterion that Künne suggests to accept for facts is the empirical criterion of *necessary coexistence*, meaning by this that, necessarily, one fact exists (or obtains) just in case the other does (see pp. 167–168 above). This is confirmed by the following:

Generally, taking 'a' and 'b' to be place-holders for atomic singular terms, if a is identical with b then the state of affairs that Fa is the same as the state of affairs that Fb. (Künne, 2003, 253)

But this is awkward. The explanation that seems plausible to Künne for *why* Fa and Fb are the same fact if 'a' and 'b' are coreferential singular terms, is that Fa and Fb are *composed* of the same constituents arranged in the same way. The criterion of fact identity that goes with this view is necessary coexistence. This criterion, as we have seen, is said to be an 'empirical' one because the reasoning supporting it is empirical: if facts *x* and *y* are empirically indistinguishable, then they are one and the same fact.[25] It is on the basis of this criterion that (1), (2), and (3) above hold. But the empirical criterion of identity is not appropriate for the conception of propositional facts that is apparently consistent both with our everyday use of 'fact' and with Vendler-like semantic analyses of that-clauses, for on that conception facts are ideal entities: the question of whether they are empirically indistinguishable or not is nonsense. As we saw while discussing Vendler's take on 'know', it is the quasi-structural criterion of facts and *not* the empirical identity criterion that best squares both with ordinary use and with the propositional facts that our ordinary use suggests.[26] Once again:

> But when it comes to truths [propositional facts], ordinary usage seems to favour the structural criterion. Thus we acknowledge that someone may be surprised at the truth of Gödel's Incompleteness Theorem yet not at some simple arithmetical truth, even though both truths necessarily obtain. (Fine, 1982, 59)

"Ordinary usage" and everyday use of 'fact' stand here for anything revealed by the analysis of the use of the word 'fact' in ordinary language: this is the use that we are scrutinizing in these pages and also the one that Künne, apparently, associates with the expression. I conclude that Künne (or the 'Künne correspondentist'), and anyone in his position, must choose between

(a) keeping the claim that some (i.e., factive) that-clauses refer to facts and accepting (extremely fine-grained) propositional facts (compatible with the strong version of option A for blocking the Slingshot);

and

(b) rejecting the claim that some (i.e., factive) that-clauses refer to facts, and accepting some kind of (more coarse-grained) 'empirical' facts (compatible with the anti-Slingshot correspondentist option B in some version).

Option (a) deprives Künne of his favorite argument to distinguish true propositions from facts, namely, the difference in their granularity. Option (b) deprives him of arguments for acknowledging facts based on the reference of that-clauses. Defending (a) basically entails appealing to how that-clauses function in language, leaving linguistic analysis to decide on its own whether true propositions and facts are two different kinds of entities. Defending (b), and at the same time accepting propositions and holding that facts are more coarse-grained than propositions, means defending facts on other counts, for example, that they are needed to do metaphysical work that cannot be done by propositions (which requires developing an account of what kind of entities such facts are, if they are neither propositional nor compositional). Now, (b) does not seem viable for Künne especially because abandoning the referential role of that-clauses would deprive him of an important argument for *propositions* that—out of the advice to the correspondentist—are much more important entities to him than facts, and because facts don't do any metaphysical work on his account. Nevertheless, Künne defends (b). To do so is legitimate, of course, but it cannot be done without arguments. These arguments are difficult to find, though they're crucially important for one who holds, like Künne, that the Sling-shot can be blocked by assuming the following principles:

No Additional Object   Two assertoric utterances state the same fact only if there is no object that is referred to in only one of them.

No Additional Property   Two assertoric utterances state the same fact only if there is no property that is introduced in only one of them.

A legitimate question arises here: are there any good grounds for assuming these principles other than a desire to block the Slingshot? One cannot simply restate the point by saying things such as:

Two definite descriptions which apply to the same object are not intersubstitutable *salvo facto* if one of them introduces a property (e.g. being a husband) into discourse which is not introduced by the other. (Künne, 2003, 140)

What we need to know is *why* this should be the case. These principles can be argued for only on the basis of further arguments. As mentioned, the main reason Künne suggests that one could offer in favor of the principles above is that in some cases two assertoric utterances "intuitively ... do not state the same fact."[27] But it is not enough merely to say this, because work-ing with the empirical conception of facts means working with a theoreti-cal posit, a philosopher's invention. 'Intuitions' cannot stand in for theoretical inquiry, since intuitions are often in conflict either with them-selves or with theoretical inquiry.[28] If our use of 'fact' is technical, then "a new class of entities is introduced in order to meet a certain theoretical demand—in this case, from ontological inquiry" (Fine, 1982, 60). What ontological inquiry entitles us here to accept those principles? Künne's sug-gestion does not go so far as to provide an ontological inquiry about facts, nor are such inquiries generally available for the kind of facts he seems to have sympathy for himself, that is, the propositional ones. From this we must conclude that we are not entitled to accept the principles above, and that Künne's suggested way out is ad hoc. An additional problem in this respect is not only that no good grounds have been given for the difference in granularity that Künne proposes to stipulate between propositions and facts, but that no good reasons have been given either for the *degree* of that difference in granularity: the degree is just enough to block the Slingshot. Instead, to block the Slingshot by rejecting A in its strongest version is to block it on independent and more general grounds: since propositional facts obey a quasi-structural criterion of identity, they depend for their identity (and thus for their granularity) strictly on the identity (and thus granularity) of the propositions they are paired off with. But then the question still stands: what reasons do we have to accept propositional facts as different from true propositions?

If we reject Künne's suggested way out from the Slingshot because the difference in granularity between facts and true propositions is ungrounded, then, in doing so, we are also rejecting his main argument for assuming a difference between facts and true propositions. This now leaves us where we started, for the option left is (a), that is, to hold on to the claim that some (i.e., factive) that-clauses refer to facts and to accept (extremely fine-grained) propositional facts. The restriction on granularity vanishes, and I conclude that this second attempt at distinguishing propositional facts from true propositions is a failure just as the first was. In fact, Künne—as far as his own acceptance of facts in the framework of *Conceptions of Truth* is concerned—should simply not acknowledge propositional facts. Note that this, for him, would be no debacle at all, but rather an attractive position: since, on Künne's conception, facts do no job anyway, he does not need them. This would be compatible with having all that-clauses refer to propositions, which is a plausible position (*if* one is able to show that that-clauses are singular terms by rejecting my argument in chap. 4).

It does not follow from the above that propositional facts cannot exist as different from true propositions. Neither does it follow that this second attempt is useless; quite the contrary. What we know from it is that *if* good reasons for assuming *propositional* facts exist, *then* propositional facts block the Slingshot because they are extremely fine-grained. And we know too that if we find good reasons to block the Slingshot by accepting coarse(r)-grained facts, then we can do so only at the price of renouncing the claim that factive that-clauses refer to facts.

The upshot of all this is that we have not yet seen any good reasons for allowing propositional facts in our ontology alongside propositions, and we still need such good reasons. The good reasons I am speaking about can be found only by considering the metaphysically explanatory *roles* facts can play once they are assumed in our catalog of the world (I come back to this point in my general conclusion at the end of the book). One problem with this is that propositional facts seem to do no work at all, except for allegedly serving as the referent of that-clauses or in similar linguistic roles. It seems to me very dubious that we should consider such roles important in the absence of any other reason to assume facts. But suppose we do think that this is important. Then the whole issue depends on whether Peterson's Fact Reference$_{Power!}$ alone can establish that propositional facts are different from true propositions.

But before we explore this in the next chapter, are we sure that propositional facts do not play any philosophical role other than a parasitic one on the use of language? Some insist that propositional facts have a role in causation. This suggests a third attempt to distinguish propositional facts from true propositions.

5.4.3   Third Attempt

The third attempt is due to an important variant of the propositional view. For Searle, who like Künne places restrictions on granularity to block the Slingshot, facts can have causal effects (Searle, 1998, 389). Searle's is an important position, because the role of propositional facts in causality seems to be the only metaphysically explanatory role that happens to be given by philosophers to propositional facts. Nevertheless, as Künne and Strawson have convincingly argued, the arguments given by defenders of this position do not support the view that facts are causally efficacious. As above, we could again describe this attempt as being based on Leibniz's principle. In this case, the relevant property thanks to which facts should be different from true propositions is their causal powers (Searle's φ, say). Now, as such, this position is unappealing to many philosophers to begin with since propositional facts are ideal and, by a considerably large consensus, neither causes nor effects are ever ideal.[29] It is important to note, however, that the reason philosophers such as Searle favor facts as the kind of items that can stand in causal relations is not so much a reason related to metaphysical considerations about real or ideal status as it is a reason internal to language. Why, according to Searle, should we take facts to be causally efficacious? Because we appropriately use sentences such as

(1)   The fact that Napoleon recognized the danger to his left flank, caused him to move his troops forward.

Künne observes that a sentence like (1) shows not that facts are causally efficacious, but only that they can be causally *explanatory* (Künne, 2003, 144; cf. P. F. Strawson, 1998, 404). That facts can be causally explanatory means that in certain cases the object that facts are (supposedly) 'about' (still in the unclear sense of 'about' we saw above, in keeping with our characteristic PF3 in section 2 above) itself stands in causal relations. In a case like (1),

what is causally efficacious … is not the fact … but rather the event which is reported by that statement: the event of Napoleon's recognizing the danger to his left flank at a certain location on a certain date. What is causally efficacious belongs to the natural order of datables and locatables, but the explanans in an explanation (even if it is a causal explanation) does not belong to this order. ... Facts are indeed, like propositions and unlike events, abstract entities. (Künne, 2003, 144; note that we have used 'ideal' for what Künne calls 'abstract')

However, although Künne agrees with Strawson here, there is an important difference in their understandings of what facts are. Strawson sides with a position we mentioned already endorsed by the early Moore, Slote, and Fine: facts are truths, that is, the being true of a proposition (Strawson, 1998, 404). Whoever endorses this view of facts, as we saw, sees facts as fine-grained as propositions, and has a plausible account of their aboutness as being parasitic on the aboutness of the propositions they fit. This enables one to have a coherent position on the reference of that-clauses and easily to block the Slingshot, but at a price, namely, that of abandoning a distinct category of facts as different from either propositions or (their) qualities.[30] And so the question remains: why should we take facts and not true propositions to play the explanatory role in causal claims, and admit facts along-side true propositions in our ontology? On what grounds should we take facts rather than true propositions to be causally explanatory? The observation made by Strawson and Künne to the effect that facts cannot be causally efficacious does not necessarily lead to the conclusion that *facts* are causally explanatory. It can lead just as well to the conclusion that *true propositions* are causally explanatory, namely on account of being about objects that are causally efficacious. There must be some reason why Strawson and Künne think that this explanatory role cannot be taken up by true propositions, but must be taken up by facts instead. What is this reason? I guess that it's simply that, in (1), the expression 'the fact that *p*' occurs. Indeed, it seems that their reasons consist in the following: it is appropriate to speak like this:

(1)   The fact that Napoleon recognized the danger to his left flank, caused him to move his troops forward;

while it is *in*appropriate to speak like this:

(2)   The true proposition that Napoleon recognized the danger to his left flank, caused him to move his troops forward.

But now, if *this* is the counterargument for why propositional facts and not propositions are the relata of explanation—if the mere appearance of the words 'the fact that' in language should decide the issue—then we need to consider this counterargument as a fourth attempt to distinguish true propositions from facts.

5.4.4 Fourth Attempt

A fourth attempt to avoid the collapse is discussed by Künne (who, how-ever, is not much convinced by it; Künne, 2003, 11). This attempt commits what Russell called the *fallacy of verbalism*, "the fallacy that consists in mis-taking the properties of words [or beliefs] for the properties of things" (Russell, 1923, 62).

Künne observes that certain forms of speech are improper if 'fact' and 'true proposition' are substituted for one another. Consider, he says, the following pairs (Künne, 2003, 10):

(1a)   True propositions are true.
(1b)   *Facts are true.

(2a)   The Pythagorean theorem is true.
(2b)   *The Pythagorean theorem is a fact.

(3a)   The victory of the Labour Party is a fact.
(3b)   *The victory of the Labour Party is a true proposition.

If facts are nothing but true propositions, so goes the argument, why is that (1a) is trivial while (1b) has an awkward ring, (2a) makes sense while (2b) does not, and (3a) is significant while (3b) is nonsense?

Note first of all that, although these are examples of three different kinds, none of which involves that-clauses, two of them (2b and 3a) involve apparently predicative uses of 'is a fact' and one (1b) involves the use of 'facts' in subject position. I already mentioned case (3a–b) and the use of 'is a fact' relevant to (2b) in chapter 4, sections 4.1.1 and 4.3. What is relevant at the moment is whether these examples give us reasons to reject the iden-tification of true propositions with facts. I argue that they don't.

First, Künne seems to take for granted the following:

(i)   that 'fact(s)' in everyday language has 'natural' reference to what he, as a professional philosopher, takes to be facts: obtaining states of affairs; and (ii)   that the predication *ad* (3a) is a substantial predication in which 'is a fact' is correctly applied to 'the victory of the Labour Party', which presup-poses that 'the victory of the Labour Party' refers to an object that can be called 'a fact'.

The reasoning at (ii) is far from convincing. First of all, according to Künne, who here follows Vendler, 'the victory of the Labour Party' does not necessarily refer to a fact: 'the victory of the Labour Party' is ambigu-ous between an event and a fact, like 'the death of Caesar'. Now, as I have shown in chapter 4, the reason (3a) works is not because it is a substantial predication—that is, a predication in which 'is a fact' is predicated of 'the victory of the Labour Party' just as 'is a hedgehog' is predicated of Hargle. The reason (3a) works is that victories are events, and that in these cases, as we saw in section 5.4.3, 'is a fact' means something like 'has happened' or 'occurred' or 'takes place', which is what we say of events. We could eventually employ this very line of argument to explain why, on one reading, (2b) 'The Pythagorean theorem is a fact' does not make sense: theorems don't occur because they are not events. But on another reading, however, a reading we also saw in chapter 4, section 4.1.1, such expressions are perfectly fine in everyday language, namely when 'is a fact' means for instance 'has been proved, approved, ratified' ('there is no way back'): the Pythagorean theorem can very well be a fact in that sense, just like Berlusconi's immunity law and the Georgia evolution lawsuit are (see p. 154).

As to (1a–b):

(1a)   True propositions are true.

(1b)   *Facts are true.

I don't know why it is that (1a) is trivial while (1b) has an awkward ring. But, philosophically speaking, I wonder what we could ever make of such awkwardness, supposing that (1b) does indeed sound awkward. It does not seem to be an explanation to say that the awkwardness arises because facts are not true propositions. There are several possible reasons for the awkwardness, not all of them necessarily to the advantage of the position Künne defends. The question we should ask, however, is this: what is the rule according to which (1b) should *not* have an awkward ring? (As we know, things can get pretty complicated whenever the predicate 'true' is involved, but never mind this for now.) I venture that the rule we're looking for must be something like:

Awkward Ring Rule Phrases denoting the same objects must be interchangeable in all contexts while yielding the same linguistic effects.[31]

This strikes me as obviously wrong. Consider this counterexample:

(4a)   Obtaining states of affairs are obtaining.

(4b)   *Facts are obtaining.

For Künne, facts are obtaining states of affairs (Künne, 2003, 253). If the Awkward Ring Rule were true, then 'obtaining states of affairs' and 'facts' would be substitutable in all contexts yielding the same linguistic effects. But they are not. Sentences (4a) and (4b) are a perfect parallel of (1a) and

(1b). Do (4a) and (4b) show that facts are not obtaining states of affairs? No, they do not. I say that the Awkward Ring Rule is entirely arbitrary.

The fourth attempt is also a failure.

5.4.5   Fifth Attempt

A fifth attempt to avoid the collapse of propositional facts into true propositions is Slote's and Fine's construal of propositional facts as *truths* (inspired by Moore, 1953, 261). When Moore, Slote, and Fine maintain that a propositional fact is the same as a truth, they do not mean a truth in the sense of a true proposition, but in the sense of a *proposition's being true* (Slote, 1974, 98–99; Fine, 1982, 52). This is the most interesting attempt to avoid the collapse of propositions into propositional facts, because at the same time it allows one to hold that factive that-clauses refer to facts and that nonfactive that-clauses refer to propositions. From a *methodological* point of view, this represents the strongest possible position on propositional facts—but, significantly, from the point of view of *content*, it is the weakest possible position. I will argue that it is, like the other attempts, ineffective to establish that one should assume a category of propositional facts alongside that of propositions.

Propositional facts in the sense of truths—a sense one might call 'Pickwickian', were we in McTaggart's and Broad's times—clearly obey PF1–PF5. If propositional facts are Fine's truths, as we saw above (see sec. 5.3 above), then PF3 is not much of a problem, since the aboutness of facts is fully parasitic on that of propositions. As we saw, accounting for the 'aboutness' of facts in other theories of propositional facts is problematic. But not so for propositional facts in this sense (i.e., the sense in which, for all true p, the fact that p is identical with the being true of p): truths obey PF3 by being about the objects that p is about, and not about p itself.

But this view is not unproblematic from other points of view. If one accepts that propositional facts are truths, then one accepts that there are only facts of the form *p's being true* (or *a is F's being true*). One problem with a view of this kind is that it has implications for the notion of truth that are unacceptable for even the weakest correspondence or truthmaker theorist. Most defenders of Fact Reference$_{Power!}$ would be bothered by that, but not all: philosophers who accept propositional facts do not normally do so in order to make them play truthmaker roles (see, e.g., Künne, 2003, 145; exception: Searle, 1995, 202). The question is rather whether those for whom the view of facts as truths is acceptable aren't *also* those who, like Künne, could actually dispense with facts altogether.

But if the aim is to keep propositional facts apart from true propositions, as is the aim we're discussing here, then the biggest problem with this view of propositional facts as truths is something else. Barring verbal differences, this view *entails* that there are no facts as a separate category of entities alongside true propositions in the catalog of the world (they are either true propositions or properties); alternatively, it entails that they are a special kind of compositional fact. Let's have a look at this. Propositional facts as truths are conceived in this way:

> There will be a simple operation C of concretization, that applies to a property P and an individual x had by P to yield a new object C (P, x), the P-ness of x. The facts will then result from applying this operation to the property of truth and a proposition. (Fine, 1982, 52)

Taking facts to be truths in the sense of the being true (P) of a proposition (x) (obtained from propositions by 'concretization') can mean one of two things. First, it might mean that facts as truths are reduced to a special subset of other items, that is, properties, and that therefore there are no facts alongside true propositions as a special category of items: the property of truth would do. This meaning of 'the truth of proposition x' seems consistent with what Fine says here:

> Truths are derived from true propositions, not identical to them; the truth of a proposition is no more a true proposition than the wisdom of a man is a wise man. (Fine, 1982, 52)[32]

The second thing one might mean when saying that facts are truths in the sense indicated is that truths are a special kind of compositional fact, namely those of the form *the being true of p* (Fine, 1982, 65). By the very same reasoning according to which the being cute of Hargle is not a property of hers but rather a special reticulation of an object and a property, facts in this sense are compositional, and to them, again, all the problems we saw in part 1 apply. Moreover, if we now accept that that-clauses refer to facts as truths in this compositional sense, then the question becomes whether the object we are referring to is not, in fact, exactly the same as a true proposition, when a true proposition is taken to be a thick particular in Armstrong's sense (though an *ideal* thick particular). I contend that truths in this compositional sense are identical to true propositions. So, as to the fifth attempt, I conclude that, regardless of whether propositional facts are truths in Fine's sense, they are not a different category of entities: they are reducible either to properties or to a subspecies of compositional facts.

Let's take stock. At this point we have seen that Fact Reference*Power*, namely the thesis that factive that-clauses refer to facts and nonfactive that-clauses refer to propositions, requires (that the facts to which factive that-clauses refer are) *propositional facts*. We saw that facts of this kind are ideal objects, which are as fine-grained as propositions and which are fully parasitic on propositions for their individuation, for their composition (if they are composed at all), and for their relation to the objects they 'talk about'. This prompted the question of whether propositional facts genuinely differ from propositions or do so only nominally. We have reviewed five attempts to support the claim that there are both propositional facts and propositions, and all of these, far from being compelling, are unsuccessful. There is one thing left to see in a final attempt to distinguish propositional facts from propositions. One might argue that language itself, that is, the working of that-clauses, compels us after all to accept propositional facts and propositions as two categories of entities. It is on the basis of such findings, after all, that Peterson, relying on Vendler and the Kiparkys, sets up what we have called Fact Reference*Power*. I shall show in the following chapter, however, that this final attempt is as unsuccessful as the others.

The sixth attempt is somewhat different from the other five, although they are two sides of the same coin. So far the question has been whether— supposing that there is reference from that-clauses to objects x (facts) and y (propositions), and taking into account the constraints put on x by the referential role of that-clauses—we have two (kinds of) objects and not just one. We have tried to answer this question by examining the kind of x and y from a metaphysical point of view. Now the question will be whether linguistic evidence *alone* is able to detect an appreciable difference between the referent of a factive that-clause and the referent of a nonfactive that-clause and, if so, whether the linguistic data for this difference are strong enough to conclude that the referent of a factive that-clause and the referent of a nonfactive that-clause belong to two different categories (propositional facts and propositions), or even whether they might *require* this. As we shall see, the outcome is negative: linguistic evidence alone does not establish that propositional facts must be accepted alongside (true) propositions.

6 A Fallback Position (2)

In the previous two chapters, I have critically investigated the claim that we have good reasons to accept facts on the basis of an argument I have called the argument for facts from nominal reference. In chapter 4, I showed that the argument is to be rejected because the first as well as the third of its three conjuncts are to be rejected. The first conjunct is the claim, briefly put, that natural language has the means to successfully refer to facts in virtue of being capable of expressing truths displaying genuine quantification over facts: this claim is to be rejected because the necessary condition for it, namely that that-clauses are referential parts of speech, does not hold (as we have seen, the argument is much more complicated, but it comes down to what I have just said). I have also shown that this conclusion also affects the third conjunct, namely the claim that (genuine) quantification over facts in natural language is ineliminable, since this claim supposes—wrongly, as I have argued—that we *do* appropriately quantify on facts in natural language. In chapter 5, I explored a fallback position and showed that even if that-clauses were referential parts of speech, and if we thus assumed, per absurdum, that the first conjunct of the argument holds, that is, that we have (successful) reference to facts in natural language, the facts to which there would be reference by means of that-clauses could only be so-called *propositional facts*, and not the compositional facts we saw in the first part of this book. I have reconstructed the notion of propositional facts as the notion of entities that are not in the world, not 'about' something, unstructured, and as fine-grained as propositions, though (allegedly) not identical to propositions. I have argued that propositional facts play no metaphysical role, and that we have no good reason to accept them as entities alongside (true) propositions. This conclusion comes down to rejecting the second conjunct of the argument from nominal reference, namely the claim that we have (good) identity conditions for facts as entities in their own right: we don't have appropriate identity conditions for propositional facts, since they collapse into (true) propositions. I reviewed five arguments to avoid this collapse and rejected them all. The conclusion is therefore that even if there is, per absurdum, reference to propositional facts via that-clauses (and thus even if the first and the third conjuncts hold), the argument from nominal reference is to be rejected because its second conjunct is to be rejected: there are no acceptable identity conditions for propositional facts such that we can avoid their collapsing into true propositions.

There is one last cluster of arguments left to review that might be invoked to block the collapse of propositional facts into propositions. I called this cluster the sixth attempt (the final one) to avoid the collapse between propositional facts and propositions. The nature of this sixth attempt is somewhat different from the other five, although the two clusters are two sides of the same coin. In the previous chapter the question has been the following: suppose there is reference from that-clauses to objects x (facts) and y (propositions), and suppose we take into account the constraints put on x by the referential role of that-clauses: do we have *two* (categories of) objects x and y, or just one? In chapter 5 we tried to answer this question by examining what kind of objects x and y are from a metaphysical point of view, assuming the following thesis about the reference of that-clauses holds:

Fact Reference$_{Power!}$ Factive that-clauses refer to facts whereas nonfactive that-clauses refer to propositions.

In the present chapter the question will be whether linguistic evidence *alone* is able to detect an appreciable difference between the referent of a factive that-clause and the referent of a nonfactive that-clause and, if so, whether the linguistic data for this difference are strong enough to conclude that the referent of a factive that-clause and the referent of a nonfactive that-clause belong to two different categories (propositional facts and propositions), or even whether they might *require* this. The conclusion is negative: linguistic data do not support Fact Reference$_{Power!}$. Having shown this, I consider my task in this book complete: after having seen that we have no reason to assume compositional facts in part 1, we will have now seen in part 2 that we have no reason to assume propositional facts, either.

This chapter is organized as follows. In the next subsections I will first critically examine arguments for and against the claim that factive that-clauses refer to propositional facts and nonfactive that-clauses to propositions (i.e., Fact Reference$_{Power!}$). In 6.1.1, I will consider evidence in favor of Fact Reference$_{Power!}$; and in 6.1.2, 6.1.3, 6.1.4, and 6.1.5, I shall discuss evidence against it. In 6.1.2, I will first examine counterexamples to Peterson's analysis of factivity (presupposed by Fact Reference$_{Power!}$) that involve communication and conjecture verbs and emotives, inquisitives, and the awkward circumstance that 'is a fact' is not a factive; in 6.1.3, 6.1.4, and 6.1.5 I then present and discuss two problematic cases of factive that-*p*/nonfactive that-*p* anaphora, one involving 'know'/'believe' (6.1.3) and one involving 'predict'/'is a surprise' (6.1.4). My conclusion will be that evidence supposedly in favor of Fact Reference$_{Power!}$ is actually unable to support it. The counterexamples disprove the claim that we are able to detect, through the use of that-clauses, two different categories of entities, propositional facts and propositions; therefore, we cannot successfully claim that factive that-clauses refer to propositional facts and nonfactive that-clauses to propositions on the basis of linguistic evidence.

This means that like the other five, the sixth and final attempt to show that propositional facts and propositions are two categories of entities fails. First, no satisfactorily general clear-cut difference in reference between factive and nonfactive that-clauses can be established; second, and more important, even assuming that such a clear-cut difference in reference exists, it can at most be concluded that factive that-clauses signal the pretense of truth rather than the presence of a fact: there is no evidence that factive that-clauses refer to propositional facts as distinct from true propositions (if they refer at all); rather, the opposite is the case.

The overall conclusion of chapters 5 and 6 is thus that *if* that-clauses are singular terms, then they can refer at most to propositions, and indeed only to propositions. As is clear from the conclusion of chapter 4, this is not a stance I myself endorse, for I hold that that-clauses are not singular terms; it is a conclusion coming, rather, from a fallback position, a position one could hold in the event that that-clauses were shown to be singular terms after all. Both my preferred stance and the fallback position support my aims in this book: they both give us reason not to accept propositional facts.

6.1 Sixth and Final Attempt: Linguistic Evidence Cannot Motivate the Acceptance of Propositional Facts alongside True Propositions

6.1.1 Arguments for Fact Reference$_{Power!}$ Fail

I know of two arguments in favor of Fact Reference$_{Power!}$ by Parsons and by Künne. They are both arguments to the best explanation and neither works.[1] Parsons notices that simultaneous quantification across factive and nonfactive contexts gives odd results (here below I append 'f' and 'p' to expressions for factive and nonfactive contexts):

(a.i)   *She believes$_p$ everything her mother regrets$_f$.

(a.ii)   *She says$_p$ everything that is tragic$_f$.

(a.iii)   *Whatever amuses$_f$ him is likely$_p$.

And yet homogeneous cross-quantification of factives (b.i–b.ii) and nonfactives (b.iii–b.iv), continues Parsons, is fine:

(b.i)   She is amused$_f$ by everything her mother regrets$_f$.

(b.ii)   Whatever amuses$_f$ him distresses$_f$ us.

(b.iii)   She says$_p$ everything that is probable$_p$.

(b.iv)   Whatever he proposes$_p$ is likely$_p$.

From all these examples Parsons concludes that we need both propositions and facts as referents of that-clauses (Parsons, 1993, 455). This is a bad argument, for two reasons. First, we also get odd results with quantification across factives:

(c)   *There is something that Bargle saw$_f$ and that Dargle confessed$_f$ (King, 2002, 368).

Besides, some speakers take the following free relative clause constructions (on the relevant reading!) to be odd (Moltmann, 2003, 91–92):

(d.i)   *John believes$_p$ what Bill asserted$_p$ (namely that p).

(d.ii)   *John said$_p$ what Mary believes$_p$ (namely that it is raining).

(d.iii)   *John remembered$_f$ what Mary noticed$_f$ (namely that Bill had shut the door).

(d.iv) *John saw$_f$ what Mary knows$_f$ (namely that it is raining).

(d.v) *John saw$_f$ what Mary heard$_f$ (namely that the door was being opened).

The oddity of (c) and (d) suggests that the oddity of (a) depends on the meaning of the specific predicate-pairs in cross-quantification and therefore on the choice of examples we make, not on the structural confusion of (terms for) facts and (for) propositions as Parsons claims.[2] Hence, Parsons' data are poor evidence for Fact Reference$_{Power!}$.[3] The second reason why Parsons's argument fails is that there are *no* that-clauses in the examples above, and so no grounds for claiming that the argument tells us anything about that-clauses. Parsons seems just to *assume* that we are quantifying over propositions and facts here, for instance in (a.iii), which he apparently reads as 'whatever (*fact*) amuses him distresses us', and which in turn can perhaps be taken as the conclusion of inferences of the form '(the fact) that p amuses him and distresses us', '(the fact) that s amuses him and distresses, etc.'. The analyses provided in chapter 4 show that this interpretation of quantification over that-clauses is at least unwarranted and at worst question begging. Although I am not arguing on the basis of those results here, it can of course very well be claimed that the reason why the arguments in this section do not work is *because* that-clauses are nonreferring expressions.

An argument similar to Parsons's is put forward by Künne, and it suffers from similar problems. The following case, says Künne, is odd:

(P1) What Ben first thought was that Ann survived the accident.
(P2) That Ann survived the accident is a miracle.
(C) Therefore (?), what Ben first thought is a miracle.

If all that-clauses referred to propositions, so the argument goes, we would be able to conclude (C), but we can't, and so some that-clauses refer to facts (Künne, 2003, 9). But this is a non sequitur: again, the argument by no means compels us to accept that there are (factive) that-clauses that refer to facts alongside (non-factive) that-clauses that refer to propositions; this example can be used equally well to argue that that-clauses do not refer at all, that is, to argue that (P1) is not an identity statement and that (P2) is not a predication.[4] Also, we can observe that in cases such as Parsons's, the same problem arises with quantifying across what Künne takes to be propositional that-clauses: for substituting the nonfactive 'what Annabella claimed' for 'is a miracle' in (P2) yields no uncontroversially good results either (again, on the relevant reading):

(C') Therefore (?), what Ben first thought is what Annabella claimed.

Hence, Künne's argument above does not establish Fact Reference*Power!* either. I conclude, then, that the arguments in favor of Fact Reference*Power!* are not convincing. Let us turn to arguments against Fact Reference*Power!*.

In the following I present three clusters of problems as evidence against Fact Reference*Power!*. First, in 6.1.2, I consider some problems posed by classes of counterexamples to the analysis of factivity on which Peterson bases Fact Reference*Power!* (communication and conjecture verbs, emotives, inquisitives)—including the awkward circumstance that 'is a fact' is a nonfactive, contrary to what one might expect. Then in 6.1.3 and 6.1.4, I analyze two cases of anaphora that are hard for defenders of Fact Reference*Power!* to explain, and for which the most straightforward solution is simply to abandon Fact Reference*Power!*.

6.1.2 Against Fact Reference*Power!* I: Counterexamples to Peterson's Analysis of Factivity

Difficulties are posed for Fact Reference*Power!* by several families of counterexamples. First, as Peterson points out, all communication verbs ('say', 'tell', 'show', 'indicate') and some conjecture verbs ('guess', 'predict', 'estimate') are *half-factives*, that is, they are significantly ambiguous between factive and nonfactive uses.[5] Consider the following:

(1)   John said that Mary refused the offer.

(2)   John didn't say that Mary refused the offer.

The use in (1) is ambiguous: there is a typical, preferred nonfactive reading of it as an indirect quote (John said, "Mary refused the offer," and we don't know whether she did), but there is also a reading that presupposes the truth of the embedded clause. Thus in the nonfactive reading (1) merely expresses that John said what he said. This reading is clear when we look at (2), which is the negation of (1) and does not presuppose the truth of the sentence following the that-clause.

In their nonfactive uses, however, both conjecture and communication verbs pass the syntactic *wh*-test, the test we saw at the beginning of chapter 5, according to which complement clauses of factive predicates can be transformed into *wh*-nominals (clauses introduced by *when, who, what, why,* and *how*) preserving grammaticality, whereas complement clauses of nonfactives cannot. Consider, for instance:

(3)   Bargle indicated that Argle bought the colander.

(3.4)   Bargle indicated what Argle bought.

(3.5)   Bargle indicated who bought the colander.

But passing this test should make these verbs factive, not nonfactive. To solve the problem, Peterson complicates the picture by introducing a distinction between genuine and nongenuine indirect questions (where the latter are only 'indirect quotations of questions'), and then by claiming that the indirect questions involved in such cases are not genuine, which is supposed to rescue their classification as nonfactives. The problem with this strategy is that it works only with communication verbs—since conjecture verbs admit of genuine indirect questions—and Peterson is left with no solution for conjecture verbs (he just says he's right; see Peterson, 1997, 79).

Second, emotive predicates that take factive clauses in the object, but not in the subject ('regret', 'resent', 'deplore') fail the syntactic *wh*-test, or at best the grammaticality of the result is speaker relative (Peterson, 1997, 79). Consider:

(4) *I regret (it) who left the meeting earlier.

(5) *Cargle regretted how Dargle wrote the letter.

These emotives, by Peterson's own admission, are genuine counterexamples (see also sec. 6.1.4 below).

Third, as we saw, 'know' is a factive verb. But like *inquisitive* verbs that admit of the whether-construction ('ask', 'wonder'), and which according to Peterson are nonfactives, the negation of 'know' admits, in addition to a factive reading (6 below) a nonfactive reading (7 below):[6]

(6) Cargle did not know that Argle had enough money;

(7) Cargle did not know whether Argle had enough money.

The three difficulties above with conjecture verbs, emotives, and the nonfactive use of 'know' require a patch to the analysis of factivity with which Peterson operates, and the patch is fairly unsuccessful, since some cases remain genuine counterexamples. Is this a problem? It might be said that it isn't, and that the mere lack of a clear-cut analysis of which clauses are factive is a problem only for a linguistic theory of the phenomenon of factivity, which might be improved. This is correct, but it is unproblematic only so long as one does not expect the analysis of factivity to decide on the reference of that-clauses. But if one does expect this, as Peterson and others do, then the lack of a clear-cut analysis is a serious problem for the reference of that-clauses. I argue for this point in 6.1.4 below. For if one accepts the claim that factivity determines whether that-clauses refer to facts or to propositions—these being taken as items of different ontological categories—then a shaky theory of factivity becomes a shaky theory of reference, and one cannot rely on it as evidence on the basis of which to accept propositional facts alongside propositions.[7] One cannot just ignore this point. And since we saw that the difference in the reference of that-clauses that is given by language in this sense is the only remaining argument that could establish a detectable difference between propositional facts and propositions, a firm linguistic basis for this difference is crucial. Take the nonfactive use of 'know': it is not clear, in this picture, what happens to the reference of a that-clause if a factive verb behaves differently when negated. If it is only the factivity of a verb that is at stake, then not much is going on. But if *reference* is at stake, then the question is more serious. For example, if it's the context given by the *predicate* that determines a complement clause's reference to a fact or a proposition, and if 'know' is a factive predicate, then the reference of 'that p' should *not* change from a fact in 'x fs that p' to a proposition in 'not: x fs whether p'. A similar shift in case of negation is the case of the half-factive 'say', but in this case the shift is from a nonfactive use to a factive use.[8] Must we really conclude that we might not know or say facts as well as propositions? Or are there rather two 'know's and two 'say's? Two ways of knowing things? Or maybe there are two types of knowledge-ascription claims involving different attitudes, or perhaps two or three kinds of negation? These are open questions, and it's impossible to answer any of them on the basis of linguistic evidence alone (at least on the basis of Peterson's analysis). As to whether such questions *should* genuinely be addressed, this is doubtful, since they arise only as an internal problem: the easiest and most natural interpretation is that it is Fact Reference$_{Power!}$ itself that prompts them, and thus creates an additional layer of problems all its own.

One additional thing worth pointing out in this connection is that 'is a fact' and 'is true' are, surprisingly, both nonfactive. Although at one point Peterson classifies 'is a fact' as factive (Peterson, 1997, 91), Parsons (1993, 455) observes that 'is a fact' cannot be factive since

(8)   It is not a fact that there is life on Mars

does not imply

(9)   There is life on Mars.

Actually, (8) appears synonymous with 'It is not true that there is life on Mars' (the case with 'that p is a fact' in the subject is similar). But if this is correct (as it seems to be, and as Peterson himself elsewhere agrees; Peterson, 1997, 389), then according to Fact Reference$_{Power!}$ 'that Bargle is choppy' in 'that Bargle is choppy is a fact' *does not refer to a fact* (*pace* Fine, 1982, 44). Now this is an awkward result, for one of the assumptions we considered at the beginning of chapter 4 that makes prima facie nominal reference to facts plausible is precisely the assumption that 'that p' in 'that p is a fact' refers to a fact. Parsons takes this result to show that the facts of ordinary speech might not coincide with a philosopher's facts (Parsons, 1993, 455; Wang, 2003, 9–10 agrees). I agree with Parsons. I shall return to the similarity between fact and truth in section 6.2.

Other difficulties to the Vendler-like accounts are posed by some uses of pronouns and anaphora. I shall consider two cases: know/believe, in section 1.3 and predict/is a surprise in section 1.4.

6.1.3   Against Fact Reference$_{Power!}$ II: <that-p>$_f$/ [that-p]$_p$ Anaphora: 'Know'/'Believe'

Consider the following:

(1)   I know that you're a guy but I do not believe it.

Epistemologists consider sentences like (1) to be problematic: according to the traditional view, knowledge is justified true belief, so it's impossible to know something without believing it. On this view (1) implies a contradiction. Vendler disagrees: examples of this kind are not problematic because they involve a contradiction, as the traditional view would have it: they are problematic, he says, because a category mismatch is involved (Vendler, 1972, 91). One cannot know what one believes because the object of belief, a proposition, is not the object of knowledge, which, as noted above, Vendler considers to be a fact: the two clauses 'that-p' in 'a knows that p' and in 'a believes that p' do not refer to the same thing since the first is a factive clause and the second is not. So we have 'a knows$_f$ <that p>$_f$' versus 'a believes$_p$ [that p]$_p$'. Vendler concludes this on the basis of Fact Reference$_{Power!}$, and from this proceeds to the philosophical conclusion that knowledge does not entail belief. So from

(2)   Bargle knows that electrons have a negative charge

we should not be able to conclude

(3)   Bargle believes that electrons have a negative charge,

the situation being actually

(2′)   Bargle knows$_f$ <that electrons have a negative charge>$_f$,

(3′)   Bargle believes$_p$ [that electrons have a negative charge]$_p$.

Therefore, says Vendler, one cannot believe what one knows. What we should realize is that, so far as Vendler is concerned, Oedipus knew he married his mother, he just did not believe *that* he did so.

This rather peculiar Vendlerian position that knowledge does not entail belief has been widely criticized. But Vendler is simply biting the bullet here, for his position that 'it' in (1) is not coreferential with 'that you are a guy' is just a consequence of Fact Reference$_{Power!}$. Yet, Vendler is here again at odds with some anaphoric uses in natural language that sound perfectly fine, such as

I always believed that you were a good friend; now I know it (Williamson, 2000, 43).

So something must be given up here (if one wants to remain within the borders of 'natural language'). Again, one could drop Fact Reference$_{Power!}$ by abandoning the idea that factive that-clauses refer to facts (while nonfactive that-clauses refer to propositions): this is what Parsons (Parsons, 1993, 456–457) and Harman suggest (see sec. 6.2). Another option is finding a way to keep Fact Reference$_{Power!}$ by making it work for anaphoric cases such as these (which allows us to maintain that knowledge does entail belief). And this is what Peterson tries to do. As we shall see, however, it is doubtful that Peterson's proposal, which is defensible only at a high theoretical and ontological cost, can make Fact Reference$_{Power!}$ work satisfactorily for the problematic cases of anaphora.

Let's have a look at this proposal. First of all, Peterson wants to defend both Fact Reference$_{Power!}$ and the thesis that knowledge entails belief, which means that the inference from (2) to (3) must go through. How does he manage? He finds a step to interpolate in the inference, namely (2.1) below:

(2)   Bargle knows that electrons have a negative charge.

(2.1)   Bargle knows that it is true that electrons have a negative charge.

(3)   Bargle believes that electrons have a negative charge.

According to Peterson, here (2) entails (3) via the first that-clause in (2.1). He maintains that the expression 'that electrons have a negative charge' refers in (2) to a fact and in (3) to a proposition. In (2.1) 'that electrons have a negative charge' refers again to a proposition, while 'that it is true that electrons have a negative charge' refers to a fact, but the latter that-clause embeds another that-clause that refers to the proposition believed in (3). Put more perspicuously, perhaps, the situation is as follows:

(2′)   Bargle knows$_f$ <that electrons have a negative charge>$_f$.

(2.1′)   Bargle knows$_f$ <that it is true$_p$ [that electrons have a negative charge]$_p$>$_f$.

(3′)   Bargle believes$_p$ [that electrons have a negative charge]$_p$.

What is the fact referred to in (2.1')? A fact that "consists of a certain proposition's *being true*" (Peterson, 1997, 14–15).[9] Does Peterson's way out reach its aim, that is, does knowledge here entail belief while Fact Reference*Power!* still holds? This is not immediately clear. For the that-clauses in (2) and (3) to be coreferential, the referents must be identical. For the referents to be identical, you must assume that (the proposition) that p is true, (the fact) that p is true, and (the proposition) that p are all the same object. This is exactly what Peterson denies. Since this directly contradicts Fact Reference*Power!*, Peterson's way out must consist in modifying something else. It seems that what is modified is, conveniently, the working of anaphora in combination with 'believe' and 'know'. And to get this, Peterson must make assumptions about the structure and nature of knowledge attitudes with no other motivation than the preservation of Fact Reference*Power!*. To see this, note that for (2')–(3') to go through while keeping Fact Reference*Power!*, as Peterson sees it, an array of strong and complicated adjunctive assumptions is required and so made by Peterson, though he never makes these explicit. The first three can be reconstructed as follows:

(i)   'True' expresses a property/truth is a property.

(ii)   There is a one-one relation between facts and the true propositions they 'fit' (or: to which they 'correspond'. or: that are their 'counterparts').

(iii)   There are facts of the form (*the fact*) *that the proposition p is true*, which are not identical to (*the fact*) *that p*.

Assumption (i), that truth is a property (though a property that may be rather unique), is a comparatively weak one, but it nonetheless implies that p and p *is true* are different propositions. A much stronger assumption is the second, that to *every* proposition exactly one fact corresponds, and vice versa (ii). This is *the one-one thesis* we saw in chapter 5, section 5.3, and it plays a fundamental role in Peterson's way-out. To see that assumption (ii) is needed, notice that the inference would not go through otherwise. For consider again:

(2')   Bargle knows$_f$ <that electrons have a negative charge>$_f$.

(2.1')   Bargle knows$_f$ <that it is true$_p$ [that electrons have a negative charge]$_p$>$_f$.

(3')   Bargle believes$_p$ [that electrons have a negative charge]$_p$.

For the solution advanced by Peterson to be a convincing alternative to coreferential anaphora, the fact we need to work with in (2.1') must embed the proposition believed in (3'), and the fact in (2') must mirror part of the fact in (2.1'). We saw that accepting Fact Reference*Power!* means accepting that a factive 'that *p*' accommodates *whatever p* we might be pleased to embed. This means that the referent of the factive that-clause is as fine-grained as the nonfactive 'that *p*' that it fits. (Assuming at this point that the relation is one-many means departing from language in a way that is not justified by prima facie language analysis, as I pointed out in the case of Vendler at the end of chap. 5, sec. 5.3, and would make Peterson's stance identical to Vendler's: i.e., both would hold that we cannot believe what we know.) Assumption (iii), that *the fact that p* and *the fact that p is true* are different facts, follows as a direct corollary from (i) and (ii). But there is more. If *the fact that p* and *the fact that p is true* are different facts, the reason for this difference can be one of two. *Either* the reason is that there is a property—truth—involved in the second fact that is not involved in the first, *or* the reason is that the concept of truth appears in one proposition but not in the other: since the identity of propositional facts is parasitic on that of the propositions to which they correspond, *the fact that p* and *the fact that p is true* are different because *the proposition that p* and *the proposition that p is true* are different propositions. Either way, if those are different facts, and, as we know, since 'know' is factive, we cannot say that knowing the first fact entails knowing the second—for example, that anyone knowing that electrons have a negative charge thereby also knows that it is true that electrons have a negative charge. Hence, to pass from (2.1) to (3) we are forced to *stipulate* what knowledge attitudes are and how they work in relation to belief attitudes. In other words, we need an adjunctive assumption, (iv):[10]

(iv)   Whenever a subject *a* has a knowledge attitude *k* toward a fact *a's being F*, she (also) has a knowing attitude k_1, distinct from *k*, directed toward a fact of the form *proposition a is F is true*, a part of which, *p*, is the object of a belief attitude *b*, and both k_1 and *b* always accompany *k*.

As is clear, accepting theses (i)–(iv) above does *not* mean that one is taking language at face value; it means doing exactly the contrary. We are not establishing by empirical findings that factive that-clauses refer to facts and that nonfactive that-clauses refer to propositions: we are in fact (1) denying an empirical finding (the working of coreferential anaphora), which denies a consequence of the thesis we want to establish (Fact Reference*Power!*), and doing so by (2) assuming otherwise unmotivated philosophical views about knowledge, belief, truth, facts, and propositions—these views being part of exactly what we want to prove.

The upshot of all this is not, again, that accepting Fact Reference*Power!* and the four assumptions we just saw taken together cannot be done or that it is never sensible and useful. It does mean, however, that Peterson's proposal is a package that amounts to committing oneself to an entire philosophical theory, and goes far beyond what ordinary language prima facie commits us to.

This might be useful and interesting in some cases, namely when we don't want to look at prima facie language commitments since our aim is the hypothetical one of just establishing what to put in the package. But it is useless if we want to defend and prove right one of the theses in the package, in our case Fact Reference$_{Power!}$, by looking at prima facie language commitments.

We are trying now to prove the thesis that propositional facts should be accepted alongside true propositions (the last attempt to do so) by examining the behavior of that-clauses, under the hypothesis that factive ones refer to something other than what nonfactive ones do. We have found one problematic consequence of this hypothesis, namely, anaphoric factive/ nonfactive cross-reference. Because anaphora requires coreferentiality, it seems that language forces us to admit that both factive and nonfactive that-clauses refer, after all, to the same thing. We cannot solve this problem by just stipulating that propositional facts are different from true propositions, because that is what we want to prove.

So far, we saw that Peterson can save Fact Reference$_{Power!}$ from the 'know'/'believe' anaphora counterexample only at a high price. But does he at least buy a solution? This is doubtful. His solution has already started to seem question begging. Is it question begging? Not exactly—perhaps. But more problems are arising. Another counterexample involving anaphora awaits a solution.

6.1.4   Difficulty 2.2: <that-p>$_f$/ [that-p]$_p$ Anaphora: 'Predict'/'Is a Surprise'

As should be clear, the problem Peterson and Vendler have with anaphora is that the most natural, prima facie interpretation of its functioning (i.e., coreference, meaning that there is only one thing referred to), is precluded by Fact Reference$_{Power!}$. We just saw that Peterson's choice for saving the anaphora in cases like

(*)   Bargle believes that electrons have a negative charge, and he knows it

is to make costly stipulations, among which is (iv), in terms of what epistemic contents and their functioning are with respect to their interrelation with facts and propositions. The stipulation functions to establish a link between the referents in such a way that the anaphora still makes sense. Now consider:

(1) Bargle believes that electrons have a negative charge, and Argle knows it.

The stipulation *ad* (*) regarded only one agent (Bargle). In this case, however, we need an adjustment of (iv) to a two-agent situation. To save the anaphora, Peterson's interpretation would have to modify (iv) in such a way that—roughly put—a reading of 'it' as 'that that's true' ('Argle knows that that's true') is allowed. We would thus need to stipulate a new, modified (iv) to allow for an explanation of this case as well so that, again, the anaphora would work because a certain connection is stipulated between what a certain agent knows and what another agent believes. The link we need to stipulate is that Argle knows something—*the very same thing* which Bargle believes—to be true. At this point, one might start wondering whether we would not be forced into providing a cascade of stipulations similar to (iv) for each case that would be even slightly different from our initial one. Perhaps this particular modification—from a one-agent (iv) to a two-agent variant—is not such a big deal. But there are more problematic cases than this one that cannot be dealt with in the way sketched above.

Indeed, take this example (cf. Peterson, 1997, 22):

(2) Though he didn't predict$_p$ it$_p$, <that Bargle broke the plate with the crackers>$_f$ was no surprise$_f$ to Argle.

Here 'it' and that 'Bargle broke the plate with the crackers' are coreferential, but the package proposed for (1) does not seem to work. Suppose indeed we forced the following:

(2′) *Though he didn't predict$_p$ [that Bargle broke the plate with the crackers]$_p$, <that [it]$_p$ was true$_p$>$_f$ was no surprise$_f$ to Argle.

This is hardly meaningful. But there is more. Suppose we leave aside the question whether the result is grammatical or not. To proceed with the solution, we would once again need to adjust to the 'predict'/'surprise' case clause (iv), which in the 'knowledge'/'believe' case guarantees by stipulation the link between the workings of knowledge and belief. In the case of (2′), clause (iv) would have to look quite different from the original (iv), more or less as follows:

(iv′) Whenever a subject *a* has a surprise attitude *k* toward a fact *a's being F*, she also has a surprise attitude k_1, distinct from *k*, which is directed toward the *proposition a is F is true*, a part of which, *p*, might happen to be the object of a prediction attitude k_2 of an agent *b* (possibly identical with *a*) and k_1 always accompanies *k*.

This complicated and artificial-sounding (iv′) is meant to deal with the 'predict'/'surprise' case *in particular* (again, disregarding the ungrammaticality of the attempt). But surely we can't do that—we can't accept (iv′). For doing that comes down to assuming a special clause to account for the special link we need to stipulate between 'is a surprise' and 'predict' to provide an explanation of why the anaphora works in this specific case, that is, to provide an alternative to the identity of referents. This would be a very specific, ad hoc solution for this particular case, one that would get us nowhere with other cases; other, similar cases with different emotive and conjecture predicates in cross-anaphoric reference would require a similarly different solution. Therefore, the solution cannot be generalized. Therefore, it is not a good solution; it is rather a very suspicious patch.

Let us look at the situation from a general point of view. There are two methodological problems here.

First, it is apparent that these cases of anaphora, (1) and (2), are problematic under Fact Reference$_{Power!}$ because anaphora supposes a strong relation, usually identity, between the referents of the terms that are anaphorically linked. The relation of identity of reference in these cases is denied by Fact Reference$_{Power!}$, so, as mentioned, if we want to keep Fact Reference$_{Power!}$ and have an explanation for the problematic cases of anaphora, we need to establish a link between the referents in a way that does not involve assuming identity. In the 'knowledge'/'believe' case, the link is directly stipulated in (iv), either in the one-agent or two-agent variant. Now, introducing a similar yet distinct (iv′) in the case of 'predict'/'is a surprise' is not just a slight adjustment: this time, (iv′) has to allow for a correlation not only of different agents but of *totally different attitudes*. This suggests that we should be trying to find an alternative solution for the 'knowledge'/'believe' case as well, a solution that takes care of *all* cases. We cannot keep making ad hoc stipulations for each case we encounter.

The second methodological problem is that although he deems these cases of anaphora to be nongenuine, Peterson accepts that there are also genuine cases. But the general grounds on which we decide which cases are genuine and which cases are not seems, for him, to depend on whether anaphora behaves in the way predicted by Fact Reference$_{Power!}$: and this begs the question. Given these problems, the best—since the most general— solution is to reject Fact Reference$_{Power!}$. But before concluding this, let's see whether there are really no alternatives left.

Once again: to keep Fact Reference$_{Power!}$ in the face of the counterexamples we saw, we need two things. First, we need a general explanation of how to understand

(2)   Though he didn't predict$_p$ it$_p$, <that Bargle broke the plate with the crackers>$_f$ was no surprise$_f$ to Argle.

Second, this general explanation must allow us to understand (2) and the following case *together*:

(1)   Bargle believes$_p$ [that electrons have a negative charge]$_p$, and Argle knows $_f$ <it>$_f$.

Two options can be advanced based on the literature. According to the first, the relation linking the two referents is such that one *is an instance of* the other. The second option brings us back to Fine's idea that facts are *truths*, that is, they are the being true of the propositions referred to in the (corresponding) nonfactive that-clauses. I have already argued that the second solution is untenable if our aim is (and it is) to show that facts are a different category of entities alongside propositions. So this solution would not deliver what it is supposed to deliver, and I shall not discuss it any further. It is worth observing that Peterson's solution to the 'know'/'believe' anaphora that we saw in section 6.1.4 comes quite close to Fine's idea of taking facts to be truths, but differs from it in being more costly in terms of ad hoc assumptions and seemingly less close to empirical findings. In particular, the major difference is that Fine assumes that there are *only* facts of the form *p's being true (the fact that p is true)*, whereas Peterson apparently assumes that there are, alongside these facts, also facts of the form 'the fact that *p*' that are not identical to the former.

The only solution left is to take facts to be instances of propositions. As I will show in the next subsection, this solution is incoherent.

6.1.5   Facts as Instances of Propositions?
According to Peterson, (2) below is a case analogous to (3) and (4) below (see Peterson, 1997, 22–23; I repeat (1) here as well):

(1)   Bargle believes$_p$ [that electrons have a negative charge]$_p$, and Argle knows $_f$ <it>$_f$.

(2)   Though he didn't predict$_p$ it$_p$, <that Bargle broke the plate with the crackers>$_f$ was no surprise$_f$ to Argle.

(3)   Bargle ate his lunch on Monday but on Tuesday he did not eat it.

(4)   In 1987 Argle didn't go to the International Conference on Topology and its Applications but in 1999 he did attend it.

The analogy rests on the fact that 'his lunch' and 'it' in (3), and 'it' and 'the International Conference on Topology and its Applications' in (4), are, says

Peterson, *only apparently* coreferential. Peterson does not explain exactly what he means by this, but I guess this is how he reasons: there isn't numerically one lunch and one International Conference on Topology and its Applications, but many, and Bargle and Argle just missed one of them.[11] But now, in what does the analogy between (2) on the one side and (3) and (4) on the other consist? If Peterson wants to show that not all cases of anaphora are genuine (i.e., coreferential), that's fine, but it does not help us solve the problem. For instance, it would not help to say that in some case 'the chameleon's tail' might refer to different parts of bodily tissue of a chameleon at different times, so that it is not strictly speaking the same thing in number that the chameleon regenerates, but different portions of tissue—to which, however, we still apply the terms 'the chameleon's tail'. This won't help us at all in understanding how (2) is supposed to fit the overall picture *unless* we explain how we should conceive of the link between the different portions of tissue from a metaphysical point of view, in such a way that this reasoning can be applied to propositional facts and propositions. There must be more to the analogy than just claiming that there are cases of nongenuine anaphora. What we need to see, as I said, is what view of facts and propositions could provide an explanation of *both* (1) and (2) together, that is:

(1)   Bargle believes$_p$ [that electrons have a negative charge]$_p$, and Argle knows$_f$ <it>$_f$.

(2)   Though he didn't predict$_p$ it$_p$, <that Bargle broke the plate with the crackers>$_f$ was no surprise$_f$ to Argle.

—under the assumption that (2) works like (3) and (4):

(3)   Bargle ate his lunch on Monday but on Tuesday he did not eat it.

(4)   In 1987 Argle didn't go to the International Conference on Topology and its Applications but in 1999 he did attend it.

In other words, we must have a clear, general, and systematically unified idea of how the items referred to in all of them are related from the metaphysical point of view.

Notice first of all that on the reading that interests us, the analogy between (2) and (3) and (4) fails. The items involved in the anaphoric reference in (3) and (4) fall in the same category, real objects (the Gruyère sandwich constituting Bargle's lunch) and events (a conference), while the items in (2) fall into two different categories, propositions and facts. At least this is what *must* be assumed, no matter what the parties involved might have had in mind, if we want to maintain a distinction in category between two kinds of that-clauses as claimed in Fact Reference$_{Power!}$. I will come back to this point at the end of this section with an alternative (but unhelpful) reading of Peterson's point.

Since there is no obvious way to put (1)–(4) together in the way we need if we want to save Fact Reference$_{Power!}$, in this, our last attempt to do so, we need to supply a fitting metaphysical account of facts and propositions according to which they fall into different categories. Let's try this: one could read the anaphora in (2) and (4) as having as one referent a series of possible events or an event-type, and the other as an event-token, that is, an instance or an actualization or a concretization of (one of) the first; in (3) there (is) are a (series of) possible lunches or a lunch-type and lunch-tokens that get *actualized*. This comes down to claiming by analogy that in (2) the anaphora can be saved by accepting that *facts are instances of propositions*. If this interpretation holds water, then we can determine whether it can be applied to (1) as well.

Unfortunately, it is not clear what it means to claim that facts are instances of propositions. It could mean two things. It could mean (option 1) that facts are to propositions as event-types are to event-tokens, or as individual qualities are to universal qualities. Or it could mean (option 2) that facts are to propositions as particulars are to the properties they instantiate. Option 2 has been defended by John Baylis (1948) and more recently by Angelika Kratzer (2002). However, Baylis's facts are not the right candidates for the role, because they are worldly: they are actual, real, located entities that have properties, and are more coarse-grained than propositions. Thus they do not obey the one-one thesis and cannot be propositional facts. Actually, they look very much like events, and I agree with Clark that a position like Baylis's needs to be supplemented with an account of whether there are states, events, and processes *in addition* to facts and what their relation is to propositions (Clark, 1975, 5; see also Wang, 2003, 13). Likewise, Kratzer's facts are not apt for the role: they do not obey the one-one thesis, since her facts are more coarse-grained than the propositions they correspond to, and thus cannot be propositional facts. We saw that the only kind of facts that are compatible with Fact Reference$_{Power!}$ are propositional facts, not worldly facts, since the latter cannot be as fine-grained as propositions.

As to option 1, I do not know of any position that defends it, but this is not relevant. What is relevant is the question how many adherents of Fact Reference$_{Power!}$ would be happy with it, since on such a view the border between propositions and facts looks not sharpened but fuzzier. It's debatable whether on this view facts and propositions can be considered items of different categories, if the analogy is that facts are to individual properties as propositions are to universal properties. For the latter are both *properties*, that is, variants of the same category. The point of Fact Reference is that there are two different kinds of that-clauses referring to items in *two different categories*. If we now abandon this fundamental idea, then much of the discussion of this chapter and the previous is pointless, and we should jump directly to the next section. But let this pass: more is problematic with option 1, and it has to do, again, with the notion of instantiation at issue. So far, we have seen a construal of facts only for (2)–(4). Can it be extended also to (1)? No. The view of facts as instances of propositions is incompatible with Fact Reference$_{Power!}$. Let's see why this is so.

Recall, once again, that the only view of facts compatible with Fact Reference$_{Power!}$ is that according to which facts are propositional facts. This, now, has two immediate problematic consequences, one for the way out that Peterson offers to save the claim that knowledge entails belief, or better, to provide a plausible account of the workings of natural language claims such as

(1)   Bargle believes$_p$ [that electrons have a negative charge]$_p$, and Argle knows$_f$ <it>$_f$,

and another problem for the way out Peterson proposes for cases such as

(2)   Though he didn't predict$_p$ it$_p$, <that Bargle broke the plate with the crackers>$_f$ was no surprise$_f$ to Argle.

The first consequence is this. If we want a general account for both (1) and (2) we must construe (1) as saying that one knows an instance of what another believes. This means we must change Peterson's assumption (our (i)–(iv)) into the following:

(i)   Facts are instances of propositions.
(ii)   Whenever a subject *a* has a knowledge attitude *k* toward a fact *a's being F*, one has also a belief attitude *b* toward a proposition *a is F*.

What we have now is that the 'fitting' of propositions and facts is explained as instantiation. But how can we hold this together with what we know about propositional facts? The notion of instantiation as applied to ideal objects outside time and space does not seem coherent. Propositional facts are ideal: how can we take them to be *instances of propositions*? What sense can there be in this? Mind that my assumption here is not that there is *no* sense of 'instantiation' according to which we might say that ideal entities instantiate other ideal entities, for I would not want to be committed to saying that, say, propositions as ideal objects cannot instantiate properties such as the property of being ideal or of truth, or that mathematical objects cannot instantiate mathematical properties (no matter what we think of such objects). This notion of instantiation is a different notion from the notion that is relevant here: this was the sense of option 2. The difference here is between 'instantiate' in the sense of having (or coming to have) properties, and 'being an instance of' in the sense in which a *trope* of sharpness or an abstract qualitative particular in space and time can be said to be (in some theories having both tropes and universals) an instance of the universal Sharpness. *That* instantiation (of universals into tropes or in universalia in re) means nothing other than *particularization*, which comes down to *getting located*, and brings with itself such characteristics as the perceivability of what gets instantiated. But all this is alien to the view that sees facts as ideal entities—it's just the opposite view. Perhaps some sense can be made of this position, but so far no metaphysically acceptable explanation seems to be available.

I conclude that these attempts to give a general explanatory account of cases of recalcitrant anaphoric uses such as (1) and (2)—one that is such that we can keep Fact Reference$_{Power!}$—all fail. Trying to make Fact Reference$_{Power!}$ work for all cases of anaphora forces an account acceptable only to those prepared to let facts and true propositions collapse.

One could observe that anaphora *is* a difficult phenomenon to handle for philosophers of language. And so, perhaps, one could accept that in some cases anaphora is not genuinely coreferential. But the problem is not that anaphora is a difficult phenomenon: the problem for what we are discussing is that there is a straightforward *alternative* explanation for the counterexamples we saw, a solution that is indifferent to anaphora being a complicated phenomenon. Here it is: it consists in construing anaphora for 'know'/'believe' as genuinely coreferential without assuming two kinds of that-clauses. We assume in the latter case that *all* that-clauses, if referential, refer to propositions, thus taking factive verbs to presuppose or imply truth. Before I say more about this possibility in the next section, let us state the conclusion of this section by way of summary: the sixth and last attempt to distinguish propositional facts from true propositions fails.

Before I close this discussion, I wish to note one last thing. My attempt at explaining above what Peterson might have had in mind in drawing attention to cases of nongenuine anaphora like 'Bargle ate his lunch on Monday but on Tuesday he did not eat it' overlooks one possibility. It is likely that Peterson is not thinking of facts as instantiations of propositions, but rather of something else, namely, he is hypothesizing that *both* facts and propositions are instantiations of a higher category of, say, *states of affairs* or *propfacts* or whatever.[12] This, however, would be a self-defeating move, for it entails a flat-out abandonment of the idea that there are *two* kinds of referents of that-clauses—an idea fundamental to Fact Reference*Power!*. Far from being a solution, this position would push the problem even further back, for it would raise not one but a plethora of questions similar to the one we have unsuccessfully tried to answer in section 5.4 of the previous chapter: in what respect is an ideal proposition different from an ideal fact if both are instances of the same category? Next to this, we would need an answer also to the following questions: What, if they are different, makes a propfact into a fact instead of making it into a proposition? What kinds of ideal entities are propfacts, insofar as they differ from *both* ideal facts and ideal propositions? On what grounds can we argue that we need an utterly complicated analysis of cases such as 'Though he didn't predict it, that Bargle broke the plate with the crackers was no surprise to Argle' using three different ideal entities instead of going for the simplest analysis on offer?

This simplest analysis is discussed briefly below.

6.2   No Reference to Propositional Facts as Distinct from True Propositions

If propositional facts, are, like (Fregean) propositions, ideal, about objects, and as fine-grained as propositions, then there is nothing that distinguishes them from true propositions. But, if so, then propositions and propositional facts do not belong to *two* categories of items to which the two kinds of that-clauses refer. There is only *one* category. In this case, Fact Reference becomes identical with

Reference   All that-clauses refer to propositions. Nonfactive that-clauses *refer to propositions* whereas factive that-clauses *refer to true propositions*.[13]

We may call 'propositions' the entities referred to by that-clauses, and we may call true propositions 'facts', but this isn't necessary; it's just one terminological option. To be clear, in general I am neither endorsing the identification of true propositions and facts nor denying it. I am just saying that the identification of propositional facts with propositions cannot be blocked *by linguistic means alone* by whoever endorses Fact Reference*Power!*. A theory in which facts are identical with true propositions and which includes Reference is a theory one could be perfectly happy with. One option might be the following. All that-clauses have the same *reference*, that is, a proposition, but nonfactive that-clauses have a different *sense* or *meaning* or *connotation* from factive that-clauses (thus two connotations—or two names, if you like—do not secure for us two different [kinds of] *objects*, i.e., propositions and facts). That-clauses with the first kind of connotation would refer to a proposition, and that-clauses with the second kind of connotation would refer to proposition as well, but in the second case we would be able to detect that the proposition is a *true* one, and the latter we would call a fact. So, in this theory, if I believe that Argle bought the colander and you know it, what I believe and what you know are one and the same thing: the proposition that Argle bought the colander. And this proposition is what the factive that-clause following 'know' and the nonfactive that-clause following believe *both* refer to. Factive that-clauses would thus signal a pretense of truth, rather than the presence of a fact. Peterson *himself* concedes that this is how things might very well be:

> Our word patterns in English very strongly suggest that there can be some reduction of facts to propositions (or *vice versa*), or that there might be some generic category (state of affairs?) to which both facts and propositions belong. For the difference between facts and propositions as manifested in such linguistic data is slight. (Peterson, 1997, 38)

As I remarked at the end of the previous section, if this means arguing that there are three kinds of ideal entities, then it is indefensible, because there are no non-question-begging ways to do it *unless* we show why we need all these entities to play certain particular metaphysical roles. If this means that we have only one category of entities, say, propositions, and the difference is simply that some of these (those that are true) we *call* facts, then there is no problem. But then we are saying that Fact Reference$_{Power!}$ is identical with Reference (it goes without saying, in light of chap. 4, that I do not endorse Reference).

Among those who seem near enough to defending the view that all that-clauses refer to propositions (while not defending a view of Russellian view of propositions, which are hybrids of propositions and states of affairs) are Parsons and Harman. Their positions are different in one important aspect, however, namely that for Parsons facts still play a peculiar role in the semantics of that-clauses, while for Harman this is not the case. Parsons, who seems to endorse Fact Reference$_{Power!}$ (Parsons, 1993, 441, 454–455), is actually unhappy with the idea that there are two kinds of that-clauses:

> A more natural assumption is that individual words work the same in both contexts, always yielding a proposition for the whole, but that in factive contexts there is deferred reference to a fact intimately related to the proposition. (Parsons, 1993, 455)

So Parsons reads '*x* knows that *p*' as '*x* knows [*the fact corresponding to the proposition] that p*', so that every factive *f* becomes *f-the-fact-corresponding-to-the-proposition-that*. On this reading, the sentence

(1) Bargle knows what Dargle believes, namely that Argle bought the colander

should be read, arguably, in a way similar to the following:

(1′) Bargle knows$_f$-the-fact$_f$-corresponding-to-the-proposition$_p$ [that Dargle believes$_p$], namely [the proposition that Argle bought the colander]$_p$.

On Parsons's proposal, factive verbs no longer have their natural reading: there is no 'know', but rather 'know-the-fact-corresponding-to-the-proposition' (in the relevant reading). There are two problems with this. First, it changes the subject, like Vendler's views on 'know'; Parsons wants to keep the view that that-clauses are singular terms because of linguistic arguments similar to those offered by the standard view on propositional attitudes we saw in chapter 4. Despite the fact that he restricts the referential role of that-clauses to propositions, Parsons still assumes that facts play a role in the semantics of factive predicates (though not as referent of that-clauses), and ascribes to the latter a different meaning from the one they have in natural language. It goes without saying that, as in Vendler's case, this interpretation is not something that can be read off language. Second, it remains a mystery what exactly the deferred reference is due to. Taking up this solution is more costly and more roundabout than just assuming that facts are true propositions (since the two, as I showed in chap. 5, sec. 5.4, are identical anyway).

Harman's suggestion is to read expressions like 'desire', 'hoping', and 'being sad that *p*' as follows: 'desire-true', 'hoping-true the proposition that *p*', and 'being sad-about-the-truth-of the proposition that *p*'. This translates directly into language the phenomenon of factivity without assuming facts (Harman, 2003, 172). So, Harman's position might, perhaps, be an acceptable way to defend the view that that-clauses are referential (i.e., Reference) while still accommodating factivity (although it does strain natural language a bit).

The position according to which all that-clauses refer to propositions, and according to which we can detect a presumption of truth in some interesting cases, is open to a reasonably vast array of philosophers, not only to a correspondentist who happens to have managed to find a way to show that that-clauses are singular terms and has acceptable truthmakers (e.g., tropes or mereological complexes; see part 1). This position is also open, interestingly, to those who identify facts with true propositions. As is well known, the view according to which facts are true propositions is well represented. A famous defender is Frege:

"Facts, facts, facts," cries the scientist if he wants to bring home the necessity of a firm foundation of science. What is a fact? A fact is a thought that is true. (Frege, 1918, 342)

This is a position defended by Ducasse (1940, 710), Carnap (1947, 6–4, 28), and Shorter (1962, 301), and it is at the core of such identity theories of truth as those proposed by Jennifer Hornsby ('true thinkables are the same as facts'; Hornsby, 1999), John McDowell (1999, 93–94; 2005, 83–85), and Julian Dodd (2000).

Let's sum up. On a view that accepts both (Fregean) propositions and Fact Reference$_{Power!}$, the latter *entails* that reference to facts is reference to propositional facts, and propositional facts collapse into propositions. The propositional fact, say, that Bargle is choppy and the (true) proposition that Bargle is choppy are both ideal; they are both about Bargle and choppiness, and they both have the same grain. They are, then, very similar entities, so similar that there seems to be nothing that distinguishes them. We did not see any convincing argument to the effect that propositional facts are not true propositions. We saw no grounds for defenders of Fact Reference$_{Power!}$ to say that we have *two* things here rather than one. If such items are said to be distinct, there must be a difference. Still, we didn't find a way to argue convincingly for this difference, and to avoid the collapse of facts and true propositions ignited by Fact Reference$_{Power!}$. In chapter 5, I reviewed five attempts at rejecting the identification of facts with true propositions, three discussed by Künne, one by Searle, and one by Fine. All these arguments fail. Finally, in chapter 6 I have considered, as a final, sixth attempt, whether the linguistic evidence backing up Fact Reference$_{Power!}$ itself provided convincing evidence to block the identification, but it didn't. In fact, linguistic evidence rather disproved that Fact Reference$_{Power!}$ can be convincingly held. Thus I reached the conclusion that, should that-clauses eventually turn out to be singular terms and should we in that case want to keep the idea of factivity, the best position regarding the reference of that-clauses would be captured by saying that all that-clauses refer to propositions, with factive that-clauses referring to true propositions (I called this: Reference). Of course, this would hold, as I said, with the proviso that that-clauses are shown to be singular terms, contrary to the results of chapter 4, and that a plausible theory of factivity is offered. Instead, though, Fact Reference$_{Power!}$ should be abandoned. There is no convincing argument for the view that propositional facts, as a distinct category of entities, deserve a place in our catalog of the world alongside propositions.

This should be confirmed to be true: for sure there could still be arguments to the effect that facts exist, but that-clauses wouldn't take us anywhere near them. There could be nothing that we could learn about facts by inspecting that-clauses. We do know, in fact, that the real reason Fact Reference$_{Power!}$ fails in such cases is that that-clauses are not singular terms.

In the last three chapters, I have dismissed that-clauses as devices of reference to propositional facts and the claim that there is genuine quantification over such facts. As far as I am concerned, the case is closed and my job done, for the only serious candidate for a theory of facts is the theory that sees them as Armstrongian compositional facts. But, as I have shown in part 1, compositional facts are implausible ad hoc entities.

One question remains: is Fact Reference$_{Power!}$ really affected in the same way that Fact Reference is by the results of this and the previous chapter if we show that-clauses to be singular terms (contrary to the results of chap. 4)? It is indeed fair to recall that it was the assumption of Fact Reference$_{Power!}$, not Fact Reference, that has made our life so complicated since section 5.1 of the previous chapter. Whoever defends Fact Reference is not committed to any definite view as to *which* that-clauses refer to facts, but only to the view that *some* do. As I pointed out in section 5.1 of chapter 5, however, Fact Reference is by no means better than Fact Reference$_{Power!}$. Let's see, then, whether Fact Reference$_{Power!}$ must indeed be abandoned if Singular Term theory is abandoned.

6.3 Exit Fact Reference$_{Power!}$, Together with Singular Terms

In chapter 4, I argued that that-clauses do not refer to anything insofar as they are not singular terms, as the No Singular Term theorists claim. I also argued that if this is the case, then Fact Reference, that is, the thesis that some that-clauses refer to facts and other that-clauses refer to propositions, is false, because this thesis depends on that-clauses being singular terms. The question now is whether the finding that that-clauses are not singular terms also disproves the thesis I consider in this and the previous chapter, namely Fact Reference$_{Power!}$, the thesis that *factive* that-clauses refer to facts and *nonfactive* that-clauses refer to propositions. The point is not exactly trivial, because Fact Reference$_{Power!}$ is a thesis conceived in the context of some results from linguistics, and the terminological and theoretical apparatus of philosophers on the one hand and of linguists on the other hand are not the same.

There are two differences worth mentioning between the No Singular Term theory we saw in chapter 4 and the Vendler-like analyses we saw in the previous section.

The first difference is that, as I mentioned, the No Singular Term theory takes the factive/nonfactive distinction into account only very rarely while discussing substitution failures. However, the examples offered by No Singular Term theory can easily be adjusted to take that distinction into account, as I have done in chapter 4, section 4.1.

The second difference is more relevant and a little confusing. The No Singular Term theory puts a lot of emphasis on substitution tests purporting to disprove that that-clauses are singular terms on the basis of the substitutability of coreferential singular terms salva veritate and congruitate, that is, the substitution failure *ad* ($\overline{NecSingularTerms\,1}$) (see chap. 4, sec. 4.1). In the tests, we freely substituted 'the proposition that' for nonfactive that-clauses and 'the fact that' for factive that-clauses, a procedure known as head noun interpolation. There is, however, a difference between the two interpolation cases. Head noun interpolation with 'the fact that' does play a role in the account given by the Kiparskys, but the Kiparskys do not append any technical consideration to head noun interpolation with 'the proposition that'. Let's look at this in some detail.

a. The Kiparskys examine predicates that can always be preceded or followed by 'the fact that'. They call these predicates *syntactically factive*. There are also *syntactically nonfactive* predicates: these cannot be followed by 'the fact that'. Although syntactically factive verbs do play a crucial role in their general account (Kiparsky & Kiparsky, 1971, 347–348), the Kiparskys find their own account inconclusive, and warn the reader that the syntactically factive/nonfactive distinction (as they present it) is speaker relative.[14]

b. Parsons, who is one of the few who discusses factivity explicitly in connection with singular terms, hastily takes the substitutability of 'the fact that *p*' to 'that *p*' as a test for *semantic* factivity (though not as the best test; Parsons, 1993, 453). Note that although Parsons seems to endorse Fact Reference*Power!* unproblematically (Parsons, 1993, 441, 454–455), it can be shown that he actually does *not* endorse it, though he does endorse the view that that-clauses are singular terms (see sec. 6.2 above).

c. None among Parsons, Peterson, Vendler, and the Kiparskys claim that the test to see whether a that-clause is (semantically) nonfactive consists in substituting 'the proposition that *p*' for 'that *p*', and I know of no such tests in any other relevant literature on factivity.[15] Peterson claims that head interpolation tests for factivity are unwarranted:

All of these kinds of forms with head nouns interpolated—e.g., 'the proposition' in propositional clauses, 'the fact' in factive clauses ...—will *not* see a simple deletion transformation as suggested by Kiparsky & Kiparsky. We think these cases with head nouns interpolated should be assimilated to structures for names and definite descriptions, where we hold that the basic fact, proposition ... expressions are neither proper names nor definite descriptions. (Peterson, 1997, 93)

So the question arises of whether the substitution tests *ad NecSingular-Terms 1* are not after all unwarranted, that is, whether they rest on a misunderstanding on the side of the No Singular Term theory—perhaps partially prompted by Parsons's work. I show below that these tests *are* warranted.

The considerations in *a*, *b*, and *c* are all correct, but they do not show that the criticism of the No Singular Term theory rests on a mistake, and they do not show that rejecting Singular Term theory (i.e., showing the falsity of the thesis that that-clauses are singular terms) does not disprove Fact Reference$_{Power!}$. For in fact it does disprove it, and here's why. Recall that there is an important difference between Factivity and Fact Reference$_{Power!}$; only the latter, and not the former, rests on Singular Term theory. Peterson is right that the *factivity* tests are not substitution tests of the kind invoked by the No Singular Term theory in the substitution failures ('the fact'-interpolation for factive that-clauses and 'the proposition'-interpolation for nonfactive that-clauses). But the point is that the substitution failures do not arise because of Factivity; they arise because of Singular Terms, that is, the assumption that that-clauses are (singularly) referring expressions. The latter, and not Factivity, is the fundamental assumption of Fact Reference$_{Power!}$. I did not use the tests, in chapter 4, to show that Factivity is wrong, but to show that that-clauses are not singular terms. What I did was merely to ensure that the tests were not vitiated by factivity/nonfactivity mismatch so that they could not be dismissed on that ground. For the point is this: if one's theory claims that that-clauses are singular terms, then that theory *is* vulnerable to substitution failure, no matter which tests for factivity one puts forward. The substitution failures with head interpolation are a problem for Fact Reference$_{Power!}$ because that thesis depends on the assumption that that-clauses are singular terms.

One might still wonder whether Peterson, Vendler & co. *really do* adhere to Singular Terms. Peterson says in the quote above that that-clauses are neither proper names nor definite descriptions. By this he could mean either that he takes that-clauses to be singular terms of a new kind, a kind that behaves in a different way from any other kind of singular terms, or else that that-clauses are not singular terms but that their *semantic value* is a fact or a proposition. The second option, put in our terms, would mean accepting the far weaker

Semantic Value   At least some that-clauses have facts as their *semantic value*.

To my knowledge, there is no support for Semantic Value in Peterson's or Vendler's writings, but there is support for Fact Reference:

A. A noun phrase NP_i *refers to a fact* if and only if (i) there is a full-sentence structure S_i embedded in the deep structure (or one nearly identical to it) of the sentence NP_i occurs in and S_i is the de-vendlerization of NP_i, and (ii) S_i can be replaced by at least one corresponding indirect question structure S_i' preserving grammaticality in the ultimate surface form based on this revised deep structure. B. if NP_i satisfies (i) ... but fails the test in (ii) then *the referent of NP_i is a PROPOSITION*. (Peterson, 1997, 76; emphasis added)

Certainly, according to Vendler, 'the word *term* belongs to the logician's, not to the linguist's vocabulary' (Vendler, 1967, 35). Yes, but so does reference: and *if* we want to argue that a factive 'that *p*' successfully refers to one and only fact, the fact that *p*, while a nonfactive 'that *p*' successfully refers to one and only proposition, the proposition that *p*, then what we want (and need) to argue is that that-clauses *are* singular terms. Since we can rule out the supposition that Semantic Value is all Peterson and Vendler want, the only option left to us to interpret what is going on is, arguably, that they take that-clauses to be a new kind of singular term. But if this is their position, as I pointed out in chapter 4, section 4.2, they beg the question.

So, yes, if Singular Term theory must be abandoned, Fact Reference*Power!* must be abandoned as well. If that-clauses are not singular terms, it is not the case that factive that-clauses refer to facts and nonfactive that-clauses refer to propositions; therefore, theories based on the latter, such as Vendler's and Peterson's, must be abandoned.

6.4   Conclusion

In chapter 4, we saw that Fact Reference is false, that is, that that-clauses do not refer to facts because that-clauses are not singular terms. As far as I am concerned, the rebuttal of the argument from nominal reference for facts was concluded at that point. In chapters 5 and 6, I have offered a fallback position leading to the conclusion that all that-clauses refer to propositions.[16] Here I have assumed the contrary of chapter 4, that is, that that-clauses *are* singular terms, and explored a fallback position while ignoring the problem posed by Singular Term theory. The conclusion of this exploration is that Fact Reference$_{Power!}$ is problematic even on its own—even if we accept that that-clauses are singular terms.

In chapter 5, section 5.1, we saw that if we combine the view that language exhibits a phenomenon called factivity, which is intrinsically linked to the implication or presupposition of the truth of certain embedded clauses (i.e., Factivity), with the idea that there are two kinds of that-clauses, one referring to facts and another referring to propositions (i.e., Fact Reference), we obtain the claim that factive that-clauses refer to facts whereas nonfactive clauses refer to propositions (i.e., Fact Reference$_{Power!}$). Fact Reference$_{Power!}$ is a stronger and more reliable claim than Fact Reference because it gives us an explanatory account of which that-clauses refer to facts. (As we just saw, Fact Reference$_{Power!}$ and Fact Reference have the same problem as Singular Term theory, and thus both Fact Reference$_{Power!}$ and Fact Reference as false as well.) In chapter 5, sections 5.2–5.3, we saw that the view of the relationship between facts and propositions that Fact Reference$_{Power!}$ implies (since its facts are facts of the propositional kind, i.e., items that are, like propositions, not in the world, and are as fine-grained as propositions) is such that there is no difference between propositional facts and true propositions. In chapter 5, section 5.4, through chapter 6, section 6.2, we tried to find a convincing argument to establish a difference between propositional facts and true propositions, but we did not manage to do so: all attempts to block the identification have failed. Moreover, in section 6.2 of chapter 6, we considered counterexamples involving anaphora (such as the 'knowledge'/'belief case' and the 'predict'/'surprise' case) that cannot be coherently accounted for by the proponent of Fact Reference$_{Power!}$.

The upshot of all this is that holding onto Fact Reference$_{Power!}$ forces us to identify true propositions with (propositional) facts after all. So, even if that-clauses were singular terms (and they are not), the view that there are two kinds of that-clauses, one referring to facts and one referring to propositions, entails that propositional facts are the only type of facts there are, and propositional facts are identical to true propositions.

Hence, to assume Fact Reference$_{Power!}$ is pointless *unless* we are ready to accept the identification of propositional facts with true propositions. On the basis of these findings, if we really want to hold on to Fact Reference$_{Power!}$ and keep using the word 'fact' as a technical term, then we must accept that facts are true propositions. This can count as a rebuttal of the argument from nominal reference for those who reject this identification. Those who endorse this identification, by contrast, would likely use these conclusions to support their own view. But this means, of course, that the linguistic evidence that backs up Fact Reference*Power!* cannot support any philosophical view of facts as different from propositions. To be convincing, Fact Reference*Power!* must be supplemented with a theory of propositional facts in which one ascribes to them a metaphysical role that cannot be played by any other category of entities, such as propositions. We did not see even the shadow of such a theory, however, and to the best of my knowledge none is on offer.

This means that, after having said farewell to compositional facts, we can now say farewell to propositional facts as well.

Conclusion: Farewell to Facts

Recall Russell's quote cited at the very beginning of this book:

The first truism to which I wish to draw your attention ... is that the world contains facts, which are what they are whatever we may choose to think about them, and that there are also beliefs, which have reference to facts, and by reference to facts are either true or false. ... If I say 'It is raining', what I say is true in a certain condition of weather and is false in other conditions. The condition of weather that makes my statement true (or false as the case may be), is what I should call a 'fact'. (Russell, 1918–1919, 500)

Is it, as Russell says, a *truism* that the world contains facts? No, it is not. It is implausible that the world contains facts. It is implausible that there are compositional facts, as I argue in part 1 (chapters 1–3), and it is implausible that there are propositional facts, as I argue in part 2 (chapters 4–6).

It is important to point out that I have used two quite different strategies to come to these conclusions. In part 1, I criticized views of compositional facts in such a way that no discrepancy had to be assumed between my own methodological stance and the stance of my opponents. By contrast, in part 2, I reasoned against propositional facts by reductio, that is, I assumed a methodological framework I don't share, the framework of what is called *descriptive* metaphysics, while in fact I endorse a view of metaphysics known as *revisionary*.[1] My reductio argument aimed to show from within the descriptive framework, so to speak, that the arguments put forward for propositional facts fail on grounds internal to that very framework.

The discrepancy between how I reasoned for such an extended portion of this book and my own methodological convictions, as well as the connection between the results of the two parts, calls for comment.

In my reductio, I first introduced a Quine-inspired argument: the argument for facts from nominal reference. This argument is built around three conditions for ontological commitment that facts allegedly fulfill: one regarding singular reference to (propositional) facts (first conjunct), one regarding identity conditions for facts (second conjunct), and one regarding the eliminability of quantification on facts in natural language (third conjunct). Roughly, in chapter 4 I discussed the first of these, and argued that there is no reference to facts; here I performed what we might call an *elimination* of facts: that-clauses, we found—and so the expression 'the fact that p'—do not refer at all (which implies that 'the proposition that p' does not refer at all, either). In chapters 5 and 6 I discussed the second condition, and argued that, under the assumption that there is, per absurdum, reference to facts via that-clauses, there are no acceptable identity conditions for propositional facts such that we can avoid their collapsing into true propositions. In chapter 5 and 6 I performed what we might call a *reduction* of facts to something else: facts are reduced to true propositions, so what 'fact' refers to is what 'true proposition' refers to, and this item is at most what I have called in chapter 1 a *Fregean proposition* (notice that this is not the same as saying that any of these words can be exchanged in all contexts). This result is also close to common use in natural language, in which, when 'facts' are contrasted with 'opinions', they fall in the same category of *grounded* statements (or *empirically corroborated*, if one prefers) that are held long enough by a large number of people. As to the third condition (third conjunct), the eliminability of quantification over facts in natural language, I argued in section 4.3 of chapter 4 that genuine quantification over facts in natural language depends on the first condition (first conjunct), that is, our having singular terms for facts in natural language. Since the first condition is unfulfilled, I concluded that the overall strategy underlying the argument from nominal reference is unsuccessful.

Now, what one may wonder on the basis of the above, independently of the descriptive framework underlining this strategy, is this: what if the argument succeeded on its own linguistic grounds, or could be strengthened sufficiently in order to do so? Would it be useful evidence for facts? No, it would not. Linguistic arguments—arguments that rely essentially on the use of linguistic expressions—*presuppose* an ontology of facts just to get off the ground (and I say that they must do so). It seems clear that at most arguments of this kind can be no more than articulations of the very ontological position they assume—as Quine thought. But such arguments cannot then be *both* articulations of an already assumed ontological position *and* drawn upon to support that very position, on pain of circularity. One cannot have it both ways. This, one may note, can easily be generalized: the only conclusion we can derive from linguistic arguments, it seems, is that such evidence is useful only to philosophers already convinced by whatever ontology the 'evidence' itself presupposes (Varzi, 2002, 2007). This means that, to be methodologically sound, linguistic enterprises in metaphysics must not only be explicitly descriptive, but also always explicitly *hypothetical*. That is, we have first to make clear that we are performing linguistic analysis (say, on the functioning of that-clauses) under the hypothetical assumption that certain entities exist (say, propositions, facts, and what have you).

I do not say that the methodology of descriptive metaphysics is faulty. It can be perfectly legitimate, but it has its rules, and those rules cannot be changed ad libitum when the game is already on. For example, the attempts we saw in chapters 5 and 6, aimed at blocking the identification of facts with true propositions, are methodologically unsound because they cannot reach their aim without breaking the rules of the game. The position we examined in those chapters according to which there are two kinds of that-clauses, one referring to facts and another to propositions, would thus, in theory, stand a chance as an honestly descriptive enterprise only if that enterprise is hypothetical: that is, all a descriptive metaphysician can say is that our conceptual schemes as expressed in language are such that some that-clauses refer to propositions and others refer to (propositional) facts—first, only under the hypothesis that that-clauses are singular terms, and second, only under the hypothesis that (propositional) facts and propositions exist as items of different categories. Two hypotheses are thus involved here: one in philosophy of language, about the reference of that-clauses, and another in metaphysics, about the existence of a certain category of propositional facts distinct from the category of propositions. Now, we saw in the chapter 4 that the hypothesis in philosophy of language is untenable: that-clauses aren't referential for reasons internal to language itself. In chapter 5, I showed that the metaphysical hypothesis is untenable as well. In chapter 6, I investigated whether one could defend the latter in, say, a nonhypothetical way, namely by letting it depend ultimately on language itself giving us reasons to think that (propositional) facts exist alongside propositions as items of different categories, only to find that this did not get us anywhere. For we saw that language itself gives us no reason to think that propositional facts exist alongside propositions as items of a different category. On the contrary, language shows that if we suppose that that-clauses are referential, then in the best case they refer to facts only if facts are true propositions. Propositional facts cannot be established by a descriptive strategy reliant upon the workings of that-clauses or other linguistic phenomena themselves reliant upon the use of the word 'fact'. On the face of this, descriptive metaphysicians have two options to be methodologically kosher. Either they bite the bullet and accept that there are no propositional facts alongside propositions; or they show where I go wrong, by playing the same descriptive game by the same descriptive rules. What they cannot do, in the second case, is to deny that the whole enterprise is hypothetical, for that would beg the question; or, in the first case, to forget that the enterprise is descriptive, because that would be cheating.

It is not difficult to show the circularity of philosophical positions defending propositional facts nonhypothetically on the basis of the workings of that-clauses. While philosophers adhering to such positions rely on what linguists such as Vendler say about facts and propositions, linguists such as Vendler rely on what those very philosophers say. But this, of course, is Münchhausen's pulling himself out of the marsh by his own hair. Let's consider, for instance, how the analyses of Vendler and Peterson from chapters 4 through 6 really work. Peterson argues along the following lines: in philosophy (in particular in the work of Austin as taken up by Vendler) there's talk of facts, propositions, events, states of affairs, and the like; let's see whether we can find any empirical support for such items in linguistics. This means that, according to this reasoning, one begins by assuming facts: linguistic analyses themselves nowhere require anything like the technical notions of *reference*, *proposition*, and *fact*. The linguist's declared aim here is that of using linguistics to support an ontology of facts and propositions, where, methodologically speaking, such an ontology (of some barely specified kind) is already taken for granted. But the only thing we can show on this basis is that the linguistic data in question fit this position. We can't fool ourselves into thinking that we are *discovering* something about facts and propositions by citing such linguistic analyses. As Noam Chomsky rightly observed about the method of applying results of linguistics to specific philosophical problems like causation and knowledge, it would be "a lucky accident if acquaintance with linguistics proved to be of substantial help in this inquiry" (Chomsky, 1969, 57). There is no hope to pull an ontological rabbit out of a linguistic hat. There is hope only to pull linguistic rabbits out of linguistic hats (and here 'linguistic' is about natural language).

In light of the above, the only methodologically acceptable position on reference to facts, if we find the latter nonnegotiable, is one according to which facts are taken to be the semantic value of certain expressions *by stipulation*. In this scenario, we take 'That p is a fact' to be true (in virtue of 'that p' referring to facts) in a regimented language that matches an ontology of facts that we assume from the outset: we just stipulate that the semantic value of 'that p' (in some cases) and 'the fact that p' are facts when we speak in the regimented language of the philosopher, no matter what natural language suggests.

So far, so good? Yes, but also no. And this is where my metaphysical conclusions about compositional facts and propositional facts (as distinct from true propositions) in both parts of the book come in. Since taking facts to be the semantic values of certain expressions requires facts in our ontology, we must now show by means other than linguistic arguments that we have good reasons to assume facts. But we don't have such reasons. As I have shown that no notion of fact as an item at the level of reference is metaphysically acceptable, it follows that taking our fact-talk seriously as involving propositional or compositional facts is metaphysically misguided. Propositional facts alongside propositions could reasonably be assumed if we could argue successfully that propositional facts (as different from true propositions) are needed to play a metaphysical role—that is, on the basis of arguments to the best explanation. But, as I have argued in chapter 5, propositional facts play no such role. A fortiori, they can't be established by any such arguments, because there is nothing for them to explain. Stipulating that that-clauses refer to them is thus not a sensible thing to do. Compositional facts could reasonably be assumed if compositional facts were the best candidate to play the roles of unifier of the world and truthmaker. But, as I have argued in chapters 2 and 3, they aren't. So stipulating that that-clauses refer to them is also not a sensible thing to do.

To sum up, at least in case of technical philosophical terms like 'fact', 'proposition', 'event', and the like, reference collapses into semantic value, and the latter is something we fix by stipulation. We can't specify what refers to what unless we have already made up our mind as to what there is in the world. At this point one might ask: how then do we know what there is in the world? It is not my aim here to answer this question. I shall offer some concluding remarks, however, on how I think we should answer it. As I also pointed out in my methodological remarks in chapters 2 and 3, arguing for the inclusion of any entity in our catalog of the world—answering: what is there?—depends first of all on how well that entity performs in certain fundamental roles that we agree *must* be played in view of important theoretical aims that we might indicate as basic. Basic theoretical aims tend to be maximally general, and the agreement as to which roles should be played has to be as large and as neutral as possible. Once we establish that certain important theoretical roles must be played by introducing entities, we then select from among available entities the ones that can play those roles in the best way. The criteria to decide what are the best ways an entity can play a role are certain theoretical virtues such as coherence, simplicity, economy, minimization of ad hoc moves, and so on. These virtues are normally relative: theories that possess them fare relatively better than others when we compare the costs and benefits. These two points— choosing roles and fixing the reference of an expression as its semantic value—are therefore related. We first set up an ontological scenario, and then match a more or less regimented language to this scenario. And in all this, the role of natural language is limited. It is doubtful that we should have any constraints of linguistic naturalness on the regimentation I am talking about here, because requiring that our regimentation should not bring us far from natural language seems hard to justify, if only because natural language is not designed for theoretical enterprises of this kind. Such a request would bring us back to the problem of assessing 'naturalness'. How can we do that? Recall that when we do philosophy, we speak in a language containing technical terms: it is an illusion to think that we can assess the naturalness of a language of this kind without being biased by ontological preferences. What we may well require of the regimented language at issue, however, is that it endeavor to keep our conceptual apparatus to a minimum ("minimize ideology," as Lewis and Quine would say).

We might fix what a metaphysician needs to show as follows:

(i)   The roles that are deemed necessary to be played really do need to be played by entities in order to achieve certain general theoretical aims.

(ii)   Choosing some entities to play such roles has certain important advantages over choosing other entities.

(iii)   The importance of these advantages is determined by certain meta-metaphysical values shared by the largest possible community (such as economy, simplicity, absence of ad hoc and question-begging reasoning, etc.).

As to (i), what are the roles that should be played by entities? Again, it is not my intention to be more than tentative and sketchy on this matter. In chapter 1, I did introduce, along with seven ontological characteristics possessed by facts, five semantic roles that I believe are taken to be played by entities in general (sentence-subject, sentence-sense, sentence-object, truth-bearer, and truthmaker), and in chapter 2 I introduced the ontological role of the 'unifier of reality', on which, as I have shown, the truthmaker role depends. And so one might want to ask whether I think that any of these roles represent roles that *must* be played, if perhaps not by facts.[2] Without being able to quantify this claim in any sufficiently objective way, the situation seems to me to be the following: there is little agreement among philosophers that we need a special entity to play the role sentence-sense; there is less agreement than there may seem to be that we need a special entity to play the role of truthmaker (ditto for unifier of reality); and there may be relatively broad, implicit agreement that there must be sentence-objects. There is very broad agreement, by contrast, that we need truthbearers, and I'd say the same applies to sentence-subjects. It seems to me, therefore, that among the semantic roles I've introduced, the least controversial are the truthbearer role[3] and the sentence-subject role. None of the others seem general and neutral enough; they make sense only within particular theories of the relationship between language and world.

If we now come back specifically to facts, it seems clear from the previous chapters that whoever defends facts does not seem to be working in agreement with the methodological desiderata of metaphysics just sketched. As said, it is doubtful that the roles of truthmaker and possibly sentence-object must be played, and in any case facts are not the best entities to play the roles of truthmaker and sentence-object.[4] We might argue that *every* theory of truth needs truthbearers, just as *every* theory of reference seems to postulate sentence-subjects. But that does not require facts. However, if truthmaker and sentence-object are roles to be played at all, our best choice is to say that they are played by certain mereological complexes including relata-/bearer-specific relations/properties. If so, then we can just stipulate that the reference of expressions like *Hargle's being happy* and *the being happy of Hargle* are mereological complexes, not facts. So far, defenders of facts have failed to show that facts should be given any place in metaphysics, let alone that it is a truism that the world contains facts.

Notes

Synopsis

1. The function of this chapter is similar to that of Reicher (2009).

1 Compositional Facts

1. The example, repeated by Russell (1919, 278), is controversial because weather sentences like 'It's raining' pose adjunctive problems concerning their logical form, which does not seem to allow for analysis in terms of object-quality predication. I will disregard this complication here.

2. These "semantic roles" (Simons, 1988; Morscher & Simons, 1982; Morscher, 1986) appear in the interplay of language, mind, and world. I follow this terminology but it is very important to make clear that facts are *not* entities that themselves have semantic or representational aspects. See also n. 7 below.

3. For a brief discussion of the notion of existence in metaphysics that I accept, and of the criteria to decide whether we are able to claim that (it is plausible that) certain categories of entities exist, see the introduction, pp. xvi–xviii.

4. On the fact/value dichotomy, see Herbst (1956); Anscombe (1958); Foot (1958–59).

5. I will disregard the role of the objects of mental states and acts (*judgment-objects*) because it won't play any role in this book. However, there are arguments against facts in which it is a crucial element that facts can (or cannot) play the role of that which judgments in our mind are about. For more on this, see Betti (2013).

6. One may wonder where this list of conditions comes from. Lists of this kind are always set up by way of a mix of methods and aims. For the most part, the list comes from a descriptive and empirical—if one may say so—study of a variety of texts from different periods and traditions about facts and other entities, that is, of what philosophers themselves have said about facts and what is implied by this. In smaller

part, the list is a tool designed normatively via conceptual analysis on the basis of systematic choices, but still with interpretive aims in mind, and especially well suited for use in doing history of philosophy. The list of conditions can be also seen as a *model* in Betti and van den Berg's (2014) sense. See also n. 40 and the list of characteristics for propositional facts I give in chap. 5, sec. 5.2.

7. This list is adapted from Simons (1988, 97–101). I follow Simons rather closely here for the presentation of (some of) the semantic roles. See also n. 2 above.

8. Therefore, following existing terminology, in chapters 1 through 3 I won't use 'sentence-subject' to mean the grammatical subject of a sentence. In chapters 4 through 6, however, I shall need to talk of 'subjects', 'structural subjects', and 'null-subject languages' in a purely grammatical sense. I hope that the difference across chapters is not too confusing.

9. On reference, see Reimer (2010) and chap. 4 below.

10. Translation courtesy of @clarocada.

11. A good general introduction to propositions is Loux (2006, 121–139).

12. The idea of projection is quite new. Until the end of the nineteenth century there was no room for a relation of projection of this kind. For more on this, see Betti (2013).

13. Thoughts and ideas have also been considered to be primary truthbearers (see Künne, 2003, 100, 249; David, 2009, sec. 2.1). I do not deal with theories of this kind here.

14. On sentences versus judgments as truthbearers, see again Betti (2013).

15. Smith (1999, 274). See also Bigelow (1988); Fox (1987); Mulligan, Simons, & Smith (1984); Armstrong (1997, 13). These works do use the word 'correspondence', but they reason as if correspondence is reduced to truthmaking only, namely a relation of necessitation from the world to truthbearers, and do not, as Smith (1999) does, take truthmaking to have a dual nature (necessitation *and* projection). For a rather exhaustive overview on truthmaking theory positions, see MacBride (2014).

16. In sec. 1.4 below I call these truthbearers *Aristotelian propositions*.

17. To be sure, there are theories in which some sort of factlike entities are taken (also) to play the role of sentence-sense (role 1) and of truthbearer (role 4). However, as we shall see in sec. 1.4.2 below, these are theories that acknowledge not facts or states of affairs, but certain hybrid entities that are a mix of states of affairs and (Fregean) propositions: Meinongian *Objective* or Russellian propositions. As we shall see in chap. 3, sec. 3.3, theories in which such entities feature inherit all the problems I shall consider for facts *plus* certain other problems.

18. Note also that the claim that a single unified entity is needed does not mean that it is always the case that *one* single unified entity—a fact—is needed. This point depends on the extent to which a philosopher adheres to *logical atomism*, namely the position according to which *molecular* predications such as 'Hargle is sick and Bargle is choppy' do not require a single truthmaker, but can be made true by more than one fact. See also n. 23 below.

19. In chapter 2, I shall address this point without making a separate case for properties, but not everyone agrees that we can do that without further ado, i.e., agrees that we can treat properties as monadic relations (as Russell, 1918–1919, 522, saw them), because, it is argued, relations are "categorically different" from properties. See Meinertsen (2008, sec. 4).

20. This is not entirely Armstrong's view, but this need not concern us yet. See the introduction to chap. 2.

21. By using 'reticulate', I do not wish to select any particular view of facts. Different kinds of facts that differ in reticulation will be discussed in chap. 2.

22. For this reason I shall ignore the option of being a reductionist about relations, i.e., transforming all relations into *relational properties*.

23. As noted (see n. 18), some friends of facts also accept nonbasic, i.e., *molecular* states of affairs—negative, disjunctive, conjunctive, conditional, existential, and general states of affairs. See for a first approach Wetzel (2003, sec. 4). Since my arguments apply to basic characteristics of compositional facts, I will not need to consider molecular states of affairs in this chapter and the rest of part 1 (chaps. 2–3). I will need to consider molecular *propositional* facts in chaps. 5 and 6 instead.

24. See Loux (1998, 40, and 56–57).

25. Throughout this book I am completely disregarding matters concerning time and space indexes in predication and their ontological systematization.

26. Cf. Grossmann (1992, 20).

27. This means that if there is just one property or relation in number, it would be both particular and universal or neither. This is unproblematic for what I have to say in this book.

28. Paul (2002) calls these 'logical parts', but in the tradition at least up to the nineteenth century they were called 'metaphysical parts' (tropes): the 'logical parts' were the parts of the definition of (the concept) of an object. In the following I will freely speak of tropes as (metaphysical) parts of objects.

29. On tropes, see the excellent Maurin (2002).

30. This is a bit quick. As is known, universals come in two sorts, Aristotelian and Platonistic (Loux, 2002, 40–43). Since Aristotelian universals are time bound, the

notion of *ideal* introduced in this section is inapplicable to them unless tweaked as follows: "Objects are ideal if they are timeless, or if, time bound, are universal" (see the previous condition for a characterization of 'universal'). Granted, this sounds rather artificial. The point is of little relevance, however, because my discussion of the unity problem in chap. 2 is independent of Aristotelianism or Platonism about universals. Still, since Armstrong's position on facts is the best available and that position relies on Aristotelian universals, I'll come back to the issue in condition 5 below.

31. To be absolutely clear: I am speaking of lowest-order or rock-bottom cases of reference. The sense/reference distinction is of course a distinction of roles similar to the one I made between roles 2 and 3 in the previous section, so one can have cases of semantic ascent in which we talk about entities that normally play the role of sense (as when you say '*Gedanken* are sentence-senses according to Frege'). But these cases are generated from the rock-bottom, most normal cases. See also condition 4 below.

32. Recall that I am speaking about *compositional* facts. As we shall see, defenders of *propositional* facts deny this point (see chap. 5, sec. 5.2), as they deny other characteristics I am here attributing to facts. However, I will argue in chapter 6 that propositional facts are (Fregean) propositions, and that there is no convincing story to tell to show that the aboutness of propositional facts is a distinct phenomenon from the aboutness of Fregean propositions. See also n. 54 below.

33. Again, I am speaking of rock-bottom cases. Depending on how we look at semantics, some events could be considered semantically non-idle, but those will be quite special cases—such as the event of someone's (or her expressions') referring to something—and such cases might arguably be generated from or depend on other, nonsemantic events, such as uttering words or engaging in mental activity. How this would actually work, I leave undiscussed.

34. A similar problem arises if propositions and facts are merged, as they are in theories accepting Meinongian *Objektive* and Russellian propositions. On these factlike entities, see sec. 1.4.2 below.

35. Imperceptible events are a difficult case—so much so that even philosophers who have devoted extensive efforts to understanding events avoid dealing with imperceptible events at the outset (see, e.g., Bennett, 1988, 2).

36. "As well as having no considerable rivals, this view about what events are is hardly even controversial" (Bennett, 1988, 93). Note that Bennett acknowledges facts but identifies them with propositions. For positions of this kind, which are left untouched by my arguments against facts (though possibly vulnerable to my arguments against that-clauses in chap. 4), see chap. 6, sec. 6.2.

37. Note that this point is important for philosophers who are action theorists. If actions are a subcategory of events, then accepting the distinction I make here

between facts and events is important because my arguments do not apply to events, and thus to actions. If, however, actions are not a subcategory of events but are relations between agents and events (see Casati & Varzi, 2010, sec. 2.3, and the literature quoted there), then depending on what such relations are taken exactly to be, actions might very well be facts, and thus fall prey to the arguments of this book.

38. I return to the identity conditions of facts in chap. 5, sec. 5.2.

39. The existing versus subsisting distinction as time-bound versus time-unbound (or timeless) being is perhaps most famously associated with Meinong (Meinong, 1902, 189; 1910, 74–75), but it can be found in Twardowski as well, and even earlier in Bolzano (see Betti & Raspa, forthcoming).

40. Note that here the tweaked notion of *ideal* from n. 30 above applies. Given this tweaked notion, condition 5 also applies to Armstrongian facts. Since Armstrong accepts Aristotelian universals, an Armstrongian fact and its reticulated constituents are all time bound (thanks to Anna-Sofia Maurin for discussion on this point). Still, at least one of the constituents of an Armstrongian fact has an ontological character-istic that both the whole and at least one of its other constituents do *not* have: *exist-ing as wholly present as one in number at different places and different times and possibly scattered in both time and space*. It should also be said for completeness that although condition 6 happens to be obeyed by the major positions on facts, one could insist that this condition is not strictly necessary for facthood. The same applies to condi-tion 2. For instance, within a variant of trope monism one could consistently defend facts that obey conditions 1, 3, 4, and 6, but not 2 and 5, i.e., facts with all and only abstract and real tropes as constituents. My arguments also apply to these fact-vari-ants. Thanks to Jeroen Smid for discussion on this point.

41. 'Sachverhalt', the German term for state of affairs, expresses this relational aspect more transparently than 'state of affairs'. See Mulligan (1985, 145). I take the term 'reticulation' from Smith (1989), 421. On states of affairs, see below, sec. 1.4.2.

42. *Pace* Vallicella (2004), see Wieland and Betti (2008).

43. See, e.g., Fine (1982, 73).

44. Note that Russell's approach bears more than a vague conceptual resemblance to Bolzano's notion of the form of a proposition. See Bolzano (1837, §§ 12, 69, 81, 147).

45. See, e.g., Dodd (1999, 154); Horgan (1978, 42).

46. To take into account this complication and try to make the point clearer for the moment, consider this. Suppose you say that actually there are three things: (1) Hargle, (2) sadness, *and* (3) the loose, mere collection Hargle *plus* sadness of which both (1) and (2) are parts, as we might say there are 345 sheep *and* the flock of them. A fact would be a *fourth* thing, composed such as to yields a real unity; a unity like

that which a sheep has, and not like the loose composition of the flock. For more on this, see chap. 2, introduction and sec. 2.2.

47. The clearest example is perhaps my labeling of singular or Russellian propositions below as 'blurs', 'hybrids,' or 'propfacts', and my classification of them, given the framework I am using, as variants of states of affairs.

48. This makes clear that my 'propositions' are *structured* propositions (see King, 2011). There are views according to which propositions aren't structured, e.g., views taking propositions to be sets of possible worlds. In this book I leave aside such views (i.e., *noncompositional* views).

49. Note that, historically speaking, it would be more accurate to call this view 'Bolzanian' since it is uncontroversial that Bolzano's *Sätze an sich* are structured, whereas some dispute that Frege held his *Gedanken* to be structured (see, e.g., Kemmerling, 2010). However, since today the position acknowledging such entities goes commonly under the name of "Fregeanism," this terminology has the advantage of departing less from contemporary systematic usage.

50. As noted, Fregean and the Aristotelian (one could also call it, with some reason, *Quinean*) propositions are variants of the notion of structured proposition as I have introduced it; they should not be considered the two notions of structured propositions that are considered paradigmatic today. These are, rather, the notions of Fregean and Russellian (or *singular*) propositions (see Fitch & Nelson, 2009). I treat the notion of Russellian (or singular) proposition below as a variant of the notion of state of affairs.

51. Problems for compositionalist theories of propositions are, among others, the *reduplication problem*. See Textor (2008, 106); Vickers (2004, 502); Frege (1923, 15; 1918, 361).

52. See also Simons (1988, 100).

53. As in the case of facts, in some cases propositions (at least in approaches that admit of them) are sentence-subjects (role 1), but these are cases in which it can be argued that nominalizations of propositions figure as terms in sentences, namely in *second-order* cases such as

(1)   That Miss Caswell had a point, idiotic, but a point was what Addison said,

where *that Miss Caswell had a point, idiotic, but a point* is the sentence-*subject* of (1). By contrast, note that the *object* of (1) is *that Miss Caswell had a point, idiotic, but a point's being what Addison said.* I will reconsider critically nominalization in chapter 5.

54. Cf. also Olson (1987) versus Fine (1982, 45). There is, to be sure a *third* sense of 'about', due to Russell, according to which saying that a fact is 'about' Socrates means that the fact has Socrates has a constituent (Russell, 1919, 278). This sense

has been influential on so-called propositional views of facts, in which facts are unstructured ideal objects that have *no* constituents but are still said to be 'about' the worldly entities they 'contain'. These views feature in chapters 4 through 6 (see esp. chap. 5, sec. 5.2) below. As I shall argue, it does not seem possible to make sense of this (fourth?) sense of 'about' of propositional facts.

55. Prior (1976, 26). In Prior (1948) he puts this as follows: a true propositions expresses a fact, a false proposition denies it (see p. 64). Prior's propositions should be taken to be rather *Aristotelian* propositions. Prior's position recalls here that of the so-called middle Russell (1918–1919, 507), in which propositions and belief can be *true to the fact* or *false to the fact*.

56. The most famous philosopher who accepted obtaining and nonobtaining states of affairs is Wittgenstein (1921/1962, 2.04, 2.062 [2]). See also Grossmann (1992, 73).

57. See Olson (1987, 2).

58. On obtaining, see also chap. 5, sec. 5.4, n. 23.

59. See Simons (1988, 100–101).

60. Not surprisingly, this is exactly what direct reference theorists maintain; see, e.g., King (1996). Other possibilities are mentioned in King (2002, 365, n. 1).

61. Chisholm (1970, 21). Russell's influential notion of proposition comes from Russell (1903). Russell himself abandoned it a few years later, around 1907. Kaplan (1989) seems to have been particularly influential in the renaissance of this notion.

2   The Unity Problem

1. This *lectio* is only in some manuscripts. Others reconstruct the line as "Stat Roma pristina nomine, nomina nuda tenemus."

2. The word *complex* is Russell's translation of Meinong's *Komplexion*. Russell did not distinguish between complexes and facts.

3. For the debate on the difference at issue here, see Thomson, 1983; Wiggins, 1968. Philosophers who have argued against the difference have used two arguments: (1) *x* and *y* cannot differ in their *modal* properties if their *actual* properties coincide (same location, same shape, same weight, same color, etc.). For in virtue of what would their modal properties diverge (Burke, 1992; Zimmerman, 1995; Olson, 2001; Sider, 1999; for replies: Rea, 1997, Lowe, 1998a, 223; Bennett, 2004; Koslicki, 2004)? (2) When we say that *x* and *y* are different, there is a de dicto and a de re reading, and the latter is question begging (Lewis, 1971; Robinson, 1985; Noonan, 1991; Jubien, 1993; and—from a slightly different perspective—Della Rocca, 1996, Varzi, 2005; for replies: Fine, 2003, 198).

4. In Varzi 2010 the principle is formulated as follows:

(P15) $\exists w \varphi w \rightarrow \exists z \forall w \, (Ozw \leftrightarrow \exists v(\varphi v \wedge Ovw))$

where φ stands for any condition, i.e., a predicate applying to any kind of objects in the universe, O ('overlap') is defined $Oxy =_{df} \exists z(Pzx \wedge Pzy)$ and P stands for 'part', for the following which axioms (forming so-called *ground mereology*, the basis of any comprehensive part-whole theory) are given:

(P1) *Reflexivity* Pxx
(P2) *Transitivity* $(Pxy \wedge Pyz) \rightarrow Pxz$
(P3) *Antisymmetry* $(Pxy \wedge Pyx) \rightarrow x=y$.

P15 and P1–3, together with

(P5) *Strong Supplementation* $\neg Pyx \rightarrow \exists z(Pzy \wedge \neg Ozx)$,

yield *general extensional mereology* (the powerful theory of Stanisław Leśniewski, and of Henry Leonard and Nelson Goodman).

5. This means that the problem I deal with in this and the following chapter is neutral with respect to the question of whether there is any composition at all in the universe. According to *mereological nihilists*, there isn't—there are no parts and no wholes. In this position, 'part' is seen as a semantically empty term—which, I take it, means that 'compose' in 'x and y compose z' stands for an internal relation I introduce in chap. 3, sec. 3.1 (cf. Sider, 2013).

6. "A proposition, in fact, is essentially a unity, and when analysis has destroyed the unity, no enumeration of constituents will restore the proposition. The verb, when used as a verb, embodies the unity of the proposition, and is thus distinguishable from the verb considered as a term, though I do not know how to give a clear account of the precise nature of the distinction" (Russell, 1903, 54). To see the immediate relevance of this, read here for 'verb', 'relation'; for 'proposition', read 'complex', 'fact', or 'state of affairs'; for 'terms', read 'objects' or 'constituents'.

7. Unless noted otherwise, I take mereology to be general extensional mereology (see n. 4 above). This is by no means uncontroversial, but the issue whether general extensional mereology is the mereological calculus we should adopt, and in particular whether we should remove the extensionality of parthood from that calculus, lies beyond the scope of this book (on this, see Varzi, 2008, 2010). For this reason, and to avoid confusion, I am holding to a simple opposition between mereology and 'constitution theory', meaning by this any theory that rejects the extensionality of parthood. This determines my terminology: when I need it (though often I don't), I will keep separate *parts of complexes*, which obey extensional mereological principles such as the extensionality of parthood (see p. 67), and *constituents of facts*, which do not obey those principles. One *might* extend the meaning of 'part' in such a way to cover both, but, as Russell put it: "We may make a ... general sense, in which anything which is part in any sense, or part in one sense of part in another, is

to be called a part. This sense, however, has seldom, if ever, any utility in actual discussion" (Russell, 1903, 135).

8. This is why it is not surprising to find in the literature the same critical discussion formulated sometimes in terms of relations and sometimes in terms of facts (which, as I said, I do not distinguish from complexes, for the time being). Methodologically speaking, one can approach the issue in two ways: (1) give a critical assessment of the unity problem for facts by raising the unity problem directly for facts; (2) criticize facts as a solution to the unity problem for relations and properties by arguing that they suffer from the very problem that they are supposed to solve, or that they are not a good solution to that problem. For Armstrong's particular primitivist theory, which I consider to defend the best brand of facts, it does not really matter how we start.

9. This is also how Olson looks at the issue, if I read him correctly, although he does not put the issue explicitly in this way, nor does he speak of *roles*. See Olson (1987, iv).

10. What I handle here is most recently discussed by Maurin (2012) under the general heading of "Unity in Complexity."

11. "In addition to the cup and the saucer we have to take account of the fact that the cup is on the saucer" (Olson, 1987, iv).

12. For more on this point, see Betti (2013).

13. Here's Armstrong, quoted in Dodd (1999, 155):

If mereological composition is the only form of composition that there is in the world, then the world has no real unity. The argument for this is that when objects form a mereological whole that whole supervenes on those objects. Given a and b then the whole is there automatically. But such supervenience is, I think, ontologically innocent. It adds nothing to the world that was not there before. ... That, incidentally, is why it seems proper to take mereological fusion in a permissive fashion so that a given a and b may be 'things' falling under different categories. The Sydney Opera House and $\sqrt{-1}$ have their fusion. But if this is so, then it seems that mere mereology never really unites things at all. ... Really to unite things ..., relations are required. ... So, I argue, the state of affairs of a's being (externally) related to b by some R is required. (Armstrong, 1991, 192)

14. I shall also endorse in my reasoning a particularly strong take on the unrestricted principle of mereological composition. That is, *for sums* (and only for sums) I will assume composition to be identity in a strong sense. This means that I assume that there is no ontological difference between the objects $x_1 ... x_n$ and their sum $x_1 + ... + x_n$ such that a sum is nothing over and above $x_1 ... x_n$. For the phrase 'over and above' see chapter 3, note 3. This position is controversial, but again neutral with respect to the unity problem: one can make the point I am making just as well for the weak version, but this would complicate the reasoning since an additional object would be involved.

15. The master argument style is borrowed from Vallicella (2002, 2004). The specific master argument I present here is an adaptation from Wieland and Betti (2008). The essentials of this section and some literal formulations come from the latter paper, but the points are updated and reworked, and much is added to the mereological issues only touched upon there (which were due to me). The main and final objection against facts as ad hoc objects you find in chap. 2, sec. 2.2, of this book is new. The option of considering mereological versus nonmereological composition as itself an *ontological ground* for the difference between sums and facts (though not its ramifications, discussed here in sec. 2.2), as well as the bulk of the material on relations in chap. 3, sec. 3.1, is due to Jan Willem Wieland.

16. A supporter of (B) is Bergmann (1967, 9); defenders of (D) are Armstrong (1997, 118–119), Olson (1987, 60–61), and Hochberg (1978, 338–339). For Hochberg's difficulties with exemplification, see also MacBride (2002, 220–222).

17. If you are a nonpresentist, sums will also contain a mix of present and nonpresent objects. I ignore issues regarding time in this book.

18. Note also that under unrestricted mereological composition, the world does contain scattered sums of half Scottish salmons, half American turkeys, Sarah Palin, and *shooting synchronically*, but cannot possibly contain the *unified* complex of these things (*Sarah Palin's synchronically shooting half a Scottish salmon and half an American turkey*).

19. This reconstruction of Bradley's relation regress adopts the general structure of an infinite regress from Maurin (2007). T is the trigger-statement, followed by an infinity of steps S1–S*N*, which are question–answer pairs.

20. This conclusion is resisted in *fact-infinitism* (Gaskin, 2009; Orilia, 2007, 2009). For discussion, see García-Carpintero, 2010; Gaskin 2010a,b; Schnieder, 2010; Vallicella, 2010. According to Gaskin, Bradley's regress isn't vicious, but it is "the metaphysical ground of the unity of the proposition" (Gaskin, 2009, 345). If one accepts this, then fact-infinitism can be listed as a fifth option E under M3. In my view, fact-infinitism misconstrues the meaning of 'metaphysical ground'. My position on the issue harmonizes roughly with that of Schnieder (2010).

21. One of the options Vallicella advances for what Big Bargle could be is *God*. But this cannot be acceptable. Not only would the option be open only to theists, it would actually be a big problem for theists since it would accept a very strong form of (ontological) occasionalism, namely occasionalism about *individuals*. This cannot be reconciled with theodicy. Even Malebranche defended, for this reason, only a generic form of occasionalism; see Schmaltz (2009).

22. See Olson (1987), vi, chap. 3.

23. See n. 3 above.

24. Note that although the criticism just mentioned is shared by Vallicella, he does accept unmereological composition, since he thinks that the complex and the sum

might share the same parts and yet be different. But for him, there can be no unmereological composition *without an external composer*, that is, in the case at issue, the *U*-operator (Vallicella 2000, 246–247)—Big Bargle. I do not think Vallicella needs to assume unmereological composition if he assumes Big Bargle, but I will leave this issue aside here.

25. This is a general problem with metaphysical positions in which controversial notions are taken as primitive. It is a bad move, for the simple reason that if our primitive notions are problematic, we will sooner or later end up in question-begging reasoning. For a similar complaint, see sec. 5 of Betti (2010) against the primitivity of 'because' as proposed by Benjamin Schnieder (2006b).

26. An ad hoc ontology might be defined as one made up of "those entities postulated by a theory T the only or main reason to believe in which is that they, in the context of T, play a certain theoretical roles (e.g. contribute to the explanation of a phenomenon X or the solution of a problem Y)" (Rodríguez-Pereyra, 2002, 211).

27. A case in which this constraint is not in place is that of propositional facts, which, as I shall argue in chaps. 5 and 6, do not even play a metaphysical role.

28. As Vallicella puts it, "An argument for truthmakers is not automatically an argument for states of affairs as truthmakers; but given the rest of [Armstrong's] ontology, states of affairs are the only sort of entity that could do the truthmaker job" (Vallicella, 2000, 237).

29. One could object that the truthmaker argument is an argument to the best explanation based on (6) as a definitional step (one of the ontological conditions I have listed in chap. 1) and hold that such a definitional step can't be criticized for being *false*. We can reply to this by attacking the notion of nonmereological composition involved in the definition (and for this resort to the arguments I offer in this chapter). (Thanks to Jonathan Lowe for discussion on this point.) To put it in terms of best explanation, I rather see the conclusion of the argument (facts as the best explanation of truthmaking) as based on the claim that facts are the best explanation of world unity; since the latter is implausible, as I show, the whole argument is implausible. On a more radical critical take of the truthmaker argument (which I am not taking here), one could claim that not the *two* roles of truthmaker and unifier of the world, but just *one* issue is involved, namely nonmereological composition, which is presumed in (6) to the effect of showing its very need in the conclusion; by this reasoning, the argument is clearly question begging.

30. This is also why formal systematization (see, e.g., Suszko, 1968) does not bring the problem nearer a solution. For, again, the problem is not whether a more or less formally adequate theory can or cannot be developed once nonmereological composition is given, but whether we can plausibly assume such composition in the first place.

31. This third point (but not the objection to it) is due to Jan Willem Wieland.

32. For these modes of combination, see Russell (1904/1994). See the next chapter for more on option B, *Resist*, as a mereological alternative.

33. Note that the status of facts under option D as nonmereological complexes of *constituents* neutralizes as question-begging Lewis's 'Humeanist' objection against this kind of facts. Lewis (1998, 215–216; see also MacBride, 2014, sec. 2.4) argues that since the mereological parts of a fact have (separately or together in a sum) distinct existence from that fact, then it cannot be the case that the fact cannot exist without them. The defender of facts under options D can reply that it is not without its mereological parts that a fact cannot exist, because it has none; the fact cannot exist *without its constituents*—without the constituents it reticulates. Since its constituents are not distinct existences with respect to the fact, there is nothing mysterious in the circumstance that the fact ontologically depends on them. As we shall see in sec. 2.2.2., although this 'reduplication of the world' characteristic of facts saves them from the Lewis's Humeanistic objection we just saw, it makes them vulnerable to my *ad hocness* objection.

34. Strictly speaking, following Varzi (2008), three principles can be distinguished that are normally identified in the literature:

(1)   *Extensionality of Parthood*: If x and y are composite objects with the same proper parts, then $x = y$. (A composite object is anything that has proper parts, i.e., parts distinct from the whole.)

(2)   *Uniqueness of Composition*: If x and y are sums of the same things, then $x = y$, where x is a sum of the zs $=_{df}$ the zs are all parts of x and every part of x has a part in common with at least one of the zs.

(3)   *Extensionality of Composition*: If x and y are composed of the same things, then $x = y$, where x is composed of the zs $=_{df}$ x is a sum of the zs and the zs are pairwise disjoint (i.e., no two of them have any parts in common). It is important to Varzi's defense of (1) to distinguish these three principles, but nothing here hinges on keeping them separate.

35. On this issue, see also McDaniel (2009). Note in particular that option D does not exclude that mereological composition also applies to facts. Indeed, Armstrong writes: "But of course if states of affairs are taken as units, as atoms one might say, and one does not dive within these states of affairs, then they are susceptible of themselves being put together in a way that obeys the mereological rules" (Armstrong, 1997, 122). Although facts are *unmereologically* composed units (and so composed of atoms that have unmereological composition), they are themselves the atomic building blocks of the world obeying *mereological* composition. For instance, a conjunction of two Armstrongian facts such as *Hargle's being happy* and *Bargle's being choppy* is not itself another fact, not a *third* fact over and above these two; rather, it is just a mereological sum of these two facts (themselves unmereologically composed). As noted, I am ignoring here the question of the exact relationship between composition and identity. I have some sympathy for the strong take on the

issue (composition *is* identity), but the topics I discuss in this chapter and the next are neutral with respect to this point. See n. 14 above. As to 'over and above': sometimes (as in Armstrong, 1997, 90) Armstrong uses '*a* supervenes on *b*' to mean that there is *only b*, not *a* as well (so that we have one, not two objects: but we do have two *names*, *a* and *b*, referring to the same object). At some points he suggests that when *a* supervenes on *b* it does name a *second* object distinct from the object named by *b* (see also Simons, 2009). On 'over and above', see the introduction to this chapter and chap. 1, sec. 1.3, condition 7.

36. Note that there is a slight difference between the kind of modal talk in Armstrongian or D-dualism and the kind of modal talk I discussed in the introduction to this chapter. The former is expressed in terms of existence conditions for sums and facts in all generality from the point of view of parts/constituents, while the latter (as in the example of the pawns in the introduction) is formulated under the assumption that a certain specific fact is given. The modal difference in the latter case is one between the constituents of a sum that *can* form a certain specific fact *f* and those constituents that *do* form this fact *f*. This difference has no bearing on my argument.

37. As noted, the debate on material constitution concerns mainly the issue of whether extensional mereology is generally applicable to the world. Usually, to show that mereology is not extensional, philosophers in this debate come up with alleged counterexamples to principles of extensional mereology, which are normally cases of colocated objects that, it is argued, are nonidentical, such as the statue and the lump of clay of which it is composed. This is a (subtle) further difference with Armstrong, but not a problematic one for my reasoning. See also n. 3 above.

38. Incidentally, note that if objects span across times and worlds, EP stands, as α, β would not have the same temporal/modal parts (see Varzi, 2008). As I said, I am not taking into account questions about time in this book.

39. Note that my point is general, and independent of the assumption that the world is or is not atomistic. If we are dealing with nonatomistic theories, we can simply take the constituents to be of relative simplicity, i.e., we can reason as if they are simple.

40. See also n. 28 above.

3   Solving the Unity Problem

1. This account of the three feature-pairs comes from Wieland and Betti (2008). It is mainly due to Jan Willem Wieland, and inspired by Maurin's asymmetric dependence theory of relations (Maurin, 2010a, sec. 5; see also Maurin, 2002, sec. 4.4.1).

2. This take on the internal/external distinction derives from Russell (1907, 139–146).

3. Peter van Inwagen has criticized the use of the phrase 'being nothing over and above' on the grounds that nobody explains what this means (van Inwagen 2001, 99). Here is an explanation. The phrase 'x is nothing over and above y' means this. Suppose at t you take Sicilian caciocavallo, marinated eggplant, a roll, and arrange them into a sandwich. Do you thereby create at t a new entity—say, the caciocavallo-and-marinated-eggplant-sandwich entity? If you do *not*, the sandwich is nothing over and above the ingredients taken together. If you do create a new entity, than the sandwich is an entity over and above its parts or constituents. If the sandwich is nothing over and above its ingredients, however you count them at t, it is not the case that there are the following *four* things: caciocavallo, marinated eggplant, roll, and sandwich.

4. This is a very strong take on the internality of relations, but I won't deal with this issue here. We can just retain this characterization and assume that all the relations I will discuss are external.

5. Reasons for preferring (relata-specific) tropes over universals are given in Wieland (2008) and Maurin (2010b).

6. Actually, it seems possible to consider Big Bargle at option C in a different way (which is arguably not the one Vallicella thinks of, see chap. 2, n. 24) as nothing more than a subspecies of the mode of combination option in the second sense described on pp. 65–66 and thus a case of B: a very big mode of combination one can add to any $a + R + b$ mereological sum. For, at any given time, all-purpose Big Bargle keeps together the very same constituents in a certain specific way. If at time t_1 Argle precedes Bargle and at time t_2 Bargle precedes Argle instead, Big Bargle is *not* keeping the constituents Argle, Bargle, and *preceding* by self-determination in the same way at both times: the sum Argle+*preceding*+Bargle will be the same in both cases but BigBargle$_{apb}$+Argle+*preceding*+Bargle at t_1 and BigBargle$_{bba}$+Argle+*preceding*+Bargle at t_2 will be different.

7. "We surely don't want to say that a relation that relates a and b, by its very nature as a relation, could not have related any other pair. That would contradict the fact that R is external to its terms" (Vallicella, 2000, 240; cf. Vallicella, 2002, 14–15, 31; 2004, 164).

8. See Wieland and Betti (2008) where we discuss a second explanation of why Vallicella disregards the two solutions just mentioned, namely his objection to relata-specificity in Mertz's work, and offer a rebuttal of Vallicella's objection.

9. These relata-specific slots of the relations I am considering should not be confused with the positions of positionalism (from Fine, 2000, sec. 3). For instance, if a is on top of b, positionalism analyzes the relation between a and b as $_{upper}R_{lower}$. But these positions can still be relata-unspecific (or not). I am leaving aside here special problems posed by nonsymmetric relations and their implications for relata-specific relations.

10. In Wieland (2008, chap. 1), the criterion of ad hoc avoidance sums up three *desiderata*: the carefulness, uniformity, and generality of a metaphysics theory. Wieland also argues there that ad hoc avoidance rests on arguments from increased utility, fundamentality, and credibility.

11. Note that by saying that option D assumes a (complex) special kind of entity (facts) *and* a special kind of composition (nonmereological composition) I am not double counting: under option D we find positions, such as Armstrong's, according to which there are objects other than facts with a special kind of nonmereological composition, namely structural universals, which differ, again, from their coincident sum of universals in virtue of a difference for which no grounds can plausibly be given.

12. For the notion of ad hoc entities and theory choice in metaphysics, see Rodríguez-Pereyra (2002) and Wieland (2008). Note that, besides, *Comply*'s world is open to monism, i.e., a world in which there is only one category of entities, either tropes or universals, which can therefore act as the only sort of mereological atoms. The best-known example of an option D world, Armstrong's, has four kinds of mereological atoms: three of them (thin particulars, structural universals, and universals) suitable for both mereological and nonmereological composition, and one of them, facts, suitable only for mereological composition.

13. Note that, although after Mulligan, Simons, and Smith (1984) it is known that nontransferable tropes (which in that paper are defined as *not* being parts, by contrast with what I do here) can serve as truthmakers, the question I raise here is whether my complexes, which are mereologically composed of *parts* and admit of both tropes and universals as parts, can serve as such.

14. It would also require being prepared to abandon some deeply ingrained assumptions in present-day metaphysics. For more on this, see Betti (2010). See also Daly (2005), Schnieder (2006a,b), and Schulte (2010). For a defense against Hornsby (2005), see Rodríguez-Pereyra (2008).

15. This can be seen, for instance, in Maurin (2011).

16. I address this issue in Betti (2013).

II Propositional Facts

1. According to a famous stance taken by Strawson, *expressions* don't refer: *speakers* do. According to Kent Bach, this "flies in the face of common philosophical lore" (for "common philosophical lore," read: the mainstream position in philosophy of language); there is "general consensus" that at least some expressions (successfully) refer, although there is "considerable dispute" on *which* ones these are (Bach, 2006, 517). Nothing I say here depends on this issue, and I will switch back and forth between (so-called) common philosophical lore and Strawson's position.

2. For the elimination of singular names in Quine, see Quine (1960, §38), esp. p. 186: "the atomic sentences have the form 'Fx', 'Fxy' etc." On Quine and names, see Decock (1999).

3. Notice that throughout this book I nowhere go beyond the boundaries of first-order classical predicate logic. Singular terms in, e.g., free logics behave differently. However sympathetic I might be to alternative accounts such as that of free logics or of Leśniewski's systems, these are nonstandard approaches far removed from the apparatus of mainstream analytic philosophy of language, which is my frame of reference here. An assumption commonly made in this frame, but by no means uncontroversial, is that classical first-order predicate logic is the paradigm of translation against which the validity of arguments in ordinary language must be measured.

4. Notice that this reasoning requires from the start that a (in natural language) is not an empty term: this is exactly the assumption made for expressions such that '(the fact) that p', namely that they are singular terms in natural language for facts (and as I have said we won't go beyond the boundaries of first-order classical predicate logic as far as the translation of s is concerned, and will not allow empty terms in the calculus). Given this supposition, the circularity of this reasoning starts to become apparent (I come back to this point in my general conclusion). It must be said, however, that although having singular terms for facts is the quickest way to get step 2, it is a sufficient condition and not a necessary one. See "The Argument for Facts from Nominal Reference" below and Fine (1982, 45), quoted in the next section.

5. See Varzi (2002, 2007) and Betti (2014) for reflection on language-based methodology in metaphysics.

6. By, e.g., Baylis (1948, 460). The psychological, mental counterpart of this position is Twardowski's position. It has to be said, however, that the reason Russell adduced for his claim is appealing only to those who reject nonobtaining states of affairs, and it wasn't particularly mystical: Russell argues that facts cannot be named because for each fact there correspond two propositions: there is one fact in the world that makes 'Socrates died' true and one that makes 'Socrates did not die' false (Russell, 1918–1919, 507).

7. As Prior writes, commenting on Russell's point, "to state a fact is not to name an object," and to this he adds that neither sentences nor their nominalizations such as that-clauses are names of anything (Prior, 1967, 228b–229a; see also Prior, 1971, 17). I shall come back to the question of whether that-clauses are names or singular terms for facts (and propositions) in chap. 4.

8. This point was already and convincingly made by Bolzano in *Wissenschaftslehre* (1837, §64), in which he speaks against a structural mirroring between parts of propositions in themselves, i.e., ideas in themselves, and parts of objects referred to by the latter.

9. The idea that the complexity of the grammatical structure of sentences is mirrored by facts comes near to a version of fact-correspondentism (or whole-correspondence, as I call it in Betti, 2013): a theory of truth according to which truth is a matter of structural correspondence with something out there (or at least with something objective), and that this something is a fact. The idea is also connected, albeit more loosely, to Armstrong's truthmaker argument (which is not, strictly speaking, a correspondentist argument and makes no mention of 'reference'). I offered a rebuttal of Armstrong's truthmaker argument in chap. 2, and do not have anything to add to that account here. Note that the notion of projection from chap. 1 can be put in the same group as positions defending the claim that sentences are special referring names.

10. The standard reference in linguistics for this analysis is Rosenbaum (1967).

11. It's worth mentioning already at this point that the linguistic background theory of Fine's paper is generative semantics—a theory is by no means innocent from the point of view of its semantical assumptions. I return to this point in chap. 4 at the end of sec. 4.1 (see ($\overline{NecSingularTerms\,4}$)).

12. The privileged status of subject position over predicate position is a *topos* of analytic philosophy that is part and parcel of the heritage of Quine's original criterion of ontological commitment, and derives, in turn, from Frege's logical analysis of language in terms of functions and arguments. For a connection between these topics and linguistics, see chap. 4, sec. 4.1, ($\overline{NecSingularTerms\,4}$).

13. On these matters, see also Varzi (2002, 2007) and Cameron (2008, 4). See also this book's introduction, xvi–xviii. Note that both *Quine-Like* and the biconditional following it are meant as definitory claims. Strictly speaking, only one direction is needed in the argument for what I want to show (thanks to Cleo Condoravdi, Elisabeth Coppock, Stefan Roski, and Martin Stokhof for discussion on the structure of the argument).

14. For more on this issue, see Betti (2014).

4   Reductio

1. In particular, 'that' is a "term-forming operator that turns meaningful sentences of the language into complex singular terms" (Moffett, 2003a, 1). Among those who agree that that-clauses are singular terms are Anderson (1984), Salmon (1986, 5–6), Schiffer (1992, 504, 2006, 267–269), Bealer (1993, 18), and David (2002, 140). To this list, the literature quoted in nn. 3 and 5 below should be added.

2. I use 'syntactic unit' in the way in which a linguist would use 'syntactic constituent'. Among those who reject that that-clauses are syntactic units are Quine (1960, 216), Prior (1963, 191; 1971, 19), Davidson (1968, 142), Belnap, Camp, and Grover

(1975, 103 [3.3], 109–111 [4.4]), Williams (1981, 228), Hugly and Sayward (1996, chap. 1), Recanati (2000, 23), and Mulligan (2010, 577).

3. See Vendler (1972, 81–82, 111), Peterson (1997, 9), and Künne (2003, 9). Other positions are possible: some alleged adherents of *Fact Reference* do not distinguish facts from propositions (Bennett, 1988, 7); Künne and Peterson accept, along with facts and propositions, a third kind of that-clauses referring to events; some would reject *Fact Reference* because they reject propositions but keep facts (Black, 1934, 42); others would perhaps object to the formulation I use because they hold that that-clauses are, rather, ambiguous in themselves, and it is head-interpolation that disambiguates the fact (that *p*) from the proposition (that *p*) (David, 2002, 140).

4. Or an expression canonically serving to *identify* exactly one object for an audience (see Strawson, 1968, 104). Quick and snappy characterizations with which everyone is happy do not seem to be on offer, and the question has been long and hotly debated. See sec. 4.1 below.

5. Those who reject *Fact Reference* while keeping *Singular Terms* maintain that that-clauses are singular terms referring univocally to *propositions*; see Moffett (2005, 105), and, notwithstanding impressions to the contrary, Cresswell (1973, 165–169), Delacruz (1976, 184), and Parsons (1993). On Cresswell (1973) and Delacruz (1976), however, see n. 6 below.

6. For more on this point, see Rosefeldt (2008, 303). Note that *Semantic Value* also requires the apparatus of a model-theoretical semantics of some kind. This is a view for which I have little sympathy, but I have no intention to criticize it here. Positions such as those defended by Cresswell (1973, 165–169), Delacruz (1976, 184), and Chierchia (1982, 304, 338) are arguably to be considered as adhering to *Semantic Value* rather than to *Singular Terms*, insofar as what they offer is a *modeling* of that-clauses in formal grammars (such as Montague grammar or its modifications).

7. "If facts cannot be the objects of singular reference, it seems to follow that there are no facts. For, surely, anything there is can be singularly referred to" (Clark, 1975, 7).

8. On nonnominal quantification in connection with that-clauses, see also Hugly and Sayward (1996, 178), Harman (2003, 177), and Pryor (2007, 226).

9. See the first condition of the Dummettian criterion given by Bob Hale as reported in Stirton (2000, 194).

10. Wolfram Hinzen has attracted my attention to another element (which might perhaps make for a fifth necessary condition): the lack of finite tense in phrases that can be taken to be singular terms. See Hinzen (2011).

11. The mismatch is in Bach (1997, 225) and Rosefeldt (2008, 304).

12. This is my reformulation of P2* of Rosefeldt (2008, 309).

13. One might note that these examples are all cases of that-clauses in object position (i.e., *b* in *Rab*). For cases of failure in subject position, see the discussion of *NecSingularTerms 4* in 4.4 below.

14. This is my reformulation of P1* of Rosefeldt (2008, 306).

15. On ad hoc reasoning and principles in metaphysics in connection with theory choice, see Rodríguez-Pereyra (2002), Wieland (2008), and chapter 3, and section 3.2 above.

16. For the examples in (l), see Rundle (1979, 283); for (m), thanks to Bjørn Jespersen; for (n), I used a suggestion in Fara (2000), sec. 3; for (o)–(p), see Alrenga (2005, 179, 177, n. 3), followed by Takahashi (2010, 368); for (q), see Schiffer (2003, 93).

17. To explain incongruities such as (k.ii), Schiffer (2003, 93) invokes, among others, phenomena of substitution failure of synonymous expressions involving dative movement. From 'Betty gave her tiara to Oxfam' we can pass to 'Betty gave Oxfam her tiara', while you cannot pass from 'Betty donated her tiara to Oxfam' to 'Betty donated Oxfam her tiara' in American English, so *give/donate* cannot be substituted although they are synonymous. But, first of all, Schiffer's *give/donate* example is not relevant here because it involves verbs allowing or not allowing dative movement, not the substitution of singular terms. Second, irrespective of the peculiarities of dative movement (a contingent feature of languages without cases such as English), examples (l)–(p) are very different from Schiffer's cases of substitution failure, since none of these cases is a double object (direct object/indirect object) construction; examples (o.i)–(o.ii) involve a secondary predication where a predicate nominal follows and modifies the direct object (see Emonds & Whitney, 2006, 75).

18. "In 'He complained that *P*', 'that' does not denote or introduce what was complained of or objected to, it simply prefaces a report of the terms in which the person complained or objected. As such, it has something of the force of 'to the effect that', and it is interesting to note that sense, if not idiom, is often retained if we replace 'that' by this phrase, or by 'thus': '*A* complained (reasoned, guessed) thus: *P*'—a version which brings out the intransitive, act-describing role of the verb" (Rundle, 1979, 286).

19. For other examples see Pryor (2007, 226) and Rosefeldt (2008, 312–428), who also points out that a behavior similar to that displayed by that-clauses is found in interrogative clauses (*wh*-questions): we have substitution failure connected to nonnominal functioning for 'the question who will get an Oscar nomination'/'who will get an Oscar nomination'.

20. For a formal account of how to deal with (c) and (d) when that-clauses are interpreted nonnominally (one that hangs on to propositions and classes as the *semantic values* of that-clauses and predicate), along with several alternative strategies, see Rosefeldt (2008, 318–328). As I pointed out at the beginning of this chapter, the

view that that-clauses have propositions or facts as semantic values is not the same as the one that takes that-clauses to be referring to propositions or facts.

21. For more on nonnominal quantifiers in this connection, see again Rosefeldt (2008, 311–318).

22. Bear in mind that I am not denying that in *some* specific cases Rule 2 applies. For instance:

(*.i)   Dargle will always remember that Argle stole the colander.
(*.ii)   There is some fact that Argle will always remember (namely that Argle stole the colander).

Something similar can also be said for *NecSingularTerms 1*. But the point is that the defenders of the Singular Term theory make an unmotivated generalization on the basis of the positive cases only, and forget about the bad cases. The No Singular Theory has instead a general explanation for *all* cases.

23. See Alrenga (2005), where a solution is given to the 'the Suck/Seem problem' by rejecting the view that that-clauses are true structural subjects and taking them as topic phrases. The Suck/Seem problem is the odd circumstance that *seem* (like *appear, happen, turn out*), in contrast with *suck* (*stink, blow, bite*) and despite the superficial similarities between the two verbs, cannot occur with sentential subjects:

(p.i)   It seems that the Giants lost the World Series.
(p.ii)   *That the Giants lost the World Series seems.

Compare:

(q.i)   That the Giants lost the World Series really sucks.
(q.ii)   It really sucks that the Giants lost the World Series (Alrenga, 2005, 175).

24. For a recent account, see Takahashi (2010, 368): "Various facts have been pointed out in the literature which appear to show that clausal complements cannot reside in the canonical subject and object positions that DP complements [NP, A. B.] can occupy (see Emonds 1972; Stowell 1981, among many others)." That that-clauses are not nominal complements, but sentential complements was also argued for by Rundle 1979: 287 and *ff*. Like Emonds and Koster, Rundle takes 'It is a fact that *p*' to be prior to 'That p is a fact'. See p. 153.

25. Assumption 1 is at the core of the so-called linguistics wars (see Harris, 1995, 82; I owe this reference to Lieven Decock and valuable discussion on this point to Wolfram Hinzen). Assumption 1 can be seen as conflating three different assumptions: one about grammatical structure, one about meaning, and one about logical form. These distinctions apparently do not play any role in Fine's reasoning, but I find it important to keep these three claims distinct. Claims to the effect that logical form and meaning are revealed by a paraphrased sentence where certain terms do or do not appear, for instance, belong to a family of principles that philosophers have very

often assumed while doing metaphysics. For a critical view of such methods, see Varzi (2002, 2007), and Betti (2014).

26. It should be remarked that in Lexical Functional Grammar (a version of generative grammar), Bresnan's claim that *all* that-clauses are COMP (roughly, not singular terms) has been contested on the basis of the fact that *some* that-clauses in *some* languages in sentences of the form '*x f*s that *p*' are OBJ (roughly: singular terms). However, whereas Dalrymple and Lødrup's (2000) hypothesis cannot explain why the following is unacceptable in English:

(*) On the roof was written that enemies are coming,

this incongruity can be explained by Bresnan's theory that in English *no* that-clause is ever of category OBJ; they are all COMP (Bresnan, 1995; Dalrymple & Lødrup, 2000, 8–9).

27. The terminology comes from Schnieder (2006c, sec. 2b).

28. Note that I remain neutral throughout this book as to whether any of these forms are indeed singular terms, and in particular as to whether definite descriptions are singular terms. I am just considering the most inclusive list of singular terms that one could propose, i.e., I am granting as much as I can, namely that all these expressions are such, for the sake of argument.

29. J. Williamson (1976, 205); T. Williamson (2000, 43); Neale (2001, 87, n. 5).

30. Or rather, according to some, 'è un fatto che a Hargle non piace il latte'. Of sentences like 'It rains' one could give a Brentano-like existential reading ('There is raining', 'Raining exists') and make a parallel with the assertion-reading of 'is a fact' I favored in the previous section. Exactly as in Brentano's claims that 'exists' is not a predicate, but rather something like a sign of assertion, 'That *p* is a fact' would say exactly the same as *p*. For an interpretation of 'it' here as a dummy *predicate*, see Moro (1997).

31. Another objection to seeing 'the fact that *p*' as a definite description emerges from "scepticism about the implication of *uniqueness* and *individuability*" conveyed by the expression, because fact-identity is fishy (Lowe, 1998b, 231–232). This second objection is of a rather different kind from the first: perhaps we might say that while the first objection challenges that 'the fact that p' is a description, the second challenges that it is definite. Note, *en passant*, that the objection fits particularly well Austin's position insofar as his sentences correspond to *types* of facts, so that "by itself, the phrase 'the fact that *S*' may not refer to a unique fact at all" (Olson, 1987, 9, n. 8).

32. *Pace* David (2002, 140, n. 18) and Hochberg (2001, 124). For discussion, see Betti (2014).

33. See also Neale (1990, 116, n. 55).

34. Two other objections to treating expressions such as 'the fact that p' as appositions, are made by Gennaro Chierchia, Barbara Partee, and Nicholas Asher. Asher
(1993, 171) notes that the appositive construction is symmetric, but the noun that-
clause construction is not:

(i)   John, a friend, took me home last night.
(ii) A friend, John, took me home last night.
(iii) The thought that Fred is insane has crossed my mind.
(iv) *That Fred is insane, the thought, has crossed my mind.

Chierchia (1982, 347), following Partee, observes that the following inference pat-
tern is valid for appositions:

a. the lawyer J. Smith runs for the presidency
b. J. Smith is a university professor
c. the university professor J. Smith runs for the presidency

But it does not apply to noun that-clause constructions:

a. the rumour that J. Smith is running for the presidency bothers Mary
b. that J. Smith is running for the-presidency is Jane's claim
c. Jane's claim that J. Smith is running for the presidency bothers Mary.

35. For this see the introduction to this book, pp. xvii–xviii. For an example of
philosopher defending the claim that 'the fact that p' is a singular term, see Sider
(2011, 111).

36. We could also take 'There is a fact' or 'There is at least one fact' to be the closest
equivalent. This would not alter my point.

37. Note that Tillman (1966) is written in the spirit of Vendler (1967), although it
reaches different conclusions.

38. Against my reasoning here, one could claim the following: 'Something is my
mother' sounds as bad as 'Something is a fact', but from this it does not follow that
there are no mothers. Against this I say that this observation supposes an analogy
between 'Something (someone) is my mother' and 'Something is a fact' that is not
there: a singular term (namely a proper name) can be substituted for 'my mother' in
'Something (someone) is my mother' (e.g., Tina Betti is my mother), but no singular
term can be substituted for 'something' in 'Something is a fact'.

39. For Rundle, verbs preceding that-clauses do not have a genuinely transitive use:
that-clauses do not function as objects of the verb, but have rather an adverbial
status (Rundle, 1979, 330). For Vendler, *I know that that p is a fact* and *I know for a
fact that p* are 'emphatic forms of *I know that p*' (Vendler, 1972, 108).

40. This analysis is also directly supported by historically oriented work in synchronic linguistics relying on transformations from Old and Middle English; see

Hsieh (1977). It seems this link has so far gone unnoticed. See Betti (2014) for more on this point.

41. This use is well documented in current English: "After his meeting with Ayatollah Khamenei, Mr. Velayati announced that the Holocaust is a fact of history and chastised those who question its reality." Abbas Milani, "What Scares Iran's Mullahs?" *New York Times*, February 23, 2007.

42. http://articles.latimes.com/2004/nov/09/nation/na-evolution9. This use of 'is a fact' is also quite common in Dutch/Flemish newspapers, "Immuniteit Berlusconi is een feit [Berlusconi's Immunity Is a Fact]" (*De Morgen*, July 3, 2008), http://www.demorgen.be/dm/nl/990/Buitenland/article/detail/356122/2008/07/22/Immuniteit-Berlusconi-is-een-feit.dhtml.

43. For more on this point, see Betti (2014).

44. "We have some evidence for holding that the word 'fact' is a certain kind of emphatic device" (Tillman, 1966, 127).

45. Ducasse (1940, 710); Prior (1971, 5–6); Parsons (1993, 455). For a different view, see Vendler (1972, 113–114).

5 A Fallback Position (1)

1. Peterson's analysis differs from other analyses to the effect that some predicates that are factive in Peterson's analysis turn out to be nonfactive on other accounts (and vice versa). For instance, the verb 'regret', usually considered a factive, is nonfactive for Peterson (Peterson, 1997, 8).

2. Although Peterson argues explicitly that factivity does not link to *implication*, but rather to Strawsonian *presupposition* (Peterson 1997, 67), he speaks in his introduction (ibid., 9) of 'imply, implicate or presuppose'.

3. As for Peterson, for the Kiparskys a (semantically) factive predicate is a predicate such that whenever a speaker utters a sentence with an embedded 'that *p*' following (or preceding) it, the utterance carries the presupposition that *p* is true (Kiparsky & Kiparsky, 1971, 348). In contrast with Peterson, the Kiparskys have, alongside *semantically* factive predicates (presupposing the truth of the embedded clause), also *syntactically* factive predicates. See chap. 6, sec. 6.3, below.

4. One can argue that, although the phenomenon of factivity is empirically detectable via recognition by agents, including children (Schulz, 2000; Hollebrandse, 2002), the issue of whether certain specifically technical predicates are factive is a matter of philosophy (or for scientific research), and not something to be decided by reference to language (or common use). The Kiparskys admit, for instance, that although 'forget' in their classification is factive, it is logically possible to forget 'a false notion' (Kiparsky & Kiparsky, 1971, 360). The same reasoning can easily be

applied to many other cases. A case similar to 'forget' has indeed been made for the hotly debated 'know', since, arguably, the question of whether one can know something false should be decided by epistemology, not by language (see Hazlett, 2010).

5. Vendler does not speak of factive and nonfactive that-clauses but of 'subjective' and 'objective' that-clauses (Vendler, 1972, 111).

6. Although Fine also says that natural language does not exclude the worldly view of facts, and he himself seems happy to accept both (Fine, 1982, 54–55).

7. For more references, see White (1970, 82, n. 11).

8. There is still considerable dispute on the meaning of 'the world' in this context. I use this expression for the realm of real objects, their properties, their causes, and effects. But another respectable position is that held by identity theorists such as Hornsby and McDowell, who argue that facts are 'in the world' and yet identify facts with true thoughts. A way to settle the issue, at least terminologically, is this: identity theorists accept, in Fregean terms, that facts belong to the realm of sense, but they reject that facts belong to the realm of reference (Hornsby, 1999, 241; McDowell, 2005, 84). See also chapter 1, section 1.3, condition 3.

9. For more on the internal structure of facts and their variety, see chapters 1–3.

10. Positions similar to that of Meinong in accepting states of affairs as so-called higher-order objects, but differing in holding that states of affairs are not truthbearers, are those of Husserl (who speaks of states of affairs as *founded* on their constituents) and Twardowski. Husserl and Twardowski were, roughly speaking, Meinong's contemporaries and, like Meinong, had both been pupils of Franz Brentano in Vienna.

11. It is a moot question whether the expression 'noncompositional fact' (which in the literature sometimes is used in opposition to compositional facts) is consciously meant to cover all variants of ideal facts, including hybrid positions such as Meinong's or Clark's. Present-day works of reference are unclear in this regard, and the role of abstract (for us: ideal) facts in possible world semantics complicates the picture (see Wetzel, 2003, who ascribes noncompositional facts to Plantinga, Pollock, and Barwise; see also Mulligan & Correia, 2008). For a discussion, see Betti (2014).

12. In Betti (2014) I argue that, if common linguistic use should settle the matter, there is no empirical ground for saying that speaking of 'true facts' and 'false facts' is improper while speaking of 'true propositions' and 'false propositions' is proper.

13. Let us observe that, like PF1 (ideal), PF3 (aboutness) applies also to so-called noncompositional facts defended by Plantinga and others. Indeed, the unclarity of the relation between facts and the objects they are about is a known objection made by David Lewis to Alvin Plantinga's conception of facts (i.e., as 'states of affairs', which he accepts alongside propositions: Plantinga, 1976, 258–259). Note that the defense of Plantinga's position made by van Inwagen (1986, 201–210) is ineffective

for what I am discussing here because van Inwagen there trades Plantinga's states of affairs for propositions. But that propositions represent is not the problematic point here. Rather, the problem is this: in what exactly, in positions such as Plantinga's, where both states of affairs and propositions are accepted, do the representing capacities of states of affairs differ from those of propositions?

14. Menzies (1989, 73), among others, has suggested, similarly to defenders of Russellian propositions as ontological counterpart of true sentences, that facts ('abstract situations') are set-theoretical entities. But suggesting that the containment of object and properties in a fact is analogous to set membership does not explain anything: it just shifts the question to what it *means* to say that a real object is *contained* in a set. Set-theoretical tools are a way to *model* the world: if this is all we want them to do, that's fine; as a metaphysical explanation of what facts are, however, it is but one that purports to clarify *obscurum per obscurius*.

15. The one-one thesis entails that there are molecular facts, and it is distinctive of the position Künne calls *prodigal fact-correspondentism* that is taken up by people such as G. E. Moore (Moore 1953, 256, 261–262, 276–277; cf. Künne, 2003, 114–115). It is also shared, apparently, by John Searle (Searle, 1995, 214). In his discussion of the slingshot argument, however, Searle simply switches to a many-to-one match between propositions and facts. See n. 27 below.

16. Similar problems are faced by the so-called noncompositionalists such as Pollock (1984, 52–56) and Plantinga (1985, 88–91, 92–93).

17. Similar points are made by Fine (1982, 67; his point is based on the way in which he defines propositional facts, as a result of applying operations to construct them) and Olson (1987, 6–7, n. 60).

18. The most sensible position to assume as to the ontological status of such objects is that, like two small tables when they are brought together to make up a bigger one, they make no *third additional* piece of furniture (Russell 1918–1919, 42, 47; see also Künne, 2003, 119). As well known, it is debatable whether *everyone* accepting compositional facts takes up this mereological position (Armstrong seems to do so, though it is debatable, judging from his idea of supervenience, that he really does). Yet my point on disjunctive facts is independent of this matter. See also the introduction and section 2.1 of chapter 2.

19. Whether a plausible theory of worldly facts in which worldly disjunctive facts appear can be advanced is not something I will discuss here. I am rather skeptical that this can be achieved in a way that would take care of all the problems raised in this book, though; as such, a theory would have to be able to handle the connections between *worldly* and *disjunctive* facts on the one hand and, *at the same time*, between worldly and conjunctive facts on the other. Note that if molecular facts were worldly items, the world would be unnecessarily duplicated, for any conjunctive fact (*Cargle's being wrong and poor Argle's being a thief*) would be taken to exist

next to its conjuncts (*Cargle's being wrong, poor Argle's not being a thief*). As I mentioned in the previous note, I do not find this an appealing position, but it does have its followers.

20. Vendler insists that although knowledge-claims are opaque, knowledge is not (Vendler, 1972, 116). This has been challenged by Rosenthal (1976, 248). A somewhat similar problem to the one I am discussing here in connection with Vendler and 'know' ("what they know may appear to them in different perspectives"; Vendler, 1972, 115) is discussed by Bach (1997) in connection with *believe* (in a framework that merges propositions and facts).

21. Wang (2003, 19) also reaches the conclusion that if you have both Fregean propositions and so-called Fregean facts (i.e., ideal facts) then they are identical.

22. Fine says that some of these compelling arguments are summarized by Clark (1976). Note, however, that Clark gives no *arguments* against this identification. He just gives a list of six *claims* containing *characterizations* of what facts are, all similar to the following: "*It is not proper to say that* facts are true or false" (Clark, 1976, 261, emphasis added). As I show in Betti (2014), whatever we may think of the methodology supporting claims such as these, the latter claim is disproved by legal language.

23. This seems a particularly natural thing to hold for those who think that facts are either there, or they aren't facts at all—that is, for those who hold that there are no 'false facts', such that 'obtaining fact' is redundant and 'nonobtaining fact' is an oxymoron. Now, to be sure, Moore's φ *could* be available also to a view on which both obtaining and nonobtaining *states of affairs* are accepted, for one could argue that the difference between obtaining and nonobtaining states of affairs is an ontological difference par excellence, while, again, no such difference holds between true and false propositions. If this is indeed an option available to compositional views (though they would still be plagued by other difficulties; see chap. 3, sec. 3.3.4), it is difficult to see how there could be, *pace* Künne (2003, 253), an *ontological* difference between obtaining and nonobtaining *propositional* states of affairs: the latter are not in the world, i.e., they are neither located nor dated, nor come in and out of existence, and nor fulfill any metaphysical role once we deny them a causal role (see the sec. 5.4.3 below). Besides, the parallel between true propositions and obtaining state of affairs and between false propositions and nonobtaining states of affairs is so strong on this conception that saying that 'obtaining' has ontological import while 'true' does not can be seen as a confirmation that the issue is, indeed, merely a verbal one.

24. As Künne says:

One cannot plausibly maintain that definite descriptions which apply to the same object can never be exchanged *salvo facto*: As one can see from the following pair:

Esau is Jacob's elder brother
Esau is Israel's elder brother

such a general prohibition would be incompatible with accepting (STS). (Künne, 2003, 140)

25. On the relationship between the empirical criterion and compositional facts, see Armstrong (1997, 133–134).

26. Note that Künne does not literally endorse the view that factive that-clauses refer to facts (Fact Reference_{Power!}); he endorses the view that *some* that-clauses refer to facts (Fact Reference). But notice, also, that Künne makes use of Vendler's results, which assume Fact Reference_{Power!}. As I argued above, the position of those who hold that *some* (kinds of) that-clauses refer to facts without recourse to a general account based on a comprehensive study of language (which Vendler would no doubt say he gives) is philosophically weaker than the position of those who do give such an account, i.e., an explanatory hypothesis as to which that-clauses refer to facts and why.

27. A similar strategy to the one of the Künnian fictional correspondentist is followed by Searle. Searle's position on fact-identity oscillates incoherently between Fine's quasi-structural criterion and Fine's empirical criterion. "If it is true that the cat is on the mat, there must be something in virtue of which it is true, something that makes it true. The disquotation criterion only tells us *for each case* what that something is. The something that makes it true that the cat is on the mat is just that the cat is on the mat. And so on for any true statement" (Searle, 1995, 211, emphasis added; this suggests that Searle follows the quasi-structural criterion). This is denied by the following: "Intuitively, the fact that Tully was an orator is the very same fact as the fact that Cicero was an orator ... because exactly the same states of affairs in the world makes each statement true, and 'fact' is defined as that which makes a statement true" (Searle, 1995, 220; this suggests that Searle follows the empirical criterion). Searle agrees thus with Künne on

(1) The fact that Leah's husband is very fond of Joseph ≠ the fact that Rachel's husband is very fond of Joseph

for the same "intuitive" reasons, but this clashes with the quasi-structural criterion. Searle's reasons for holding

(2) The fact that George Eliot wrote *Middlemarch* = the fact that Mary Ann Evans wrote *Middlemarch*

are different: "The fact that Tully was an orator is a different fact from the fact that the man who denounced Catiline was an orator ... because the latter fact requires that someone have denounced Catiline for its existence, and the existence of the former fact has no such requirement" (Searle, 1995, 220). It is clear that notions such as *existence requirements for facts in dependence of (the existence of) the objects or properties a fact is about* are technical notions (in particular, notions left unclear by Searle), and have very little to do with the everyday use of 'fact'.

28. Rodríguez-Pereyra (1998) makes a somewhat similar point against Searle's discussion of the Slingshot.

29. *Pace* what Hacker (2007, 87, n. 34) seems to suggest, Mellor's position is not as problematic as Searle's in this respect: Mellor acknowledges states of affairs, but, like Chisholm, does not acknowledge propositions (Mellor, 1998, 8), and moreover Mellor's states of affairs are located (Mellor, 1998, 9). On there being no reason for having facts as causal relata on the account of their being ideal, see also Menzies (1989).

30. I take the notion of *category* I use in this chapter and the next to be fairly intuitive; the technical characterization of what I have in mind is that of contemporary metaphysical systems of categories as described by, e.g., Thomasson (2009, 1.4). In this sense, events, facts, propositions, properties, substances (or individuals), etc. all may constitute different (and possible) categories.

31. The Awkward Ring Rule is inspired by this: "The things that are true are propositions, and they cannot sensibly be said to be the case. The things that are the case (or that obtain) are states of affairs, and they cannot sensibly said to be true. *So* the predicates 'is the case' and 'is true' have not even overlapping extensions" (Künne, 2003, 257; emphasis added). It has to be said, in fairness, that Künne would not adhere *unrestrictedly* to a rule of this kind (ibid., 11, n. 25).

32. Interestingly, in view of phenomena such as perception and emotions, truths in the sense of properties in this sense would arguably need to be bearer-specific properties (and would perform better as tropes than as universals). For suppose you are surprised by something—say, that your birth certificate disappeared, and that the fact that your birth certificate disappeared scares you awfully. Then, first, if it is the truth of *this* proposition that scares you, then it is not the truth of the proposition that you still have your passport that scares you. For *that* does not scare you. And, second, it would be the truth of a proposition *in use* that scares you, either thought, imagined, whispered, or spoken. Many would not be happy with truths as bearer-specific in this sense but, as a matter of fact as we saw in part 1, truths in Fine's sense *must* be bearer-specific to fulfill the role he ascribes to them and thus to avoid the unity problem (see chap. 3, sec. 3.1.2).

6   A Fallback Position (2)

1. Neither Parsons nor Künne (as I already mentioned) literally endorse Fact Reference$_{Power!}$; they endorse Fact Reference (see chap. 5, introduction). But, once again, as I argued above, the position of those who wish to defend the position that *some* that-clauses refer to facts (Fact Reference) is philosophically vaguer, and philosophically less convincing than the position of those who give an account of *which* that-clauses refer to facts based on a systematic, in-depth study of language.

2. In case of attitude verbs, at least, sharing objects in similar constructions requires "shared perceptual, epistemic, or communicative 'mode' (with possible differences in the strength of the attitude)" (Moltmann, 2003, 92).

3. Note also that the emotive 'regret' in (a.i) is a peculiar case: the verb is normally considered a factive, but in Peterson's analysis is a half-factive (and it is taken to be a counterexample), and in (a.i) its use is a nonfactive one; 'say' in (a.ii, b.iii, d.ii) is a half-factive. See sec. 6.1.2.

4. There are alternative analyses to the relational one defended by Künne, Parsons, and others. One is the adverbialist analysis (see Kriegel, 2008), which extends to intentionality what Chisholm (1957, 145) and Ducasse (1942) hold about perception. For other nonrelational analyses of that-clauses, see Moltmann (2003, 108–113). See also chap. 4, sec. 4.1.

5. Peterson (1997, 78, 325); see also the many *indifferent* verbs of Kiparsky and Kiparsky (1971, 360).

6. Peterson (1997, 324); Vendler (1972, 96–97).

7. Recall that Fact Reference$_{Power!}$, i.e.,

Fact Reference$_{Power!}$ Factive that-clauses *refer to facts* whereas nonfactive that-clauses *refer to propositions*

presupposes Factivity:

Factivity Language exhibits a phenomenon called factivity; this phenomenon is linked to the implication or presupposition of truth of certain embedded clauses.

8. Peterson (1997, 79, 325). On 'predict', see sec. 6.1.4.

9. Peterson is not consistent throughout: in 'Mary's refusal of the offer was significant', he says, the expression 'Mary's refusal of the offer' "refers to a fact" or "presupposes the truth of a proposition or is a factive clause" (1997, 75). See also Peterson (1997, 45, 52), where propositions as bearers of truth-values are said to be the 'contents' of *both* beliefs and knowledge.

10. Note that this way of handling knowledge attitudes remains unjustified. Why should knowledge have that double structure? One could just as well insist that the inference goes, e.g., as follows:

(2)   Bargle knows$_f$ <that electrons have a negative charge>$_f$.
(2.1)   Bargle knows$_f$ <that it is true$_p$ [that electrons have a negative charge]$_p$>$_f$.
(2.2)   Bargle believes$_p$ [that it is true$_p$ [that electrons have a negative charge]$_p$]$_p$.
(3)   Bargle believes$_p$ [that electrons have a negative charge]$_p$.

No grounds are given for preferring (2)–(3) in the shorter version above to this one (one could even argue that in this version things with (iv) get somewhat simpler). I do not mean to suggest, however, that one choice would be less arbitrary than the other.

11. Peterson offers, at most, the following: "The chameleon lost its tail in January, but grew it back in March. ... (Given the nature of reptiles, their tails, etc.) two different tails are referred to. No chameleon ever grows back the numerically same tail it lost" (Peterson, 1997, 156).

12. Both Iris Loeb and Jan Willem Wieland have independently suggested this option (pers. comm.), either as an alternative systematic position or as an interpretation of what Peterson might have had in mind.

13. A defender of this position is Cresswell, his mention of Vendler and the Kiparskys notwithstanding: Cresswell introduces two operators, that and that' (Cresswell, 1973, 166, 168), which correspond to factive and nonfactive that-clauses of Reference.

14. "There are speakers for whom many of the syntactic and semantic distinctions we bring up do not exist at all. Professor Archibald Hill has kindly informed us that for him factive and non-factive predicates behave in most respects alike and that even the word *fact* in his speech has lost its literal meaning and can head clauses for which no presupposition of truth is made" (Kiparsky & Kiparsky, 1971, 348, n. a). Indeed, the Kiparskys are unhappy with '*I know the fact that John is here' (though 'know' is for them semantically factive), and so are Parsons (1993, 459) and Moltmann (2003, 85); others find instead 'Laura knows the fact that Adele left the room' perfectly fine (Moffett, 2003b, 81).

15. *Pace* Moffett (2003b, 81, 83; 2005, 106, n. 5); Parsons (1993, 453).

16. I discuss yet another fallback position, the one arguing that the mere circumstance that we have the word 'fact' in natural language is an argument to accept facts, in Betti (2014). There I offer critical considerations on the methodology (similar to the one I have considered in these three chapters) that purports to use linguistic evidence to fix our catalog of the world and, in general, to do metaphysics.

Conclusion: Farewell to Facts

1. The dichotomy between descriptive and revisionary metaphysics comes from Peter Strawson: "Descriptive metaphysics is content to describe the actual structure of our thought about the world, revisionary metaphysics is concerned to produce a better structure" (Strawson, 1959, 9). Mind that on at least one reading this characterization is not fully apt to capture the contrast I want to capture between the two parts of this book (thanks to the participants of the Gothenburg High Seminar in March 2014 for discussion on this point).

2. Facts can play certain semantic roles (say, truthmaker), because they are endowed with certain ontological characteristics (nonmereological composition, first of all)—

something that, as we have seen, was important to showing that the truthmaker argument is unsound. But it is not too difficult to see that these ontological characteristics themselves are not meant to be basic roles that must be played. For instance, one might think that something must be in the world (condition 3) and that something must be complex (condition 1). Now, for a minimal realist approach, it is trivial that there must be something in the world (1), but I do not think that there is enough agreement that complexity or composition needs to be a role played by an *entity* that is composed (3). See chap. 2, n. 5.

3. In particular, none of my arguments touches Aristotelian propositions: among all entities that appear in this book, they are the entities best equipped to serve as truthbearers.

4. See also Betti (2013), where I discuss this issue in historical perspective and defend more neutral theories of correspondence in which the roles of truthmaker and sentence-object do not need to be played.

References

Alrenga, P. (2005). A sentential subject asymmetry in English and its implications for complement selection. *Syntax, 8*, 175–207.

Anderson, A. C. (1984). General intensional logic. In D. Gabbay & F. Guenther (Eds.), *Handbook of philosophical logic IV*. Dordrecht: Reidel.

Anscombe, G. E. M. (1958). On brute facts. *Analysis, 18*, 69–72.

Aquila, R. (1977). *Intentionality: A study of mental acts*. University Park, PA: Pennsylvania State University Press.

Armstrong, D. M. (1989). *Universals: An opinionated introduction*. Boulder: Westview.

Armstrong, D. M. (1991). Classes are states of affairs. *Mind, 100*, 189–200.

Armstrong, D. M. (1997). *A world of states of affairs*. Cambridge: Cambridge University Press.

Armstrong, D. M. (2004). *Truth and truthmakers*. Cambridge: Cambridge University Press.

Asher, N. (1993). *Reference to abstract objects in discourse*. Dordrecht: Kluwer.

Austin, J. L. (1961). Unfair to facts. In *Philosophical papers* (pp. 102–122). Oxford: Clarendon Press.

Bach, K. (1997). Do belief reports report beliefs? *Pacific Philosophical Quarterly, 78*, 215–241.

Bach, K. (2006). What does it take to refer? In E. Lepore & B. C. Smith (Eds.), *The Oxford handbook of philosophy of language* (pp. 516–554). New York: Oxford University Press.

Baylis, C. A. (1948). Facts, propositions, exemplification, and truth. *Mind, 57*, 459–479.

Bealer, G. (1993). A solution to Frege's puzzle. *Philosophical Perspectives, 7*, 17–61.

Belnap, N. D., Camp, J. L., & Grover, D. L. (1975). A pro-sentential theory of truth. *Philosophical Studies*, *27*, 73–125.

Bennett, J. (1988). *Events and their names*. Oxford: Clarendon Press.

Bennett, K. (2004). Spatio-temporal coincidence and the grounding problem. *Philosophical Studies*, *118*, 339–371.

Ben-Yami, H. (2004). *Logic and natural language: On plural reference and its semantic and logical significance*. Burlington: Ashgate.

Bergmann, G. (1967). *Realism: A critique of Brentano and Meinong*. Madison: University of Wisconsin Press.

Betti, A. (2010). Explanation in metaphysics and Bolzano's theory of ground and consequence. *Logique et analyse*, 211, 281–316.

Betti, A. (2013). On the history of facts. Unpublished ms.

Betti, A. (2014). The naming of facts and the methodology of language-based metaphysics. In A. Reboul (Ed.), *Mind, values, and metaphysics*. Berlin: Springer.

Betti, A., & van den Berg, H. (2014). Modeling the history of ideas. *British Journal for the History of Philosophy*, *22*, 812–835.

Betti, A. (Ed.), Venanzio, R. (Ed.), & Twardowski, K. (Forthcoming). *Logik: Wiener Logikkolleg 1894/95*. Berlin: De Gruyter.

Bigelow, J. (1988). *The reality of numbers: A physicalist's philosophy of mathematics*. New York: Oxford University Press.

Black, M. (1934). A propos of "facts." *Analysis*, *1*, 39–43.

Blanshard, B. (1984). Bradley on relations. In A. Manser & G. Stock (Eds.), *The philosophy of F. H. Bradley* (pp. 211–226). Oxford: Clarendon Press.

Bodomo, A. B., & Lee, Y. M. (2003). On the function COMP in Cantonese. In A. B. Bodomo & K. K. Luke (Eds.), *Journal of Chinese Linguistics, Monograph Series 19: Lexical-Functional Grammar Analysis of Chinese*, 96–116.

Bolzano, B. (1833/1935). *Der Briefwechsel B. Bolzano's mit F. Exner* (E. Winter, Ed.). Prag: Královská česká společnost nauk.

Bolzano, B. (1837). *Wissenschaftslehre*. Stuttgart/Bad Canstatt: Friedrich Frommann Verlag/Günther Holzboog.

Bradley, F. H. (1893). *Appearance and reality*. London: Swan Sonnenschein.

Bradley, F. H. (1910). On appearance, error, and contradiction. *Mind*, *19*, 178–185.

Bresnan, J. (1995). Category mismatches. In A. Akinlabi (Ed.), *Theoretical approaches to African linguistics* (pp. 19–45). Trenton: Africa World Press.

Burke, M. (1992). Copper statues and pieces of copper: A challenge to the standard account. *Analysis, 52,* 12–17.

Cameron, R. P. (2006). Tropes, necessary connections, and non-transferability. *Dialectica, 60,* 99–113.

Cameron, R. P. (2008). Truthmakers and ontological commitment: Or how to deal with complex objects and mathematical ontology without getting into trouble. *Philosophical Studies, 140,* 1–18.

Carnap, R. (1947). *Meaning and necessity.* Chicago: University of Chicago Press.

Cartwright, R. (1987). A neglected theory of truth. In *Philosophical essays* (pp. 71–93). Cambridge, MA: MIT Press.

Casati, R., & Varzi, A. (2010). Events. In E. N. Zalta (Ed.), *The Stanford encyclopedia of philosophy* (Spring 2010 Ed.). http://plato.stanford.edu/archives/spr2010/entries/events/.

Chierchia, G. (1982). Nominalization and Montague grammar: A semantics without types for natural languages. *Linguistics and Philosophy, 5,* 303–354.

Chisholm, R. M. (1957). *Perceiving: A philosophical study.* Ithaca: Cornell University Press.

Chisholm, R. M. (1970). Events and propositions. *Noûs, 4,* 15–24.

Chisholm, R. M. (1973). Parts as essential to their wholes. *Review of Metaphysics, 26,* 581–603.

Chisholm, R. M. (1976). *Person and object: A metaphysical study.* London: Allen & Unwin.

Chomsky, N. (1969). Linguistics and philosophy. In S. Hook (Ed.), *Language and philosophy* (pp. 54–91). New York: New York University Press.

Church, A. (1956). Propositions and sentences. In I. M. Bochenski, A. Church & N. Goodman (Eds.), *The problem of universals* (pp. 3–11). Notre Dame, IN: University of Notre Dame Press.

Clark, R. W. (1975). Facts, fact-correlates, and fact-surrogates. In P. Welsh (Ed.), *Fact, value, and perception: Essays in honor of Charles A. Baylis* (pp. 3–18). Durham: Duke University Press.

Clark, R. W. (1976). What facts are. *Southern Journal of Philosophy, 14,* 257–267.

Cresswell, M. J. (1973). *Logic and languages.* London: Methuen.

Dalrymple, M., & Lødrup, H. (2000). The grammatical functions of complement clauses. In *LFG00 Conference Proceedings.* Berkeley, CA: CSLI Publications.

Daly, C. (2005). So where's the explanation? In H. Beebee & J. Dodd (Eds.), *Truth-makers: The contemporary debate* (pp. 85–103). Oxford: Clarendon Press.

David, M. (2002). Truth and identity. In M. O. Campbell Joseph K. David Shier (Eds.), *Meaning and truth: Investigations into philosophical semantics* (pp. 124–141). New York: Seven Bridges Press.

David, M. (2009). The correspondence theory of truth. In E. N. Zalta (Ed.), *The Stanford encyclopedia of philosophy* (Fall 2009 Ed.). http://plato.stanford.edu/entries/truth-correspondence/.

Davidson, D. (1968). On saying that. *Synthese, 19*, 130–146.

Davidson, D. (1969). True to the facts. *Journal of Philosophy, 66*, 748–764.

Decock, L. (1999). Quine on names. *Logique et Analyse, 167–8*, 373–379.

Delacruz, E. B. (1976). Factives and proposition level constructions in Montague grammar. In B. Partee (Ed.), *Montague grammar* (pp. 177–199). New York: Academic Press.

Della Rocca, M. (1996). Essentialists and essentialism. *Journal of Philosophy, 93*, 186–202.

Dodd, J. (1999). Farewell to states of affairs. *Australasian Journal of Philosophy, 77*, 146–160.

Dodd, J. (2000). *An identity theory of truth*. London: Macmillan.

Ducasse, C. J. (1940). Propositions, opinions, sentences, and facts. *Journal of Philosophy, 37*, 707–711.

Ducasse, C. J. (1942). Moore's refutation of idealism. In P. Schilpp (Ed.), *The philosophy of G. E. Moore* (pp. 225–251). Chicago: Northwestern University Press.

Emonds, J. (1972). A reformulation of certain syntactic transformations. In S. Peters (Ed.), *Goals of linguistic theory* (pp. 21–61). Englewoods Cliffs, NJ: Prentice-Hall.

Emonds, J., & Whitney, R. (2006). Double objects constructions. In H. van Riemsdijk & Everaert M. Van (Eds.), *The Blackwell companion to syntax* (pp. 73–144). Oxford: Blackwell.

Fara, D. G. (2000). Comments on Marian David's "Truth and identity." Commentary presented at Metaphysics Mayhem V, Syracuse University, August 14.

Fine, K. (1982). First-order modal theories III—Facts. *Synthese, 53*, 43–122.

Fine, K. (2000). Neutral relations. *Philosophical Review, 109*, 1–33.

Fine, K. (2003). The non-identity of a material thing and its matter. *Mind, 112*, 195–234.

Fitch, G. (1994). Singular propositions in time. *Philosophical Studies*, *73*, 181–187.

Fitch, G., & Nelson, M. (2009). Singular propositions. In E. N. Zalta (Ed.), *The Stanford encyclopedia of philosophy* (Spring 2009 Ed.). http://plato.stanford.edu/archives/spr2009/entries/propositions-singular/.

Foot, P. (1958–1959). Moral beliefs. *Proceedings of the Aristotelian Society*, *59*, 83–104.

Fox, J. (1987). Truthmaker. *Australasian Journal of Philosophy*, *65*, 188–207.

Frege, G. (1918). Der Gedanke. *Beiträge zur Philosophie des deutschen Idealismus*, *1*, 58–77.

Frege, G. (1923). Logische Untersuchungen: Dritter Teil: Gedankengefüge. *Beiträge zur Philosophie des deutschen Idealismus*, *3*, 36–51. Translated by R. Stoothoff as "Compound thoughts," *Mind*, *72*, 1–17 (1963). Page references are to the translation.

García-Carpintero, M. (2010). Gaskin's ideal unity. *Dialectica*, *64*, 279–288.

Gaskin, R. (2009). *The unity of the proposition*. New York: Oxford University Press.

Gaskin, R. (2010a). Précis of *The unity of the proposition*. *Dialectica*, *64*, 259–264.

Gaskin, R. (2010b). The unity of the proposition: Replies to Vallicella, Schnieder, and García-Carpintero. *Dialectica*, *64*, 303–311.

Goldman, A. I. (1976). *A theory of human action*. Princeton: Prentice Hall.

Gregory, D. (2001). Smith on truthmakers. *Australasian Journal of Philosophy*, *79*, 422–427.

Grimshaw, J. (1982). Subcategorization and grammatical relations. In A. Zaenen (Ed.), *Subjects and other subjects: Proceedings of the Harvard Conference on the Representation of Grammatical Relations* (pp. 35–56). December 1981, Indiana University, Bloomington, IN: Linguistics Club.

Grossmann, R. (1992). *The existence of the world: An introduction to ontology*. London: Routledge.

Hacker, P. M. S. (2007). *Human nature: The categorial framework*. Oxford: Wiley-Blackwell.

Harman, G. (2003). Category mistakes in M&E. *Philosophical Perspectives*, *17*, 165–180.

Harris, R. A. (1995). *The linguistics wars*. New York: Oxford University Press.

Hazlett, A. (2010). The myth of factive verbs. *Philosophy and Phenomenological Research*, *80*, 497–522.

Herbst, P. (1956). The nature of facts. In A. Flew (Ed.), *Essays in conceptual analysis* (pp. 134–156). London: Macmillan.

Hinzen, W. (2007). *An essay on names and truth*. Oxford: Oxford University Press.

Hinzen, W. (2011). Truth, deflationism, and grammar. Unpublished text of a talk given at Truth Be Told—Workshop on Philosophical and Formal Theories of Truth, Amsterdam, March 23–25. Abridged version published as chapter 9 of Wolfram Hinzen & Michelle Sheehan, *The philosophy of universal grammar*, Oxford: Oxford University Press, 2013.

Hochberg, H. (1978). *Thought, fact, and reference: The origins and ontology of logical atomism*. Minneapolis: University of Minnesota Press.

Hochberg, H. (2001). *The positivist and the ontologist: Bergmann, Carnap, and logical realism*. Amsterdam: Rodopi.

Hollebrandse, B. (2002). Review of Schulz 2000. *Glot International, 6*, 304–306.

Horgan, T. (1978). The case against events. *Philosophical Review, 87*, 28–47.

Hornsby, J. (1999). The facts in question: A response to Dodd and Candlish. *Proceedings of the Aristotelian Society, 2*, 241–245.

Hornsby, J. (2005). Truth without truthmaking entities. In H. Beebee & J. Dodd (Eds.), *Truthmakers—The contemporary debate* (pp. 33–49). New York: Oxford University Press.

Hsieh, H.-I. (1977). Synchronic syntax in historical perspective. *Lingua, 43*, 41–54.

Hugly, P., & Sayward, C. (1996). *Intensionality and truth: An essay on the philosophy of A.N. Prior*. Dordrecht: Springer.

Jubien, M. (1993). *Ontology, modality, and the fallacy of reference*. Cambridge: Cambridge University Press.

Kaplan, D. (1989). Demonstratives (typescript, UCLA, 1977). In John Perry, J. Almog, & Howard K. Wettstein (Eds.), *Themes from Kaplan*. Oxford: Oxford University Press.

Kemmerling, A. (2010). Thoughts without parts: Frege's doctrine. *Grazer Philosophische Studien, 82*, 165–188.

Kim, J. (1973). Causation, nomic subsumption, and the concept of event. *Journal of Philosophy, 70*, 217–236.

Kim, J. (1980). Events as property exemplifications. In M. Brand & D. Walton (Eds.), *Action Theory* (pp. 159–177). Dordrecht: Reidel.

King, J. C. (1996). Structured propositions and sentence structure. *Journal of Philosophical Logic, 25*, 495–521.

King, J. C. (2002). Designating propositions. *Philosophical Review, 111*, 341–371.

King, J. C. (2011). Structured propositions. In E. N. Zalta (Ed.), *The Stanford encyclopedia of philosophy* (Fall 2011 Ed.). http://plato.stanford.edu/archives/fall2011/entries/propositions-structured/.

Kiparsky, C., & Kiparsky, P. (1971). Fact. In D. Steinberg & L. A. Jakobovits (Eds.), *Semantics: An interdisciplinary reader* (pp. 345–369). Cambridge: Cambridge University Press.

Koslicki, K. (2004). Constitution and similarity. *Philosophical Studies, 117,* 327–364.

Koster, J. (1978). Why subject sentences don't exist. In S. J. Keyser (Ed.), *Recent transformational studies in European languages* (pp. 53–64). Cambridge, MA: MIT Press.

Kratzer, A. (2002). Facts: Particulars or information units? *Linguistics and Philosophy, 25,* 655–670.

Kriegel, U. (2008). The dispensability of (merely) intentional objects. *Philosophical Studies, 141,* 79–95.

Künne, W. (2003). *Conceptions of truth.* Oxford: Oxford University Press.

Künne, W. (2010). Reply to Paul Boghossian and Kevin Mulligan. *Dialectica* 64: 585–615. Enlarged and modified version published as "Truth without truths? 'Propositional attitudes' without propositions? Meaning without meanings?" In K. Mulligan, K. Kijania-Placek & T. Placek (Eds.), *The history and philosophy of Polish logic—Essays in honour of Jan Wolenski* (Basingstoke: Palgrave Macmillan, 2014).

Lewis, D. K. (1971). Counterparts of persons and their bodies. *Journal of Philosophy, 68,* 203–211.

Lewis, D. K. (1991). *Parts of classes.* Hoboken, NJ: Wiley-Blackwell.

Lewis, D. K. (1992). Armstrong on combinatorial possibility. In *Papers in metaphysics and epistemology* (pp. 196–214). Cambridge: Cambridge University Press.

Lewis, D. K. (1998). A world of truthmakers? In *Papers in metaphysics and epistemology* (pp. 215–220). Cambridge: Cambridge University Press.

Loux, M. J. (1998). *Metaphysics: A contemporary introduction.* London: Routledge.

Loux, M. J. (2002). *Metaphysics: A contemporary introduction* (2nd ed.). London: Routledge.

Loux, M. J. (2006). *Metaphysics: A contemporary introduction* (3rd ed.). London: Routledge.

Lowe, E. J. (1998a). Form without matter. *Ratio, 11,* 214–234.

Lowe, E. J. (1998b). *The possibility of metaphysics—Substance, identity, and time.* Oxford: Oxford University Press.

MacBride, F. (2002). Facts und universals. *Grazer Philosophische Studien, 65,* 207–222.

MacBride, F. (2014). Truthmakers. In E. N. Zalta (Ed.), *The Stanford encyclopedia of philosophy* (Spring 2014 Ed.). http://plato.stanford.edu/archives/spr2014/entries/ truthmakers/.

Malcolm, N. (1940). The nature of entailment. *Mind, 49,* 333–347.

Matthews, R. J. (2007). *The measure of mind—Propositional attitudes and their attribution.* Oxford: Oxford University Press.

Maurin, A.-S. (2002). *If tropes.* Dordrecht: Kluwer.

Maurin, A.-S. (2007). Infinite regress—virtue or vice? In T. Rønnow-Rasmussen, Björn Petersson, Jonas Josefsson, Dan Egonsson (Eds.), *Hommage à Wlodek: Philosophical papers dedicated to Wlodek Rabinowicz* (pp. 1–25), Lund: Lund University, Department of Philosophy.

Maurin, A.-S. (2010a). Trope theory and the Bradley regress. *Synthese, 175,* 311–326.

Maurin, A.-S. (2010b). An argument for the existence of tropes. *Erkenntnis, 74,* 69–79.

Maurin, A.-S. (2011). Exemplification as explanation. *Axiomathes, 23,* 401–417.

Maurin, A.-S. (2012). Bradley's regress. *Philosophy Compass, 7,* 794–807.

McDaniel, K. (2009). Structure-making. *Australasian Journal of Philosophy, 87,* 251–274.

McDowell, J. (1999). Responses. In M. Willaschek (Ed.), *John McDowell: Reason and nature* (pp. 93–117). Münster: Lit Verlag.

McDowell, J. (2005). The true modesty of an identity conception of truth: A note in response to Pascal Engel. *International Journal of Philosophical Studies, 13,* 83–88.

McGrath, M. (2012). Propositions. In E. N. Zalta (Ed.), *Stanford encyclopedia of philosophy* (Summer 2012 Ed.). http://plato.stanford.edu/archives/sum2012/entries/ propositions.

Meinertsen, B. (2008). A relation as the unifier of states of affairs. *Dialectica, 62,* 1–19.

Meinong, A. (1902). *Ueber Annahmen.* Leipzig: J. A. Barth.

Meinong, A. (1910). *Ueber Annahmen,* rev. ed. Leipzig: J. A. Barth.

Meinong, A. (1983). *On assumptions* (Heanue, J., Trans.). Berkeley, CA: University of California Press.

Mellor, D. H. (1998). *The facts of causation.* London: Routledge.

Menzies, P. (1989). A unified account of causal relata. *Australasian Journal of Philosophy, 67,* 59–83.

Moffett, M. A. (2003a). Are "that"-clauses really singular terms? Unpublished ms.

Moffett, M. A. (2003b). Knowing facts and believing propositions: A solution to the problem of doxastic shift. *Philosophical Studies, 115*, 81–97.

Moffett, M. A. (2005). Constructing attitudes. *Protosociology, 21*, 105–128.

Moltmann, F. (2003). Propositional attitudes without propositions. *Synthese, 135*, 77–118.

Moltmann, F. (2004). Nonreferential complements, nominalizations and derived objects. *Journal of Semantics, 21*, 1–43.

Moore, G. E. (1953). *Some main problems of philosophy*. London: Allen & Unwin.

Moro, A. (1997). *The raising of predicates: Predicative noun phrases and the theory of clause structure*. Cambridge: Cambridge University Press.

Morscher, E. (1986). Propositions and states of affairs in Austrian philosophy before Wittgenstein. In J. C. Nyiri (Ed.), *From Bolzano to Wittgenstein* (pp. 75–85). Vienna: Verlag Hölder-Pichler-Tempsky.

Morscher, E., & Simons, P. (1982). Objektivität und Evidenz. In F. W. & E. M. J. Seifert (Eds.), *Vom Wahren und vom Guten: Festschrift zum achtzigsten Geburtstag von Balduin Schwarz* (pp. 205–222). Salzburg: St. Peter Verlag.

Mulligan, K. (1985). "Wie die Sachen sich zueinander verhalten" inside and outside the *Tractatus*. *Teoria, 5*, 145–174.

Mulligan, K. (2010). The truth predicate vs. the truth connective: On taking connectives seriously. *Dialectica, 64*, 565–584.

Mulligan, K., & Correia, F. (2008). Facts. In E. N. Zalta (Ed.), *Stanford encyclopedia of philosophy* (Winter 2008 Ed.). http://plato.stanford.edu/archives/win2008/entries/facts/.

Mulligan, K., Simons, P., & Smith, B. (1984). Truth-makers. *Philosophy and Phenomenological Research, 44*, 287–321.

Neale, S. (1990). *Descriptions*. Cambridge, MA: MIT Press.

Neale, S. (2001). *Facing facts*. Oxford: Oxford University Press.

Noonan, H. (1991). Indeterminate identity, contingent identity, and Abelardian predicates. *Philosophical Quarterly, 41*, 183–193.

Olson, E. (2001). Material coincidence and the indiscernibility problem. *Philosophical Quarterly, 51*, 337–355.

Olson, K. (1987). *An essay on facts*. Stanford, CA: CSLI Publications.

Orilia, F. (2007). States of affairs: Bradley vs. Meinong. In *Meinongian issues in contemporary Italian philosophy* (pp. 213–238). Heusenstamm: Ontos Verlag.

Orilia, F. (2009). Bradley's regress and ungrounded dependence chains: A reply to Cameron. *Dialectica, 63*, 333–341.

Parsons, T. (1993). On denoting propositions and facts. *Philosophical Perspectives, 7*, 441–460.

Paul, L. A. (2002). Logical parts. *Noûs, 36*, 578–596.

Peterson, P. L. (1997). *Fact, proposition, event*. Dordrecht: Kluwer.

Plantinga, A. (1976). Actualism and possible worlds. *Theoria* 42: 139–160. Reprinted in M. J. Loux (Ed.), *The possible and the actual* (253–273). Ithaca, NY: Cornell University Press, 1979.

Plantinga, A. (1985). Self-profile. In J. Tomberling & P. van Inwagen (Eds.), *Alvin Plantinga: Profiles* (pp. 3–97). Dordrecht: Kluwer.

Pollock, J. L. (1984). *The foundations of philosophical semantics*. Princeton, NJ: Princeton University Press.

Prior, A. N. (1948). Facts, propositions, and entailment. *Mind, 57*, 62–68.

Prior, A. N. (1963). Is the concept of referential opacity really necessary? *Acta Filosofica Fennica, 16*, 189–199.

Prior, A. N. (1967). Correspondence theory of truth. In P. Edwards (Ed.), *The encyclopedia of philosophy* (Vol. 2, pp. 223–232). New York: Macmillan.

Prior, A. N. (1971). *Objects of thought*. Oxford: Clarendon Press.

Prior, A. N. (1976). *The doctrine of propositions and terms*. London: Duckworth.

Pryor, J. (2007). Reasons and that-clauses. *Philosophical Issues, 17*, 217–244.

Quine, W. V. O. (1953a). Logic and the reification of universals. In *From a logical point of view* (pp. 122–129). New York: Harper & Row.

Quine, W. V. O. (1953b). On what there is. In *From a logical point of view* (pp. 1–19). New York, Evanston: Harper & Row.

Quine, W. V. O. (1960). *Word and object*. Cambridge, MA: MIT Press.

Quine, W. V. O. (1969). Existence and quantification. In *Ontological relativity and other essays* (pp. 91–113). New York: Columbia University Press.

Rea, M. C. (1997). Supervenience and co-location. *American Philosophical Quarterly, 34*, 367–375.

Recanati, F. (2000). *Oratio obliqua, oratio recta: An essay on metarepresentation*. Cambridge, MA: MIT Press.

Reicher, M. E. (2009). Introduction. In *States of affairs* (pp. 1–37). Heusenstamm bei Frankfurt: Ontos Verlag.

Reimer, M. (2010). Reference. In E. N. Zalta (Ed.), *The Stanford encyclopedia of philosophy* (Spring 2010 Ed.). http://plato.stanford.edu/archives/spr2010/entries/reference/.

Robinson, D. (1985). Can amoebae divide without multiplying? *Australasian Journal of Philosophy, 63*, 299–319.

Rodríguez-Pereyra, G. (1998). Searle's correspondence theory of truth and the Slingshot. *Philosophical Quarterly, 48*, 513–522.

Rodríguez-Pereyra, G. (2002). *Resemblance nominalism: A solution to the problem of universals*. Oxford: Oxford University Press.

Rodríguez-Pereyra, G. (2008). Postscript to "Why truth-makers." In E. J. Lowe & A. Rami (Eds.), *Truth and truth-making*. Kingston: McGill-Queen's University Press.

Rosefeldt, T. (2008). "That"-clauses and non-nominal quantification. *Philosophical Studies, 137*, 301–333.

Rosenbaum, P. (1967). *The grammar of English predicate complement constructions*. Cambridge, MA: MIT Press.

Rosenthal, D. M. (1976). Res cogitans: An essay in rational philosophy by Zeno Vendler. *Journal of Philosophy, 73*, 240–252.

Rundle, B. (1979). *Grammar in philosophy*. Oxford: Clarendon Press.

Russell, B. (1903). *The principles of mathematics*. Cambridge: Cambridge University Press.

Russell, B. (1904/1994). On functions. In A. Urquhart (Ed.), *The collected papers 4: Foundations of logic, 1903–05* (pp. 96–110). London: Routledge.

Russell, B. (1907). The monistic theory of truth. In *Philosophical essays* (pp. 131–146). London: Allen & Unwin.

Russell, B. (1910). Some explanations in reply to Mr. Bradley. *Mind, 19*(75), 373–378.

Russell, B. (1912). *Problems of philosophy*. London: William & Norgate.

Russell, B. (1913/1984). Theory of knowledge. In E. Ramsden Eames (Ed.), *The collected papers 7, theory of knowledge: The 1913 manuscript*. London: Allen & Unwin.

Russell, B. (1918–1919). The philosophy of logical atomism. *Monist, 28*, 495–527; *Monist, 29*, 32–63, 190–222, 345–380.

Russell, B. (1919). On propositions: What they are and how they mean. *Proceedings of the Aristotelian Society, Supplementary Volume, 2*, 1–43.

Russell, B. (1923). Vagueness. *Australasian Journal of Psychology and Philosophy, 1*, 84–92. Reprinted in R. Keefe & P Smith (Eds.), *Vagueness: A reader* (pp. 61–68), Cambridge, MA: MIT Press, 1997. Page references are to the reprint.

Russell, B. (1924). Logical atomism. In J. H. Muirhead (Ed.), *Contemporary British philosophy—Personal statements* (pp. 356–383). First Series. New York: Routledge. Reprinted in Russell, *Logic and knowledge: Essays 1901–1950* (pp. 323–343). New York: Macmillan, 1956. Page references are to the reprint.

Salmon, N. (1986). *Frege's puzzle*. Cambridge, MA: MIT Press.

Schiffer, S. (1992). Belief ascription. *Journal of Philosophy, 92*, 499–521.

Schiffer, S. (2003). *The things we mean*. Oxford: Oxford University Press.

Schiffer, S. (2006). Propositional content. In E. Lepore & B. C. Smith (Eds.), *The Oxford handbook of philosophy of language* (pp. 267–294). Oxford: Oxford University Press.

Schmaltz, T. (2009). Nicolas Malebranche. In E. N. Zalta (Ed.), *The Stanford encyclopedia of philosophy* (Winter 2009 Ed.). http://plato.stanford.edu/archives/win2009/entries/malebranche/.

Schnieder, B. (2006a). Troubles with truth-making: Necessitation and projection. *Erkenntnis, 64*, 61–74.

Schnieder, B. (2006b). Truth-making without truth-makers. *Synthese, 152*, 21–46.

Schnieder, B. (2006c). Canonical property designators. *American Philosophical Quarterly, 43*, 119–132.

Schnieder, B. (2010). Propositions united. *Dialectica, 64*, 289–301.

Schulte, P. (2010). Truthmakers: A tale of two explanatory projects. *Synthese, 181*, 413–431.

Schulz, P. (2000). *Getting the facts: Finite complements, factive verbs, and their acquisition*. PhD dissertation, University of Tübingen.

Searle, J. (1995). *The construction of social reality*. New York: Free Press.

Searle, J. (1998). Truth: A reconsideration of Strawson's views. In L. E. Hahn (Ed.), *The philosophy of P. F. Strawson* (pp. 385–401). Chicago: Open Court.

Shorter, J. M. (1962). Facts, logical atomism, and reducibility. *Australasian Journal of Philosophy, 40*, 283–302.

Sider, T. (1999). Global supervenience and identity across times and worlds. *Philosophy and Phenomenological Research, 59*, 913–937.

Sider, T. (2011). *Writing the book of the world*. Oxford: Clarendon Press.

Sider, T. (2013). Against parthood. In K. Bennett & D. W. Zimmerman (Eds.), *Oxford studies in metaphysics 8* (pp. 237–293). Oxford: Oxford University Press.

Simons, P. (1988). Aristotle's concept of state of affairs. In M. W. F. O. Gigon (Ed.), *Antike Rechts- und Sozialphilosophie* (pp. 97–112). Frankfurt: Peter Lang.

Simons, P. (2009). Why there are no states of affairs. In M. E. Reicher (Ed.), *States of affairs* (pp. 111–128). Heusenstamm bei Frankfurt am Main: Ontos Verlag.

Slote, M. A. (1974). *Metaphysics and essence*. Oxford: Blackwell.

Smith, B. (1989). Constraints on correspondence. In W. L. Gombocz, H. Rutter, & W. Sauer (Eds.), *Traditionen und Perspektiven der analytischen Philosophie: Festschrift für Rudolf Haller* (pp. 415–430). Vienna: Verlag Hölder-Pichler-Tempsky.

Smith, B. (1999). Truthmaker realism. *Australasian Journal of Philosophy, 77*, 274–291.

Smith, B. (2002). Truthmaker realism: Response to Gregory. *Australasian Journal of Philosophy, 80*, 231–234.

Soames, S. (1988). Substitutivity. In J. J. Thomson (Ed.), *On being and saying: Essays for Richard L. Cartwright* (pp. 99–132). Cambridge, MA: MIT Press.

Sprigge, T. L. S. (1970). *Facts, words, and beliefs*. New York: Humanities Press.

Stalnaker, R. (1985). Belief attribution and context. In R. H. Grimm & D. D. Merrill (Eds.), *Contents of thought* (pp. 140–156). Tucson: University of Arizona Press.

Stirton, W. R. (2000). Singular term, subject and predicate. *Philosophical Quarterly, 50*, 191–207.

Stowell, T. (1981). *Origins of phrase structure*. PhD dissertation, MIT, Cambridge, MA.

Strawson, P. F. (1950a). On referring. *Mind, 59*, 320–344.

Strawson, P. F. (1950b). Truth. In *Logico-linguistic papers (1970)* (pp. 190–213). London: Methuen.

Strawson, P. F. (1959). *Individuals: An essay in descriptive metaphysics*. London: Methuen.

Strawson, P. F. (1968). Singular terms and predication. *Journal of Philosophy, 19*, 97–117.

Strawson, P. F. (1998). Reply to John Searle. In L. E. Hahn (Ed.), *The philosophy of P. F. Strawson* (pp. 402–404). Chicago: Open Court.

Suszko, R. (1968). Ontology in the *Tractatus* of L. Wittgenstein. *Notre Dame Journal of Formal Logic, 9*, 7–33.

Tabossi, P. (2006). Idioms, comprehension of. In L. Nadel (Ed.), *Encyclopedia of cognitive science*. New York: John Wiley & Sons.

Takahashi, S. (2010). The hidden side of clausal complements. *Natural Language and Linguistic Theory*, *28*, 343–380.

Textor, M. (2008). A repair of Frege's theory of thoughts. *Synthese*, *167*, 105–123.

Thomasson, A. L. (2009). Categories. In E. N. Zalta (Ed.), *The Stanford encyclopedia of philosophy* (Spring 2009 Ed.). http://plato.stanford.edu/archives/fall2010/entries/categories/.

Thomson, J. J. (1983). Parthood and identity across time. *Journal of Philosophy*, *80*, 201–220.

Tillman, F. A. (1966). Facts, events, and true statements. *Theoria*, *32*, 116–129.

Tye, M. (1989). *The metaphysics of mind*. Cambridge: Cambridge University Press.

Vallicella, W. F. (2000). Three conceptions of states of affairs. *Noûs*, *34*, 237–259.

Vallicella, W. F. (2002). Relations, monism, and the vindication of Bradley's regress. *Dialectica*, *56*, 3–35.

Vallicella, W. F. (2004). Bradley's regress and relation-instances. *Modern Schoolman*, *81*, 159–183.

Vallicella, W. F. (2010). Gaskin on the unity of the proposition. *Dialectica*, *64*, 265–277.

van Inwagen, P. (1986). Two concepts of possible worlds. *Midwest Studies in Philosophy*, *11*, 185–213.

van Inwagen, P. (2001). *Ontology, identity, and modality: Essays in metaphysics*. Cambridge: Cambridge University Press.

Varzi, A. C. (2002). Words and objects. In A. Bottani, M. Carrara, & P. Giaretta (Eds.), *Individuals, essence, and identity: Themes of analytic metaphysics*. Dordrecht: Kluwer.

Varzi, A. C. (2005). Mereological commitments. *Dialectica*, *54*, 283–305.

Varzi, A. C. (2007). From language to ontology: Beware of the traps. In M. Aurnague, M. Hickmann, & L. Vieu (Eds.), *The categorization of spatial entities in language and cognition* (pp. 269–284). Amsterdam: John Benjamins.

Varzi, A. C. (2008). The extensionality of parthood and composition. *Philosophical Quarterly*, *58*, 108–133.

Varzi, A. C. (2010). Mereology. In E. N. Zalta (Ed.), *Stanford Encyclopedia of Philosophy* (Spring 2010 Ed.). http://plato.stanford.edu/entries/mereology/.

Vendler, Z. (1967). *Linguistics in philosophy*. Ithaca, NY: Cornell University Press.

Vendler, Z. (1972). *Res cogitans—An essay in rational philosophy*. Ithaca, NY: Cornell University Press.

Vickers, J. M. (2004). Ramsey on judgment: The theory of "facts and propositions." *Dialectica, 58*, 499–516.

Wang, X. (2003). Where are facts? A case for internal factual realism. *Diálogos, 38*, 7–30.

Webelhuth, G. (1992). *Principles and parameters of syntactic saturation*. Oxford: Oxford University Press.

Wetzel, T. (2003). States of affairs. In E. N. Zalta (Ed.), *Stanford encyclopedia of philosophy* (Fall 2003 Ed.). http://plato.stanford.edu/archives/fall2003/entries/states-of -affairs/.

White, A. R. (1970). *Truth*. New York: Anchor Books.

Wieland, J. W. (2008). *Minimize ad hoc turtles*. Amsterdam: University of Amsterdam.

Wieland, J. W., & Betti, A. (2008). Relata-specific relations: A response to Vallicella. *Dialectica, 62*, 509–524.

Wiggins, D. (1968). On being in the same place at the same time. *Philosophical Review, 77*, 90–95.

Williams, C. J. F. (1981). *What is existence?* Oxford: Clarendon Press.

Williams, D. C. (1953). On the elements of being I. *Review of Metaphysics, 7*(1), 3–18.

Williamson, J. (1976). Facts and truth. *Philosophical Quarterly, 26*, 203–216.

Williamson, T. (2000). *Knowledge and its limits*. Oxford: Oxford University Press.

Wittgenstein, L. (1921/1962). *Tractatus logico-philosophicus: The German text of Ludwig Wittgenstein's Logisch-philosophische Abhandlung with a new translation by D. F. Pears and B. F. McGuinness*. London: Routledge & Kegan Paul.

Yablo, S. (1996). How in the world? *Philosophical Topics, 24*, 255–286.

Zimmerman, D. W. (1995). Theories of masses and problems of constitution. *Philosophical Review, 104*, 53–110.

Index